Health and medical professionals

The importance of personal behavior, as well as health-care quality and costs, cannot be overemphasized in managing health. Stress: Living and Working in a Changing World *is a valuable tool to help health-care organizations effectively address this challenge. Timely and useful, it will be popular with employees and employers alike.*

Daniel A. Gregorie, MD, retired, president and CEO, ChoiceCare

What topic applies both on the job and in the home? Stress. With humor and profound insight, the authors address this important subject. Managing stress is a survival skill and Stress: Living and Working in a Changing World *is the survival kit not only for patients but for patients' doctors as well.*

William Monnig, MD, president, Kentucky Medical Association

Stress: Living and Working in a Changing World *is an important book that should be on the bookshelves of all physicians, nurses, and human resource professionals who deal with the impact of stress in the workplace. Manning, Curtis, and McMillen provide profound insight into the problems faced and offer real world, practical solutions.*

M. J. Wakeman, MD, MS, director of occupational medicine
The Health Alliance of Greater Cincinnati

Stress: Living and Working in a Changing World *is equally at home in cardiac rehab., the employee lounge, and the management library.*

Kerry Gillihan, CEO, Cardinal Hill Hospital

This wonderful and timely book will give us the courage to press on to further develop our healthcare delivery system.

M. Julia Hanser, president and CEO, Mercy Regional Health System

Educators and authors

Stress: Living and Working in a Changing World *will become a staple of our training programs as we assist employees, both professionally and personally, in facing the challenges presented by an ever changing environment.*

Loretta F. Harper, PhD, associate vice chancellor for human resources
North Carolina State University

With stress increasing everywhere, we need new tools NOW . . . this book offers practical tools and ideas to increase self-awareness, reduce the impact of stress on our daily lives, and transform our perception of change from crisis to opportunity. I highly recommend it to everyone.

Michael Greenhouse, learning resources consultant, Levi Strauss & Co.

Manning, Curtis, and McMillen have given us a gift . . . a workshop in a book. They present the science of stress with a minimum of jargon, the dangers of stress with candor, and the delights of stress with warmth and humor. Along the way, we get to examine our own stress, and what we might do about it. Well done!

Dick Richards, management consultant and author of *Artful Work and Setting Your Genius Free*

It is a goldmine! If you are managing a company where employee stress affects the workplace, then give this book to all your people.

Philip M. Parker, PhD, associate professor, INSEAD France

It's all here. This is the most comprehensive and usable book I've seen on stress, peppered with wise quotations and memorable stories and chock full of exercises that will help you learn by doing. If you want to get to know yourself, understand your relationships and everything that influences them, and then make healthier choices, it's all here.

Andrea Kay, columnist, author, and career consultant

Corporate and business management

This excellent book is a handbook for living our lives. It provides insights into the causes of stress that we encounter in both our personal and professional lives. Readers are guaranteed to be more successful and happier in all aspects of their lives.

Walter M. Lovenberg, PhD, retired, president, Marion Merrell Dow Research

At Van Melle, our task is to grow successfully in the global marketplace without losing the caring work atmosphere that has guided our company. Stress: Living and Working in a Changing World provides wisdom and practical tools for employees from the front line person to the president's office.

Marius Van Melle, president, Van Melle, U.S.A.

A very readable book that succinctly captures the message of how to deal with stress and change.

Jim Spina, Director, management development, Tribune Company

Stress: Living and Working in a Changing World provides a practical summary of what individuals and organizations can do about stress . . . readers understand clearly how positive coping skills can reduce stress and enhance performance in a changing world.

Mary Ann Donahue, vice president, human development, Medtronic, Inc.

More than just a book, it is a practical approach to managing stress in a changing world. Read it— prepare yourself for future stress.

Don Carr, Manager, sales training, Merck AgVet Division of Merck & Co., Inc.

A powerful resource. This book can help organizations and individuals cope with and understand how stress impacts every aspect of a person's life . . . meaningful assessments highlight the undesirable effects of stressful living.

Suzanne Hanein, corporate communications, United Parcel Service

Timely book for managing stress in a world of accelerating change and fierce competition.

Larry W. Hitch, quality systems, Ford Motor Company

Filled with wisdom, knowledge, and insight . . . the reader is given a wonderful opportunity to coexist with the stressful challenges of work and life.

Patrick L. Burns, chairman and CEO, United Ad Label Co., Inc.

Authoritative and accurate . . . this is a must for everyone from the boardroom to the shop floor.

Robert D. Johnson, president, Imperial Adhesives, Inc.

STRESS

Living and Working in a Changing World

Manning, Curtis, & McMillen

Whole Person Associates
Duluth, Minnesota

Whole Person Associates, Inc.
210 West Michigan
Duluth, MN 55802-1908 218-727-0500
E-mail: books@wholeperson.com
Web site: http://www.wholeperson.com

Stress: Living and Working in a Changing World

Printed in the United States of America
10 9 8 7 6 5 4 3 2 1

Editorial Director: Susan Gustafson
Art Director: Joy Dey
Manuscript Editor: Kathy DeArmond
Production Manager: Paul Hapy

Library of Congress Cataloging-in-Publication Data

Stress: living and working in a changing world.
   536 pg. 27 cm.
   Edited by George Manning, Kent Curtis, and Steve McMillen.
   Includes bibliographical references and index.
   ISBN 1-57025-176-2
   1. Stress (Psychology) 2. Stress management. I. Manning, George, 1943- II. Curtis,
Kent, 1939- III. McMillen, Steve, 1953-
   BF575.S75 S7734 1999
   155.9'042—dc21

                               98-40160
                                 CIP

This book is dedicated to our families

Nancy, Page, Larry, and Heather

Mary, Lisa, Denise, and Craig

Laure, Zeina, and André

Table of Contents

Part Eight: Stress Prevention

Learning Tools

Preface

This book is for everyone. No one lives a stress-free life, and everyone has times that are truly demanding in terms of dealing with change. *Stress: Living and Working in a Changing World* has application on the job and across the life span, and is appropriate for business professionals, college students, and the general public as well. It is especially appropriate for individuals and organizations going through periods of uncertainty and change.

This is an applied book that combines theory with practice, giving common-sense answers to real-life problems. Information is presented in a format conducive to quick access on an as-needed basis. Each chapter presents concepts and skills in the important areas of managing stress and coping with change. Self-evaluation questionnaires and practical exercises to be used for personal and professional development make the impact greater.

Approach and style of the book

The difference between this book and most books on stress can be compared to the difference between a lecture and a seminar. Although both are good educational vehicles, the lecture is better for conveying large amounts of information, while the seminar is better for developing skills and attitudes. A good lecture is interesting and builds knowledge, while a good seminar is stimulating and builds competency. *Stress: Living and Working in a Changing World* emphasizes the interactive, seminar approach to learning.

The writing style is personal and conversational, with minimal professional jargon. True-life examples clarify points under consideration. Concepts are supported by facts and figures, as well as by stories and anecdotes that are meaningful and easy to remember. Each chapter includes learning activities and authors' file notes to bridge the gap between theory and real-life experience. Our goal has been to include material that is interesting to read, practical to use, and personalized to the reader's own concerns.

Focus and audience

The focus of this book is self-discovery and personal development as the reader "learns by doing." The information provided is authoritative and up-to-date, reflecting current theory and practice. This book is written for three audiences:

- Individuals and organizations interested in managing stress and dealing with change within the context of the work environment.

- Students in college and university courses in stress, change, and personal development; it is appropriate for students in four-year colleges and universities, as well as community colleges and proprietary schools.

- The individual who seeks to understand stress and change in life and who wants to use this book for personal growth.

Nature and highlights of the book

Stress: Living and Working in a Changing World takes a holistic view—personal, social, occupational, and physical. It is intended to be used as a practical resource for living and working in a changing world. Topics, questions, and activities include:

- Introduction—*How long will you live?* Add years to your life and life to your years. See pages xv–xxvii.

- Part One—*How stressful is your world* and what does this mean for your physical health? See pages 31–51.

- Part Two—What *coping techniques* do successful people use? Do you possess the *characteristics of a hardy personality?* See pages 83–99; 101–106.

- Part Three—How do you *help people through change?* What are the *challenges of adulthood* and *elements of happiness?* See pages 114–131; 138–149.

- Part Four—What gives *purpose* and *meaning to your life?* See pages 159–160, 164–179; 181–197.

- Part Five—What are the *characteristics of an effective family?* What are the *elements of a successful relationship?* See pages 220–222; 229–235; 242–244.

- Part Six—How can you avoid the *job burnout phenomenon?* Find out how to succeed at work and live to enjoy it. See pages 285; 287–289; 309–314.

- Part Seven—How do you achieve your *full potential* in life? See pages 344–346; 352–357; 359–360; 410–411.

- Part Eight—What is the 1 x 3 x 7 = 21 *readiness plan* for dealing with stress? See pages 431–473.

This book can be read two ways: from cover to cover as one would read a textbook, or with targeted reading based on personal interests. For example, for stress in the workplace, see Part Six; for interpersonal stress, see Part Five; for helping people through change, see Part Three; for stress coping techniques, see Part Two; and for a readiness plan to deal with stress, see Part Eight.

How to use this book

The best way to use this book is to *interact* with the material. Read the narrative, complete the questionnaires and exercises, examine the interpretations, and review the principles and techniques. Then ask, "How does this apply to me? How can I use this concept or lesson to manage stress and deal with change?" Then *take action.*

To increase interest and improve overall learning, try the following:

■ Share the results of your questionnaires and exercises with family, friends, and coworkers. In this way, you can make practical use of what you learn and may even help others.

■ Write in the book. Use the margins, underline, highlight passages, write your own ideas, and personalize the material. Experiment with one exercise, many exercises, or all exercises.

■ You may want to use two markers—one to underline material that applies to you and the other to underline material that applies to others. Then think about, discuss, and strive to utilize these ideas in a meaningful way.

Good luck in your learning!

We want your suggestions. If you have questions or see a way to improve this book, please write:

George Manning / Kent Curtis   Steve McMillen
Northern Kentucky University   Hillenbrand Industries
Highland Heights, KY 41099   700 State Rte 46 E
                                       Batesville, IN 47006

Acknowledgments

Theorists, practitioners, and authors per part:

Introduction: Robert Allen, Alex Comfort, Leonard Hayflick.

Part One: Walter Cannon, Norman Cousins, Robert Eliot, Susan Folkman, Thomas Holmes, James Kalat, Richard Lazarus, Adolf Meyer, Friedrich Nietzsche, Kenneth Pelletier, Richard Rahe, Paul Rosch, Hans Selye, Alvin Toffler, Mark Twain, Harold Wolff.

Part Two: John Adams, Aristotle, Harvey Brenner, Thomas Carlisle, Charles Dickens, Meyer Friedman, Susan Kobasa, John Milton, William Osler, Ray Rosenman, Martin Seligman, George Bernard Shaw, Charles Swindoll, Paul Tillich, Leo Tolstoy, Redford Williams.

Part Three: William Bridges, Willa Cather, Daryl Conner, Erik Erikson, Heraclitus, Ronald Inglehart, Dennis Jaffe, John Kotter, Harold Leavitt, Kurt Lewin, David McClelland, Ashley Montague, David Myers, John Naisbitt, Price Pritchett, Cynthia Scott.

Part Four: Gordon Allport, Joel Barker, Stephen Covey, Viktor Frankl, Buckminster Fuller, Hermann Hesse, William James, Laurie Beth Jones, Soren Kierkegaard, Gordon Lippitt, Abraham Maslow, Morris Massey, Rollo May, William Menninger, Edward Mowatt, Boris Pasternak, Bertrand Russell, Jean Paul Sartre, Maury Smith, Baruch Spinoza.

Part Five: Helen Bee, L. F. Berkman, Robert Bramson, Martin Buber, Leo Buscaglia, Dale Carnegie, Erich Fromm, Kahlil Gibran, Karen Horney, James House, Jane Howard, Sam Keen, Sheldon Kopp, Wendy Leebov, Anne Morrow Lindbergh, Dean Ornish, Scott Peck, Carl Rogers, Socrates, Robert Sternberg.

Part Six: Terry Beehr, Joseph Brady, Wayne Cascio, Cary Cooper, Mihaly Csikszentmihalyi, Fyodor Dostoyevsky, Andrew DuBrin, Benjamin Franklin, Herbert Freudenberger, Arlie Hochschild, Joseph Hurrell, Jr., John Jones, Robert Karasek, Gwendolyn Puryear Keita, Carol Krucoff, Alan Lakein, Peggy Lawless, Robert Levering, Lawrence Murphy, Steven Sauter, Jay Weiss.

Part Seven: Richard Bolles, Winston Churchill, Peter Drucker, Ralph Waldo Emerson, Jerry Eppler, Charles Garfield, Tibor Greenwalt, Edgar Guest, Kurt Hahn, Napoleon Hill, John Holland, Rudyard Kipling, Michael Korda, Richard Leider, Alac MacKenzie, Phillip Marvin, Michael O'Brien, Theodore Roosevelt, Hiram Smith, Nina Tassi, Studs Terkel, Donald Tubesing, Voltaire, Sam Walton, Marvin Weisbord, Fred Young.

Part Eight: Robert Ader, ·Herbert Benson, Kenneth Cooper, Hippocrates, Edmund Jacobson, William James, C. Everett Koop, William Shakespeare, Arthur Steinhaus.

Conclusion: John Dewey, Hans Selye, Henry David Thoreau.

Review, advice, and research:

Dale Adams, Ray Benedict, Don Blaz, Nancy Bloehmer, Terri Bonar-Stewart, Christopher Brill, Michael Campbell, Robert Caplon, Jerry Carpenter, Edward Chang, Joseph Creevy, Tom Devine, Jane Dotson, Arlyn Easton, Gary Eippert, Allen Ellis, Rudy Garns, Dan Gibbons, Sharon Glazer, Barbara Gleason, Perilou Goddard, George Goedel, Jo-ann Goodhew, Wendy Gordon, Michael Gray, Frank Hartley, Ronald Heineman, Ray Henschen, William Holloway, Meredith Howe, Alan Kalos, Angela King, David Krings, Pam Kushmerick, Walter Lovenberg, Judith Marksberry, Polly Marquette, Barbara Mathews, John McCollister, Cynthia Miller, William Monnig, Mary Jo Nead, Linda Olasov, William Oliver, Joseph Petrick, Pamela Pfaff, Wiley Piazza, Paul Quealy, Carol Rich, Susan Roth, Sally Rotondo, Ann Royalty, Vince Schulte, Louise Schwarber, Matt Shank, Jeffrey Smith, Merle-Lynn Sproul, Peggy Stapleton, Gil Steinberger, William Stewart, Ralph Tesseneer, James Thomas, Harold Utly, Mary Jo Wakeman, Robert Wallace, Earl Walz, Susan Wehrspann, Ian Wilcox, Robert Wones, Angela Woodward.

About the authors

George Manning is professor of psychology at Northern Kentucky University. Dr. Manning is a consultant to business, industry, and government, serving clients such as AT&T, General Electric, IBM, the United Auto Workers, and the National Institutes of Health. He lectures on economic and social issues including quality of work life, work force values, and business ethics. Dr. Manning maintains an active program of research and writing in organizational psychology. His current studies and interests include the changing meaning of work and coping skills for personal and social change.

Kent Curtis is professor of organizational studies and leadership development at Northern Kentucky University. Dr. Curtis has designed numerous employee and management development programs. He has served as a consultant to business, industry, and government, serving clients such as Houston Medical Center, Wendy's International, and American Electric Power. His current research includes developing the leader as an effective teacher, employee empowerment, and process management.

Steve McMillen is director of executive development and performance improvement at Hillenbrand Industries, Inc. Dr. McMillen has held senior HRD executive positions in the information, publishing, and manufacturing business sectors and has consulted for numerous organizations including General Motors, Junior Achievement, and the National Home Builders Association. His current professional interests include personal and organizational change, peak performance, creativity, and team development.

Stress

Stress (stres), noun. 1. strain; pressure; especially a force exerted upon a body that tends to strain or depress its shape. a) the intensity of such force. b) the resistance or cohesiveness of a body resisting such force. 2. tension; strained exertion: *The stress of war affected all the people.* 3. physical and emotional wear and tear from pressure, conflict, and frustration. 4. physical, emotional, and spiritual fatigue.

Introduction

3,155,414,400	Seconds
52,590,240	Minutes
876,504	Hours
36,521	Days
5,218	Weeks
1,200	Months
400	Seasons
100	Years
1	Life[1]

One life to live

You only have one life to live. What will you do with your life, and how will you live it? These are basic questions that at some point we all must face. This book deals with these questions in the context of managing stress in a changing world.

To personalize the subject, what are the sources of stress in your life? Is your world changing at this point in time? Are there new people, events, and challenges in your life?

How a person manages stress and copes with change affects both the quality and length of life a person can expect. At one pole is a life that is short and unhappy; at the other is a long and fulfilled life based on principles of good living.

How long will you live?

People are unlikely to change the habits of a lifetime unless they are in the mood and can see clearly the benefits of a new pattern of behavior. The quiz beginning on page xvi is designed to gain your attention and put you in the mood to study, learn, and apply the lessons of this book. It is a measure of how long you are expected to live.

Whatever your results on the Life Expectancy Quiz, by applying the principles of this book you can extend longevity and add years to your life and life to your years.

⊘ Application: Life Expectancy Quiz[2]*

Use a blank piece of paper. Begin with the number 76, which is based on the average life expectancy in the United States for all races and sexes combined rounded to the nearest full year. Follow these steps:

Personal facts

- If you are a white male, *subtract 3 years.*

- If you are a black male, *subtract 11 years.*

- All other U.S. males, *subtract 8 years.*

- If you are a white female, *add 4 years.*

- If you are a black female, *subtract 2 years.*

- All other U.S. females, *subtract 0 years.*

    Physical and cultural factors combine to result in different longevity statistics for different races and sexes.

- If you live in an urban area with a population over 2 million (Dade County, Cook County, New York City, Los Angeles, etc.), *subtract 2 years.*

- If you live in a town with a population under 10,000 or on a farm, *add 1 year.*

    One can see the impact of crime, traffic, and pollution on the one hand, in contrast to the idyllic and less stressful nature of rural and village living.

---

*   Health risk appraisals (HRAs) now being used by doctors, medical centers, and insurance companies provide a more accurate picture of probable longevity than old-fashioned actuarial tables that depend almost entirely on hereditary factors and medical history. Current attempts to predict longevity consider personal data and lifestyle behavior as well. Although such questionnaires are generally dependable for large groups of people, they lose precision for individual cases because of individual differences. A high salary may or may not be detrimental to a person's health. It is not how much money you earn, it is how you earn it and what you do with it that counts. Also, marriage or living with a mate is usually expected to increase life expectancy. However, embattled partners may actually increase each other's stress levels and reduce longevity.

- If any natural grandparent lived to 85 or more, *add 2 years.*

- If all four natural grandparents lived to 80 or more, *add 5 additional years.*

  Heredity is an important factor in the stress equation. People once thought that after a stressful day, one could eat a good meal and get a good night's sleep, and come back just as strong as before. This is not so. Every stressful event, good or bad, exacts a toll on the human organism, and this amounts to aging. When we are born, we inherit many characteristics—eye color, skin texture, body type, etc. We also inherit a vitality factor, analogous to a bank account for aging, one on which withdrawals—how fast you spend your life and for what purpose—can be controlled, but not one to which you can add deposits. Inherited vitality influences longevity expectation.

- If either natural parent died of a stroke or heart attack before the age of 50, *subtract 4 years.*

- If any natural parent, brother, or sister under 50 has (or had) cancer or a heart condition, or has had diabetes since childhood, *subtract 3 years.*

- Do you earn over $100,000 a year? *Subtract 1 year.*

  This shows the statistical nature of this questionnaire. There are many individuals who earn high amounts of income from interest-bearing and dividend-providing vehicles with little stress effect. But this is not the norm. Most people who earn high incomes do so as a consequence of demanding and resource-draining schedules and activities.

- If you finished college, *add 1 year.* If you have a graduate or professional degree, *add 2 more.*

- If you are 65 or over and working at something you enjoy, *add 2 years.*

  This shows the importance of an active life for a long life. If you are wondering what to do about parents or grandparents, the answer is to keep them active; keep them active physically, socially, mentally, and occupationally in activities they enjoy.

- If you live with a spouse, friend, or family member, *add 4 years.* If not, *subtract 1 year for every ten years alone since age 25,* unless you have pets.

  This shows the importance of relationships and the fact that people need belonging and love.

- If you have strong social ties, *add 1 year.*

Lifestyle status

- **If your work is sedentary, such as sitting at a desk,** *subtract 2 years.*

  Some people have desks, but they are rarely behind them (imagine the typical factory or field supervisor). Others have desks and are usually behind them (imagine an office supervisor or middle-level manager).

- **If your work requires regular physical activity, such as farm or factory labor,** *add 2 years.*

  If you have ever "put up the hay" or worked at a truly strenuous job, you know how healthful physical exertion can be.

- **If you exercise regularly and moderately (walking, running, swimming, bicycling, etc.) three to five times a week for at least half an hour (5 minutes warmup, 20 minutes aerobic activity, 5 minutes cooldown),** *add 4 years.*

- **Do you sleep more than ten hours each night?** *Subtract 3 years.*

- **If you are intense, aggressive, and easily angered,** *subtract 2 years.*

- **If you are easygoing, laid back, and peaceful,** *add 2 years.*

  If you are unsure, go by what your family would say.

- **Do you have a compelling purpose in life, something important yet to be done?** *Add 1 year.*

- **Are you happy?** *Add 1 year.* **Unhappy?** *Subtract 2.*

  At any point in time, 25 percent of Americans are depressed; chronic or episodic, they are depressed. Hans Selye, the father of stress research and education, discovered in the laboratory what all the poets of all the civilizations have always known—mood affects one's health. When you are happy, your body emits chemicals and hormones that combat disease and prolong life. In contrast, when you are sad or depressed, your body releases chemicals and hormones that can trigger disease and prematurely end life. The prescription is to be happy, and help others to be happy as well.

- **Have you had a speeding ticket in the past year?** *Subtract 1 year.* **If you always wear a seat belt,** *add 1 year.*

  Be sure to buckle up every time you drive, and use defensive driving techniques—pull over to read maps, dial a phone, or eat; and steer clear of anyone who is driving erratically.

- **Do you smoke more than two packs of cigarettes a day?** *Subtract 8 years.*

One to two packs? *Subtract 6.* **One-half to one?** *Subtract 3.* **If you regularly smoke a pipe or cigars,** *subtract 2.*

One can see that for heavy smokers, no single voluntary act has more impact on longevity than to stop smoking.

■ **If you are a male and have more than 3 drinks a day or more than 21 drinks a week,** *subtract 2 years.* **If you are a female and have more than 2 drinks a day or more than 14 drinks a week,** *subtract 2 years.*

Moderate drinking is defined as no more than two drinks a day for men and no more than one drink a day for women. A standard drink is defined as 12 oz. of regular beer, 7 oz. malt liquor, 10 oz. wine cooler, 5 oz. table wine, or 1.5 oz. of 80-proof distilled spirits such as whisky, rum, gin, or vodka. These each have about the same amount of absolute alcohol. People who should not drink alcohol include (1) women who are pregnant or trying to conceive, (2) individuals who plan to drive a car or perform tasks that require attention or skill, (3) individuals using prescription or over-the-counter medications, (4) children and adolescents, and (5) individuals of any age who cannot restrict their drinking to moderate levels.

■ **Are you overweight by 50 pounds or more?** *Subtract 8 years.* **By 30 to 50 pounds?** *Subtract 4.* **By 10 to 30 pounds?** *Subtract 2.*

Clinical obesity is defined by the National Center for Health Statistics as 20 percent more than one's ideal body weight, considering age, height, and bone structure (degrees are mild, 20 to 40 percent overweight; moderate, 40 to 100 percent overweight; severe, 100 percent or more overweight).

■ **If you feel relaxed and stress-free most of the time,** *add 1 year.* **If you feel uptight and under a high degree of stress most of the time,** *subtract 2.*

Stress is physical and emotional wear and tear resulting from real or imagined pressure, conflict, and frustration.

■ **If you are a male over 40 and have regular physical checkups,** *add 2 years.*

■ **If you are a female over 18 and/or sexually active and you see a gynecologist once a year,** *add 2 years.*

■ **If your diastolic blood pressure (the bottom number) is under 90,** *add 1 year.* **If it is from 90 to 104,** *subtract 1.* **If it is above 104,** *subtract 2.*

Note that high blood pressure can usually be reduced by maintaining a moderate weight, exercising regularly, not smoking, limiting salt consumption, and eating foods low in fat and cholesterol.

Age adjustment

- If you are from 32 to 43, *add 2 years.*

- If you are from 44 to 52, *add 3 years.*

- If you are from 53 to 57, *add 4 years.*

- If you are from 58 to 61, *add 5 years.*

- If you are from 62 to 65, *add 6 years.*

- If you are 66 or older, *add 7 years.*

Scoring and interpretation

Enter your total score on the Life Expectancy Quiz: _____. Life expectancy is the number of years, on average, that someone at a particular age is expected to live. Figure I.1 shows how your score compares with national average life expectancies.

Figure I.1 Average Life Expectancy in the United States,
All Races and Both Sexes Combined, 1994[3]

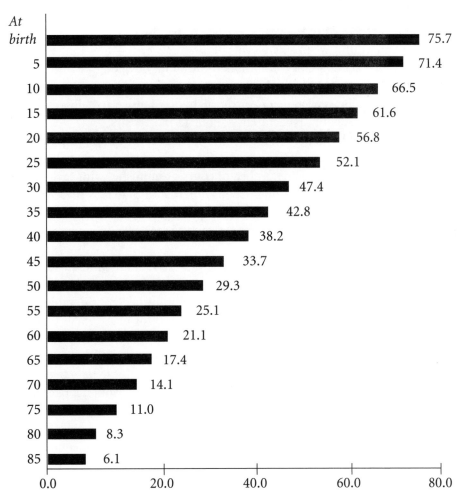

Number of years of additional life expected

Example: Current age (30) + Number of years of additional life expected (47.4) =
Average individual life expectancy (77.4)

In 1995, the average life expectancy in the United States for all races and sexes combined was 75.8 years—a full 28.5 years longer than in 1900. See Appendix A. Provisional data shows that the average life expectancy will have increased from 47.3 years in 1900 to 76.4 in the year 2000. See Appendix B.

When we are young, we think in terms of how old we are—how long we have lived. But as we get older, we begin to think more about how long we have left to live. Reassuringly, the older we are, the longer we can expect to live—up to a point. Thus, although our life expectancy at birth might be 75, if we actually reach the age of 75, we can reasonably expect to live about 11 more years.

The most-used column in a life table is the one that reveals average life expectation. It answers this question: Given a certain age, on average, how many more years can one expect to live? The number, of course, diminishes with each birthday. The life table from the National Center for Health Statistics presented in Appendix C gives the number of years of life expectation for every age from birth to age 85, assuming that the death rates for each age in 1995 are equally applicable for the next 85 years.

As Appendix C shows, 1995 life expectancies were 73.4 for white males, 65.2 for black males, 79.6 for white females, and 73.9 for black females. Life expectancy differences between whites and blacks have diminished considerably since 1900, when life expectation at birth was 15.7 years less for black males than for white males and 16 years less for black females than for white females.

Theories abound, but the fact remains—when it comes to life expectancy or the average number of years a person is expected to live: it helps to be active; good genes count; where you live is important; love is a positive attribute; it pays to be happy; one needs a purpose in life; stress management helps; physical checkups matter; exercise is important; but most dramatic of all, eat right and don't smoke. Keep your weight within healthy limits, and if you smoke, stop immediately. Finally, as food for thought and reinforcement of the importance of a positive mental attitude, ask Satchel Paige's famous question—"How old would you really be if you didn't know how old you really were?"

Life span and longevity—outer limits and life expectancy

All forms of life have a characteristic *life span*. This refers to the upper boundary of years a given species can expect to live. Examples are 3 years for a mouse, 25 years for a lion, 39 years for a chimpanzee, and 63 years for an elephant. Some organisms are extremely long-lived. The scraggly bristlecone pines of California are older than the pyramids, having lived almost 5000 years. Human beings live longer than any other mammal, with a life span in the range of 110 years and a maximum of about 120.[4]

Longevity refers to the average expected length of life at any particular time in history, in a particular culture. Figure I.2 compares modern day longevity with that of our forefathers. It is astonishing to realize that human beings survived hundreds of thousands of years, more than 99 percent of our existence, with a life expectation at birth of only 18 years, and that almost half the increase in longevity has occurred in the twentieth century. A child born in the United States in 1996 can expect to live about 29 years longer than a child born in 1900.

Longevity and life expectancy have been increasing dramatically in developed societies. In 1900, 75 percent of the people in the United States died before they reached the age of 65. Today, this figure is reversed; about 70 percent of people die after the age of 65.[5] As for the future, the Social Security Administration predicts that by the year 2050, life expectancy will rise to 76.5 for men, on average, and 83 for women. Much of this increase can be attributed to improvements in public health policy and progress in the areas of disease prevention, safe food, water and sewage, nutrition, sanitation, and health education.

Figure I.2 Human Life Expectancy at Birth from Prehistoric to Contemporary Times[6]

Time Period	Average Life Expectancy (in years)
Prehistoric Times	18
Ancient Greece	20
Middle Ages, England	33
1620, Massachusetts Bay Colony	35
19th Century, England	41
1900, United States	47
1915, United States	54
1954, United States	70
1983, United States	75
1990, United States	75.4
1991, United States	75.5
1992, United States	75.8
1993, United States	75.5
1994, United States	75.7
1995, United States	76.3
2000, United States (projected)	76.4
2005, United States (projected)	76.9
2010, United States (projected)	77.4

Despite increases in longevity and life expectancy, the human life span has remained roughly unchanged. Through healthful habits and other advances, many more people can live to be 100 and older; but, thus far, improvements in disease prevention and health care have not extended the upper boundary beyond the 110 to 120 age range.[7] In 1997, Jeanne Calment, recognized as the world's oldest person, died in Arles, France at the age of 122.

The normal process of aging cannot be prevented by any means yet devised. We begin aging even before we are born, and this process continues throughout our lives. The effects of aging result from wear and tear on the body's essential cellular functions that gradually change and become less efficient over the years. The body wears out even as the best-designed and well-maintained machine wears out. However, with care and healthful living, a person's mind and body can be vibrant and healthy for nearly the entire length of his or her life.

> In 1920, at the age of 14, Aileen Riggin became the youngest female Olympic gold medalist by winning the women's springboard diving at Antwerp. In 1924, she won a silver medal in springboard and a bronze in the 100-meter backstroke at Paris. After her Olympic career, Aileen continued an active lifestyle by becoming one of the first female sportswriters, a dancer, and a skater. To this day, Aileen Riggin Soule still leads an energetic life. She continues to write for leading magazines, and she has never stopped swimming. This may account for her being a very vibrant 90 years young![8]

Purpose of this book

If life is a stress test and change is our challenge, this book is a primer. It explains what stress is, what its causes and consequences are, and how you can deal successfully with change.

Figure I.3 shows how you can use each part of the book to improve both the length and the quality of your life by moving from problems and deficiencies toward health and happiness.

Figure I.4 shows how stress events may or may not be harmful, depending on whether they are moderated by a positive appraisal, a stress-resistant personality, healthy habits, coping techniques, and enduring social support.

Figure I.3 Positive Forces Impacting the Length and Quality of Life

Moving *from* Problems ⟶ Moving *toward* Health
and Deficiencies and Happiness

Part 1 *Understanding Stress*
Maintain balance between stress
in your world and your resources
for coping.

Part 2 *Personality and Stress*
Use wisdom of the ages and the
characteristics of a hardy
personality for managing stress.

Part 3 *Stress Across the Life Span*
View change as a challenge and
master the developmental tasks
of adulthood.

Part 4 *Personal Stress*
Know who you are and what is
important as anchor and sextant
for a long and happy life.

Part 5 *Interpersonal Stress*
Develop positive relationships
based on mutual understanding,
trust, and respect.

Part 6 *Stress in the Workplace*
Manage stress on the job; avoid
the burnout phenomenon and
experience "flow."

Part 7 *Peak Performance*
Gain control of your time and
your life; be or become your full
potential as a person.

Part 8 *Stress Prevention*
Maintain a readiness plan to deal
effectively with stress.

Figure I.4 Managing Stress

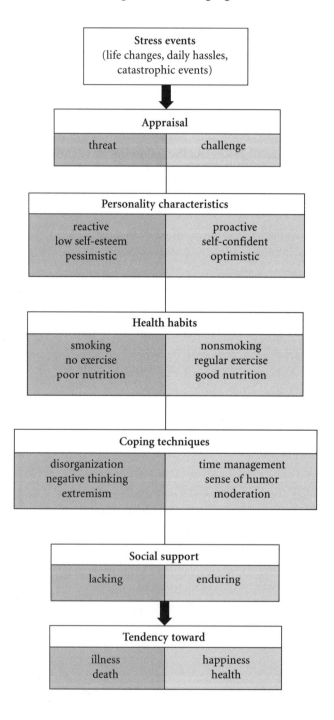

Each person plays many roles in life. Like a juggler, we must balance the demands of work and the demands of home. We must also balance the sometimes conflicting urges of our cultural and biological selves. Like an animal trainer, we must overcome internal fears with personal courage, the technique of self-talk, and bold action to overcome obstacles. Like a tightrope walker, we must deal with life's transitions from one point to another with an open mind and a positive attitude. The purpose of this book is to help you master these and other stressful roles.

The goal of this book is to develop constructive ways to manage stress both on the job and in the home. As the following story shows, you never know when you might need your stress-coping techniques.

> A young man attended his company's Christmas party where a young lady had too much to drink. Being the gentleman he was, he offered to drive her home. And being safety conscious as he was, he made sure she was deposited securely in her house.
>
> When he arrived at his own home, his wife suggested that they go out to get a bite to eat. Sure, he said; and off they drove. As they passed the local shopping district, his wife pointed to a "Sale" sign at one of her favorite stores.
>
> That's when he saw the "toe"—a woman's shoe was sticking out from under the seat. With his wife looking out the window, he rolled down his own window, reached down, grabbed the shoe, and tossed it out.
>
> Relieved, he drove on to the restaurant, pulled into a parking space, and climbed out of the car. When he looked back, he saw his wife searching everywhere. She said, "Have you seen my shoe?"
>
> As the young man was to learn, you never know when you might have to use your stress coping techniques.[9]

Introduction References

[1]   Leonard Hayflick, *How and Why We Age* (New York: Ballentine Books, 1994), 303.

[2]   U.S. National Center for Health Statistics, *Vital Statistics of the United States;* U.S. Bureau of the Census, *Statistical Abstract of the United States: 1998,* 118th ed. (Washington, D.C.: 1998); and Robert F. Allen and Shirley Linde, *Lifegain: The Exciting New Program that Will Change Your Health— and Your Life* (Norwalk, Conn.: Appleton-Century-Crofts, 1981; modified 1998).

[3]   U.S. National Center for Health Statistics, *Vital Statistics of the United States;* U.S. Bureau of the Census, "Expectation of Life and Expected Deaths by Race, Sex, and Age: 1995," *Statistical Abstract of the United States: 1998, 118th ed.* (Washington, D.C.: 1998).

[4]   Alex Comfort, *The Biology of Senescence*, 3rd ed. (New York: Elsevier North Holland, 1979); and Marvin L. Jones, registrar of The Zoological Society of San Diego, California, in Hayflick, *How and Why We Age,* 29, 32.

[5]   Hayflick, *How and Why We Age.*

[6]   Monroe Lerner, "When, Why, and Where People Die," in E. S. Shneidman, ed., *Death: Current Perspectives*, 3rd ed. (Palo Alto, Calif.: Mayfield, 1984); and U.S. National Center for Health Statistics, U.S. Life Tables and Actuarial Tables, 1959-61, and 1979-81, *Vital Statistics of the United States, annual, 1998, 118th ed.* and unpublished data (Washington, D.C.: 1998)

[7]   Leonard Hayflick, "Why Grow Old?" *The Stanford Magazine* 3, no.1 (1975): 36-43; and P. Yin and M. Shine, "Misinterpretations of Increases in Life Expectancy in Gerontology Textbooks," *The Gerontologist* 25 (1985): 78-82.

[8]   Steve Wulf, "She Has Done Just Swimmingly," *Time,* special edition, Summer 1996, p. 96.

[9]   "The Life of a Young Man," Mike Campbell, Kentucky Power Company, Ashland, Ky., 1994.

Part One

Understanding Stress

1. Stress Physiology

2. Stress in Your World

The job of managing a career isn't too bad. Deadlines, travel, and all the meetings are fine. I can handle being a father to two boys and a new baby girl. Being a husband and spending time with my wife is great. The work of keeping up a home and yard is OK too. It's doing all of these things at the same time that's killing me. I hope I can keep up.—Author's file notes (G. M.)

What you will learn in Part One

In Part One you will learn:

- the definition, causes, and consequences of stress;

- the importance of health habits and social relationships for managing stress;

- the "critical balance" between the demands you face and your resources for coping.

Chapter One
★
Stress Physiology

Introduction

In 1993 the World Health Organization spoke out on its number-one health concern for the industrialized world over the current decade. The issue had nothing to do with acute disease such as AIDS, infectious disease, cancer, or pollution. Instead, a chronic nonmedical problem—stress—was the organization's primary health concern for the 1990s.[1]

A 1983 survey found that 28 percent of Americans felt under great stress either almost every day or several days a week. Less than a decade later, the Baxter Survey of American Health Habits indicated that the percentage had risen to 33 percent. More and more people are living with high stress every day.[2]

If you do not manage stress successfully, the price can be great. The following statements are not just meaningless sayings:

"That accident took ten years off my life."

"I was sick with worry."

"This job is killing me."

"He gives me a pain in the neck."

The stress caused by an accident *can* age you prematurely; the stress caused by emotional worry *can* make you physically sick; your job *can* affect your health; and the stress from dealing with difficult people and unpleasant situations *can* cause aches and pains in the neck, stomach, and other places.

Learning to manage stress effectively is one of life's developmental tasks. It is the secret to living a long and satisfying life. For the typical person, half the source of stress is job related and half is connected to home and family. If the workplace is stressful, it helps to have a port in the storm at home; if there is stress on the home front, ideally there is smooth sailing on the job. But the person who is fighting a two-front war—problems on the job and problems in the home—has double trouble and is a candidate for what used to be called "breakdown" and is now popularly known as "burnout."[3]

What is stress?

The term "stress" has been used in various ways by many theorists. Some define stress as a stimulus or event, such as loss of a job. Others define stress as the response to or effect of physiological arousal. An approach that combines both views is to define stress as a transaction—physical and emotional wear and tear resulting from real or imagined problems. Types of problems include:

- **Pressures**, such as the effort required to raise a family and earn a living. A midcareer professional reports:

  Industrial-strength pressure
  Sometimes my chest feels like a drum and bugle corps marching and pounding. Then I know I have overdone it, and the answer is to shut down, go away, and rest, cursing myself for having let things get so bad.

- **Conflicts**, such as choosing between alternative careers, mates, and lifestyles. Conflicts include arguments with others and arguments with self. Consider a young professional experiencing four basic conflicts:[4]

  Decisions, decisions, decisions:
  Do I take job A or job B? I like them equally, and the pay is the same. (*Approach-approach conflicts* are those in which we have to choose between two equally desirable, but mutually exclusive, people, objects, or events.)

  I want to marry Bill, but if I do, I will have to move to China. (*Approach-avoidance conflicts* involve having to choose whether or not to pursue a course that has both positive and negative qualities or consequences.)

  Do I confront my boss, or do I accept these negative employment conditions? Either choice is bad. (*Avoidance-avoidance conflict* is having to choose between two undesirable options.)

  I have a choice of two homes. One is well-constructed and charming, but the location isn't good. The other is in a good location, but the home isn't as pretty and sound. (A *double approach-avoidance conflict* means having to choose between two alternatives, each of which has positive and negative attributes.)

- **Frustrations**, such as wanting but not being able to afford a home of your own, or wanting but not having good relations with someone you love. Consider the case of one man, married more than thirty years:

  We have met the enemy, and he is us
  I love my wife with all my heart, and she loves me. In fact, we each think the other is the best person a person can be. Yet life together is filled with stress. We talk *at* each other, *around* each other, or *fail* to talk at all. For both of us, it is the single biggest frustration in our lives. Others can't understand it. They think she is an angel and I'm a saint. But we both know, it isn't easy.

The human organism wears down with problems and age much the same as physical structures deteriorate from weather and time. Problems may be caused by self or caused by others. They may occur on the job or in the home. They may be large or small. They may develop early in life or late. Yet each problem exacts a toll; each results in physical and emotional wear and tear on the person. Like a metal bridge that deteriorates from the effects of weather and time, the human organism wears down and tears down with pressure, conflict, and frustration.

Stressors can be *acute*, such as the death of a loved one; *sequential*, such as a series of events leading to a marriage or move; *intermittent*, such as monthly bills and chores; or *chronic*, such as the daily commute through rush-hour traffic or the daily stress involved with one's job.

Each person has a breaking point for dealing with stress. A period of too much pressure, too many conflicts, and too much frustration can take one closer and closer to that point. That is why it is important to anticipate potential stressors and plan how to deal with them.

Consider yourself: What is your major source of stress, and is this primarily a pressure, conflict, or frustration? One can see that it is possible to have an interaction effect. For example, pressure to perform can lead to interpersonal conflict, and this can lead to feelings of frustration.

Stressors tend to be different for different ages and types of people. A recent survey of college students revealed the following top ten sources of stress: (1) final exam week, (2) test anxiety, (3) academic workload, (4) future plans, (5) putting off assignments, (6) financial pressures, (7) grades received, (8) guilt from not performing better, (9) worrying about not exercising, and (10) competitiveness for grades.[5]

The general adaptation syndrome

A clumsy scientist can be blamed for introducing stress into our lives. Hans Selye, a young endocrinologist in the 1930s, had a habit of dropping his laboratory rats on the floor, chasing them around the room, and trapping them beneath the sink. Soon they developed ulcers and shrunken immune systems. Selye did many tests and came to the realization that his clumsiness was making them sick. Selye, a Hungarian born in Vienna and working in Canada, searched for an English word to describe this response to life under tension. Borrowed from the field of engineering, the term "stress" was born.[6]

Our knowledge of stress has been greatly influenced by Selye, who served his entire professional life at McGill University in Montreal. Selye began his research on stress in 1936. By the time of his death in 1982, he had published more than sixteen hundred articles and thirty-three books, and was recognized as the father of stress physiology and stress education.

Selye's data provided evidence that the body goes through a predictable response to any kind of demand. He identified this response as the "general adaptation syndrome" (GAS). The GAS is triggered by any threat to the physical or emotional well-being of the organism. The response occurs in three phases—the alarm reaction, the resistance stage, and the exhaustion stage.[7]

The alarm reaction

In the first phase, the *alarm* reaction, the body's physiological resistance dips slightly below normal as preparation is made to fight the stressor. With initial shock, temperature and blood pressure, as well as blood fluid and potassium levels, decline and muscles slacken. This is followed by an arousal response that includes the release of powerful hormones called catecholamines (adrenaline, noradrenaline, etc.), which create a defense for survival. Important reactions include:

- surges in heart rate that increase the heart's pumping ability, thus delivering additional power and blood volume at a moment's notice;

- elevated blood sugar levels that supply instant muscle energy;

- diversion of blood from the digestive organs to the skeletal muscles and brain, allowing for a quick getaway or knockout blow;

- faster blood clotting that reduces the likelihood of bleeding to death from wounds;

- increased breathing rate, so that more oxygen is available to the body's vital organs.

In addition to the catecholamines, the alarm reaction stimulates production of other substances, including endorphins, which decrease the body's sensitivity to pain, and hormones, which can increase both visual and auditory alertness. In the alarm phase, the body shows generalized stress arousal, but no one specific organ system is affected, although most and sometimes all of the body systems show measurable changes.[8]

The organism cannot maintain high levels of shock and arousal for long. Indeed, under severe stress, the alarm reaction can lead to sickness and even death. Prolonged high blood sugar level has the effect of decreasing resistance to infection, and the alarm reaction to intense fear may result in heart stoppage.[9]

Stage of resistance

Under less severe conditions, the organism enters into a second phase, a stage of *resistance*. In the stage of resistance, the organism may appear to adapt; however, it is vulnerable. The stress response is channeled into the specific organ system or process most appropriate for dealing with it. However, this adaptation process contributes to stress-related illness. The specific organ system becomes activated, and with prolonged activation it may wear out and malfunction. If additional stress is introduced, it may overload capacity to resist. This is how the phenomenon of constant vigilance can lead to fatigue, sickness, and the third phase of the GAS, exhaustion.[10]

Stage of exhaustion

If stress continues, the final phase, the stage of *exhaustion*, may be reached. During this stage, the immune system is considerably weakened, increasing the likelihood of infection and tissue breakdown. As with stress on a Holland dike, too much overload, and the sea pours in. Physiologically, this can mean breakdown of the body's weaker systems. In modern society, the heart and blood vessels of the cardiovascular system are most often weakened.[11] In the stage of exhaustion the body's resources are depleted, breakdown occurs, and death may result. See Figure 1.1.

Although research shows individual differences in the appraisal of stress and subtle differences in the body's reaction to different stressors, few medical experts today quarrel with Selye's basic point that prolonged stress produces physical deterioration. This leads to the practical concerns of this book: What causes stress? What are the consequences of stress? And how can stress be managed?

Figure 1.1 The General Adaptation Syndrome

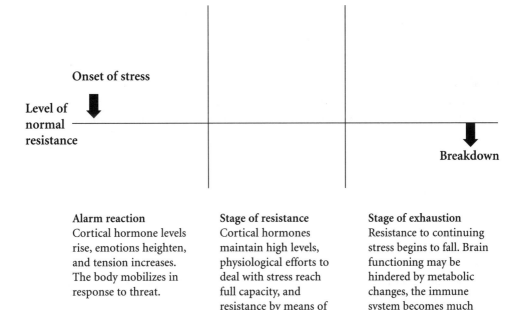

Onset of stress

Level of normal resistance

Breakdown

Alarm reaction
Cortical hormone levels rise, emotions heighten, and tension increases. The body mobilizes in response to threat.

Stage of resistance
Cortical hormones maintain high levels, physiological efforts to deal with stress reach full capacity, and resistance by means of defense mechanisms and coping strategies intensify.

Stage of exhaustion
Resistance to continuing stress begins to fall. Brain functioning may be hindered by metabolic changes, the immune system becomes much less efficient, and serious illness or disease becomes likely as the body begins to break down. Death may result.

Source: Hans Selye, The Stress of Life, *rev. ed. (New York: McGraw-Hill, Inc. 1984). Reprinted with permission.*

The fight-or-flight response

When a threat to well-being is perceived, a small area of the brain known as the hypothalamus is activated. The hypothalamus stimulates a number of physiological changes involving activity in both the endocrine system and the autonomic nervous system. You have probably felt the fight-or-flight response to stress—your heart beats faster, you feel a surge of energy, and you are mobilized to take protective action.

Specifically, the master gland of the endocrine system, the pituitary gland, sends adrenocorticotropic hormone (ACTH) into the bloodstream. ACTH activates the outer layer, or cortex, of the adrenal gland, and this results in the production of numerous glucocorticoids, including cortisol, a chemical that increases blood sugar and speeds up body metabolism.

Simultaneously, nerve impulses from the sympathetic branch of the autonomic nervous system reach the core, or the medulla, of the adrenal glands, resulting in the release of adrenaline (also called epinephrine), which helps supply glucose to be used as fuel for increased muscle and nervous system activity, and noradrenaline (also called norepinephrine), which speeds up the heart rate and raises blood pressure. Within seconds, the entire organism is brought into an aroused physical state.[12]

In addition, the individual experiences a state of general mental anxiety. No matter what you are consciously thinking, the endocrine system and autonomic nervous system have alerted and prepared your body to take action so that you can either combat the threat or run away. If you do fight or flee, chemicals and hormones that have been generated are metabolized quickly. This biological response to stress, known as the fight-or-flight syndrome, was first described by Walter B. Cannon of Harvard Medical School in the early 1900s. His book, *The Wisdom of the Body,* published in 1932, is one of the most important books ever written on the subject of stress.

> As a matter of routine, I have long trusted unconscious processes to serve me. . . . [One] example I may cite was the interpretation of the significance of bodily changes which occur in great emotional excitement, such as fear and rage. These changes—the more rapid pulse, the deeper breathing, the increase of sugar in the blood, the secretions from the adrenal glands—were very diverse and seemed unrelated. Then, one wakeful night, after a considerable collection of these changes had been disclosed, the idea flashed through my mind that they could be nicely integrated if conceived as bodily preparations for supreme effort in flight or in fighting.—Walter B. Cannon

See Figure 1.2 for an illustration of brain-body pathways during times of stress.

For early men and women threatened by large predators, forest fires, and adverse climatic conditions, the fight-or-flight syndrome was an excellent aid for survival. When they rounded a bend and saw danger staring at them, a quick and automatic response prepared them to either fight or flee and thus cope with the problem. However, as explained by Selye in his 1956 book, *The Stress of Life*, response can be hazardous for modern men and women. Times have changed, but human physiology has not.

Today, most of the threats we face are psychological instead of physical (a difficult boss, for example); fighting is inappropriate (it just makes a bad situation worse); and escape is not feasible (running away is usually not possible). Yet our bodies react just as did our ancestors'—hormones and chemicals are automatically activated as a response to threat. Having been taught not to fight and being unable or unwilling to flee, we usually "sit tight." In this state, the level of metabolites in the bloodstream increases, and internal organs experience harmful wear and tear. Damage may result in a heart attack, stroke, ulcerative colitis, or some other harmful disease, depending on what heredity and history have predisposed for the individual.

Figure 1.2 Brain-Body Pathways During Stress

In times of stress, the hypothalamus sends signals along two pathways. The pathway through the autonomic nervous system controls the release of catecholamine hormones, which help mobilize the body for action. The pathway through the pituitary gland and the endocrine system controls the release of corticosteroid hormones, which increase energy and ward off inflammation of the tissues.[13]

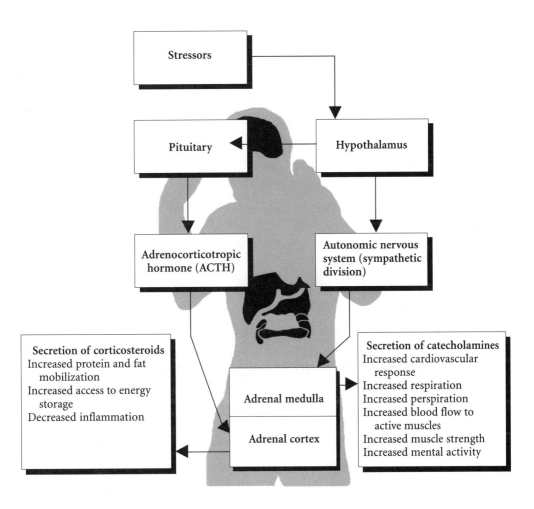

Figure 1.3 shows the effects of short- and long-term stress. Eventually we reach an adaptability limit that produces a need for a greater recovery period. This has implications for people who are confronted with multiple and seemingly endless problems both at home and at work.

Selye concludes that the fight-or-flight syndrome, so useful to our ancestors, can be a destructive force for people today unless it is managed properly. This is why stress has been called the dominant disease of modern times. Selye writes:

> We are just beginning to see that many common diseases are largely due to errors in our adaptive response to stress, rather than to direct damage by germs, poisons, or life experience. In this sense, many nervous and emotional disturbances, high blood pressure, gastric and duodenal ulcers, and certain types of sexual, allergic, cardiovascular, and renal derangements appear to be essentially diseases of adaptation.[14]

Costs of stress—disease and aging

During the 1930s, Harold Wolff of Cornell Medical College found that colds, flu, ulcers, arthritis, heart disease, and tuberculosis are stress related.[15] Physical and emotional wear and tear weaken the organism; fatigue results; and the person becomes susceptible to illness. In fact, according to the American Academy of Family Physicians, 75 to 90 percent of all office visits to health care professionals are for stress-related symptoms and disorders.[16]

Stress-related disorders include tension and migraine headaches, cardiovascular disease, stomach and intestinal problems, rheumatoid arthritis, and pains in the neck and back. Unfortunately, prolonged stress also leads to a weakening of the body's immune system, which makes recuperation from illness difficult. People experiencing emotional stress can have difficulty shaking a common cold or recovering from pneumonia. Accumulating evidence also indicates that some forms of cancer, including leukemia and lymphomas, are related to prolonged stress reactions.[17]

Figure 1.3 Recovery Periods for Short- and Long-Term Stress

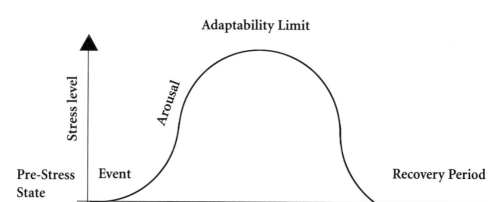

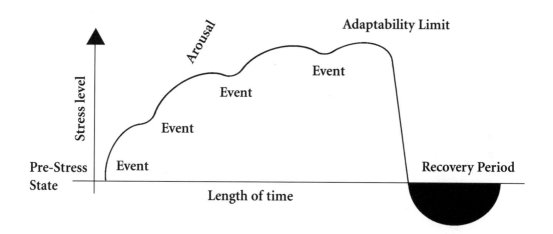

Note: Recurring stress over a long period of time produces the need for a greater recovery period.

A pattern of illness unfolds when people perceive (1) overwhelming stressful situations that (2) cannot be resolved effectively, leading to (3) a sense of helplessness, anger, and depression, which (4) weakens resistance to disease and (5) raises vulnerability to ever-present pathogenic agents, resulting in (6) illnesses ranging from heart attack to the common cold.[18]

What disease a person may develop depends on both genetic makeup and environmental exposure, not on either factor alone. For example, cholera is rare in America today, but flu viruses are common. Everyone has some idea of his or her own weakest area—for one, it may be the kidneys; for another, the heart; yet another may be susceptible to respiratory problems.

Ulysses S. Grant wrote in his Civil War diary that on the night before Appomattox, when Robert E. Lee refused to surrender, he had gone to bed with an excruciating headache. However, as soon as word arrived that Lee had changed his mind, Grant's headache disappeared. Everyone, even Civil War generals, experiences headaches, and often they are the direct result of the stress that is a part of our daily lives.[19]

Aging is also stress related. Perhaps the best definition of the aging process is "the wearing down and tearing down of the organism." Think of your own parents, for example. When did they seem to age the most rapidly? It was probably when they were under the most stress. And when was that? It was probably when you were a teenager. If you are a parent yourself, you may have noticed yourself aging before your very eyes.

It is interesting to know that the bio-markers or physiological signs of aging are manageable. This helps explain why one forty-year-old may look fifty while another forty-year-old may not even look thirty. Selye explains the relationship between stress and the aging process:

> True age depends largely on the rate of wear and tear, on the speed of self-consumption; for life is essentially a process which gradually spends the given amount of adaptation energy that we inherited from our parents. Vitality is like a special kind of bank account which you can use up by withdrawals but cannot increase by deposits. Your only control over this most precious fortune is the rate at which you make your withdrawals. The solution is evidently not to stop withdrawing, for this would be death. Nor is it to withdraw just enough for survival, for this would permit only a vegetative life, worse than death. The intelligent thing to do is to withdraw and expend generously, but never wastefully for worthless efforts.

> Many people believe that after they have exposed themselves to very stressful activities, a rest can restore them to where they were before. This is false. Experiments on animals have clearly shown that each exposure leaves an indelible scar, in that it uses up reserves of adaptability which cannot be replaced. It is true that immediately after some harassing experience, rest can restore us almost to the original level of fitness by eliminating acute fatigue. But the emphasis is on the word almost. Since we constantly go through periods of stress and rest during life, even a minute deficit of adaptation energy every day adds up—it adds up to what we call aging.[20]

The philosophical question faced by every person is, are you aging at the rate you want and for the purposes you want? You only have one life to live—are you spending your life on what is important to you and at the pace you desire?

The consequences of stress can be high. Costs can be understood in terms of four stress-associated Ds: disorders, drugs, dollars, and death.

Disorders

- More than 60 million Americans—more than one in four—have one or more types of cardiovascular disease.

- About 50 million Americans age six and older have high blood pressure (hypertension).

- As many as one and a half million Americans will have a new or recurrent heart attack each year, and about one-third of them will die.

- More than 30 million Americans have chronic conditions of diabetes, ulcers, migraine, and stomach disorders.

Drugs

- Approximately 25 percent of Americans 18 and older are currently smoking cigarettes.

- Billions of doses of tranquilizers, amphetamines, and barbiturates are prescribed each year.

- From youth to old age, millions of Americans are abusing drugs ranging from cocaine to hallucinogens.

Dollars

- The annual cost of hospital care in the United States exceeds $358 billion.

- The yearly cost of physician services is more than $202 billion.

- Drugs and other medical nondurables cost more than $91 billion each year.

- The overall national health expenditures increased from $26 billion a year in 1960 to $1035.1 billion a year in 1996.

Death

- More than 150,000 Americans die of stroke each year.

- More than 730,000 deaths occur each year due to heart disease.

    2,000 deaths occur each day
    83 deaths occur each hour
    More than 1 death occurs every minute

- More than 31,000 Americans commit suicide each year.

Although statistics such as these are staggering, they are somewhat impersonal. They do not communicate the suffering of the victims of stress and their loved ones. True understanding comes from personal exposure to the costs of stress—premature aging and the four Ds (disorders, drugs, dollars, and death).[21]

To personalize the subject of stress, health, and aging—if you were to become ill, what would your illness probably be; what have history and heredity predisposed for you? What about the aging process? What is your true age, based on the amount of wear and tear you have experienced? Perhaps most importantly, are you spending your adaptive energy at the rate you wish and for the purposes you value?

Personal signs of stress

People react to stress in different ways. Warning signals are varied and are unique to the individual. One person may have a nervous tic or bite her fingernails; another may crack his knuckles or grind his teeth.

Whatever your symptoms are, your body will usually tell you when you are experiencing too much stress, if you will only pay attention. Learn what your warning signals are; then, when you notice them, act to relieve the problem. Common physical, behavioral, and psychological signs of stress include:

- **Aches and pains.** When a person complains, "I have a headache," it may be caused by pressure, conflict, and frustration, resulting in body tension.

- **Sweating hands and paling or flushing of the face.** Many people experience these physical symptoms of too much stress. Do you know someone who gets sweaty palms, sweaty feet, or sweaty other things as a sign of stress?

- **Inability to sleep or sleeping too much.** Some people toss and turn and cannot sleep because of too much stress. Others wake up in the morning, look at the world, say "Oh, no!"—and go right back to sleep. Both insomnia and sleeping too much are common signs of too much stress.

- **Inability to eat or eating too much.** Some people have upset stomachs and do not want to eat when they are under stress. Others have the opposite response—the refrigerator reaction: When they experience stress, they may consume enormous amounts of candy, baked goods, salted snacks, or pizzas. Overeating is a common reaction to too much stress.

- **Skin disorders.** Can you remember your first date? It may have gone like this: Five o'clock on a Saturday afternoon, you went into the bathroom to get ready to go. You looked in the mirror, and right in the middle of your forehead…there was a big pimple. This may have been your sign of too much stress. Both psychologists and dermatologists have long known that emotional problems can trigger skin disorders.

- **Mental and emotional blanks.** Your mind may go blank for short periods of time, or you may become temporarily numb to feelings because of stress. If continued over a long period of time, these mental and emotional blanks may result in a general lack of interest in people, ideas, and events in life.

- **Mistakes and accidents.** Have you ever forgotten something for no apparent reason? Have you ever had an accident for seemingly no cause at all? With severe or prolonged stress, objective thinking and problem-solving abilities decrease. Forgetfulness, errors, and accidents are common signs of too much stress.[22]

Mind-blank

As I was finishing graduate school and starting to work on the dissertation, I was trying to locate an organization that would provide me with a research population. One day I was meeting with a senior executive and discussing the possibility of doing research at her firm. The executive started asking me questions about my references and previous work experiences. She was very assertive and I found myself getting nervous. At one point, she asked me to describe some work I had mentioned on my resume. My mind went blank and I started to sweat. I could not think of any work I had done for that organization and my interviewer became increasingly suspicious. She quickly concluded the interview and skeptically said, "If you can ever think of the work you did, please call me and let me know about it." It wasn't until two hours later that I remembered. This was a significant and memorable experience for me in that it showed the very real impact stress can have on the functioning of mind and body.—Author's file notes (S. M.)

In addition to physical, behavioral, and psychological signs of stress, social problems such as family abuse, alcohol and drug addiction, and irritability with others can be signs of too much stress. When a situation becomes overly stressful, some people turn to alcohol and drugs for relief, and many become chemically dependent. Statistics show that 14 percent of Americans abuse or are dependent on alcohol and that 5 percent abuse or are dependent on other drugs.[23]

When stress levels are high, some people displace their feelings onto close or safe targets. These are often the people they care about the most, such as family and friends. Perhaps you have kicked the dog, husband, wife, or other family member when you have been under stress. Whether you kick someone physically or psychologically, the blow usually hurts the relationship and results in increased stress.

To personalize the subject, what are your signs of stress? How do you know when you are experiencing too much pressure, conflict, or frustration; and, importantly, do you act upon this awareness, or do you deny reality until *pressures* reach the breaking point, *conflicts* erupt harmfully, or you explode in *frustration*? Also, do you experience stress at a certain time of the day (morning, afternoon, evening); at a particular place (work, home); with certain people (family, coworkers, boss)? Knowing your signs of stress and acting to defuse stressful situations in a positive way are important elements in effective stress management. Figure 1.4 shows signs of stress at each stage of the general adaptation syndrome.

Figure 1.4 Signs of Stress

Stage 1—Alarm Reaction: The Stress-Arousal Stage (includes the following symptoms)

Physical
High blood pressure
Unusual heart rhythms (skipped beats)
Sweating; cold chills
Headaches; stomachaches
Grimaces and twitches

Behavioral
Arguments/irritability
Insomnia
Crying
Resistance/lack of creativity
Bruxism (grinding the teeth)

Psychological
Anxiety
Forgetfulness
Inability to concentrate
Misplacing things
Anger

Stage 2—Stage of Resistance: The Energy-Conservation Stage (includes the following symptoms)

Physical
Decreased sexual desire
Persistent tiredness
Tightness in neck and/or shoulders

Behavioral
Lateness for work
Missed deadlines
Increased alcohol consumption
Increased coffee, tea, or cola consumption
Excess smoking
Excess sleeping
Excess eating

Psychological
Procrastination
Cynical attitude
Resentment
"I don't care" attitude
Loss of sense of humor
Constant worry
Loneliness

Stage 3—Stage of Exhaustion: The Breakdown Stage (includes the following symptoms)

Physical
Chronic headaches
Chronic physical fatigue
Chronic stomach or bowel problems

Behavioral
Inability to make decisions
Physical withdrawal from
    friends, work, and family

Psychological
Chronic sadness or depression
Chronic mental fatigue
Desire to "drop out"
Sense of hopelessness

Source: Based on the work of Daniel A. Girdano and George S. Everly Jr., Controlling Stress and Tension, 3rd ed. *(Englewood Cliffs, N.J.: Prentice-Hall, Inc., 1990).*

The importance of health habits and social conditions

A wellness cushion involving good *health habits* and *supportive social conditions* can be an important ally in managing stress in your life. Although some health and social problems may be unavoidable, many problems are self-induced and can be easily corrected.

Health habits

Actuarial statistics and death records show that few people die of old age. Instead, they die because of poor health habits. Their hearts have been underdeveloped and overworked because of lack of exercise; their livers have been abused by too much alcohol; their lungs have been ruined by cigarette smoke; their blood vessels have been clogged by a poor diet; or some other harmful health practice has accelerated wear and tear and contributed to their death.[24] Selye states:

> To die of old age would mean that all the organs of the body had worn out proportionately, merely by having been used too long. This is never the case. We invariably die because one vital part has worn out too early in proportion to the rest of the body. Life, the biologic chain that holds our parts together, is only as strong as its weakest vital link. When this breaks—no matter which vital link it is—our parts can no longer be held together as a single living being.[25]

In 1979, U.S. Surgeon General Julius B. Richmond issued Healthy People: The Surgeon General's Report on Health Promotion and Disease Prevention. The report stated that as many as half the premature deaths in the United States could be traced to unhealthy behaviors or lifestyles.

The U.S. Public Health Service reports that more than half of all deaths continue to be caused by lifestyle—patterns of consumption, reactions to stress, and health-related behaviors. According to a 1993 study, the three biggest culprits are tobacco, lack of exercise, and a high-fat diet, with these three factors accounting for at least $200 billion of the $1 trillion in annual U.S. health care costs.

Figure 1.5 shows the leading causes of death in the United States from about 1900 to the 1990s. Since 1900 the number-one killer has been cardiovascular disease in every year except one (1918). Every 33 seconds an American dies of cardiovascular disease; that is more than 40 percent of all deaths annually.[26] Note that risk factors for diseases of the heart are well known—cigarette/tobacco smoke, high blood pressure, high blood cholesterol, physical inactivity, diabetes, and obesity.[27]

Figure 1.5 Changing Causes of Death

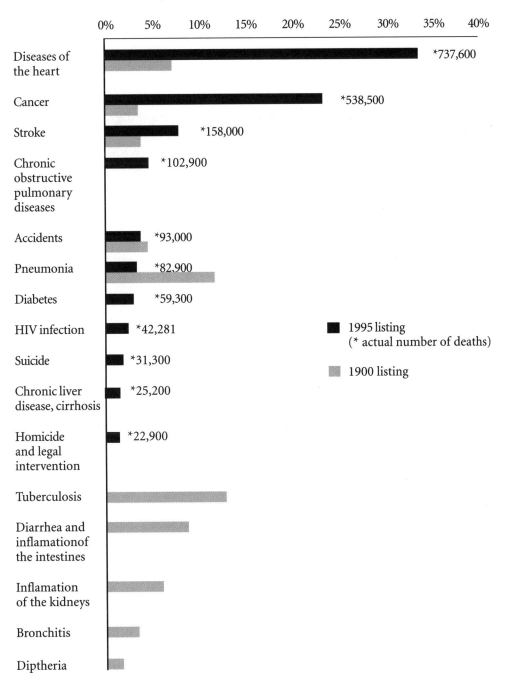

Source for 1900 data is the U.S. Department of Health and Human Services, Health United States 1987, and source for 1995 data is the U.S. National Center for Health Statistics, Vital Statistics of the United States, Annual, 1998, 118th ed.; and unpublished data. (Washington, D.C.: 1998)

Cigarette/tobacco smoke—Smokers' risk of heart attack is more than twice that of nonsmokers. In fact, cigarette smoking is the biggest single risk for sudden cardiac death: from two to four times the risk of nonsmokers. Smokers who have a heart attack are more likely to die suddenly (within an hour) than nonsmokers. It should be noted that chronic exposure to environmental tobacco smoke (secondhand smoke) increases the risk of heart disease by about 30 percent.

High blood pressure—High blood pressure (hypertension) increases the heart's workload, causing the heart to enlarge and weaken over time. For most adults a blood pressure reading that is less than 140/90 mm HG (millimeters of mercury) indicates no cause for worry. However, the harder it is for blood to flow, the higher the numbers will be. This means the heart is working harder than normal to pump blood and oxygen to the body's organs and tissues to meet their needs, putting both the heart and arteries under a greater strain. High blood pressure contributes to heart attacks, strokes, kidney failure, and atherosclerosis. More than one in four American adults have high blood pressure that is easily detected and usually controllable.

High blood cholesterol—The risk of coronary heart disease rises as blood cholesterol levels increase. Based on large population studies, blood cholesterol levels below 200 mg/dl (milligrams per deciliter) in middle-aged adults indicate a relatively low risk of coronary heart disease. A level of 240 mg/dl and higher approximately doubles the risk. Blood cholesterol levels from 200 to 239 mg/dl indicate moderate and increasing risk. The problem of high blood cholesterol is not limited to adults. Millions of children also have high levels, and thus may be at increased risk of atherosclerosis and coronary heart disease later in life.

Physical inactivity—Regular aerobic exercise plays a significant role in preventing heart and blood vessel disease. Thirty to 60 minutes of physical activity (including 20 minutes of aerobic exercise) promotes cardiovascular fitness. Even modest levels of low-intensity physical activity are beneficial if done regularly and over a long term. Such activities include walking, dancing, housework, and gardening. People who are inactive should consult a physician before significantly increasing physical activity.

Diabetes—Diabetes is the inability of the body to produce or respond to insulin properly. More than 80 percent of people with diabetes die of some form of heart or blood vessel disease. Part of the reason for this is that diabetes affects cholesterol and triglyceride levels. When diabetes is detected, a doctor may prescribe changes in diet, weight control, exercise programs, and even drugs as a treatment plan.

Obesity—People who are overweight or obese are more likely to develop cardiovascular disease than normal weight individuals. Excess weight increases the strain on the heart and is linked with coronary disease mainly because it raises blood pressure and blood cholesterol and can lead to diabetes. A weight reduction program is required to restore physical health.

What should be done to maintain good health? The simple acts of exercising regularly, eating sensibly, obtaining needed rest, not smoking, and avoiding drug and alcohol abuse are within the control of every person. If these basic practices are followed, increased longevity and better health can be expected. They can have important influences on whether or not you will have heart disease, stroke, diabetes, cancer, and accidents. Test yourself to see how well you follow seven healthy habits.

⊘ Application: Seven Healthy Habits

The following habits increase your chances of living a long and healthy life. Indicate whether or not you practice these basic health habits. Give yourself one point for each "yes" answer.

Health Habit	Yes	No	Explanation
No smoking	___	___	As the ads state, it is a matter of life and breath. Conclusive findings indicate that smoking harms your health and shortens your life. Nothing will add more years to your life than not smoking. Estimated reduction in heart attack risk is 50 to 70 percent within five years. The percentage of U.S. smokers 18 years of age and older equals 25.6: 28.4 male and 22.8 female.
Moderate or no drinking	___	___	Three or more drinks a day (males) or two or more drinks a day (females) can shorten your life. If you drink, do so in moderation. You can't save your "one a day" for seven on Friday nights.[28] The percentage of U.S. adults having two or more drinks in any day equals 5.5: 9.7 male and 1.7 female.
Sufficient sleep	___	___	Although some people can exist on less, most adults require seven to eight hours of sleep each day to recharge their batteries. If you need less, OK; but check how you respond to stress if you sleep less.
Good nutrition	___	___	Problems may result from poor eating habits. For example, someone with poor eating habits may develop diabetes. The best strategy is to eat balanced meals in proportion to your body size and activity level. A good way to maintain a healthy weight is to cut out snacks and keep a regular schedule for meals.
Breakfast every morning	___	___	Although this sounds like a cereal commercial, ideally we should live by the adage "eat breakfast like a king/queen, lunch like a prince/princess, and dinner like a pauper." We need energy in these proportions throughout the day. The percentage of U.S. adults who regularly eat breakfast equals 56.3: 54.6 male and 58.0 female.

Normal weight	___ ___	Maintain a weight that is no more than 5 percent underweight and no more than 10 to 15 percent overweight. Excess weight puts strain on internal organs, especially the cardiovascular system. Therefore, it is no mystery why being overweight shortens one's life. The percentage of U.S. adults who are 20 percent over ideal body weight considering age, height, and bone structure equals 35: about 33 percent of men and 36 percent of women.
Moderate, regular exercise	___ ___	Note the words moderate and regular. Moderation by most doctors' standards means not increasing your heart rate beyond a safe level, depending on your age, exercise history, etc. Regular translates into three to five times a week. The one-time weekend workout does little to increase health and longevity. Estimated reduction in heart attack risk is 45 percent for active vs. sedentary people. The percentage of U.S. adults who exercise regularly equals 40.7; 44 percent of men and 37.7 percent of women.

TOTALS ___ ___

Sources: Berkman, L. F. and L. Breslow, 1983, Health and Ways of Living, The Alameda County Study, *(New York: Oxford University Press, 1983) and Guralnik and Kaplan, "Predictors of Healthy Aging: Prospective Evidence from the Alameda County Study,"* American Journal of Public Health, *79, 703-708, 13 and U.S. National Center for Health Statistics,* Health Promotion and Disease Prevention: United States, 1990, Vital and Health Statistics, *series 10, no. 185.*

Scoring and interpretation

How did you do on the Seven Healthy Habits test? If you scored six or seven, be glad. Research shows that you are likely to live 7.2 (women) to 11.5 (men) years past your normal life expectancy.

Imagine adding years to your life by simply exercising regularly, eating properly, and getting enough sleep. Research indicates that the physical health of people over 75 years of age who follow these seven health habits can be as good as, if not better than, that of 35- to 45-year-olds who follow fewer than three of the habits. If you practice five or fewer of these habits, keep reading, and take special note of the 1 x 3 x 7 = 21 plan presented in Part Eight of this book.

To underscore the importance of following basic health habits, consider the following story:

Eternal truths

One cold and stormy night, a light appeared in the sealane of the battleship Missouri. The captain ordered "Send a signal. Tell them to move starboard." The signal was sent. But a signal came back, "Move starboard yourself."

Taken aback, the captain commanded, "Send another signal. Tell them to move starboard. This is the battleship Missouri, the mighty Missouri." The signal came back, "Move starboard yourself. This is the lighthouse!"

When it comes to living a long and healthy life, some truths are eternal. Seven health habits are beacons of light to live by. These represent the *lighthouse.*

Social conditions

Social conditions help account for extra stress and accelerated aging for many people. Boredom, forced retirement, and a lack of meaningful relationships are a few harmful social conditions. The following research emphasizes the importance of meaningful relationships, showing that "people need people":

Nearly seven thousand adults were surveyed to determine health and health-related behaviors, as well as other background factors and the extent of their social relationships. Mortality (death rate) data were collected for a nine-year period on 96 percent of this original sample.

A "social network index" was computed for each person consisting of the number and relative importance of social contacts. This index of social disconnection was significantly correlated with overall mortality rates as well as each specific cause of death.

For every age group and both sexes, more people with minimal social contacts died than people with many social contacts. This effect was independent of health status at the time of the initial survey or of socio-economic status. Furthermore, people who were socially isolated were more likely to engage in poor health behaviors (smoking, drinking, over-eating, irregular eating, inadequate sleep, etc.).

But the extent of one's social contacts still predicts mortality over and above the effects of any or all of these poor health practices. Thus, likelihood of death can be predicted better by knowing how isolated or connected a person is than by knowledge of the person's smoking history, even though smoking clearly increases mortality.

The data warrant the researcher's conclusion that social and community ties [are] powerful determinants of consequent health status.[29]

Paul Rosch of the American Institute of Stress emphasizes the importance of social interaction: "The most significant observation is that widows die at rates three to thirteen times as high as married women for every known major cause of death."[30] Also, the mortality rate for death from cardiovascular disease is ten times higher for widowers than for married men of the same age.[31]

One factor working against socialization benefits in American society is the lack of a common community place in addition to a home place and a work place. Unlike some other cultures, which have a three-legged stool for meeting social needs, contemporary American society has relatively little tradition for a village-wide or other common gathering location where people meet and give social support. When the European homemaker goes to the store once a day for bread and milk, it is not because she needs the supplies; it is to interact even briefly with another human being. Efforts to satisfy the third leg of the stool in American culture are varied, including churches, fraternal organizations, and neighborhood gathering places.

Establishing contact with people who are important to you and who give you pleasure is an effective antidote to too much stress. Also, relationships with animals can be important in the stress-management equation. Many people find that dogs, cats, horses, and other pets add happiness and meaning to their lives and help them cope with the pressures, conflicts, and frustrations they encounter.

Types of stress

Stress is inevitable from the moment of birth. One definition of life is "the continual process of solving problems," and all problem solving involves pressure, conflict, and frustration—in other words, stress. Selye writes:

> No one can live without experiencing some degree of stress all the time. You may think that only serious disease or intensive physical or mental injury can cause stress. This is false. Crossing a busy intersection, exposure to a draft, or even sheer joy are enough to activate the body's mechanism to some extent. Stress is not even necessarily bad for you; it is also the spice of life, for any emotion, any activity, causes stress.[32]

Selye goes on to explain that there is a difference between good stress (eustress) and bad stress (distress) and that while the mind is aware of the difference, the body is not and will experience wear and tear in any case. For example, if an active family life, winning a competitive event, or realizing significant achievement in your work are meaningful and satisfying, these experiences represent good stress, but also wear and tear. On the other hand, to the degree loneliness, sickness, or war are undesirable experiences, these represent distress—also wear and tear.

In the case of either good stress or distress, the wear and tear will be the same because even though the mind knows the difference and may choose good experiences over bad, the body reacts in the same way. Heart rate and blood pressure go up; brain activity is altered; and stress hormones, particularly epinephrine, norepinephrine, and ACTH, appear in the bloodstream.

Selye describes two additional variations of stress. *Hyperstress*, or excessive stress, usually occurs when events pile up and stretch the limits of our adaptability. *Hypostress*, or insufficient stress, can occur when we lack stimulation. As a result, bored people may resort to sensation-seeking behaviors such as experimentation with drugs. See Figure 1.6 for four variations of stress.

Figure 1.6 Four Variations of Stress

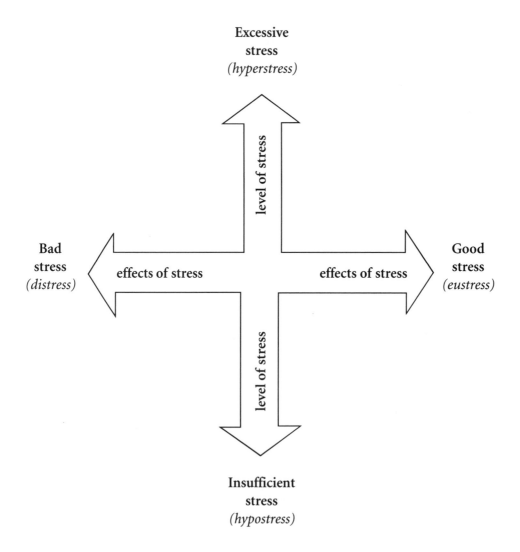

The question is, if stress is unavoidable and wear and tear is inevitable, what should be your goal? How should you cope? What should be your philosophy and practices regarding stress? The answer is to maximize good-stress experiences up to, but not beyond, the point at which they become harmful to others or yourself and to minimize distress whenever possible.

An analogy illustrates this point. Imagine an empty cup that represents your life. It is sitting between two pitchers—a pitcher of good stress, full of satisfying experiences and pleasurable events, and a pitcher of distress, full of unhappy experiences and unpleasant events. You should pour from the good-stress pitcher into your life's cup. Fill it as full as possible, but not to the point of overflowing. Remember, too much of even a good thing (hyperstress) can be harmful. Remember also, a half-full cup represents a half-full life, and too little stress (hypostress) is undesirable as well. And never, if at all possible, pour from the distress pitcher. Although it can be character building, distress isn't something you would sign up for.

The difference between good stress and distress is detailed in the two stress cycles in Figure 1.7. Good stress is positive, resulting in a full and satisfying life; distress is negative, resulting in decreased happiness and effectiveness.

Figure 1.7 Two Stress Cycles

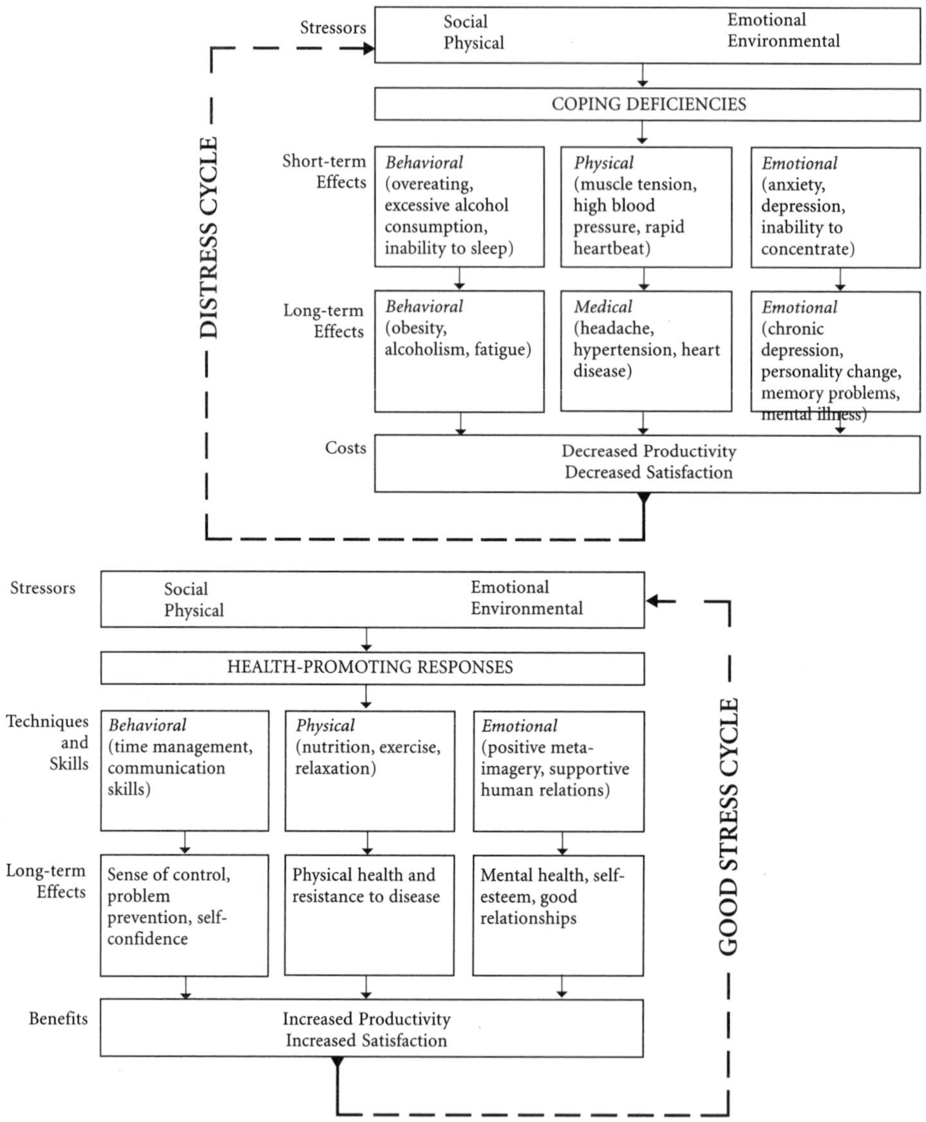

Source: Adapted from Edward A. Charlesworth and Ronald G. Nathan, Stress Management: A Comprehensive Guide to Wellness *(New York: Ballentine Books, 1984).*

In summary, the proper amount of stress keeps you alert and interested in what you are doing. It helps you to be both healthy and satisfied. Indeed, some of your best moments in life are accompanied by stress. Think of a wedding, a birth, or some special feat you have performed. Finally, remember Selye's words: "Stress . . . is also the spice of life," and "Complete freedom from stress is death."[33]

Chapter One References

1   Gerald P. Elovitz, "Life Management," *Fitness Management*, October 1993.

2   Lou Harris & Associates, Poll Conducted for Rodale Press, 1988; and B. Kerber, ed., *How Employers Are Saving through Wellness and Fitness Programs*, 2nd ed. (Wall Township, N.J.: American Business Publishing, 1994), 31.

3   Gwendolyn Puryear Keita and Joseph J. Hurrell Jr., *Job Stress in a Changing Workforce: Investigating Gender, Diversity, and Family Issues* (Washington, D.C.: American Psychological Association, 1994).

4   Sari Biklen and Diane Pollard, *Gender and Education* (Chicago: National Society for the Study of Education/University of Chicago Press, 1993).

5   H. S. Bush, M. Thompson, and N. Van Tubergen, "Personal Assessment of Stress Factors for College Students," *Journal of School Health* 55, no. 9 (1985): 370-95.

6   B. Paulson, "A Nation Out of Balance," *Health* (October, 1994): 50-55; and Leonard Zusne, ed., *Biographical Dictionary of Psychology* (Westport, Conn.: Greenwood Press, 1984).

7   Hans Selye, *The Stress of Life*, rev. ed. (New York: McGraw-Hill, 1976) 1, 173-78.

8   Robert S. Eliot, *From Stress to Strength* (New York: Bantam Books, 1994), 23.

9   Robert S. Eliot and Dennis L. Breo, *Is It Worth Dying For?* (New York: Bantam Books, 1989), 24.

10   Eliot, *From Stress to Strength*, 24-25.

11   Eliot, *From Stress to Strength*, 29.

12   James W. Kalat, *Biological Psychology*, 5th ed. (Pacific Grove, Calif.: Brooks/Cole, 1995).

13   Walter B. Cannon, *The Wisdom of the Body* (New York: W. W. Norton, 1932); Harold G. Wolff, *Stress and Disease* (Springfield, Ill.: Thomas, 1953); and Judith Green and Robert Shellenberger, *The Dynamics of Wellness: A Biopsychosocial Approach* (Fort Worth, Tex.: Holt, Rinehart and Winston, 1991), 99.

14   Selye, *The Stress of Life*, xvi–xvii.

15   Harold G. Wolff, *Stress and Disease*, 2nd ed. (Springfield, Ill.: Thomas, 1968); and C. F. Stroebel, *Q. R., The Quieting Reflex* (New York: Berkley, 1982).

16   Stroebel, *Q. R., The Quieting Reflex*.

17   Green and Shellenberger, *The Dynamics of Health and Wellness*, ch. 4.

18   Blair Justice, *Who Gets Sick?* (Houston: Peak Press, 1987).

19   David Bresler, *Free Yourself from Pain* (New York: Simon and Schuster, 1979).

20   Selye, *The Stress of Life*, 428-29.

21   U.S. National Center for Health Statistics, *Vital Statistics of the United States, Annual, 1998, 118th ed.;* and unpublished data. (Washington, D.C.: 1998)

22   Selye, *The Stress of Life*, 173-78.

23   J. Kahn, ed., "Mental Health in the Workplace: A Practical Psychiatric Guide," *Drug Abuse and Dependence* 1993: 346-47.

24   Selye, *The Stress of Life*, 432.

25   Selye, *The Stress of Life*, 432.

[26] American Heart Association, *Heart and Stroke Facts: 1996 Statistical Supplement* (Dallas, Tex.: American Heart Association, National Center, 1996).

[27] Thomas R. Dawber, *The Framingham Studies: The Epidemiology of Atherosclerotic Disease* (Cambridge, Mass.: Harvard University Press, 1980); and American Heart Association, *Heart and Stroke Facts.*

[28] R. G. Victor and J. Hansen, "Alcohol and Blood Pressure—A Drink a Day . . . ," *The New England Journal of Medicine* 332, no. 26: 1782-83, 1995; and R. D. Moore and T. A. Pearson, "Moderate Alcohol Consumption and Coronary Heart Disease: A Review," *Medicine* 65, no. 4: 242-67, 1986.

[29] L. F. Berkman, "Psychological Resources, Health Behavior and Mortality: A Nine Year Follow-Up Study" (paper presented at the annual meeting of the American Public Health Association, Washington, D.C., October 1977), 7.

[30] Claudia Wallis, Ruth Mehrtens Galvin, and Dick Thompson, "Stress: Can We Cope?" *Time* 121, no. 23 (June 1983): 48-53.

[31] Marian Osterweis, Fredric Solomon, and Morris Green, eds., *Bereavement: Reactions, Consequences, and Care* (Washington: National Academy Press, 1984), 22.

[32] Selye, *The Stress of Life,* xv.

[33] Selye, *The Stress of Life,* xv; and Hans Selye, *Stress without Distress* (Philadelphia: J. B. Lippencott, 1974), 32.

Chapter Two
★
Stress in Your World

Catastrophes and stress

We experience stress every day. Noise, crowding, delays, and setbacks are a normal part of life. On top of these daily stressors, situations occasionally occur that add even more stress. Extreme stress can come from traumas associated with war, for example. Combat produces both physical and psychological casualties. People experience prolonged fear and anxiety when placed in situations of extreme unpredictability in which killing and perhaps being killed are expectations. During World War I, the term "shell shock" was used to describe traumatic reactions to combat. This was later called "operational fatigue" and "war neurosis" during World War II, and eventually "combat fatigue" or "combat exhaustion" in the Korean and Vietnam wars. Whatever it is called, combat exhaustion is a serious problem. During World War II, it was the single greatest cause of the loss of personnel. Today, this condition is called post-traumatic stress disorder (PTSD).[1]

A 1997 long-term study reported in the journal *Psychosomatic Medicine* compares PTSD veterans with other army men serving in Vietnam at the same time. Those with PTSD had: (1) more than double the rate of infectious and nervous system diseases such as hepatitus and tuberculosis; (2) nearly twice the odds of getting muscle and skeletal diseases such as arthritis and fibromyalgia; (3) a 62 percent higher rate of circulatory ailments such as strokes, hypertension, and coronaries.

The extremes of war are not the only catastrophes of modern life. The daily news brings reports of natural disasters such as earthquakes, floods, tornadoes, droughts, and fires. We also see human-caused calamities—toxic spills, nuclear accidents, and senseless horrors, including murder, rape, drive-by shootings, and even bombings. These events, unlike war, are often sudden and short-lived, but they are nonetheless stressful.

Oklahoma City bombing

The bombing of the Murray Federal Building in Oklahoma City affected every worker in the United States, especially federal workers. While going to work was once a fact of life, employees are now concerned if it could mean a fact of death. Even children are not immune from this catastrophe. One six-year-old girl wants to know if her "mommy will get blown up going to work today." Now, this child hesitates to kiss her mother good-bye in the morning because she fears her mother may not come home.

Catastrophes are different from everyday stressors. In general, they are distinguished by eight characteristics: (1) type (natural event versus human-caused event); (2) duration (short-term accident versus long-term sickness); (3) personal impact (losing one's family versus losing one's hair); (4) damage (visible and widespread versus hidden and localized); (5) occurrence (one-time lightning strike versus annual tax season); (6) degree of warning (sudden disaster versus one anticipated or predicted); (7) presence of a low point at which the worst is over (certain versus uncertain); and (8) perception of control (external versus internal locus of control).[2] An understanding of these characteristics can help determine the severity of a catastrophe and the type of assistance that may be required. For example, a victim of a long and brutal kidnapping may require considerable psychological assistance. Problems may be severe because the pain was inflicted by another person over an extended period and had a personal impact. See Figure 2.1.

Figure 2.1 Characteristics of Catastrophes and Everyday Stressors

Characteristic	Catastrophe	Everyday stressor
1) Type	Usually natural and sometimes man-made	Usually man-made
2) Duration	Up to a year, most acute	Long-term, often chronic
3) Personal impact	Usually powerful	May be powerful
4) Degree of damage	Often causes visible and widespread damage	Often causes hidden and localized damage
5) Occurrence	Usually one time, often sudden	Often recurring, may be sudden
6) Degree of warning	Low predictability	Some predictability
7) Low point	Clear low point	Unclear low point
8) Perception of control	Uncontrollable, lack of control	Uncontrollable but potentially controllable

Source: Stress and Coping, *A. Monat and R. S. Lazarus, eds., (New York: Columbia University Press, 1991). Reprinted by permission.*

In a general sense, studies of catastrophes reveal some of the basics of stress management. Aids to survival include strong personal values that anchor the individual, commitments that provide purpose and direction, effective coping skills or living habits, personal and professional competencies to solve problems, and good health habits. These factors, along with social support, are valuable aids in today's stressful world.

Appraisal of stressful events

One of the most interesting concepts in stress and coping is the notion of *appraisal*. Researchers Richard Lazarus and Susan Folkman have shown that the impact of a stressful event is often a function not only of the event itself, but also of the individual's appraisal of his or her ability to cope with the event. Events that are viewed as exceeding one's coping resources are perceived as *threats*, whereas events that are seen as manageable, although difficult, are considered to be *challenges*. The effective individual chooses to be proactive, seeing life as a challenge, versus apathetic, seeing life as a threat. A positive appraisal of one's own abilities to cope can be a key determinant of stress outcomes.[3]

People in a world of change

Alvin Toffler, author of *Future Shock*, writes that change is descending upon people today at such a rate and volume that breakdown may result. He defines future shock (breakdown) as "the distress, both physical and psychological, that arises from an overload of the human organism's physical adaptive systems and its decision-making processes."[4]

An important factor in the stress equation is life changes—events that somehow require one to adapt or cope. The idea that people can be victims of too much change, and can get sick as a result, began with Adolf Meyer of Johns Hopkins University around 1900. Meyer kept detailed life charts on his patients that indicated that many illnesses occurred when people experienced clusters of major events in their lives.[5] The concept was expanded in the 1930s and 1940s by Harold Wolff, who studied the life settings and emotional states surrounding many specific illnesses.[6]

Beginning in 1949, Thomas Holmes of the University of Washington School of Medicine applied Meyer's concept of life charts to the case histories of over five thousand patients. He identified forty-three common changes that occurred over and over in the lives of these patients. He found that these changes tended to take place shortly before the onset of major illness. Some of the changes were desirable, such as marriage and vacations, while others were undesirable, such as the death of a spouse or loss of employment. Holmes assigned an arbitrary number (50) to marriage to represent the amount of readjustment required for this life change. Based on a survey of a cross section of the adult population, the readjustment values of the other forty-two items were determined. Readjustment values were based on the amount, duration, and severity of change.

In 1965, Holmes and Richard Rahe developed the Social Readjustment Rating Scale (SRRS), an evaluation instrument based on this research. To determine how stressful your world is, complete the following questionnaire.

◎ Application: Social Readjustment Rating Scale (SRRS)

All of the events in your life, both good and bad, exact a penalty in the form of stress. The amount of stress you experience could affect your health. This test was developed to help predict (and prevent) physical problems that can come from too much change and stress in your life.

Under Number of Occurrences, indicate how many times in the past year each of the events has occurred. Multiply the number under Life Change Units (LCU) by the number of occurrences of each event, and place the answer under Your Score. Add the figures under Your Score to find your total for the past year.

Life event	Number of occurrences	LCU	Your score
1. Death of a spouse	___	100	___
2. Divorce	___	73	___
3. Marital separation	___	65	___
4. Detention in jail or other institution	___	63	___
5. Death of a close family member	___	63	___
6. Major personal injury or illness	___	53	___
7. Marriage	___	50	___
8. Loss of job	___	47	___
9. Marital reconciliation	___	45	___
10. Retirement from work	___	45	___
11. Major change in the health or behavior of a family member	___	44	___
12. Pregnancy (self or spouse)	___	40	___
13. Sexual difficulties	___	39	___
14. Gaining a new family member	___	39	___
15. Major business readjustment	___	39	___
16. Major change in financial state	___	38	___
17. Death of a close friend	___	37	___
18. Changing to a different line of work	___	36	___
19. Major change in the number of of arguments with spouse	___	35	___
20. Taking on a large mortgage or loan for a major purchase	___	31	___
21. Foreclosure on a mortgage or loan	___	30	___
22. Major change in responsibilities at work	___	29	___
23. Son or daughter leaving home	___	29	___
24. Trouble with in-laws	___	29	___
25. Outstanding personal achievement	___	28	___

26.	Spouse beginning or ceasing work outside the home	___	26	___
27.	Beginning or ceasing formal schooling	___	26	___
28.	Major change in living conditions	___	25	___
29.	Revision of personal habits	___	24	___
30.	Trouble with boss	___	23	___
31.	Major change in working hours or conditions	___	20	___
32.	Change in residence	___	20	___
33.	Changing to a new school	___	20	___
34.	Major change in usual type and/or amount of recreation	___	19	___
35.	Major change in church activities	___	19	___
36.	Major change in social activities	___	18	___
37.	Taking on a small mortgage or loan	___	17	___
38.	Major change in sleeping habits	___	16	___
39.	Major change in number of family get-togethers	___	15	___
40.	Major change in eating habits	___	15	___
41.	Vacation	___	13	___
42.	Christmas	___	12	___
43.	Minor violations of the law	___	11	___

This is your total life change score for the past year   ___

Source: Reprinted with permission from T. H. Holmes and R. H. Rahe, "The Social Readjustment Rating Scale," Journal of Psychosomatic Research *11 (1967): 213–18. Copyright © 1967, Pergamon Press, Ltd. Recent Life Changes Questionnaire, 1997.*

Scoring and interpretation

If your total score on the Social Readjustment Rating Scale is 149 or below, you are on fairly safe ground. Life events and changes in your world are not causing undue stress. On the other hand, a score between 150 and 199 indicates mild life changes, with a 37 percent chance that you will feel the impact of stress through physical symptoms. Scores from 200 to 299 represent moderate stress in your world, with a 51 percent chance that you will experience stress-related illness in the near future. Finally, a score of over 300 points represents a serious threat to your well-being, with a 79 percent chance of sickness in the near future unless you take corrective action.

If you have a high score, you may wonder what this means in terms of illness. What kind of illness? How serious? Holmes and his associates researched the answer to this question. They studied patients who had been inflicted with different diseases. A list showing sixteen disorders appears in Figure 2.2. Column 1 identi-fies the disorder; column 2 shows its relative seriousness; and column 3 lists the accumulated scores on the Social Readjustment Rating Scale during the two years prior to onset of the illness.

The higher the score, the more serious the health problems. Not only does a person with an average score of over 300 have a 79 percent chance of falling ill, it is also probable that the type of disorder will be serious as well. People with the highest scores are more likely to suffer chronic illness—cancer or heart disease. In contrast, those with lower scores tend to have minor disorders that are acute and short in duration—headaches and skin disorders.

Figure 2.2 Life Changes and Disorders

Column 1 Illness	Column 2 Seriousness of Illness (Units in Parentheses)	Column 3 Average Life Changes (Accumulated Scores During Two Years Preceding the Illness)
Headache	(88)	209
Psoriasis	(174)	317
Eczema	(204)	231
Bronchitis	(210)	322
Anemia	(312)	325
Anxiety reaction	(315)	482
Gallstones	(454)	563
Peptic ulcer	(500)	603
High blood pressure	(520)	405
Chest pain	(609)	638
Diabetes	(621)	599
Alcoholism	(688)	688
Manic-depressive psychosis	(766)	753
Schizophrenia	(785)	609
Heart failure	(824)	772
Cancer	(1020)	777

Source: A. R. Wyler, M. Masuda, and T. H. Holmes, "Magnitude of Life Events and Seriousness of Illness," Psychosomatic Medicine *33 (1971), 115-22; Walter H. Gmelch,* Beyond Stress to Effective Management. *(New York: John Wiley & Sons, Inc., 1982). Reprinted with permission.*

Discussion

There are a number of points to remember about measures of life change such as the Social Readjustment Rating Scale:

- Research has documented the relationship between individual life changes and physical and psychological health.[7] The overall pattern of findings shows that the greater the number, clustering, and intensity of life changes, the greater the probability of illness, injury, and psychological problems.[8] In both retrospective and prospective investigations, statistically significant relationships are found between mounting life change and the occurrence of physical illness and psychological disorders.[9]

- The purpose of evaluation is to heighten your awareness of the relationship between life events, stress, and physical problems. You should share your results with family and friends—those who influence you and who are influenced by your life changes, stress levels, and health.

- If your score alarms you, do something about it. For example, if you have a high score because you have recently graduated from school, moved to a new residence, taken a new job, married, lost a loved one, and changed your eating and sleeping habits, and you are now considering pregnancy, you may decide to postpone such an important decision. Allow time to pass so the fatigue of previous adjustments can wear off and your body can rest before you add more stress to your world. Your cup may already be overflowing, and the additional stress of a new event, no matter how satisfying, may result in physical problems.

- On the other hand, you may have a low score, which may reflect a half-full cup. In such a case, perhaps you should proceed with the room addition you have been considering, accept the challenge of leading a 4-H club or a Girl Scout troop, or go back to school to complete your education. If these activities would be satisfying, get involved and live life more fully. Lack of stimulation can be boring and can lead to the distress of stagnation and depression. Remember, your goal is to pour from the pitcher of good-stress experiences into your life's cup up to, but not beyond, the point of overflowing.

- Recognize that some stress is self-made and some stress is made for you. You may not have asked for some of your life changes; forces beyond your control may have caused them. In any case, you must cope with the stress. It is the total score and its impact on your health that counts, not who causes it.

- Both good and bad events can wear a person down, cause fatigue, and increase susceptibility to physical disorders. For example, marital reconciliation (45 points) and gaining a new family member (39 points) are both positive events that take a great deal of adaptive energy. It is interesting to note that of the forty-three stressful events included in the questionnaire, only thirteen are clearly negative, six are positive, and the other twenty-four are essentially neutral.

- Although everyone experiences some amount of stress, not everyone experiences the same consequences. Some people will get headaches, others backaches. In some people, stress and digestive problems go together. The kind of disorder a person develops depends on both the individual and environment. Regarding the individual, heredity may predispose one person to arthritis and another to ulcers. Regarding environment, the chance of anyone getting bubonic plague today is low, but respiratory ailments are not unusual. It is important to note that change itself does not cause illness. As Holmes emphasizes, "it takes a germ."[10]

- Perception plays an important part in managing stress. In a sense, stress is in the eye of the beholder. One person may view divorce as a positive event, while another may view it negatively.[11] Research shows that the perceived desirability of an event can have impact on its ultimate stressfulness.[12]

- Some people perceive change in general as negative; others welcome new experiences and challenges. This quality is important for hardiness.[13] It should be noted that even the most hardy individual has physical and emotional limits and should consider the health consequences of continuous and major life changes.

- The items, scores, and probabilities of the Social Readjustment Rating Scale are based on a cross section of the population and may not apply for a particular individual. For example, some people are "turtles" by temperament. Imagine Albert Einstein—deliberate, contemplative, and unhurried. The following reflects his humble and relaxed temperament: "Before God we are all equally wise and equally foolish" and "I never think of the future. It comes soon enough."

On the other hand, some people are "racehorses" by temperament. Consider Thomas Alva Edison, who, at the age of 67, connected the camera and the phonograph to produce "talking pictures," which he hoped to use for educational purposes. Full of energy and action, Edison wrote: "Genius is one percent inspiration and 99 percent perspiration" and "Show me a satisfied man, and I will show you a failure."

Individual temperament has little to do with hardiness, and each temperament (the turtle and the racehorse) can be equally happy, productive, wise, and healthy. But if we try to speed up the turtle, it will be distressful; and it is likely that a person like this could tolerate fewer life changes than could the average person. Similarly, if we try to slow down the racehorse, it will be distressful. Racehorses love variety and activity and thrive on more life change than does the average person. Before you say, "Aha! That explains my high stress score. I am a racehorse!", you should realize that most people fall somewhere between the extreme turtle and extreme racehorse temperaments. Therefore, the foregoing scores and predictions would apply.

Stress and change have attracted much interest by researchers over the past thirty years. The indication after more than a thousand studies is that dimensions that increase the relationship between life events and disorders are undesirability, unpredictability, uncontrollability, event magnitude, and time clustering.[14]

In 1977, Richard Rahe developed an updated version of the Social Readjustment Rating Scale entitled the Recent Life Changes Questionnaire (RLCQ). In 1995 a more current survey of the RLCQ was developed by Rahe and Mark Miller. Their research indicates that life stress, as estimated by recent life change scores, has increased markedly over the past thirty years. An increase of 45 percent was found across scaling studies performed in 1965, 1977, and 1995. In other words, our worlds are becoming more stressful. Also, women are reporting higher levels of stress than are men, either because they are experiencing more stress or because men tend to repress and deny the effects of stress.[15] Figure 2.3 shows the changing rank order of the 43 life events and the increasing amount of stress reported over thirty years.

Figure 2.3 Life Changes Scaling Across 30 Years

Life events	1965 Rank	1965 LCU	1977 Rank	1977 LCU	1995 Rank	1995 LCU
Death of spouse	1	100	1	105	1	119
Divorce	2	73	4	62	2	98
Marital separation	3	65	8	52	4	79
Jail term	4	63	6	57	7	75
Death of close family member	5	63	2	73	3	92
Major personal injury or illness	6	53	16	42	6	77
Marriage	7	50	10	50	19	50
Fired from work	8	47	3	64	5	79
Marital reconciliation	9	45	17	42	13	57
Retirement	10	45	11	49	16	54
Change in health or behavior of family member	11	44	9	52	14	56
Pregnancy	12	40	5	60	9	66
Sexual difficulties	13	39	12	49	21	45
Gain of new family member	14	39	14	47	12	57
Major business readjustment	15	39	21	38	10	62
Change in financial state	16	38	13	48	15	56
Death of close friend	17	37	15	46	8	70
Change to different line of work	18	36	22	38	17	51
Change in number of arguments with spouse	19	35	24	34	18	51
Mortgage or loan greater than $10,000	20	31	18	39	23	44
Foreclosure on a mortgage or loan	21	30	7	57	11	61
Change in responsibilities at work	22	29	32	30	24	43
Child leaving home	23	29	36	29	22	44
Trouble with in-laws	24	29	34	29	28	38
Outstanding personal achievement	25	28	25	33	29	37
Spouse begins or ends work	26	26	23	37	20	46
Begin or end school	27	26	28	32	27	38
Change in living conditions	28	25	19	39	25	42
Change in personal habits	29	24	30	31	36	27
Trouble with boss	30	23	20	39	33	29
Change in work hours or conditions	31	20	27	33	30	36
Change in residence	32	20	26	33	26	41

Life events	1965 Rank	1965 LCU	1977 Rank	1977 LCU	1995 Rank	1995 LCU
Change in schools	33	20	39	28	31	35
Change in recreation	34	19	33	30	34	29
Change in church activities	35	19	35	29	42	22
Change in social activities	36	18	40	28	38	27
Mortgage or loan less than $10,000	37	17	42	26	35	28
Change in sleeping habits	38	16	31	31	40	26
Change in number of family get-togethers	39	15	41	26	39	26
Change in eating habits	40	15	38	29	37	27
Vacation	41	13	37	29	41	25
Christmas	42	12	*	*	32	30
Minor violations of the law	43	11	29	32	43	22
Grand mean LCU values (for all events)		34		42		49

* The event "Christmas" was not scaled in 1977.

Source: Mark A. Miller and Richard H. Rahe, "Life Changes Scaling for the 1990s." Journal of Psychosomatic Research, 43, no. 3, *(1997): 279–92. Reprinted with permission.*

Attempts to improve life stress measurements have led to the development of event inventories for specific target populations—athletes (Bramwell, 1971), children (Greene, Walker, Hickson, and Thompson, 1985), and teachers (Harington, Burry, and Pelsma, 1989). Of interest to college-age adults is the Student Stress Scale, a modification of Holmes and Rahe's Recent Life Changes Questionnaire. See Figure 2.4.

Figure 2.4 Student Stress Scale

The Student Stress Scale has been developed to apply to college-age adults, and should be considered a general indication of stress levels and health consequences. Each event, such as beginning or ending school, is given a stress value that represents the amount of readjustment a person has to make as a result of change. Multiply the number under Life Change Unit (LCU) by the Number of Occurrences of each event and place the answer under Your Score. Add your answers to find your total for the past twelve months.

Life event	Number of occurrences	LCU	Your score
1. Death of a close family member	___	100	___
2. Death of a close friend	___	73	___
3. Divorce among parents	___	65	___
4. Jail term	___	63	___
5. Major personal injury or illness	___	63	___
6. Marriage	___	53	___
7. Firing from a job	___	50	___
8. Failure in an important course	___	47	___
9. Change in health of a family member	___	45	___
10. Pregnancy	___	45	___
11. Sex problems	___	44	___
12. Serious argument with a close friend	___	40	___
13. Change in financial status	___	39	___
14. Change in major	___	39	___
15. Trouble with parents	___	39	___
16. New girlfriend or boyfriend	___	38	___
17. Increase in workload at school	___	37	___
18. Outstanding personal achievement	___	36	___
19. First quarter/semester in college	___	35	___
20. Change in living conditions	___	31	___
21. Serious argument with an instructor	___	30	___
22. Lower grades than expected	___	29	___
23. Change in sleeping habits	___	29	___
24. Change in social activities	___	29	___
25. Change in eating habits	___	28	___
26. Chronic car trouble	___	26	___
27. Change in number of family get-togethers	___	26	___
28. Too many missed classes	___	25	___
29. Change of college	___	24	___
30. Dropping of more than one class	___	23	___
31. Minor traffic violations	___	20	___

Total score ___

Interpretation

If your total score is 300 or higher, you have a high risk for developing stress-related health problems. If your score is between 150 and 300, you have a fifty-fifty chance of experiencing stress-related health problems. If your score is below 150, you have a one-in-three chance of having health problems related to stress in your world.

Source: Adapted from Kathleen Mullen and Gerald Costello, Health Awareness Through Self-Discovery *(Minneapolis: Burgess, 1996); and T. H. Holmes and R. H. Rahe, "The Social Readjustment Rating Scale,"* Journal of Psychosomatic Research *11 (1967): 213.*

Little hassles mean a lot

In addition to life events, "little hassles" make a difference in the amount of physical and emotional wear and tear we experience. This was the conclusion of a study done by Richard Lazarus and his associates at the University of California at Berkeley. Lazarus reports:

> In short, we found that major events do have some long-term effects, but in the short term, hassles seem to have a much stronger impact on mental and physical health. . . . In sum, it is not the large, dramatic events that make the difference, but what happens day in and day out, whether provoked by major events or not. It is not the large things that send a man to the madhouse . . . no, it's the continuing series of small tragedies . . . not the death of his love but a shoelace that snaps with no time left.[16]

Figure 2.5 is a summary of the most common hassles and uplifts for the average adult.

Figure 2.5 Life's Top Ten Hassles and Uplifts

What are the most common sources of pleasures and hassles in life? It all depends on who you are. When Lazarus and his colleagues asked 100 white, middle-class, middle-aged men and women to keep track of their hassles and uplifts over a one-year period, they got one set of candidates for the top ten annoyances and joys. When they asked a group of college students, they got another. Canadian health professionals gave still another list.

The ten most frequent hassles and uplifts in the middle-aged group were, in order of frequency:

Hassles	Uplifts
1. Concern about weight	1. Relating well with spouse or lover
2. Health of a family member	2. Relating well with friends
3. Rising prices of consumer goods	3. Completing a task
4. Home maintenance	4. Feeling healthy
5. Too many things to do	5. Getting enough sleep
6. Misplacing or losing things	6. Eating out
7. Yard work or outside home maintenance	7. Meeting responsibilities
8. Property, investment, or taxes	8. Visiting, phoning, or writing someone
9. Crime	9. Spending time with loved ones
10. Physical appearance	10. Pleasing home atmosphere

People differ widely in the problems and pleasures typical of their lives. Only three hassle items rated among the top ten for all three groups. The big three: misplacing or losing things, physical appearance, and too many things to do.

Each group had certain hassles common to its station in life. For the middle-aged, middle-class group, the predominant theme was economic concern—worries about investments and rising prices. The Canadian health professionals tended to check off hassles that reflect the anxieties and pressures of their careers: too much to do, not enough time to do it all, too many responsibilities, and trouble relaxing. Students were most hassled by anxiety over wasting time, meeting high standards, and being lonely.

As for pleasures, there again the groups diverged. The uplifts of the middle-aged are the joys of a home-body: being in good health; enjoying hearth, home, and kin. Students, on the other hand, tend to be more hedonistic; their uplifts include having fun, laughing, and entertainment. The only two uplifts shared by young and middle-aged alike were completing a task and having good times with friends.

Source: Richard Lazarus, "Little Hassles Can Be Hazardous to Your Health," Psychology Today (July 1981): 58-62.

For a measure of your hassle level, complete the following questionnaire.

@ Application: What is Your Hassle Quotient?

For each statement, circle Y if it is true or mostly true, and circle N if it is false or mostly false.

	Y (Yes)	N (No)
1. I am concerned about my weight (either too heavy or too light).	Y	N
2. I have a good relationship with a spouse or lover.	Y	N
3. The rising cost of living bothers me.	Y	N
4. I have a sense of accomplishment.	Y	N
5. I have a lot to do to maintain my home.	Y	N
6. I have good friends.	Y	N
7. Misplacing or losing things is a problem for me.	Y	N
8. I am in good health.	Y	N
9. I have too much to do and too little time to do it.	Y	N
10. I get enough sleep.	Y	N
11. I am not satisfied with my physical appearance.	Y	N
12. I spend a lot of time with the people who are important to me.	Y	N
13. Managing finances and keeping records take a lot of my time.	Y	N
14. My home is pleasant.	Y	N
15. Someone close to me is in poor health.	Y	N
16. I eat out (in) often enough.	Y	N
17. I am concerned about crime and safety.	Y	N
18. I have a sense of satisfaction in meeting my responsibilities.	Y	N

Source: Adapted from Bethesda Hospitals: Stress Management Program *(St. Louis, Mo.: Department of Health Promotion, St. Louis University Medical Center).*

Scoring and interpretation

Count the odd-numbered statements on the What is Your Hassle Quotient test for which you have circled Y (Yes). This is your hassle score. _____ Count the even-numbered statements for which you have circled Y (Yes). This is your up-lift score. _____ .

Your stress level is high if your hassle score is either greater than four or greater than your uplift score. In this case, life's little hassles are causing you extra pressure, conflict, and frustration, with corresponding physical and emotional wear and tear.

It is difficult to determine which stressors are more important, life changes or little hassles, because they often happen at the same time. Indeed, life changes can cause hassles, and vice versa. Divorce, for example, may result in many hassles such as loneliness, reduced income, and too many things to do. Similarly, joblessness often interferes with family relations, feelings of self-worth, and personal health.

The critical balance

How you handle stress depends on the demands you face—life changes and hassles—and your resources for meeting these demands, not on any one factor alone. Just as physical health depends partly on the number and strength of germs you are exposed to and partly on your body's ability to resist these invaders, psychological health depends to some degree on the people and problems in your life and partly on your mental and emotional strength. If you have strong physical, psychological, and spiritual resources, you can deal with tremendous amounts of change in your life and many little hassles. Figure 2.6 shows the relationship between the demands we face and our resources for coping.

Figure 2.6 The Critical Balance

Demands we face— events, hassles, and handicaps	Resources for coping— physical, psychological, and economic assets
Low status	TLC
Unhappy marriage	Happy marriage
Sexual problems	Close friends
Boredom	Self-confidence
Unrealistic goals	Adequate income
Job problems	Mental health
Quarrels with associates	Physical fitness
Debts, money trouble	Realistic frame of reference
Loss of loved ones	Satisfactory status
Inadequate competencies	Adequate competencies
Physical handicaps	Satisfactory living conditions (e.g. housing, food)
Sickness	Satisfying job
Inferiority feelings	
War	
Unsatisfactory living conditions (e.g. food, shelter)	

Source: Data from James C. Coleman, Personality Dynamics and Effective Behavior *(Glenview, Ill.: Scott, Foresman & Company, 1960), 183. Reprinted with permission.*

Selye describes the critical balance as a process of adaptation:

Life is largely a process of adaptation to the circumstances in which we exist. A perennial give-and-take has been going on between living matter and its inanimate surroundings, between one living being and another, ever since the dawn of life in the prehistoric oceans. The secret of health and happiness lies in successful adjustment to the ever-changing conditions . . . the penalties for failure in this great process of adaptation are disease and unhappiness.[17]

An important point in the "demands-resources" equation is the need for renewal. The person who expends resources (time, energy, and emotion) without replenishment ultimately experiences physical, psychological, and spiritual fatigue, and burnout may occur. The solution is to reach a balance. A tree needs sun and rain, and a person must receive to give. In your own life, what are you doing both to meet demands and to replenish your resources?

The following exercise provides an estimate of your critical balance at this time.

◎ Application: Who's on Top—the World or You?

For an evaluation of your critical balance, compare the demands you face in the left column and your resources for coping in the right. Circle the number between each pair that reflects conditions as they are now. Add your total score.

Demands		Resources
Low self-esteem	1 2 3 4 5 6 7 8 9 10	High self-esteem
Pessimism	1 2 3 4 5 6 7 8 9 10	Optimism
Loneliness	1 2 3 4 5 6 7 8 9 10	Close friends
Job problems	1 2 3 4 5 6 7 8 9 10	Job success
Unhappy marriage (relationship)	1 2 3 4 5 6 7 8 9 10	Happy marriage (relationship)
Debts, money troubles	1 2 3 4 5 6 7 8 9 10	Financial security
Poor health	1 2 3 4 5 6 7 8 9 10	Good health
Boredom	1 2 3 4 5 6 7 8 9 10	Excitement
Inner turmoil	1 2 3 4 5 6 7 8 9 10	Peace of mind
Sexual problems	1 2 3 4 5 6 7 8 9 10	Sexual satisfaction
Low social status	1 2 3 4 5 6 7 8 9 10	High social status
Quarrels and conflict	1 2 3 4 5 6 7 8 9 10	Smooth relationships
Physical problems	1 2 3 4 5 6 7 8 9 10	Physical fitness
Low self-confidence	1 2 3 4 5 6 7 8 9 10	High self-confidence
Meaningless work	1 2 3 4 5 6 7 8 9 10	Meaningful work

Too little rest	1 2 3 4 5 6 7 8 9 10	Sufficient rest
Poor eating habits	1 2 3 4 5 6 7 8 9 10	Good eating habits
Feeling out of control	1 2 3 4 5 6 7 8 9 10	Feeling in control
Confusion, lack of goals	1 2 3 4 5 6 7 8 9 10	Clarity of direction
Unsatisfactory living conditions (food, shelter, etc.)	1 2 3 4 5 6 7 8 9 10	Satisfactory living conditions (food, shelter, etc.)

Scoring and interpretation

Everyone faces demands, and everyone has resources for coping. Also, times and conditions change for each of us. Based on your answers to the Who's on Top test at this time:

If your score is:	Your balance is:
20–40	Poor; major resources and coping skills are needed.
41–100	Negative to average; additional resources and coping skills are needed.
101–160	Average to positive; you are doing well, but should continue to improve.
161–200	Excellent; your critical balance is strongly in your favor.

Take action

If your score is low, you should take steps to improve your critical balance. Identify your weakest areas and address those deficiencies first. For example, you could develop a better sense of control by clarifying your goals in life and following good time management principles.

Note that each pair in the critical balance test has the potential to act as either a demand or a resource. For example, a marriage may be unhappy and distressful, or it may be a source of joy and comfort. Making improvements in any area can have a positive affect on your overall well-being.

The importance of humor

One of the best ways to maintain a positive balance between stress in your world and your resources for coping is to have a good sense of humor. With humor, you can keep difficult situations in perspective and can take yourself lightly while taking life seriously. This helps one maintain grace under pressure and helps on a basic physiological plane as well.

You simply cannot be distressed while you are laughing. A lively sense of humor and a good laugh a few times a day put a healthy distance between you and life's problems. Remember, laughter is like jelly—when you spread it around, you can't help getting some on yourself.

The philosopher Friedrich Nietzsche noted that the most acutely suffering animal on earth invented laughter as an antidote. The root of the word humor is "umor," which means fluid, like water. Humor relieves tension; it keeps us fluid and flexible instead of rigid and breakable in the face of stress and change. Laughter has the effect of making fears manageable and fueling hope.

It is important to note that good humor is constructive and involves laughing with others or at ourselves, never at the expense of another person, which in itself is stressful and destructive. A role model at this was Yogi Berra, the famous baseball player and manager. His convoluted but memorable misuses of language were humorous, healthful, and wise all at the same time:

"Baseball is 90 percent mental. The other half is physical."
"The other team could make trouble for us if they win."
"If you can't imitate him, copy him."
"Always go to other people's funerals, otherwise they won't come to yours."
"If you come to a fork in the road, take it."

In his influential book *Anatomy of an Illness,* Norman Cousins describes the value of humor in healing. Told that all medical avenues had been exhausted in the treatment of a debilitating connective tissue disease, Cousins developed his own technique for healing. With his doctor's support, he checked out of the hospital and began watching old TV comedies—*I Love Lucy, The Honeymooners,* and others. He said that he substituted laughter for depression—"Ten minutes of good laughter gave me an hour of pain-free sleep. . . . The more I laughed, the better I got." In time, his fever and pain diminished and the disease itself dissipated. Cousins discovered that humor, cheerfulness, and other positive emotions can have a dramatic therapeutic value. Along these lines and predating Cousins, Mark Twain noted the importance of humor in promoting health:

> The old man laughed loud and joyously, shook up the details of his anatomy from head to foot, and ended by saying such a laugh was money in a man's pocket, because it cut down the doctor's bills like anything.[18]

Such anecdotal accounts are supported by research data. Healing, in fact, can be aided by the simple act of smiling. Scientists have identified a physical connection between the nerves of the facial muscles and a specific area of the brain that is capable of releasing health-enhancing chemicals. Humor is a form of communicating on a high level of complexity that produces a positive response on a physiological level.[19] Read the following story and notice the feeling of well-being you experience when you smile and laugh.

A letter written in a childish scrawl came to the post office addressed to "God." An employee, not knowing what to do with the letter, opened it and read: "Dear God, my name is Jimmy. I am six years old. My father is gone and my mother is having a hard time raising me and my sister. Would you please send us $500?"

The postal employee was touched. He showed the letter to his fellow workers and all decided to kick in a few dollars each and send it to the family. They were able to raise $300.

A couple of weeks later they received a second letter. The boy thanked God, but ended with this request: "Next time would you please deliver the money directly to our home? If you send it through the post office they deduct $200."[20]

Humor can take a variety of forms, including surprise, exaggeration, absurdity, incongruity, word play, or tragic twists. In all of its forms, a sense of humor can be an excellent stress-coping technique, a release for tension, and a survival mechanism.

Cousin's first-hand account of the importance of humor is presented on page 55. As you read, ask yourself, "If I were to become ill, would I turn to humor to help make me well?" What form of humor would you use? Have you ever personally experienced the positive effects of humor?

Personal Thoughts on Understanding Stress

Answer the following questions to personalize the content of Part One. Space is provided for writing your thoughts.

■ Is the stress in your life primarily *good stress* or *distress?*

■ What are your "health habits" and "aging influences"? Are you aging at the rate you want and for the purposes you want?

■ How stressful is your world at this time? Is your cup overflowing, or not yet full?

■ What "little hassles" do you have to deal with? How do you cope?

■ Who's on top—the world or you? Are your resources for coping keeping up with the demands you face?

■ If it is true that taking on responsibility for holidays and vacations is like taking on a part-time job, who in your family usually assumes this additional stress?

■ Do you use humor as a stress-coping technique to enhance your life?

Chapter Two References

1. H. S. Bloch, "Army Clinical Psychiatry in the Combat Zone 1967-1968," *American Journal of Psychiatry* (1969): 126, 289.

2. M. R. Berren, A. Beigel, and G. Stuart, "A Typology for the Classification of Disasters," in R. H. Moos, ed., *Coping with Life Crises* (New York: Plenum, 1980), 295-305; R. Bolin, "Responses to Natural Disasters," in M. Lystad, ed., *Mental Health Response to Mass Emergencies* (New York: Brunner-Mazel, 1988); and E. L. Quarantelli, "What is Disaster? The Need for Clarification, Definition, and Conceptualization in Research," in B. J. Sowder, ed., *Disasters and Mental Health: Selected Contemporary Perspectives* (Rockcastle, Md.: U.S. Department of Health and Human Services, 1985), 41-73.

3. Richard S. Lazarus and Susan Folkman, *Stress, Appraisal, and Coping* (New York: Springer, 1984), 22-52; also, M. F. Scheier and C. S. Carver, "Effects of Optimism on Psychological and Physical Well-being: Theoretical Overview and Empirical Update," *Cognitive Therapy and Research* 16 (1992): 201-28.

4. Alvin Toffler, *Future Shock* (New York: Random House, Inc., 1970), 290.

5. Adolf Meyer, "The Life Chart and the Obligation of Specifying Positive Data in Psychopathological Diagnosis," in E. G. Winters, ed., *The Collected Papers of Adolf Meyer,* vol. 3, *Medical Teaching* (Baltimore: Johns Hopkins, 1951).

6. Harold G. Wolff, *Stress and Disease,* 2nd ed. (Springfield, Ill.: Thomas, 1968).

7. B. S. Dohrenwend and B. P. Dohrenwend, eds., *Stressful Life Events: Their Nature and Effects* (New York: John Wiley and Sons, 1974); B. S. Dohrenwend and B. P. Dohrenwend, eds., *Stressful Life Events and Their Contexts* (New York: Prodist., 1981); and B. P. Dohrenwend, "Note on a Program of Research on Alternative Social Psychological Models of Relationships between Life Stress and Psychopathology," in Mortimer H. Appley and Richard Trumbull, eds., *The Dynamics of Stress: Physiological, Psychological, and Social Perspectives* (New York: Plenum Press, 1986), 283-94.

8. Richard Rahe, *Stress: How Much Can You Take?* (Augusta, Maine: Maine Department of Mental Health and Mental Retardation, 1987).

9. J. G. Rabkin and E. L. Struenins, "Life Events, Stress and Illness," *Science* 194 (1976): 1013-20; and C. David Jenkins, "The Mind and the Body," *World Health,* March/April 1994, pp. 6-7.

10. Claudia Ruth Merhtens Galvin and Dick Thompson, "Stress: Can We Cope?" *Time* 121, no. 23 (June 1983): 48-53.

11. David A. Chiriboga and Linda S. Catron, *Divorce: Crisis, Challenge, or Relief?* (New York: New York University Press, 1991).

12. D. P. Mueller, D. W. Edwards, and R. M. Yarvis, "Stressful Life Events and Psychiatric Sympotomatology: Change or Undesirability?" *Journal of Health and Social Behavior* 18 (1977): 307-17.

13. S. C. Kobasa, "Stressful Life Events and Health: An Inquiry into Hardiness," *Journal of Personality and Social Psychology* 37 (1979): 27-38.

14. Leo Goldberger and Shlomo Brenitz, eds., *Handbook of Stress,* 2nd ed. (New York: The Free Press, 1993).

15. Mark A. Miller and Richard H. Rahe, "Life Changes Scaling for the 1990s," *Journal of Psychosomatic Research,* 43, no. 3 (1997): 279-92.

[16] A. DeLongis, J. C. Coyne, G. Dakof, S. Folkma, and R. S. Lazarus, "Relationship of Daily Hassles, Uplifts, and Major Life Events to Health Status," *Health Psychology* 1 (1982): 119-36; A. D. Kanner, J. D. Coyne, C. Schaefer, and R. S. Lazarus, "Comparisons of Two Modes of Stress Measurement: Daily Hassles and Uplifts Versus Major Life Events," *Journal of Behavioral Medicine* 4 (1981): 1-39; and Lazarus and Folkman, *Stress, Appraisal, and Coping.*

[17] Hans Selye, *The Stress of Life* (New York: McGraw-Hill, 1976), xv-xvi.

[18] Mark Twain, *The Adventures of Tom Sawyer* (New York: Heritage Reprints, 1936).

[19] Robert S. Eliot, *Stress to Strength* (New York: Bantam Books, 1994),130; and Norman Cousins, *Head First: The Biology of Hope* (New York: Dutton, 1991).

[20] Marvin Gregory, ed., *Bits and Pieces* (Fairfield, N.J.: The Economic Press, Inc.).

Part One Reading

Anatomy of an Illness as Perceived by the Patient

This . . . is about a serious illness that occurred in 1964. I was reluctant to write about it for many years because I was fearful of creating false hopes in others who were similarly afflicted. Moreover, I knew that a single case has small standing in the annals of medical research, having little more than "anecdotal" or "testimonial" value. However, references to the illness surfaced from time to time in the general and medical press. People wrote to ask whether it was true that I "laughed" my way out of a crippling disease that doctors believed to be irreversible. In view of those questions, I thought it useful to provide a fuller account than appeared in those early reports.

In August 1964, I flew home from a trip abroad with a slight fever. The malaise, which took the form of a general feeling of achiness, rapidly deepened. Within a week it became difficult to move my neck, arms, hands, fingers, and legs. My sedimentation rate was over 80. Of all the diagnostic tests, the "sed" rate is one of the most useful to the physician. The way it works is beautifully simple. The speed with which red blood cells settle in a test tube—measured in millimeters per hour—is generally proportionate to the severity of an inflammation or infection. A normal illness, such as grippe, might produce a sedimentation reading of, say, 30 or even 40. When the rate goes well beyond 60 or 70, however, the physician knows that he is dealing with more than a casual health problem. I was hospitalized when the sed rate hit 88. Within a week it was up to 115, generally considered to be a sign of a critical condition.

There were other tests, some of which seemed to me to be more an assertion of the clinical capability of the hospital than of concern for the well-being of the patient. I was astounded when four technicians from four different departments took four separate and substantial blood samples on the same day. That the hospital didn't take the trouble to coordinate the tests, using one blood specimen, seemed to me inexplicable and irresponsible. Taking four large slugs of blood the same day even from a healthy person is hardly to be recommended. When the technicians came the second day to fill their containers with blood for processing in separate laboratories, I turned them away and had a sign posted on my door saying that I would give just one specimen every three days and that I expected the different departments to draw from one vial for their individual needs.

I had a fast-growing conviction that a hospital is no place for a person who is seriously ill. The surprising lack of respect for basic sanitation; the rapidity with which staphylococci and other pathogenic organisms can run through an entire hospital; the extensive and sometimes promiscuous use of X-ray equipment; the seemingly indiscriminate administration of tranquilizers and powerful painkillers, sometimes more for the convenience of hospital staff in managing patients than for therapeutic needs; and the regularity with which hospital routine takes precedence over the rest requirements of the patient (slumber, when it comes for an ill person, is an uncommon blessing and is not to be wantonly interrupted)—all these and other practices seemed to me to be critical shortcomings of the modern hospital.

Perhaps the hospital's most serious failure was in the area of nutrition. It was not just that the meals were poorly balanced; what seemed inexcusable to me was the profusion of processed foods, some of which contained preservatives or harmful dyes. White bread, with its chemical softeners and bleached flour, was offered with every meal. Vegetables were often overcooked and thus deprived of much of their nutritional value. No wonder the 1969 White House Conference on Food, Nutrition, and Health made the melancholy observation that a great failure of medical schools is that they pay so little attention to the science of nutrition.

My doctor did not quarrel with my reservations about hospital procedures. I was fortunate to have as a physician a man who was able to put himself in the position of the patient. Dr. William Hitzig supported me in the measures I took to fend off the random sanguinary assaults of the hospital laboratory attendants.

We had been close friends for more than twenty years, and he knew of my own deep interest in medical matters. We had often discussed articles in the medical press, including the *New England Journal of Medicine (NEJM)* and *Lancet.* He was candid with me about my case. He reviewed the reports of the various specialists he had called in as consultants. He said there was no agreement on a precise diagnosis. There was, however, a consensus that I was suffering from a serious collagen illness—a disease of the connective tissue. All arthritic and rheumatic diseases are in this category. Collagen is the fibrous substance that binds the cells together. In a sense, then, I was coming unstuck. I had considerable difficulty in moving my limbs and even in turning over in bed. Nodules appeared on my body, gravel-like substances under the skin, indicating the systemic nature of the disease. At the low point of my illness, my jaws were almost locked.

Dr. Hitzig called in experts from Dr. Howard Rusk's rehabilitation clinic in New York. They confirmed the general opinion, adding the more particularized diagnosis of ankylosing spondylitis, which would mean that the connective tissue in the spine was disintegrating.

I asked Dr. Hitzig about my chances for full recovery. He leveled with me, admitting that one of the specialists had told him I had one chance in five hundred. The specialist had also stated that he had not personally witnessed a recovery from this comprehensive condition.

All this gave me a great deal to think about. Up to that time, I had been more or less disposed to let the doctors worry about my condition. But now I felt a compulsion to get into the act. It seemed clear to me that if I was to be that one in five hundred I had better be something more than a passive observer.

I asked Dr. Hitzig about the possible origin of my condition. He said that it could have come from any one of a number of causes. It could have come, for example, from heavy-metal poisoning, or it could have been the aftereffect of a streptococcal infection.

I thought as hard as I could about the sequence of events immediately preceding the illness. I had gone to the Soviet Union in July 1964 as chairman of an American delegation to consider the problems of cultural exchange. The conference had been held in Leningrad, after which we went to Moscow for supplementary meetings. Our hotel was in a residential area. My room was on the second floor. Each night a procession of disel trucks plied back and forth to a nearby housing project in the process of round-the-clock construction. It was summer, and our windows were wide open. I slept uneasily each night and felt somewhat nauseated on arising. On our last day in Moscow, at the airport, I caught the exhaust spew of a large jet at point-blank range as it swung around on the tarmac.

As I thought back on that Moscow experience, I wondered whether the exposure to the hydrocarbons from the diesel exhaust at the hotel and at the airport had anything to do with the underlying cause of the illness. If so, that might account for the speculations of the doctors concerning heavy-metal poisoning. The trouble with this theory, however, was that my wife, who had been with me on the trip, had no ill effects from the same exposure. How likely was it that only one of us would have reacted adversely?

It seemed to me, as I thought about it, that there were two possible explanations for the different reactions. One had to do with individual allergy. The second was that I could have been in a condition of adrenal exhaustion and less apt to tolerate a toxic experience than someone whose immunologic system was fully functional.

Was adrenal exhaustion a factor in my own illness?

Again, I thought carefully. The meetings in Leningrad and Moscow had not been casual. Paper work had kept me up late nights. I had ceremonial responsibilities. Our last evening in Moscow had been, at least for me, an exercise in almost total frustration. A reception had been arranged by the chairman of the Soviet delegation at his dacha, located thirty-five to forty miles outside the city. I had been asked if I could arrive an hour early so that I might tell the Soviet delegates something about the individual Americans who were coming to dinner. The Russians were eager to make the Americans feel at home, and they had thought such information would help them with the social amenities.

I was told that a car and driver from the government automobile pool in Moscow would pick me up at the hotel at 3:30 P.M. This would allow ample time for me to drive to the dacha by 5:00 when all our Russian conference colleagues would be gathered for the social briefing. The rest of the American delegation would arrive at the dacha at 6:00 P.M.

At 6:00, however, I found myself in open country on the wrong side of Moscow. There had been a misunderstanding in the transmission of directions to the driver, the result being that we were some eighty miles off course. We finally got our bearings and headed back to Moscow. Our chauffeur had been schooled in cautious driving; he was not disposed to make up lost time. I kept wishing for a driver with a compulsion to prove that auto racing, like baseball, originally came from the U.S.S.R.

We didn't arrive at the dacha until 9:00 P.M. My host's wife looked desolate. The soup had been heated and reheated. The veal was dried out. I felt pretty wrung out myself. It was a long flight back to the states the next day. The plane was overcrowded. By the time we arrived in New York, cleared through the packed customs counters, and got rolling back to Connecticut, I could feel an uneasiness deep in my bones. A week later I was hospitalized.

As I thought back on my experience abroad, I knew that I was probably on the right track in my search for a cause of the illness. I found myself increasingly convinced, as I said a moment ago, that the reason I was hit hard by the diesel and jet pollutants, whereas my wife was not, was that I had had a case of adrenal exhaustion, lowering my resistance.

Assuming this hypothesis was true, I had to get my adrenal glands functioning properly again and to restore what Walter B. Cannon, in his famous book. *The Wisdom of the Body*, called homeostasis.

I knew that the full functioning of my endocrine system—in particular the adrenal glands—was essential for combating severe arthritis or, for that matter, any other illness. A study I had read in the medical press reported that pregnant women frequently have remissions of arthritic or other rheumatic symptoms. The reason is that the endocrine system is fully activated during pregnancy.

How was I to get my adrenal glands and my endocrine system, in general, working well again?

I remembered having read, ten years or so earlier, Hans Selye's classic book, *The Stress of Life*. With great clarity, Selye showed that adrenal exhaustion could be caused by emotional tension, such as frustration or suppressed rage. He detailed the negative effects of the negative emotions on body chemistry.

The inevitable question arose in my mind: what about the positive emotions? If negative emotions produce negative chemical changes in the body, wouldn't the positive emotions produce positive chemical changes? Is it possible that love, hope, faith, laughter, confidence, and the will to live have therapeutic value? Do chemical changes occur only on the downside?

Obviously, putting the positive emotions to work was nothing so simple as turning on a garden hose. But even a reasonable degree of control over my emotions might have a salutary physiologic effect. Just replacing anxiety with a fair degree of confidence might be helpful.

A plan began to form in my mind for systematic pursuit of the salutary emotions, and I knew that I would want to discuss it with my doctor. Two preconditions, however, seemed obvious for the experiment. The first concerned my medication. If that medication were toxic to any degree, it was doubtful whether the plan would work. The second precondition concerned the hospital. I knew I would have to find a place somewhat more conducive to a positive outlook on life.

Let's consider these preconditions separately.

First, the medication. The emphasis had been on pain-killing drugs—aspirin, phenylbutazone (butazolidine), codeine, colchicine, sleeping pills. The aspirin and phenylbutazone were antiinflammatory and thus were therapeutically justifiable. But I wasn't sure they weren't also toxic. It developed that I was hypersensitive to virtually all the medication I was receiving. The hospital had been giving me maximum dosages: twenty-six aspirin tablets and twelve phenylbutazone tablets a day. No wonder I had hives all over my body and felt as though my skin were being chewed up by millions of red ants.

It was unreasonable to expect positive chemical changes to take place so long as my body was being saturated with, and toxified by, pain-killing medications. I had one of my research assistants at the *Saturday Review* look up the pertinent references in the medical journals and found that drugs like phenylbutazone and even aspirin levy a heavy tax on the adrenal glands. I also learned that phenylbutazone is one of the most powerful drugs being manufactured. It can produce bloody stools, the result of its antagonism to fibrinogen. It can cause intolerable itching and sleeplessness. It can depress bone marrow.

Aspirin, of course, enjoys a more auspicious reputation, at least with the general public. The prevailing impression of aspirin is that it is not only the most harmless drug available but also one of the most effective. When I looked into research in the medical journals, however, I found that aspirin is quite powerful in its own right and warrants considerable care in its use. The fact that it can be bought in unlimited quantities without prescription or doctor's guidance seemed indefensible. Even in small amounts, it can cause internal bleeding. Articles in the medical press reported that the chemical composition of aspirin, like that of phenylbutazone, impairs the clotting function of platelets, disc-shaped substances in the blood.

It was a mind-boggling train of thought. Could it be, I asked myself, that aspirin, so universally accepted for so many years, was actually harmful in the treatment of collagen illness such as arthritis?

The history of medicine is replete with accounts of drugs and modes of treatment that were in use for many years before it was recognized that they did more harm than good. For centuries, for example, doctors believed that drawing blood from patients was essential for rapid recovery from virtually every illness. Then, midway through the nineteenth century, it was discovered that bleeding served only to weaken the patient. King Charles II's death is believed to have been caused in part by administered bleedings. George Washington's death was also hastened by the severe loss of blood resulting from this treatment.

Living in the second half of the twentieth century, I realized, confers no automatic protection against unwise or even dangerous drugs and methods. Each age has had to undergo its own special nostrums. Fortunately, the human body is a remarkably durable instrument and has been able to withstand all sorts of prescribed assaults over the centuries, from freezing to animal dung.

Suppose I stopped taking aspirin and phenylbutazone? What about the pain? The bones in my spine and practically every joint in my body felt as though I had been run over by a truck.

I knew that pain could be affected by attitudes. Most people become panicky about almost any pain. On all sides they have been so bombarded by advertisements about pain that they take this or that analgesic at the slightest sign of an ache. We are largely illiterate about pain and so are seldom able to deal with it rationally. Pain is part of the body's magic. It is the way the body transmits a sign to the brain that something is wrong. Leprous patients pray for the sensation of pain. What makes leprosy such a terrible disease is that the victim usually feels no pain when his extremities are being injured. He loses his fingers or toes because he receives no warning signal.

I could stand pain so long as I knew that progress was being made in meeting the basic need. That need, I felt, was to restore the body's capacity to halt the continuing breakdown of connective tissue.

There was also the problem of the severe inflammation. If we dispensed with the aspirin, how would we combat the inflammation? I recalled having read in the medical journals about the usefulness of ascorbic acid in combating a wide number of illnesses—all the way from bronchitis to some types of heart disease. Could it also combat inflammation? Did vitamin C act directly, or did it serve as a starter for the body's endocrine system—in particular, the adrenal glands? Was it possible, I asked myself, that ascorbic acid had a vital role to play in "feeding" the adrenal glands?

I had read in the medical press that vitamin C helps to oxygenate the blood. If inadequate or impaired oxygenation was a factor in collagen breakdown, couldn't this circumstance have been another argument for ascorbic acid? Also, according to some medical reports, people suffering from collagen diseases are deficient in vitamin C. Did this lack mean that the body uses up large amounts of vitamin C in the process of combating collagen breakdown?

I wanted to discuss some of these ruminations with Dr. Hitzig. He listened carefully as I told him of my speculations concerning the cause of the illness, as well as my layman's ideas for a course of action that might give me a chance to reduce the odds against my recovery.

Dr. Hitzig said it was clear to him that there was nothing undersized about my will to live. He said that what was most important was that I continue to believe in everything I had said. He shared my excitement about the possibilities of recovery and liked the idea of a partnership.

Even before we had completed arrangements for moving out of the hospital we began the part of the program calling for the full exercise of the affirmative emotions as a factor in enhancing body chemistry. It was easy enough to hope and love and have faith, but what about laughter? Nothing is less funny than being flat on your back with all the bones in your spine and joints hurting. A systematic program was indicated. A good place to begin, I thought, was with amusing movies. Allen Funt, producer of the spoofing television program "Candid Camera," sent films of some of his CC classics, along with a motion-picture projector. The nurse was instructed in its use. We were even able to get our hands on some old Marx brothers films. We pulled down the blinds and turned on the machine.

It worked. I made the joyous discovery that ten minutes of genuine belly laughter had an anesthetic effect and would give me at least two hours of pain-free sleep. When the pain-killing effect of the laughter wore off, we would switch on the motion-picture projector again, and, not infrequently, it would lead to another pain-free sleep interval. Sometimes, the nurse read to me out of a trove of humor books. Especially useful were E. B. and Katharine White's *Subtreasury of American Humor* and Max Eastman's *The Enjoyment of Laughter*.

How scientific was it to believe that laughter—as well as the positive emotions in general—was affecting my body chemistry for the better? If laughter did in fact have a salutary effect on the body's chemistry, it seemed at least theoretically likely that it would enhance the system's ability to fight the inflammation. So we took sedimentation rate readings just before as well as several hours after the laughter episodes. Each time, there was a drop of at least five points. The drop by itself was not substantial, but it held and was cumulative. I was greatly elated by the discovery that there is a physiologic basis for the ancient theory that laughter is good medicine.

There was, however, one negative side-effect of the laughter from the standpoint of the hospital. I was disturbing other patients. But that objection didn't last very long, for the arrangements were now complete for me to move my act to a hotel room.

One of the incidental advantages of the hotel room, I was delighted to find, was that it cost only about one-third as much as the hospital. The other benefits were incalculable. I would not be awakened for a bed bath or for meals or for medication or for a change of bed sheets or for tests or for examinations by hospital interns. The sense of serenity was delicious and would, I felt certain, contribute to a general improvement.

What about ascorbic acid and its place in the general program for recovery? In discussing my speculations about vitamin C with Dr. Hitzig, I found him completely open-minded on the subject, although he told me of serious questions that had been raised by scientific studies. He also cautioned me that heavy doses of ascorbic acid carried some risk of renal damage. The main problem right then, however, was not my kidneys; it seemed to me that, on balance, the risk was worth taking. I asked Dr. Hitzig about previous recorded experience with massive doses of vitamin C. He ascertained that at the hospital there had been cases in which patients had received up to 3 grams by intramuscular injection.

As I thought about the injection procedure, some questions came to mind. Introducing the ascorbic acid directly into the bloodstream might make more effective use of the vitamin, but I wondered about the body's ability to utilize a sudden, massive infusion. I knew that one of the great advantages of vitamin C is that the body takes only the amount necessary for its purposes and excretes the rest. Again, there came to mind Cannon's phrase—the wisdom of the body.

Was there a coefficient of time in the utilization of ascorbic acid? The more I thought about it, the more likely it seemed to me that the body would excrete a large quantity of the vitamin because it couldn't metabolize it fast enough. I wondered whether a better procedure than injection would be to administer the ascorbic acid through slow intravenous drip over a period of three or four hours. In this way we could go far beyond 3 grams. My hope was to start at 10 grams and then increase the dose daily until we reached 25 grams.

Dr. Hitzig's eyes widened when I mentioned 25 grams. This amount was far beyond any recorded dose. He said he had to caution me about the possible effect not just on the kidneys but on the veins in the arms. Moreover, he said he knew of no data to support the assumption that the body could handle 25 grams over a four-hour period, other than by excreting it rapidly through the urine.

As before, however, it seemed to me we were playing for bigger stakes: losing some veins was not of major importance alongside the need to combat whatever was eating at my connective tissue.

To know whether we were on the right track we took a sedimentation test before the first intravenous administration of 10 grams of ascorbic acid. Four hours later, we took another sedimentation test. There was a drop of nine full points.

Seldom had I known such elation. The ascorbic acid was working. So was laughter. The combination was cutting heavily into whatever poison was attacking the connective tissue. The fever was receding, and the pulse was no longer racing.

We stepped up the dosage. On the second day we went to 12.5 grams of ascorbic acid, on the third day, 15 grams, and so on until the end of the week, when we reached 25 grams. Meanwhile, the laughter routine was in full force. I was completely off drugs and sleeping pills. Sleep—blessed, natural sleep without pain—was becoming increasingly prolonged.

At the end of the eighth day I was able to move my thumbs without pain. By this time, the sedimentation rate was somewhere in the 80s and dropping fast. I couldn't be sure, but it seemed to me that the gravel-like nodules on my neck and the backs of my hands were beginning to shrink. There was no doubt in my mind that I was going to make it back all the way. I could function, and the feeling was indescribably beautiful.

I must not make it appear that all my infirmities disappeared overnight. For many months I couldn't get my arms up far enough to reach for a book on a high shelf. My fingers weren't agile enough to do what I wanted them to do on the organ keyboard. My neck had a limited turning radius. My knees were somewhat wobbly, and off and on, I have had to wear a metal brace.

Even so, I was sufficiently recovered to go back to my job at the *Saturday Review* full time again, and this was miracle enough for me.

Is the recovery a total one? Year by year the mobility has improved. I have become pain-free, except for one shoulder and my knees, although I have been able to discard the metal braces. I no longer feel a sharp twinge in my wrists when I hit a tennis ball or golf ball, as I did for such a long time. I can ride a horse flat out and hold a camera with a steady hand. And I have recaptured my ambition to play the Toccata and Fugue in D Minor, though I find the going slower and tougher than I had hoped. My neck has a full turning radius again, despite the statement of specialists as recently as 1971 that the condition was degenerative and that I would have to adjust to a quarter turn.

It was seven years after the onset of the illness before I had scientific confirmation about the dangers of using aspirin in the treatment of collagen diseases. In its May 8, 1971 issue, *Lancet* published a study by Drs. M. A. Sahud and R. J. Cohen showing that aspirin can be antagonistic to the retention of vitamin C in the body. The authors said that patients with rheumatoid arthritis should take vitamin C supplements, since it has often been noted that they have low levels of the vitamin in their blood. It was no surprise, then, that I had been able to absorb such massive amounts of ascorbic acid without kidney or other complications.

What conclusions do I draw from the entire experience?

The first is that the will to live is not a theoretical abstraction, but a physiologic reality with therapeutic characteristics. The second is that I was incredibly fortunate to have as my doctor a man who knew that his biggest job was to encourage to the fullest the patient's will to live and to mobilize all the natural resources of body and mind to combat disease. Dr. Hitzig was willing to set aside the large and often hazardous armamentarium of powerful drugs available to the modern physician when he became convinced that his patient might have something better to offer. He was also wise enough to know that the art of healing is still a frontier profession. And, though I can't be sure of this point, I have a hunch he believed that my own total involvement was a major factor in my recovery.

People have asked what I thought when I was told by the specialists that my disease was progressive and incurable.

The answer is simple. Since I didn't accept the verdict, I wasn't trapped in the cycle of fear, depression, and panic that frequently accompanies a supposedly incurable illness. I must not make it seem, however, that I was unmindful of the seriousness of the problem or that I was in a festive mood throughout. Being unable to move my body was all the evidence I needed that the specialists were dealing with real concerns. But deep down, I knew I had a good chance and relished the idea of bucking the odds.

Adam Smith, in his book, *Powers of the Mind,* says he discussed my recovery with some of his doctor friends, asking them to explain why the combination of laughter and ascorbic acid worked so well. The answer he got was that neither laughter nor ascorbic acid had anything to do with it and that I probably would have recovered if nothing had been done.

Maybe so, but that was not the opinion of the specialists at the time.

Two or three doctors, reflecting on the Adam Smith account, have commented that I was probably the beneficiary of a mammoth venture in self-administered placebos.

Such a hypothesis bothers me not at all. Respectable names in the history of medicine, like Paracelsus, Holmes, and Osler, have suggested that the history of medication is far more the history of the placebo effect than of intrinsically valuable and relevant drugs. Such modalities as bleeding (in a single year, 1827, France imported 33 million leeches after its domestic supplies had been depleted); purging through emetics; physical contact with unicorn horns, bezoar stones, mandrakes, or powdered mummies—all such treatments were no doubt regarded by physicians at the time as specifics with empirical sanction. But today's medical science recognizes that whatever efficacy these treatments may have had—and the records indicate that the results were often surprisingly in line with expectations—was probably related to the power of the placebo.

Until comparatively recently, medical literature on the phenomenon of the placebo has been rather sparse. But the past two decades have seen a pronounced interest in the subject. Indeed, three medical researchers at the University of California, Los Angeles, have compiled an entire volume on a bibliography of the placebo. (J. Turner, R. Gallimore, C. Fox, *Placebo: An Annotated Bibliography.* The Neuropsychiatric Institute, University of California, Los Angeles, 1974.) Among the medical researchers who have been prominently engaged in such studies are Arthur K. Shapiro, Stewart Wolf, Henry K. Beecher, and Louis Lasagna. (Their experience is discussed in the next chapter.) In connection with my own experience, I was fascinated by a report citing a study by Dr. Thomas C. Chalmers, of the Mount Sinai Medical Center in New York, which compared two groups that were being used to test the theory that ascorbic acid is a cold preventative. "The group on placebo who thought they were on ascorbic acid," says Dr. Chalmers, "had fewer colds than the group on ascorbic acid who thought they were on placebo."

I was absolutely convinced, at the time I was deep in my illness, that intravenous doses of ascorbic acid could be beneficial—and they were. It is quite possible that this treatment—like everything else I did—was a demonstration of the placebo effect.

At this point, of course, we are opening a very wide door, perhaps even a Pandora's box. The vaunted "miracle cures" that abound in the literature of all the great religions all say something about the ability of the patient, properly motivated or stimulated, to participate actively in extraordinary reversals of disease and disability. It is all too early, of course, to raise these possibilities and speculations to a monopoly status—in which case the entire edifice of modern medicine would be reduced to little more than the hut of an African witch doctor. But we can at least reflect on William Halse Rivers' statement, as quoted by Shapiro, that "the salient feature of the medicine of today is that these physical factors are no longer allowed to play their part unwittingly, but are themselves becoming the subject of study, so that the present age is serving the growth of a rational system of psychotherapeutics."

What we are talking about essentially, I suppose, is the chemistry of the will to live. In Bucharest in 1972, I visited the clinic of Ana Aslan, described to me as one of Romania's leading endocrinologists. She spoke of her belief that there is a direct connection between a robust will to live and the chemical balances in the brain. She is convinced that creativity—one aspect of the will to live—produces the vital brain impulses that stimulate the pituitary gland, triggering effects on the pineal gland and the whole of the endocrine system. Is it possible that placebos have a key role in this process? Shouldn't this entire area be worth serious and sustained attention?

If I had to guess, I would say that the principal contribution made by my doctor to the taming, and possibly the conquest, of my illness was that he encouraged me to believe I was a respected partner with him in the total undertaking. He fully engaged my subjective energies. He may not have been able to define or diagnose the process through which self-confidence (wild hunches securely believed) was somehow picked up by the body's immunologic mechanisms and translated into antimorbid effects, but he was acting, I believe, in the best tradition of medicine in recognizing that he had to reach out in my case beyond the usual verifiable modalities. In so doing, he was faithful to the first dictum in his medical education: above all, do not harm.

Something else I have learned. I have learned never to underestimate the capacity of the human mind and body to regenerate—even when the prospects seem most wretched. The life-force may be the least understood force on earth. William James said that human beings tend to live too far within self-imposed limits. It is possible that these limits will recede when we respect more fully the natural drive of the human mind and body toward perfectibility and regeneration. Protecting and cherishing that natural drive may well represent the finest exercise of human freedom.

Questions

1. If you were to become ill, would you turn to humor to help make you well? What forms and types of humor would you use?

2. Have you ever witnessed the phenomenon of mind over body? How could you utilize this notion to help you with stress?

Part Two

Personality and Stress

3. Personality Plays a Part

4. Wisdom of the Ages

5. Characteristics of a Hardy Personality

It is not the delicate, neurotic person who is prone to angina, but the robust, the vigorous in mind and body, the keen and ambitious man, whose engine is always at "full speed ahead," the well set man of from forty-five to fifty-five years of age, with military bearing, iron gray hair, and florid complexion. —William Osler

What you will learn in Part Two
In Part Two you will learn:

- the ways that living habits, personality traits, and behavior patterns can make you susceptible to stress;

- coping techniques or wisdom of the ages for dealing with stress;

- the characteristics of a hardy personality.

Chapter Three
ᛝ
Personality Plays a Part

The stress-prone person

An important factor in the stress equation is the role of personality. Some people are able to handle tremendous amounts of pressure, conflict, and frustration and reduce this down to size, while others actually create stress and suffer negative consequences.

In the nineteenth century, William Osler wrote, "I believe that the high pressure at which men live, and the habit of working the machine to its maximum capacity, are responsible for arterial degeneration." He described one of his patients as follows:

> Living an intense life, absorbed in his work, devoted to his pleasures, passionately devoted to his home, the nervous energy of the patient is taxed to the uttermost, and his system is subjected to that stress and strain which seems to be a basic factor in so many cases of angina pectoris.[1]

This general description is an old version of the modern concept of the stress-prone person. Note that it makes direct connections between mind and body, and between lifestyle and health.

As early as the seventeenth century, physician William Harvey (1578–1657) described the relationship between mind and body when he wrote:

> Every affection of the mind that is attended with either pain or pleasure, hope or fear, is the cause of an agitation whose influence extends to the heart.[2]

Research over the past forty years has extended our understanding of stress and health. One of the outcomes of this research has been to demonstrate scientifically that living habits, personality traits, and behavioral patterns can influence the body. Another has been to show that stress does not generally occur in isolation and is often tied to social relationships. Part Two of this book examines the difference between the stress-prone and the stress-resistant personalities and provides effective coping techniques or wisdom of the ages for managing stress.

Behavior patterns

People react differently to stress. One person may fly into a rage after being cut off by a motorist, while another simply shrugs it off. Consequently, a key issue about stress is not how much of it there is, but how well it is handled. Are you the type of person who takes a small amount of stress and makes it into a mountain? Or are you the type who can handle many little hassles and major life changes while keeping things in perspective?

Research shows that personality plays an important part in determining a person's susceptibility to stress and stress-related problems. Some people are "hardgoing" and live their lives in ways that increase physical and emotional wear and tear. Others are easygoing in their approach to life and its problems. Whether a person is a "turtle" or a "racehorse" by temperament, certain personality traits and living habits, formed largely through the influence of culture, correlate positively and significantly with heart disease. That these traits and habits can and should be modified is the central point of *Type A Behavior and Your Heart* by Meyer Friedman and Ray Rosenman.

Friedman and Rosenman, two cardiologists in private practice in San Francisco during the 1950s, became interested in the connection between personality types and heart disease almost by accident. Needing the chairs in their waiting room reupholstered, they scheduled the work to be done. As the upholsterer departed, he asked the doctors what line of work they were in. They answered that they were heart specialists. He said, "I was just wondering, because it is so strange that only the front edges of your chair seats are worn out"—patients had been sitting on the edges of their chairs.

The doctors were initially puzzled by this, but after reflecting on the many diagnostic sessions they had conducted with their patients and their patients' families, they thought they understood the reason. Time after time, they could remember having a conversation something like this: "Doctor, I know your tests tell you this, and your instruments tell you that, but if you want to know my Jim's problem, it is . . ." In almost every case, the family would go on to describe an almost identical constellation of behaviors and personality characteristics that they believed had caused the heart disease.[3]

Basing their conclusions on the Western Collaborative Group Study, an epidemiological project completed in 1964, Friedman and Rosenman label high-stress behaviors as type A and their opposites as type B. Included in the list of type A, coronary-prone, behaviors are the following:[4]

- **An intense drive to advance oneself or one's causes and to "beat the competition."** Whatever the occupation, trade, or profession, the type A's mental set is to be "number one." The goal may be related to work, family, or personal life, but in any case, the type A person is intensely driven to succeed.

- **An adversarial and competitive manner in interpersonal relationships.** Opinionated and often rigid, the type A person seemingly likes to argue, talks "at" others instead of "with" them, and is subject to vocal outbursts. The type A is easily irritated and seems to be in a constant struggle with other people and events.

- **Continuous involvement in a variety of activities at several levels of demand.** The type A person has a history of simultaneous work on big-picture, middle-picture, and little-picture matters, with little or no rest in between. The type A is like an octopus, wishing to have ten arms in order to get more things accomplished. As a rule, the type A person avoids repetitive chores and routine work.

- **A quick pace in walking, eating, speaking, and gesturing.** The type A person has a habitual sense of time urgency. Such a person moves through the day at an intense pace. It might be said that type A people have the "hurry-up disease." They seem to be in mortal conflict with Father Time, constantly working against impossible deadlines and time constraints.

- **Physical and mental alertness.** The type A person is characteristically tense and poised for action. Although extreme alertness may be necessary at times, constant excitement of the body—a high level of hormonal and chemical activity—without constructive physical release can be self-destructive.

- **Impatience in interpersonal relations.** The type A can be extremely demanding in human relationships (especially with people they care about). Expecting perfection from others, who rarely match up, a type A becomes critical and is prone to argument. This person often shouts and has even been known to throw things. Although this colorful personality may attract others and people may care for him or her, the type A's intolerance for the imperfections of others often harms these relationships.

- **Inability to relax.** The type A is subject to a condition known as "Sunday neurosis," an inability to relax without feeling guilty. When a type A person finds him- or herself with a day of rest, the person quickly becomes restless, feeling that he or she is wasting time. A type A person has a strong need to be doing something useful and does not equate free time and relaxation with being useful.

- **Dislike for waiting.** The type A hates waiting in lines. If he or she has to wait in a line, such as at the store, bank, or theater, the type A becomes irritated. If forced to wait in a traffic jam, a type A will typically experience increased blood pressure as he or she dwells on the lost time and productivity caused by the delay. It is common to see type A people honking the horn, leaning out of the window, making hand gestures, and talking to themselves.

This behavior contrasts with that of type B people, who consider that if they want to get to their destinations, they must wait; there is no alternative. They cannot get out of their cars and throw the others out of the way, so they avoid thinking about the delay. Instead, the type B uses forced waiting time to do something constructive, which might even involve relaxation.

In summary, type A people tend to be success oriented, driven by internal forces to accomplish more and more in less and less time. When this urge is out of control, they become perpetually active until exhaustion occurs. Often, type A's have poor human relationships because they seem to have little or no time or patience for people, or their aggressive behavior upsets others. Also, type A's may have trouble winding down from the intense state at which they operate; muscle tension, aches and pains, and insomnia are common. Finally, type A's rarely pause to enjoy the moment, as they are typically in a hurry; their mental focus is usually on the next task, the next mountain to climb.

The primary significance of Friedman and Rosenman's work was their finding that type B personalities experience less stress and have a lower incidence of cardiovascular disease, while type A's experience greater stress and have a higher incidence of heart disease. Further, they discovered that heart disease in type A people is often exhibited early in life, sometimes when they are in their thirties and forties. Friedman and Rosenman maintain that coronary heart disease almost never occurs before seventy years of age in type B people, even if they smoke, eat fatty foods, and don't exercise.[5]

There is a common belief that heart disease is a *man's* illness, partly because research efforts have focused on men who have had heart attacks in their prime midlife earning years. The fact is, women tend to get heart disease later than men, but it is usually more severe. According to the American Heart Association, as of 1995 one in eight American women age 45 and older have had a heart attack or stroke. Also a woman's risk of dying from heart disease is one in two in contrast to 1 in 9 of having breast cancer.[6]

Although a causal relationship has not been established between personality type, stress levels, and heart disease (only a high correlation has been documented), since 1980 the National Institutes of Health have recognized type A behavior as a risk factor in coronary heart disease. It is estimated that 75 percent of men have type A personality traits and that almost twice as many men fit the type A profile as women.[7]

People should be aware of whether they have a type A or type B personality. Consider that at present, heart disease is the number one cause of death in the

United States. Forty-five percent of heart attacks and 20 percent of cardiac deaths occur before the age of 65. At least 250,000 people a year die within the first hour of attack and before they reach the hospital. A large percentage of these deaths occur between the ages of 35 and 50 and are classified as "premature" deaths. These statistics alone should encourage you to do everything you can to reduce your chances of being one of the stricken.[8]

The following is a questionnaire to help you determine your personality type.

⊚ Application: the Stress Barometer —Type A, Type B Behavior Test

What am I like? The following is a list of personality traits and behavior patterns. After each trait, check the answer that best describes you. Sometimes you will feel that you belong somewhere between the columns. This is to be expected.

	Column A	Column B
I become impatient when events move slowly.	___often	___rarely
I work overtime or bring work home.	___often	___rarely
I feel guilty when I relax and do nothing.	___often	___rarely
I find myself talking "at" people instead of "with" people.	___often	___rarely
I speak, eat, or move at a quick pace.	___often	___rarely
I can't stand waiting in lines.	___often	___rarely
I do things to extremes.	___often	___rarely
I have a strong need for perfection.	___often	___rarely
I become angry easily.	___often	___rarely
I have disagreements with others.	___often	___rarely
I try to think about or do two or more things at once.	___often	___rarely
I am number oriented (I like to count my accomplishments and possessions).	___often	___rarely
I overschedule myself.	___often	___rarely
I take little notice of my physical surroundings.	___often	___rarely
People fail to meet my standards.	___often	___rarely
I become impatient with people.	___often	___rarely
I hurry the ends of sentences, or do not speak them at all.	___often	___rarely
I feel driven to accomplish my goals.	___often	___rarely
I am tense.	___often	___rarely
I am subject to vocal outbursts.	___often	___rarely
I am occupied primarily by own interests and actions.	___often	___rarely
I am quick to challenge opposing views.	___often	___rarely

Source: Based on Meyer Friedman and Ray H. Rosenman, Type A Behavior and Your Heart *(New York: Alfred A. Knopf, Inc., 1974), 80-88; and Meyer Friedman and Diane Ulmer,* Treating Type A Behavior and Your Heart *(New York: Alfred A. Knopf, Inc., 1984).*

Scoring and interpretation

Give yourself one point for each check mark in column B in the Stress Barometer test, and circle the total on the chart in Figure 3.1. Your score is a measure of whether you are a type A or type B person and indicates your corresponding susceptibility to stress and stress-related illness.

Figure 3.1 The Stress Barometer

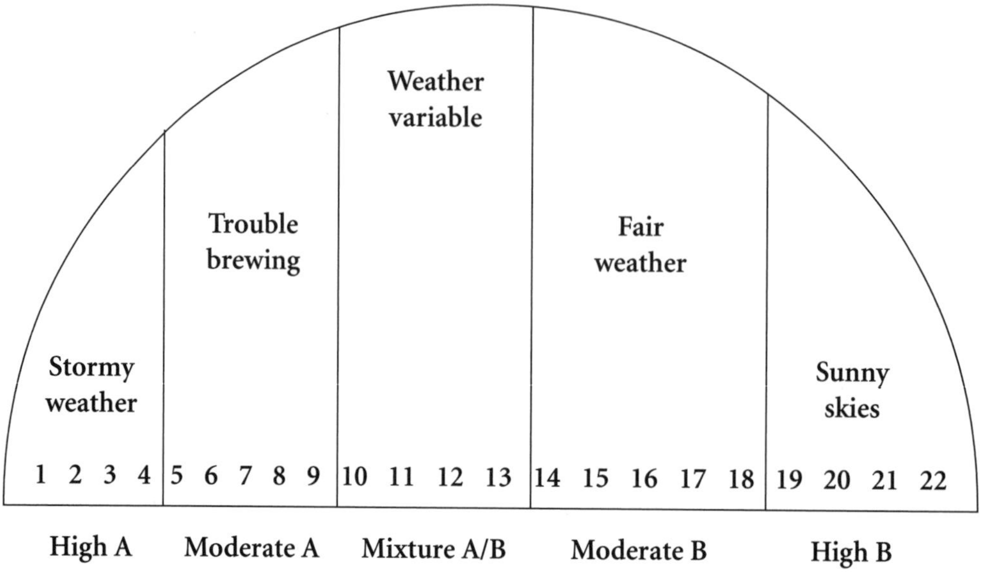

Scores	Personality type	Stress forecast
1 through 4	High A	Stormy weather
5 through 9	Moderate A	Trouble brewing
10 through 13	Mixture A/B	Weather variable
14 through 18	Moderate B	Fair weather
19 through 22	High B	Sunny skies

Discussion

There are five major points to remember about the Stress Barometer test:

- The purpose of the test is to increase your awareness of the relationship between behavior patterns and health. Scores reveal levels of susceptibility for groups of people, and these may or may not be accurate for you as an individual because (1) there is no certainty that all type A personalities (scores 1 through 9) will have heart disease and (2) there is no assurance that all type B personalities (scores 14 through 22), will not have heart disease. What is generally assured for type B's is that if you do have heart disease, your personality will not be on the list of contributing factors.

■ There are three basic elements of the type A personality: (1) speed/impulse, (2) competitiveness, and (3) anger/hostility. Of these, anger/hostility is usually the most serious problem. Acceptable outlets are often found for speed/impulse and competitiveness in the areas of hobbies, sports, and business. Anger and hostility are not as personally or socially acceptable. Thus, their effects are often experienced internally, resulting in harmful physical wear and tear.[9]

An early link between hostility and heart disease is suggested by the story of eighteenth century English medical professor Sir John Harvey when he said, "My life is in the hands of any fool who chooses to annoy me." He apparently recognized the link between his anginal chest pain and his arguments with colleagues. One evening in 1793, his prediction came true. After a heated dispute at a hospital board meeting, Dr. Harvey stormed out, collapsed, and died.[10]

To show that the connection between anger and health has been noted in other cultures as well, consider the following Chinese proverb:

The fire you kindle for your enemy often burns you more than him.[11]

Redford Williams of Duke University, author of *The Trusting Heart* and *Anger Kills*, states that anger is the most harmful component of the type A personality. His prescription for reducing anger is to put yourself in the other person's shoes, learn to laugh at yourself, relax, practice trust, listen, act as if this day is your last, and practice forgiveness.[12]

■ The toxic effects of chronic anger and continuous struggle are well documented.

If you become angered by some stimulation, your hypothalamus will almost instantly send signals to your sympathetic nervous system (that portion of the nervous system not directly under conscious control), causing the secretion of large amounts of epinephrine and norepinephrine (otherwise known as adrenaline and noradrenalin, or as a group, as catecholamines). In addition, this same anger will also induce the hypothalamus to send messages to the pituitary gland, the master of all endocrine glands, urging it to discharge some of its own exclusively manufactured hormones and also to send out chemical signals to the adrenal, sex, and thyroid glands and the pancreas as well, so that they in turn may secrete extra amounts of *their* exclusively manufactured hormones. As a consequence, not only will your tissues be bathed by an excess of catecholamines when you become angry, they may also be exposed to exceedingly large amounts of various pituitary and adrenal hormones, testosterone (or estrogen), thyroxine, and insulin. If your struggles become *chronic*, then a *chronic* excess discharge of these various hormones also occurs.[13]

- Type A and type B behaviors are determined largely by culture. Compare America with Polynesia, or compare two groups of people with the same roots—Germany and Austria. Note the contrast between America and Germany (type A) and Polynesia and Austria with their relaxed and congenial ways (type B). In any society, certain behavior patterns are rewarded and thus reinforced. This socialization process includes role modeling, identification, and habituation.

- At the family level, consider how subtle but basic actions of parents can influence children:

  Type A parents who are engaged in a chronic struggle against time and other persons may teach their children a sense of time urgency and interpersonal aggressiveness. Children are most likely to take on these behavior patterns if they value the consequences they see their parents derive from that behavior. Examples of perceived benefits include recognition, wealth, and prestige.[14]

You may be thinking, "It seems like advancements in business, engineering, transportation, etc., are achieved by type A societies and individuals, and these accomplishments are to be valued." It is true that in a world of competition and struggle, type A behavior may help you get to the top; however, four important points should be noted:

1. Although type A behavior may help you get to the top, it could be damaging your health, and you may not live to enjoy the results of your efforts unless you become more B-like somewhere along the way. The obituaries of every town newspaper tell the story of young and talented people who die because of type A behavior. Their gifts remain—but they are gone. Often, they are only sixty, fifty, forty, or even thirty years of age.

   The high stress of type A behavior increases chances of heart attack through a perpetually high heart rate, hypertension, damage to coronary artery walls, and excessive cholesterol flow in the blood. These physical processes occur in subtle, silent ways. Heart attack victims have little advance warning, although pain in or tightening of the chest is a warning in many cases. If you also smoke, do not exercise, are overweight, have a history of heart disease in your family, and eat too many high-cholesterol foods, your chances of heart attack are further increased.[15]

2. People, more than any other beings, create their world. Thus, there can be peace instead of war and concern for others versus self-centeredness if people have sufficient will to attain these. People can create societies, organizations, and families supportive of type B behavior. Imagine a family that teaches love over hate, or a company that encourages employee cooperation over internal conflict.

3. Recent studies show that as many type B as type A individuals actually obtain high levels of accomplishment. This may be due to the fact that positive A qualities, such as ambition and persistent hard work, are offset by negative A behaviors, such as impatience in decision making and argumentativeness in human relations. Indeed, there is evidence that type A's are not as good at performing some executive functions—examining alternatives, setting priorities, and enlisting the aid of coworkers and subordinates—as are their type B counterparts.[16]

4. An individual or society can be B-like without being lazy or unproductive. It is possible to achieve great feats by working efficiently and to enjoy these accomplishments by living intelligently. It is possible to be successful and live to enjoy it.

More about anger

Research points to the harmful effects of anger in terms of health consequences. One study of 255 physicians who had taken a standard personality test while attending University of North Carolina's medical school showed that over the next 25 years, those individuals whose anger/hostility scores had been in the top half were four to five times more likely to develop heart disease than those whose scores were in the lower half. A similar study of 118 lawyers found equally striking results. Of those individuals who scored in the top quarter for anger/hostility, nearly one in five was dead by age 50. Of those in the lowest quarter, only one in twenty-five died by age 50.[17]

Too often, people overreact to the minor agitations of everyday life. Feelings of anger run a range from low-level aggravation to high-level rage. Expressions of anger range from low-level arguments to high-level verbal and physical assault. The more prevalent and intense these are in a person's general pattern of behavior or approach to life, the more serious the health consequences. With heart pounding, blood pressure skyrocketing, and adrenaline surging, we are causing harm to ourselves by pushing our bodies beyond their limits.

Do men and women differ when it comes to anger? Research shows that in U.S. society incidents of anger (six to seven times a week), intensity of anger (aggravation to fury), and causes of anger (traffic jams, inconsiderate people, and waiting in lines) are generally the same for both sexes. What is different is styles of anger: Men's anger is typically straightforward and uncomplicated by restraint or guilt. Women are more likely to feel self-conscious and embarrassed, equating anger with inappropriate loss of control. After an outburst, women tell themselves, "Whoa! Get a grip." Men say, "That ought to teach them!" Either approach to anger—blowing your stack in public, which men tend to do, or seething silently in private, which women tend to do—can put your heart at risk.[18]

The banishment of anger is not possible anymore than the banishment of hunger. And who would want to? Anger can play a positive role in combating injustice and rectifying wrongs. The real problem is constant and free-floating anger, especially when it is acted out verbally or physically. An occasional flash of temper is not the problem, but a permanent state of aggravation and conflict is. The best advice is to relax, take a deep breath, count to ten, walk around the block, and decide whether an issue is worth a war. Resist getting worked up by lowering your voice, unclenching your fists and jaw, relaxing your muscles, and letting tension and anger seep away. This is not to say you should repress your feelings or deny that you are angry. Instead, simply decide, is this a hill worth dying on? If not, you should loosen up and let it go.[19]

The hot reactor syndrome

Friedman and Rosenman's work on personality and stress triggered an avalanche of interest and study on the stress-prone person. One of the best yields has been the work of cardiologist Robert Eliot and his associates at the National Center of Preventive and Stress Medicine in Phoenix, Arizona, and the Institute of Stress Medicine in Jackson Hole, Wyoming. Eliot relates a personal account that is fascinating and instructive of how the *hot reactor syndrome* can develop and have terrible consequences.

Keeping things in perspective

Wise men speak of the moment of clarity—that instant when absolute knowledge presents itself. My moment of clarity came as I was doubled up in a bathroom at a Nebraska community hospital two hundred miles from home. Earlier that morning, after conducting grand rounds in the facility's coronary care unit, I had participated in a cardiology conference before my peers. My lecture had been on heart attacks and sudden death. I had experienced some discomfort during the program but dismissed it as indigestion—or, at worst, a bout with my gallbladder.

It had been a hectic week. The day before the conference, back at my own hospital, I had argued both vehemently and unsuccessfully with administrators over the budget, manpower, and timing regarding a planned cardiovascular center. Two days before that I had flown back from an exhausting lecture series in New Orleans—where, once again, I had been the so-called expert on sudden cardiac death.

In that bathroom, the first symptom I noticed was intense pressure. It began near my breastbone; shot up into my shoulders, neck, and jaws; and surged down again through both of my arms. It was as if an elephant had plopped down on my chest. I could barely catch my breath. I started sweating. I began getting bowel cramps and then overwhelming nausea. Immediately I diagnosed my own condition: myocardial infarction. Later, as the nurses helped me into a hospital bed, I remember saying with astonishment, "I'm having a heart attack." I was forty-four years old.

During my recovery I realized my professional life had become a joyless treadmill. I had worked tirelessly for acceptance within the medical community and yet efforts to establish my own cardiovascular center had failed. This was a bitter pill for someone who had always defined life in terms of victory or defeat. My disillusionment was compounded by the knowledge that I had brought promising associates into this seemingly futile situation. I've since described my state of mind as *invisible entrapment.*

I didn't like being on the wrong side of the sheets in a coronary care unit. Something had to change; and I asked myself, "Is any of this worth dying for?" Fortunately for me, my answer was "No!" I had looked into the abyss and decided to stop sweating the small stuff. Pretty soon, I saw that it was *all* small stuff.[20]

While Friedman and Rosenman observed psychological traits and patterns of behavior, Eliot and his colleagues emphasize physiological effects. They have found that hot reactors can belong to any camp—A or B, male or female. The determining factor is the body's response to stress.

So what exactly is the "hot reactor syndrome," and how do stress practitioners test for its presence? People tend to respond to stress in one of two ways. "Cold" reactors may seem upset when confronted with a stressful situation but experience few physiological changes. In contrast, "hot" reactors to stress experience a flood of the powerful chemicals associated with the classic GAS stress response, whether or not this is visible to others.

Hot reactors are those individuals who exhibit extreme cardiovascular arousal when they are under stress. One of the most dangerous aspects of hot reacting is a dramatic rise in blood pressure as often as thirty or forty times a day. As a result, blood pressure is higher for a longer time, resulting in greater risk of developing chronic high blood pressure and heart disease. The more aroused people get physiologically, the more likely they are to suffer from cardiovascular problems. In fact, excess stress chemicals released during states of alarm and vigilance can literally rupture heart muscle fibers. This creates short circuits and malfunctional heart rhythm. When this happens, death can result.[21]

How the hot reactor stress test works

The Cardiac Performance Lab (CPL) developed by Eliot and his colleagues consists of three stages: the mental arithmetic challenge, the competitive video game, and the cold pressor test.

During the mental arithmetic challenge, the individual is placed in an isolated environment, seated in a comfortable but alert position, and attached to recording electrodes. A televised, nonthreatening guide instructs the subject to "Subtract sevens serially from 777, going as fast as possible. That is, 777, 770, 763, and so on. Keep going. You have three minutes. Don't make any mistakes."

In the same isolated environment, the individual is challenged to improve performance at a competitive video game. As the subject's skill improves, the game becomes more difficult and thus more stressful. In potential hot reactors it is an excellent tool for raising blood pressure to its highest level.

The final stage consists of the cold pressor test. It is a classic test of the body's physiological responses to a physical stress—in this case, extreme cold. In fact, studies show this test to be the best single predictor of cardiovascular catastrophes. The subject is asked to immerse his or her hand in a bucket of ice water and to try to hold this position for sixty seconds. The higher the blood pressure rises, the more likely the person is to have a premature cardiovascular catastrophe.

If the subject's mean blood pressure rises inappropriately and/or abruptly (above 107 mmHg—millimeters of mercury) during any of the three tests, then he or she is considered to be a hot reactor. This is true even if the *resting blood pressure* is normal. Such a person is at increased risk for the myriad of stress-related health problems.[22] See Figure 3.2.

The World Health Organization's criterion for high blood pressure is 140/90, which gives a mean blood pressure of 107 mmHg. This level or below indicates a physiologically safe range. Above this level, see your physician for a program of blood pressure regulation. Low blood pressure is generally an indicator of good cardiovascular health. The exception is when low blood pressure occurs with other symptoms such as lightheadedness or fainting when standing.[23]

Figure 3.2 What is a Hot Reactor?[24]

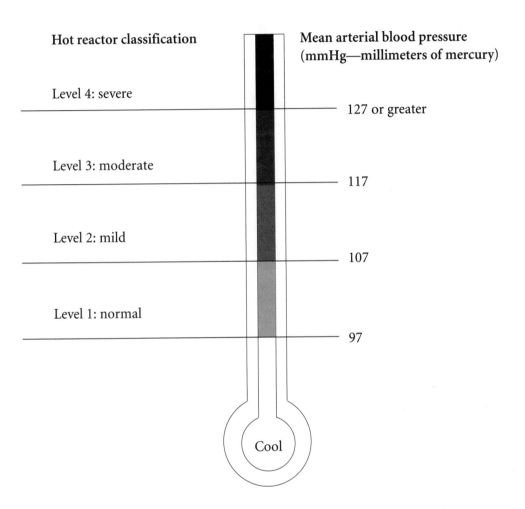

Mean Blood Pressure = $\dfrac{\text{Systolic Blood Pressure - Diastolic Blood Pressure}}{3}$ + Diastolic Blood Pressure

For example, if blood pressure is 120/80, then the mean blood pressure is:

$$\frac{120 - 80}{3} + 80,$$

or 93 mmHg.

Chapter Three References

[1] William Osler, *Aequanimitas, with Other Addresses to Medical Students, Nurses, and Practioners of Medicine* (Philadelphia: P. Blakiston's & Sons, 1910), 840.

[2] "Stress: The 'Type A' Hypothesis," *Harvard Heart Letter* . . . January 1992, p. 104.

[3] Meyer Friedman and Ray H. Rosenman, *Type A Behavior and Your Heart* (New York: Alfred A. Knopf, Inc., 1974), 55, 67-70, 193-95.

[4] Friedman and Rosenman, *Type A Behavior and Your Heart*, 51-79.

[5] Friedman and Rosenman, *Type A Behavior and Your Heart*, 70-86.

[6] American Heart Association, *Silent Epidemic: The Truth about Women and Heart Disease* (Dallas: American Heart Association, 1989).

[7] Robert S. Eliot, *From Stress to Strength* (New York: Bantam Books, 1994), 151; and Neil Wertheimer, *Total Health for Men* (Emmaus, Pa.: Rodale Press, 1995), 537.

[8] *Heart and Stroke Facts* (Dallas, Tex.: American Heart Association, 1994); and *Heart Attack and Stroke Facts: 1996 Statistical Supplement* (Dallas, Tex.: American Heart Association, 1996).

[9] J. M. MacDougall, T. M. Dembroski, J. E. Dimsdale, and T. P. Hackett, "Components of Type A Hostility and Anger in: Further Relationship to Angiographic Findings," *Health Psychology* 4 (1985): 137-52; M. H. L. Hecker, M. A. Chesney, G. W. Black, and N. Frautschi, "Coronary-prone Behaviors in the Western Collaborative Group Study," *Psychosomatic Medicine* 50 (1988): 153-64; and R. B. Williams Jr., T. L. Haney, K. L. Lee, Y. Kang, J. A. Blumenthal, and R. E. Whalen, "Type A Behavior, Hostility, and Coronary Atherosclerosis," *Psychosomatic Medicine* 42 (1980): 539-49; also C. David Jenkins, "The Mind and the Body," *World Health*, March/April 1994, pp. 6-7.

[10] Redford Williams, *The Trusting Heart: Great News about Type A Behavior* (New York: Times Books, 1989), 18.

[11] C. E. Spielberger and P. London, "Rage Boomerangs," *American Health,* March/April 1982, p. 56.

[12] Williams, *The Trusting Heart;* and Redford Williams, *Anger Kills: Seventeen Strategies for Controlling the Hostility That Can Harm Your Heart* (New York: Times Books, 1993).

[13] Williams, Haney, Lee, Kang, Blumenthal, and Whalen, "Type A Behavior, Hostility, and Coronary Atherosclerosis," 539-49.

[14] V. A. Price, *Type A Behavior Pattern: A Model for Research and Practice* (New York: Academic Press, 1982), 52.

[15] Eliot, *From Stress to Strength.*

[16] *Manage Your Stress: Participant's Workbook* (New York: McGraw Hill, 1980), 3.

[17] Edward Dolnick, "Hotheads and Heart Attacks," *Health*, July/August 1995, pp. 58-64.

[18] Dolnick, "Hotheads and Heart Attacks."

[19] Dolnick, "Hotheads and Heart Attacks."

[20] Robert S. Eliot, M.D., *From Stress to Strength*, 9-10. Copyright 1994, Reprinted with permission of the Eliot Family Trust.

[21] Eliot, *From Stress to Strength.*

[22] Eliot, *From Stress to Strength*, 74-77.

[23] Eliot, *From Stress to Strength*, 86.

[24] Robert S. Eliot, M.D., *From Stress to Strength*, 77. Copyright 1994, Reprinted with permission of the Eliot Family Trust.

Chapter Four
☈
Wisdom of the Ages

Stress coping techniques

What can be done to deal with stress? There are two basic strategies: reduce stress by changing your environment or manage stress through effective coping techniques.

Whether you are a businessperson, homemaker, parent, or student, certain principles can help you cope with the inevitable stresses of life. These apply to racehorses, turtles, and all temperaments in between. The following are sixteen principles for being a "B" as well as avoiding the hot reactor syndrome. These are coping techniques for managing stress that are timeless and apply to all types of people. In this sense, they represent Wisdom of the Ages.

One—follow the principle of moderation

Stress not only is inevitable, it is desirable. Creative tension usually accompanies great achievement, and the desire to succeed is necessary to overcome many of life's problems. The goal is not to reduce all stress, but to experience stimulation in your life that is satisfying without being destructive.

The following story shows the value of avoiding extremes:

In "How Much Land Does a Man Require," Leo Tolstoy wrote about Pakhom, a greedy man who was offered, by the Starshima of the Bashkirs, all the land he could cover by foot in a single day, from sunrise to sunset.

Lured by the fantastic offer, Pakhom set out at the crack of dawn and walked on hour after hour. It seemed as though the farther he went, the better the land became. At midday, he looked up and saw the sun overhead. It was a sign that he should turn back and head for the starting point. But then he thought of how much more land he could acquire, and the thought compelled him to keep on going.

Hour after hour passed. Now, surely, Pakhom would have to turn around and go back if he were to reach the starting point before sunset. Finally, he turned toward the starting point. But before long, he realized he had waited too long. He had been too greedy.

His heart pounded fiercely as he began to run. Soon, his breath grew shorter and shorter. Still he forced himself to run faster and faster, even though his legs were numb.

At last, Pakhom could see the Starshima and a small group of Bashkirs at the starting point awaiting his return. With his last ounce of strength, he reached the group, fell to the ground in complete exhaustion, and died.

The people buried him, saying, "This is how much land a man requires."[1]

Besides avoiding excesses such as Pakhom's, you should strive for balance in your life. You should seek balance between rest and work and thus avoid either sinking into laziness or becoming a workaholic. You should recognize that you are both a public and a private person and thus enjoy others but take pleasure in solitude as well. Daily, you should do something for each dimension of your being—spirit, mind, and body.

The Greek philosopher Aristotle prescribed, "Moderation, moderation, all things in moderation." This is a good rule to live by regarding both excesses and balance. To the romantic, this may sound unattractive. But the fact is, if your goal in life is to experience the greatest satisfaction over the longest duration, you must avoid extremes, live a balanced life, and strive for *stress without distress*.

Moderation is especially important when you are sick. Sometimes, no matter what steps you take, the flu or a cold temporarily defeats your immune system's defenses. Slow down. You can't expect your body to cope with a high activity level and combat disease simultaneously. You will get well faster if you give your body a needed break and rest.

Slow down

While I was a junior in college, I found myself going to school full time, working four part-time jobs (including twenty-five hours second shift at a local hospital), maintaining my own apartment, and doing a physical workout each day. I started to notice that my hair was falling out (I was 21, so this was very disturbing), and I felt fatigued all the time. One day in a biology class I learned that my blood pressure was high. I didn't believe this was possible—surely the instrument must be wrong. A visit to my doctor and a complete physical resulted in orders: "You've got to slow down and start taking better care of yourself, or you'll never live to enjoy the fruits of your labors." My doctor scared me enough to change my lifestyle. I quit all but one job and learned to make do with less material things. I started eating better, meditating, and leading a more healthful lifestyle. Slowing down taught me the mathematics of nature—addition by subtraction.—Author's file notes (S. M.)

Two—set priorities

People can handle enormous amounts of stress as long as they feel in control. It is only when events seem to be spinning out of control that accelerated wear and tear occurs. Have you ever felt out of control? Have you ever felt that you had too much to do and too little time? Setting priorities can help solve this problem.

You should be aware of the 80/20 rule when setting priorities: 80 percent of the value of something usually comes from 20 percent of its elements. For example, salespeople typically receive 80 percent of their business from 20 percent of their customers. Similarly, supervisors usually obtain 80 percent of their productivity from 20 percent of their workers (and 80 percent of their problems from another 20 percent). Finally, in the typical family, 80 percent of the stress is caused by 20 percent of the members.[2]

Knowing and following the 80/20 rule is an effective stress-coping technique. Realizing that 80 percent of what you value usually comes from 20 percent of what you do, you should prioritize your activities and work on the top 20 percent first. You should write these down and check them off as you complete them. Doing this will help you feel in control of situations, increase satisfaction, provide a feeling of progress, and alleviate unnecessary stress.

When setting priorities, you should consider your personal values and goals in life. Ask yourself, "What is important?"—family, work, education, and so on—and then prioritize your activities accordingly. Otherwise, you will become frustrated and feel unfulfilled, always working on matters that are relatively unimportant to you.

Look at the way your energy is used, and note especially if it is being drained away on unimportant matters. Say *yes* to high-priority items that support your values—family, health, work, and so on—and *no* to low priorities. Simplify your life by putting first things first and doing one task at a time. In this way you will avoid clutter and confusion.

Meetings can be a major source of stress in the workplace. Although meetings are essential, they can also be a waste of valuable time and resources. To ensure that your meetings are in line with your priorities, consider a technique used during World War II to conserve gasoline. In each car, a sign was affixed: "Is this trip necessary?" You may want to begin to ask: "Is this meeting necessary? Does this meeting support my critical 20 percent?" If not, stay home and conserve resources.

Three—don't try to be superhuman

The famous boxer Muhammad Ali was on a plane trip from Chicago to Las Vegas when the stewardess asked everyone to fasten their seat belts. Of course, everyone did, except Muhammad Ali. When she leaned over to ask him to please buckle his seat belt, Ali said, "Superman don't need no seat belt." The stewardess thought and sweetly said, "Yes, and Superman don't need no airplane either."[3]

No one is immune to stress. Everyone experiences pressure, conflict, and frustration in the normal course of living. And no one is superhuman, so at some point everyone has a breaking point. We all have limitations of some sort—physical, emotional, and financial. To reduce unnecessary stress, decide what is important to you and put your time and effort into those activities. Tolerate some imperfections, and don't try to be all things to all people. Avoid overpromising, overscheduling, and overcommitting.

To understand the "superperson syndrome," look at the business and social calendar of the typical type A individual. There is probably more scheduled than can ever be accomplished. The type A person commonly tries to do more, ever more, until breakdown occurs. Breakdown may take the form of failure to meet commitments, or it may mean physical and emotional exhaustion. Living beyond your means can actually make you sick, as many have discovered who have tried to maintain a lifestyle they couldn't afford financially, emotionally, or physically.

Learning when, how, and why to say *no* helps. When? Say *no* as soon as you realize that saying *yes* would be a mistake. Otherwise, others will be counting on you when they should not. How? Say *no* with compassion, because the other person's request is important to that individual. Why? Because if you do not say *no*, something you have already promised to do will suffer, or you, yourself, will break down, bringing more harm to others than the consequences of the *no* response.

Saying *no* can be difficult. You may fear disapproval or rejection from others. Sometimes, too, it may be hard to say *no* because you do not want to disappoint others. If you have a difficult time saying *no*, you might try saying, "I would like to say yes, but other things I have promised to do will suffer. We must wait until these obligations are finished." This approach should not upset the other person. Reasonable people will understand, and friends will accept it.

The average person can handle a maximum of four major commitments at any one time and do them well. Imagine an individual with four responsibilities: (1) family; (2) work; (3) education; and (4) community service. Another major commitment, no matter how worthy, could be the "straw that breaks the camel's back."

Every well has a bottom, and every person has limitations. Because we all have limits, we must make choices and concentrate our energies on doing high-priority activities well, while postponing or avoiding others. In this spirit, Salvador de Madariaga, the Spanish essayist, wrote:

Our eyes must be idealistic and our feet realistic. We must walk in the right direction, but we must walk step by step. Our tasks are to define what is desirable; to decide what is possible at any time within the scheme of what is desirable; to carry out what is possible in the spirit of what is desirable.[4]

While every individual needs some conception of the ideal, if our values and actions are not based in reality, they are likely to result in additional stress.

Four-burner living

Sometime between 1980 and 1988, I realized first-hand the meaning of the phrase "nobody is superman and everyone has limits." I saw my life as a stovetop with four burners: Burner number1 was family, number 2 was classes at the university, number 3 was consultations and studies, and number 4 was writing the books in the Human Side of Work series.

Then I thought, Where is the fifth burner? What if there is an emergency? That's when I realized there was no fifth burner, and I could not afford an emergency of any kind. For the first time, I understood the wisdom, indeed the need, for having an escape clause.

I resolved at that time to avoid scheduling all four burners with major commitments that could not be reasonably reduced in an emergency. Operationally, this meant family first, university second, and consultations and books as important but nonessential activities. It is safe to say that *Stress: Living and Working in a Changing World* would not exist if it were not for the support of the university and a much appreciated sabbatical.— Author's file notes (G. M.)

Four—share the load

An effective way to manage stress is to share the load; delegate tasks. When you are overloaded, gaining the help of others can result in three important benefits: (1) other people are developed; (2) overall performance increases; and (3) personal health improves. Figure 4.1 shows that delegation is not a new idea.

Figure 4.1 The Need to Delegate

Lack of delegation

Perhaps the earliest recognition of the importance of delegation is found in the Bible. The Book of Exodus, Chapter 18, tells how "Moses sat to judge the people; and the people stood before Moses from the morning unto the evening." Moses' father-in-law, Jethro, saw this and told him: "The thing thou doest is not good. Thous wilt surely wear away, both thou, and this people that is with thee: for the one thing is too heavy for thee; thou art not able to perform it alone." At that time the Israeli organization chart was as follows:

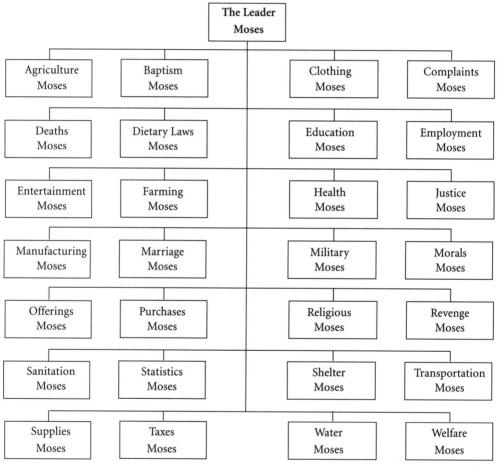

Delegation

The subordinate rulers, Jethro advised, could judge "every small matter" and bring the great matters to Moses. Up to this point, the Israelites had spent 39 years on a journey that had taken them only about halfway to the Promised Land. After delegation took place, they completed the remaining half of the journey in less than a year. The new organization chart looked like this:

Figure 4.1 (continued)

```
                    ┌──────────────────┐
                    │   The Leader     │
                    │      Moses       │
                    └──────────────────┘
          ┌──────────────────┐      ┌──────────────────┐
          │    Advisor       │      │  Staff Manager   │
          │    Jethro        │      │    Solomon       │
          └──────────────────┘      └──────────────────┘
              ┌──────────────────┐
              │ Assistant Leader │
              │     Aaron        │
              └──────────────────┘
         ┌─────────┐  ┌──────────┐  ┌─────────┐
         │  Labor  │  │Protection│  │  Tribe  │
         │ Josephus│  │  Joshua  │  │ Benjamin│
         └─────────┘  └──────────┘  └─────────┘
  ┌──────────────┐ ┌──────────────┐ ┌──────────────┐
  │Ruler of      │ │Ruler of      │ │Ruler of      │
  │Hundreds      │ │Hundreds      │ │Hundreds      │
  └──────────────┘ └──────────────┘ └──────────────┘
  ┌──────────────┐ ┌──────────────┐ ┌──────────────┐
  │Ruler of      │ │Ruler of      │ │Ruler of      │
  │Fifties       │ │Fifties       │ │Fifties       │
  └──────────────┘ └──────────────┘ └──────────────┘
 ┌────────┐┌────────┐┌────────┐┌────────┐┌────────┐
 │Ruler of││Ruler of││Ruler of││Ruler of││Ruler of│
 │Tens    ││Tens    ││Tens    ││Tens    ││Tens    │
 └────────┘└────────┘└────────┘└────────┘└────────┘
```

Source: Reprinted with permission from Ernest Dale, Management: Theory and Practice, *3d ed. (New York: McGraw-Hill, Inc., 1973), 193-94.*

Five—escape for a while

Begin to think of yourself as a balanced person who can work hard and relax as well. You should avoid scheduling your life so that you are always in a hurry, rushing from place to place, never having time for a rest or pause. Of course, you should try to accomplish as much as you can in life, but leave room for needed breaks.

When things are going badly, it often helps to escape for a while—take a walk, read a book, work in the garden, take a nap, or go fishing. You don't have to hike the Himalayas or sail around the world. Changing your activity long enough to recover breath and balance is usually sufficient. The fact is that the average work-day is not eight hours of uninterrupted labor. In order to combat fatigue and remain productive, people need breaks and will take them whether they are scheduled or not.[5]

Individuals, families, organizations, indeed whole nations, have the need to escape for a while. During World War II, immediately after the battle of Dunkirk, England was on the brink of defeat. If ever a country needed to produce, England did at that time. However, consider the following. Prior to Dunkirk, the average work week was 56 hours. After Dunkirk, the prime minister announced an increase to 69.5 hours for all workers in war-related industries. What actually resulted was a work week of barely 51 hours. The nation simply was fatigued and could produce no more; and had America not entered the war, relief might have been impossible and defeat probably would have resulted.[6]

The coffee break, the day of rest, and the annual vacation are pauses that refresh in the world of work. These breaks are useful antidotes to physical and emotional stress, and you must not feel guilty when you take one. It is interesting to note that for medium-heavy work, the optimum work week for volume produced (over extended periods of time) is 48 hours. After 48 hours, the average person is affected by fatigue and would be better served going home. Otherwise, mistakes are made, sickness occurs, and overall productivity declines.[7]

Even people who are famous for their strength and stamina need to escape for a while if they are going to be effective over the long haul. George Washington used to disappear for a time to nurse his nerves, momentarily suspending presidential chores. And consider the eloquence and humanness of another leader, Israeli prime minister Golda Meir, who after a particularly demanding and fatiguing time declared, "I have had enough."

It is interesting to note how cultures differ regarding vacations from work. In Europe five-week paid vacations and holidays are the norm, with employees required to take at least half of this time in one piece. They are told that this is to ensure that they come back with newly refreshed work spirits. Further, they are told that just a week away would not be enough time to unwind.[8]

One form of escaping for a while is a sojourn or sabbatical, during which time you review the past, evaluate the present, and plan for the future. This "mid-course correction" can be a positive force for self-renewal, which is the essence of responsibility and taking charge of your life. The second act you open and the second wind you gain can enhance and invigorate your life.

An often overlooked form of escaping for a while is the emotional release that tears can bring. Women have traditionally used this well, and with recent changes in society's attitudes, more and more men are discovering the relief crying can bring when they are truly upset. Imagine the emotional release tears can provide for one who has lost a loved one or experienced some other tragedy.

> A mother with four children, including an infant and an active toddler, would often find herself overwhelmed by the end of the evening. After the children went to bed, she found solace by taking a shower and crying away the stress. With tears streaming down her face, she would pray for the strength to make it through another day. The water of the shower renewed her physically, mentally, and spiritually, so she could face another day of challenge.

Six—use a decompression chamber technique

It is important to leave the pressures, conflicts, and frustrations of one arena of your life behind you when you enter another arena. In other words, leave home problems at home and work problems at work as much as possible. This is difficult to do unless you use a decompression chamber technique. The decompression chamber is the personal time and place you reserve to mentally unwind, physically relax, and spiritually renew yourself. Typically, the person in the decompression chamber applies the three R's—review past events, rehearse upcoming activities, and relax.

Most busy people can benefit from the decompression chamber technique as a coping mechanism. Examples include:

- the businessperson who uses the commute between work and home to forget one world and prepare for the next;

- the homemaker who sets aside personal time between daytime household chores and nighttime family activities.

Seven—talk with others

When things bother you, talk them over with a level-headed person you can trust. This helps relieve tension, adds perspective, and helps you figure out what to do. The word "catharsis"—from the Greek *kathairein*, to purge—means "cleansing." This is what happens in the talking-out process. People who are under stress report that they feel much better when they get things off their chest.[9]

To show that this is not a new observation, consider Shakespeare's words in *The Taming of the Shrew*, 1594:

> My tongue will tell the anger of my heart, or else my heart, concealing it, will break.

Talking it out is difficult for some people. Because of temperament or social conditioning, they are quiet and introverted, and talking about their problems can be uncomfortable. Other people are extroverted and find it easy to express their feelings and problems. But at times, everyone needs to talk over problems with someone. Otherwise, tension builds until the inevitable explosion occurs. Then everyone asks, "What in the world happened to Bill?" Typically, the more isolated you become, the more desperate your situation may seem.

Talking it out requires trust that the other person will not use what you say against you or be judgmental in a negative way. There is an old saying that you must be careful with whom you talk, because 70 percent of the people you may talk to don't care about your problems and 20 percent are glad that you have them. Only 10 percent truly care and want to help.

The people in your 10 percent may include your spouse, parents, or a close friend; or you may be included in someone else's 10 percent. In any case, whether you are the listener or the talker, you should remember that the good ideas, moods, and advice of others can have a comforting and constructive effect that can help you cope with stress.

People often turn to authority figures to talk over problems. Whether or not this person is helpful depends on his or her willingness to listen and personal integrity. A confidante must be worthy of another's trust and must never take advantage of another's problems and frailties.

Family and friends can be important allies against the negative effects of stress. As the following shows, the family meeting can be an effective coping technique.

> A relocated family uses a Sunday afternoon to discuss what is missing in everyone's lives. With phones and TV off, they talk together. It is a powerful experience for kids to see one parent on the verge of tears because she misses her old job, and for the other parent to say how frustrated he is with the management style of the new company, and for the kids to say how much they miss their old friends. Many families fail to grieve losses together. By grieving their losses, the family can become closer and can get unstuck and move forward with their lives.[10]

Eight—go easy with criticism

There are two kinds of criticism—criticism of self and criticism of others; go easy with both. With regard to self-criticism, you may be too demanding, expecting perfection in all you do. Because you tend to find fault, you may have trouble feeling good about yourself and your accomplishments. For example, you may perform ten tasks; if eight turn out well and two do not, you may focus enormous attention on the two unsuccessful outcomes. This results in lowered self-esteem and even depression. In this way, self-criticism is a form of self-punishment.

One way to reduce self-criticism is to avoid the "must not" syndrome. This is the tendency to think in absolutes (I must not fail; I must not cry; I must not be afraid). By replacing must nots with should nots, you preserve high goals while experiencing less guilt and shame if you happen to fall short.

With regard to criticism of others, if you expect other people to be perfect you will feel disappointed, angry, and frustrated when they fail to measure up. You should remember that everyone, including yourself, has both good and bad characteristics; no one is perfect.

If you want to be honest in your relationships and enjoy others too, and if you would like to shape behavior as well, you should state your views and preferences honestly and openly—but don't concentrate on the negative. The following is a guide for healthy relations with others:

- State what you do and do not like. You may have to repeat what you do not like several times, because people are often poor listeners and hear only what they want to hear. However, be careful not to nag the other person.

- Recognize the strengths of other people. Tell them what you admire about them. This will reinforce their good qualities, as most people want to be recognized and appreciated for what they do.

- Ignore inappropriate behavior. If the behavior is not part of the person's basic "nature," it will go away (extinguish). If it is part of his or her makeup as a *person* (an essential element of personality), it is almost impossible to change. At this point, you have two choices—either ignore the behavior or avoid the person.[11]

Type B's recognize the importance of going easy on criticism and typically take a live-and-let-live attitude. Type A's often do not. They are closed to new ideas and ways of behaving and regularly go on campaigns to change other people's behavior. Usually, these are losing campaigns that lead to health problems, poor relationships, or both. Think about it; could someone change *your* behavior if you did not want to change?

Nine—worry less and do more

The ninth principle focuses on managing your emotions. Some people are prone to worry. If they don't have something to worry about, they make up something to worry about. If you can solve a problem, do so; but don't worry about what you personally cannot change, no matter how important it may be. Starvation in under-developed countries, human rights in oppressive states, and the traffic jam you are in may be beyond your ability to solve as an individual right this minute. Nor should you worry about minor or unimportant matters. In the big picture, ask: How important is a ticking clock, a barking dog, or your mate's idiosyncrasies?

If something upsets you, do what you can to solve it, but avoid useless worry. This only makes a bad situation worse. Try following the advice of St. Francis of Assisi, later popularized by Reinhold Niebuhr in the following prayer: "Give us the serenity to accept what cannot be changed, courage to change what should be changed, and wisdom to distinguish one from the other."[12] Another saying, author unknown, makes the same point: "Of all the troubles mankind's got, some can be solved and some cannot. If there is a cure, find it; if not, never mind it."

Besides worry, two other emotions are particularly distressful. These are resentment over the past and anger in the present. A useful technique to help cope with the negative trilogy of resentment, anger, and worry is to accept three basic truths:

- You cannot change the past. (What is done is done, and being resentful is to no avail.)

- Not everyone is going to agree with you. (Being angry is a waste of precious time and energy. If you are angry, count to ten before you speak; if very angry, count to one hundred.)

- You are going to make mistakes. (Nobody bats a thousand; instead of worrying about this, use your faculties to keep your eye on the ball and concentrate on the swing.)

Like gravity, these facts are real, and the act of accepting them helps reduce nonproductive resentment, anger, and worry. The ninth principle can be summarized with the phrase "Lighten up!"

Ten—enjoy the little things in life

Research shows happiness springs primarily from feeling good over time, not from momentary peaks of ecstasy.[13] There are many small pleasures available to us. Consider how often you could enjoy your small child, read a good book, or take a walk with your mate. We tend to take for granted what we have until we lose it; then it's too late.

The following story shows how it helps to focus on the positive and natural things in life, however small:

> The historian Will Durant described how he looked for happiness in knowledge, and found only disillusionment. He then sought happiness in travel, and found weariness; in wealth, he found worry and discord. He looked for happiness in his own writing, and was only fatigued.
>
> One day he saw a woman waiting in a tiny car with a sleeping child in her arms. A man descended from a train and came over and gently kissed the woman, and then the baby, very softly, so as not to waken him.

The family drove off and left Durant with a stunning realization of the true nature of happiness. He relaxed and discovered, "every normal function of life holds some delight."[14]

When asked for advice, it is not unusual for those who have survived heart attacks or learned they have only a short time to live to say, "Take pleasure from the little things in life."

Sometimes very small things right under our noses can give us pleasure. Gary Schwartz, professor of psychology at Yale University, uses the healing power of scent in the treatment of anxiety, hypertension, and other stress-related disorders. It is interesting to note that a spicy apple scent reminiscent of cider is highly effective for many people. It is also interesting to note how pleasant smells of childhood, such as pine logs, horses, and sea air evoke happy memories that help in stressful times.

> One student found that the sweet aroma of honeysuckle on a fall morning relieved her anxiety of a new school year. Each morning before rising, she would focus on the smell of honeysuckle instead of the demands of school. Now, wherever she lives, she plants honeysuckle so she can reflect on the power of nature before starting each day.

Finding something that gives you pleasure may require a change in your environment. If so, take steps to make your work and living areas pleasant and satisfying. Surround yourself with people who give you happiness, and, every day, strive to do at least one activity that gives you peace of mind.[15]

Eleven—help another person

Self-absorption can be dangerous to both mental and physical health. While thinking about yourself is normal and healthy to a degree, the trick is to not do it so much that you lose concern for the external world, especially the care and well-being of others. As an old saying goes, "Lose yourself to gain yourself." The antidote for self-absorption is to focus on the needs and problems of others.

Related to this idea is the concept of commitment. If you have people or principles in your life to which you are committed, you will feel motivated and will be able to withstand tremendous amounts of stress. Strong personal commitments are especially important during times of change. There are three things you can do to achieve strength of commitment:

- Decide who and what are really important to you.

- Take action that supports your values and goals.

- Take action that strengthens your relationships.[16]

Twelve—handle hassles healthfully

When you feel hurried, harried, and hassled, stop and ask a few key questions that can help put things in perspective.

- What is the worst possible thing that can happen here?

- On a scale of 1 to 10, with a life-ending catastrophe as a 10, where does this hassle rate?

- Who and what are important to you, and how, if at all, does this hassle affect them?

- A month from now, will you remember this hassle?

For many people, there are predictable times when hassles tend to be high, such as holidays, vacations, and other family get-togethers. To handle stress healthfully during these occasions, follow three basic rules:

1. **Be realistic.** Set achievable goals. Don't expect every moment to be perfect and every person to be happy all of the time.

2. **Keep things simple.** Invite the people and then trust the process. Relax and remember, less can be more. Follow the advice of Beatrix Potter — the shorter, the plainer, the better.

3. **Share the tasks.** So often, one or two people shoulder most of the work. Instead, ask everyone to help in some meaningful way.

Thirteen—have a hobby

Doing something you enjoy, and doing it regularly, is an ideal stress coping technique. Find an activity that is intrinsically satisfying. It will refresh your mind and body and even improve your relationships. Consider reading, traveling, church or civic involvement, cooking, sports, and music. Think back to what you used to do when you were young. What did you enjoy doing more than anything else?

For some people, there is no passion in life, something they want to do and enjoy immensely. For others, the problem is too many passions. The number and intensity of their interests seem boundless. The answer is to manage your passions—not too many, not too few. Of course, some behavior is harmful even in moderation. The criterion is, does an activity enrich and add to the overall quality of your life without causing harm to others?

Fourteen—accentuate the positive

Attitude plays an important role in dealing with stress. To a degree, stress is determined in the mind. Two people can suffer setbacks. One may become stronger and wiser for the experience, while the other may never recover and may actually worsen. Often, the difference is that one focuses on the positive and the other on the negative. Michael Scheier and Charles Carver cite extensive research showing that optimism is an important construct that has beneficial influence on coping and well-being.[17]

Do not close your eyes to the truth, but avoid negative thinking. A positive mental attitude helps you tolerate life's ups and downs and gives you strength to overcome problems. Optimism and positive thinking are contagious. Your good attitude will rub off on others; so smile—it will help others and help yourself as well. Remember the World War II song:

> You've got to accentuate the positive,
> Eliminate the negative,
> Latch on to the affirmative,
> Don't mess with Mr. Inbetween.

The Chinese have a symbol for "crisis" consisting of two characters, each with a separate meaning (see Figure 4.2). The upper character represents danger, and the lower character stands for opportunity. The healthful view accentuates opportunity, as opposed to danger, in a crisis.

Figure 4.2 Crisis: Opportunity within Danger

"danger"

"opportunity"

A corollary to accentuating the positive is to reframe or change the way you interpret an event or situation. An event such as a job change becomes more stressful if you see it as a traumatic upheaval rather than an exciting new adventure or challenge in your life. In the process of reframing, tap the power of self-talk. Many of us are unaware of the influence of internal dialogue, much less that we have the power to change it. Instead of saying "I'm too old" or "I'm too slow," say "I am experienced and I am deliberate."

The technique of *mental music* can be a helpful application of self-talk. Imagine two job applicants preparing for an interview. The music and picture in one person's mind are from the movie *Jaws*, while the other person hears the theme from *Rocky* and imagines success. Tremendous advantage can be gained by playing positive mental music. What music do you play in your own mind to accentuate the positive?

By emphasizing the positive versus the negative, you can feel more optimistic; and this can lead to positive actions and results. Charles Swindoll explains succinctly and well the importance of attitude:

> **Attitude**
> The longer I live, the more I realize the impact of attitude on life. Attitude, to me, is more important than facts. It is more important than the past, than education, than money, than circumstances, than failures, than successes, than what other people think or say or do. It is more important than appearance, giftedness or skill. It will make or break a company . . . a church . . . a home. The remarkable thing is we have a choice every day regarding the attitude we will embrace for that day. We cannot change the past . . . we cannot change the fact that other people will act in a certain way. We cannot change the inevitable. The only thing we can do is play on the one string we have, and that is our attitude. . . . I am convinced that life is 10 percent what happens to me and 90 percent how I react to it. And so it is with you . . . we are each in charge of our own attitude.[18]

As a balance to this idea, psychologist Edward Chang cautions against overreliance on optimism and suggests that in some cases pessimism may serve a useful function. He advises striking an ideal balance between general optimism as a dominant orientation and situation-specific pessimism when conditions warrant. Popularly, this has been phrased as "Expect the best and be prepared for the worst."[19]

Fifteen—improve job proficiency

Developing technical knowledge, increasing practical experience, and learning human relations skills are excellent ways to manage stress in the workplace. Important skills that help reduce job stress are communication, teamwork, and effective use of time for all personnel, as well as leadership, delegation, and coaching skills for management personnel.

Sixteen—trust in time

Many of life's events are painful, and it may seem as though the anguish will never end. Although time may not heal all wounds, it often helps. If you suffer a loss in your personal or professional life and you feel your world has collapsed, there is a good possibility that within a year or two the pain will be gone, and you may even be stronger for the experience. As Charles Dickens wrote in *David Copperfield*, "The best metal has been through the fire." And as John Milton wrote in *Paradise Lost*, "Our torments also, in length of time, become our elements." Finally,

Ecclesiastes 3 states: "To everything there is a season, and a time to every purpose under the heaven: A time to be born, and a time to die; a time to sow seed, and a time to pluck up that which is planted." Sometimes, our only choice in a stressful period is to "trust in time."

Coping review

The whole process of managing stress requires three basic steps:

1. Be aware of stressful situations in your life.

2. Take action to reduce harmful stress.

3. Use stress-coping techniques that work for you.

Regarding point three, Mark Twain once said, "Habits cannot be thrown out the window. They must be coaxed downstairs one step at a time." With this in mind, identify the coping techniques that *you* need to try: (1) Introduce more balance and avoid extremes in your life. (2) Work smarter, not necessarily harder. (3) Share the load, and in so doing develop others. (4) Learn when, how, and why to say no. (5) Escape for a while. (6) Make the decompression chamber technique work for you. (7) Share feelings, reduce tension, and talk it out. (8) Be less critical and more accepting, both of yourself and of others. (9) Worry less and do more. (10) Slow down and enjoy the little things in life. (11) Focus on the needs of others. (12) Handle hassles healthfully. (13) Have a hobby. (14) Focus on the positive in your life. (15) Develop skills to help you reduce job stress. (16) Let time be a healer.

Notice that none of these principles promotes laziness or lack of achievement. Indeed, most accomplishments require hard work, and great achievements make life worth living. The point is not only to succeed, but to live to enjoy success. In this regard, when you consider the meaning of success, remember Cervantes' advice in *Don Quixote:* "The road is better than the inn."[20]

As the following account shows, most people can benefit by following coping techniques for managing stress:

Stress hits home
I never really knew what pain was until my wife had a stroke and I thought she might die. Then I thought she might live and feel but not be able to think. During those hours, for the first time, I knew the true meaning of grief. It is overwhelming and unbearable pain that you know will affect you forever. Only with her illness did I realize how helpful stress coping techniques could be. Until then, the subject had been academic. Now it was real. I found it ironic that I would be the one to benefit the most from the ideas we had gathered and presented in *Stress without Distress* in 1988. That's when I realized these principles truly are wisdom of the ages.— Author's file notes (G. M.)

Chapter Four References

[1] Adapted from Leo Tolstoy, *Master and Man* (London: J. M. Dent and Sons, Ltd., 1910), 65-83.

[2] Alan Lakein, *How to Get Control of Your Time and Your Life* (New York: Peter H. Wyden, 1973), 83-86.

[3] As heard on the Paul Harvey News on the ABC Radio Network.

[4] T. V. Smith and Edward R. Lindeman, *Democratic Way of Life* (New York: New American Library of World Literature, 1951), 123.

[5] Norman R. F. Maier, *Psychology in Industrial Organizations* (Boston: Houghton-Mifflin, 1973), 406-9.

[6] Maier, *Psychology in Industrial Organizations*, 74.

[7] Maier, *Psychology in Industrial Organizations*, 74.

[8] "Holidays: Why Jack is a Dull Boy," *The Economist* (December 23,1995–January 5, 1996): 112. Also, World Organizations and Working Hours 1983-92/Eu (Monograph 1995) at p. 91. IIS: 96 Fiche 1.3/96. Pages: Cover P3.

[9] J. W. Pennebaker, "Confession, Prohibition and Disease," *Advances in Experimental Social Psychology* 22 (1989): 211-44.

[10] Morris R. Shectman, *Working without a Net* (New York: Prentice-Hall, 1994), 112.

[11] Gary S. Belkin, *Practical Counseling in the Schools*, 2nd ed. (Dubuque, Iowa: Wm. C. Brown Group, 1981), 85-111.

[12] Garrison R. Benjamin, *Worldly Holiness* (Nashville: Abingdon, 1972).

[13] Robert E. Ornstein and David S. Sabel, *Healthy Pleasures* (Reading, Mass.: Addison-Wesley, 1989).

[14] June Callwood, "The One Sure Way to Happiness," *Reader's Digest* 1105, no. 630 (October 1974): 137-40, as condensed from June Callwood, *Love, Hate, Fear, Anger, and the Other Lively Emotions* (Hollywood: Newscastle Publishing, 1964).

[15] *Manage Your Stress: Participant's Workbook* (New York: McGraw-Hill, 1980), 33-35.

[16] Jerry Carpenter, "Stress and Commitment," Northern Kentucky University, 1993.

[17] Michael F. Scheier and Charles S. Carver, "Effects of Optimism on Psychological and Physical Well-Being: Theoretical Overview and Empirical Update," *Cognitive Therapy and Reasearch* 16, no. 2 (1992): 201-28.

[18] Charles Swindoll, "Attitude," *Strengthening Your Grip: Essentials in an Aimless World* (Waco, Tex.: Word Books, 1982).

[19] Edward Chang, "Cultural Differences in Optimism, Pessimism, and Coping: Predictors of Subsequent Adjustment in Asian American and Caucasian American College Students," *The Journal of Counseling Psychology* 43, no. 1 (1996): 113-23; and J. K. Norem and N. Cantor "Defensive Pessimism: Harnessing Anxiety as Motivation," *Journal of Personality and Social Psychology* 51 (1986): 1208-17.

[20] Miguel de Cervantes Saavedra, *Exploits of Don Quixote*, retold by James Reeves (New York: H. Z. Walck, 1960).

Chapter Five
Characteristics of a Hardy Personality

The stress-resistant person

Some people are stress-resistant. These are hardy individuals who are able to accomplish tremendous tasks and still remain healthy. Stress-resistant people seem comfortable in almost any situation. Their lives are full, yet unhurried. They are relaxed and confident, even when they are making critical decisions. Physically fit and seldom tired, they project a sense of control and strength.

The stress-resistant person lives a life of balance and alignment. Actions taken are consistent with thoughts and feelings. From this flows a sense of wholeness and integrity that gives the stress-resistant person the ability to be resourceful and creative even under the most difficult circumstances.

There are many models for successful living. The Danish philosopher Søren Kierkegaard thought that people could be divided into types—some are drifters and others are drivers, some are takers and others are givers. He believed that the fully functioning person would not drift aimlessly through life, but would be guided by a sense of purpose; and he believed the fully developed person would honor, protect, and care for others. Further, he believed these qualities would add to the well-being of the individual and society. To personal commitment and caring relationships, add having a sense of personal control, maintaining a positive mental attitude, and keeping life in perspective to describe the characteristics of a hardy personality.[1]

The concept of hardiness as a personality construct was first introduced by Susan Kobasa in 1979. Since then, it has been cited in hundreds of academic papers published in more than one hundred different journals. The interest in the concept stems from the fact that it addresses the mind-body relationship with a focus on health instead of illness, and with a positive image of the person as an active and purposeful agent.

◎ **Application: A Star to Live By**

The following questionnaire features the five characteristics of a hardy personality. Rate yourself on each characteristic at this time (1 is low, 20 is high).

Commitment

The Scottish philosopher Thomas Carlisle said, "We don't fear extinction, we fear extinction without meaning." This entails having a purpose in life and being true to one's values. The hardy personality thinks he knows what is important and that he is doing the right thing. This translates into *commitment* that gives tremendous strength to overcome obstacles and persevere in the face of adversity. The committed person is emotionally strong, and this emotional strength, like a wonder drug, results in physical strength as well. Where does commitment begin? It begins with choosing to be an active participant in life, not a bystander. With involvement comes understanding. Only when we understand will we care. Only when we care will we be committed. Only when we are committed will we make a difference in life. *Rate yourself on commitment.*

1 2 3 4 5   6 7 8 9   10 11   12   13   14   15   16 17   18   19   20
low   middle   high

Control

In *Don Juan in Hell,* George Bernard Shaw wrote, "Hell is to drift, heaven is to steer."[2] The hardy personality believes this idea fully, and seeks to *control* her own life. When asked the question, "Who is in charge, the world or you?", the hardy personality's answer is "Me." She sees herself as the master of her own destiny, the captain of her own ship, not the pawn of fate and not flotsam on the sea of life. What gives legitimacy to this feeling is the fact that the hardy personality has mastered and employs effective time management principles. She sets goals in line with her values, keeps a daily "to do" list with priorities indicated, works on first things first, and checks off tasks as they are completed. *Rate yourself on sense of control and practicing effective time management principles.*

1 2 3 4 5   6 7 8 9   10 11   12   13   14   15   16 17   18   19   20
low   middle   high

Attitude

The hardy personality lives by William James's prescription: "Change your *attitude*—change your life."[3] Unlike the pessimist who builds dungeons in the air, the hardy personality accentuates the positive. He recognizes the influence of mind over matter and therefore chooses to think positive thoughts that elicit positive moods that result in positive actions.[4] This doesn't mean he denies reality; the opposite is true. He sees life as it is, both good and bad. But once seen, he emphasizes possibilities over problems, strengths over weaknesses, and potentialities over deficiencies, both in the situation and in himself. In the area of attitude, the hardy personality practices three key habits—expect greatness, strive for the best, and appreciate any good that results. The hardy personality agrees with Hans Selye, who prescribed a technique for optimism—"Imitate the sundial's ways; count only the pleasant days." Because the hardy personality is an optimist, he is energized and focused; and with energy and focus, he indeed achieves his goals.[5] *Rate yourself on attitude.*

1	2	3	4	5	6	7	8	9	10	11	12	13	14	15	16	17	18	19	20
low										middle									high

Perspective

The hardy personality keeps life in *perspective* and doesn't get upset over small matters. She realizes, in the final analysis, most matters are small matters. Consequently she doesn't develop a full-blown fight-or-flight response to every minor hassle, obstacle, or setback. In this way, she avoids unnecessary states of alarm and vigilance leading to exhaustion and breakdown. The hardy personality realizes there is a need for the hot-reacting linebacker in times of defense, but she prefers to remain the cool-thinking quarterback on offense.[6] One way she does this is to remember what is important (her hills worth dying on). All else is viewed with tolerance and patience as matters of style, taste, and individual differences that can enrich the world. *Rate yourself on keeping things in perspective.*

1	2	3	4	5	6	7	8	9	10	11	12	13	14	15	16	17	18	19	20
low										middle									high

Relationships

For the masses of people most of the time, concern for others is the most important characteristic of a hardy personality. He develops caring relationships in his home life, work life, and community at large. He gives tender loving care (TLC) to all creatures, great and small; and as he sows, so he reaps. The hardy personality gives love, and in turn is beloved.[7] In this process, physiological responses are generated that are life enhancing and life prolonging, helping to explain the hardy personality's ability to overcome germs and disease and maintain good health in spite of heavy responsibilities and demanding schedules. *Rate yourself on TLC.*

1 2 3 4 5   6 7 8 9   10 11   12   13   14   15   16 17   18   19 20
low   middle   high

Scoring

Indicate your scores for each characteristic on the following star. Add your scores to obtain a total. _____

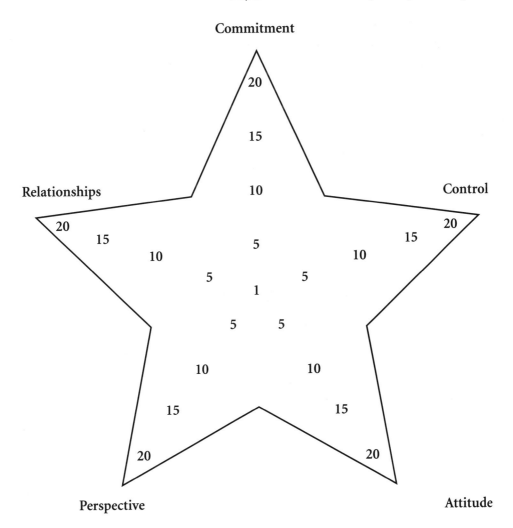

Evaluation

Scores 90–100 = A
You currently embody the characteristics of a hardy personality. You are doing all that you can do to succeed in life, plus live to enjoy it. You are a model for psychological strength and effective living.

Scores 80–89 = B
This is a high score. Your life is characterized by an effective pattern of personal commitment, sense of control, positive attitude, balanced perspective, and caring relationships.

Scores 70–79 = C
You do some things well, but need to improve in others. To improve, focus on low spots and take positive steps to change yourself or the situation.

Scores 60–69 = D
D stands for deficiencies. This means you must improve, not only to succeed in your life, but to live to enjoy it. Low scores for commitment, control, attitude, perspective, and relationships should be addressed.

Scores 59–below = F
F is for falling short. You should begin immediately to raise the quality of your life. Advice and support from others can be helpful. Attention and a sustained effort are required.

Discussion

Lives are defined largely by the points on our stars: commitment, control, attitude, perspective, and relationships. Our lives, like stars, can be bright or dim. This is determined by the choices we make. These decisions are freely made, so we are each responsible for the consequences of our own actions and reactions.

It is not the score one has that counts; it is what is done about it that matters. If you are currently low in one or more of the characteristics of a hardy personality, take concrete action to improve, and in so doing enhance your life. If you are high in an area, you should continue to capitalize on this strength and asset for effective living.

The five characteristics of a hardy personality are moving targets that you must keep your eye upon. This is a lifelong challenge, meaning that just because you have a high score today, it doesn't guarantee a high score tomorrow. Also, it is never too late to improve. Doing so at any point in time is worthwhile, resulting in a fuller and more satisfying life.

After heredity, the three most important influences in our lives are the people we are around, the messages we give ourselves, and the books we read. Along with religious and inspirational books that mean so much to so many millions, there are five books that are particularly helpful in developing the characteristics of a hardy personality. To brighten your star, read these books and apply them to your life.

For commitment, read *Man's Search for Meaning* by Viktor Frankl.

For control, read *First Things First* by Stephen Covey.

For attitude, read *Learned Optimism* by Martin Seligman.

For perspective, read *Is It Worth Dying For?* by Robert Eliot.

For relationships, read *The Art of Loving* by Erich Fromm.

The stress-prone versus the stress-resistant personality

Habits are like people, in that some are good for you and others are not. Figure 5.1 contrasts a day in the life of a stress-prone versus a stress-resistant personality. Multiply these days by weeks, months, and years, and you can see the important influence personality patterns can have in determining the quality and length of your life.

Figure 5.1 A Day in the Life of Mr. A and Mr. B

Time line	Mr. A's stress-prone path	Time line	Mr. B's stress-resistant path
7:00 A.M. Alarm goes off.	*Thoughts:* The first thing he thinks of is last night's argument. The second is the battle ahead. He resolves to be vigilant.	7:00 A.M. Alarm goes off.	*Thoughts:* The first thing he thinks of is last night's get-together. Good times should be relished. His second thought is for the day ahead. He knows he will do his best.
	Actions: He hurries through showering and dressing, and walks out the door, calling good-bye to his wife.		*Actions:* He showers and dresses and takes time to have breakfast. He gives his wife an affectionate good-bye hug and kiss.
8:15 A.M.	He sees snow on the car, and the roads are icy. He is furious, because he doesn't have a scraper.	8:15 A.M.	He sees snow on the car, and the streets are icy, but he is calm because he has a scraper and a shovel and is prepared for bad weather.
8:30 A.M. Traffic is slow.	*Action:* He honks the horn, grips the wheel, gnashes his teeth, and yells at bad drivers.	8:30 A.M. Traffic is slow.	*Action:* He goes with the flow, realizing that getting upset will not change the conditions. He listens to the radio.
	Result: Blood pressure and pulse rate go up. He arrives at work angry and tense.		*Result:* He remains calm and relaxed and arrives at work fresh and alert.

9:00 A.M.– 11:00 A.M.	*Events:* Unimportant meetings follow disorganized meetings, and frustration goes up. He becomes increasingly resentful, angry, and worried because of wasted time.	9:00 A.M.– 11:00 A.M.	*Events:* There is a sense of progress and satisfaction as well-run meetings support important goals.
11:00 A.M.– 12:30 P.M.	Emotions heat up when a customer complains and an employee gets angry.	11:00 A.M.– 12:00 noon	When a customer and an employee fail to communicate, he remains calm.
	Reaction: If people don't like the way things are, they can go elsewhere. This is a free country. Besides, complaints and problems are hassles I don't need.		*Reaction:* When people complain or get upset, it gives me a chance to share information, learn something important, and try to improve things by developing a common ground.
	Action: He delegates the problem to a subordinate and gets into a shouting match with another customer.		*Action:* He meets with the customer and employee personally. He takes the time to listen and understand their concerns. He takes their grievances seriously and is responsive to their suggestions.
12:30 P.M.– Lunch break Behind.	*Action:* He eats at his desk with a telephone in one hand and a pencil, candy bar, and coffee sharing the other.	12:00 noon– Lunch break On schedule.	*Action:* He escapes for a while by taking a walk in the park. He eats yogurt and a banana on a bench.
	Effect: Stress builds as he feels chained to his chair; indigestion sets in.		*Effect:* Exercise and nutrition are healthy, and getting away from the office helps put things in perspective.

1:00 P.M. Board meeting starts.	*Mental State:* Coming off a working lunch, he feels fragmented and ill-prepared.	1:00 P.M. Board meeting starts.	*Mental State:* He returns from lunch energized and focused, ready to give his best to the important meeting ahead.
2:30 P.M. Modest progress made.	*Thoughts:* This group couldn't change a light bulb in a weekend. We aren't accomplishing a thing! If they don't get their act together, this company's going down the tube.	2:30 P.M. Modest progress made.	*Thoughts:* We were slow today, but we did make progress. We need to celebrate these victories and learn from our shortcomings. If we work together, I think we'll succeed.
4:00 P.M. Board meeting ends.	*Action:* He goes to the bar for a quick drink and to lament the wasted day. One drink leads to another as he tries to forget his problems.	4:00 P.M. Board meeting ends.	*Action:* He goes to his office to summarize thoughts while they are fresh and to return telephone calls in a timely manner. 5:30 P.M. finds him exercising (three times a week).
7:00 P.M. Arrive home.	*Action:* He has dinner with the family. Interaction goes from polite conversation to active argument. *Effect:* Stress goes up; tension leads to headache; indigestion develops.	7:00 P.M. Arrive home.	*Action:* He has dinner with the family. Interaction goes from discussion to dialogue. *Effect:* Happiness and a sense of well-being are experienced.
8:00 P.M.	Everyone watches television—alone. *Result:* Self-absorption develops and loneliness sets in.	8:00 P.M.	He helps his son make a kite and helps his daughter with her homework. *Results:* Responsibility is taught and relationships grow.

10:00 P.M. Disagreement occurs with teenage son.	He is tired and his patience is thin. He launches into attack and "wins" by intimidation.	10:00 P.M. Disagreement occurs with teenage son.	He garners his energy and seeks the facts. He talks *with* his son, not *at* him, and gives reasons for his views. Father and son reach agreement together.
11:00 P.M. Goes to bed.	*Action:* Can't sleep; tosses and turns for two hours.	11:00 P.M. Goes to bed.	*Action:* Falls asleep quickly.
	Thoughts: What is wrong with everybody? Why can't things be smooth instead of a constant struggle? All I do is work and worry, work and worry. The truth is, I'm fed up.		*Thoughts:* This has been a good day. There is much to appreciate—family, good health, good job.
	Result: Wakes up at 7:00 A.M. exhausted and depressed.		*Result:* Wakes up at 7:00 A.M. refreshed and happy.

Personal Thoughts on Personality and Stress

Answer the following questions to personalize the content of Part Two. Space is provided for writing your thoughts.

- Of the sixteen principles for dealing with stress, which appeal to you? Which have you seen work for others?

- Think about a stressful time in your life. What did you do to improve or cope with the situation? What lessons did you learn?

- Do you currently embody the characteristics of a hardy personality? If not, what can you do to improve? What steps should you take?

- Picture yourself twenty years from today. Do you see yourself in a positive state? Are you fulfilled, at peace, a model of energy and vitality for your age? Or do you see yourself in a negative state—worn out, weakened by poor health, embittered by unfulfilled goals? Your future is largely your choice. You are busy today working full time to make one of these pictures come true.

Chapter Five References

[1] Martin E. P. Seligman, *Learned Optimism: How to Change Your Mind and Your Life* (New York: Knopf, 1991); S. C. Kobasa, S. R. Maddi, and S. Kahn, "Hardiness and Health: A Prospective Study," *Journal of Personality and Social Psychology* 42, (1982): 168-77; and S. C. Kobasa, "How Much Stress Can You Handle?" *American Health 2* (1984).

[2] George Bernard Shaw, *Don Juan in Hell* in *Man Is Superman,* Act II.

[3] William James, *The Principles of Psychology* (New York: H. Holt, 1890).

[4] Michael F. Scheier and Charles S. Carver, "On the Power of Positive Thinking: The Benefits of Being Optimistic," *Current Directions in Psychological Science* 2, no. 1 (February 1993): 26-30; and Charles S. Carver and Michael F. Scheier, *Perspectives on Personality*, 2nd ed. (Needham Hts., Mass.: Allyn and Bacon, 1992).

[5] Seligman, *Learned Optimism.*

[6] Robert S. Eliot and Dennis L. Breo, *Is It Worth Dying For?* (New York: Bantam Books, 1989).

[7] Erich Fromm, *The Art of Loving* (New York: Bantam Books, 1963).

Part Three

Stress Across the Life Span

6. Coping with Change

7. Lives in Progress

8. The Meaning of Wellness

There are only two or three human stories, and they go on repeating themselves as fiercely as if they never happened before.—Willa Cather

What you will learn in Part Three

In Part Three you will learn:

- myths, realities, and strategies for dealing with change;

- sources of stress at each stage of life;

- the meaning and dimensions of wellness.

Chapter Six

Coping with Change

Change in modern times

Nearly twenty-five hundred years ago, the Greek philosopher Heraclitus noted that one can never cross the same river twice. In other words, change is a constant in life. In *Managing at the Speed of Change,* Daryl Conner writes that the volume, speed, and complexity of change are increasing in modern times. In our personal lives, we are constantly having to adjust to family changes, job changes, and health changes. In society at large, we face escalating changes in government, education, religious, and other institutions.[1]

People are acutely aware of change in their lives and many have difficulty adjusting. Among the causes of change are a growing worldwide population, faster communication and access to information, increasing technological advancements, and breakdown of traditional rules and social order.

In dealing with change, Conner identifies three D's to avoid:

- Denial of reality: "They don't mean what they are saying."

- Distortion of facts: "Truth is what you believe it to be."

- Delusion of selves: "It could never happen here."[2]

Instead of these responses to change, managing change successfully requires (1) a focused vision, (2) guiding values, (3) personal incentives, (4) supporting resources, (5) sound judgment, and (6) an action plan. See Figure 6.1.

Figure 6.1 Building Blocks for Successful Change[3]

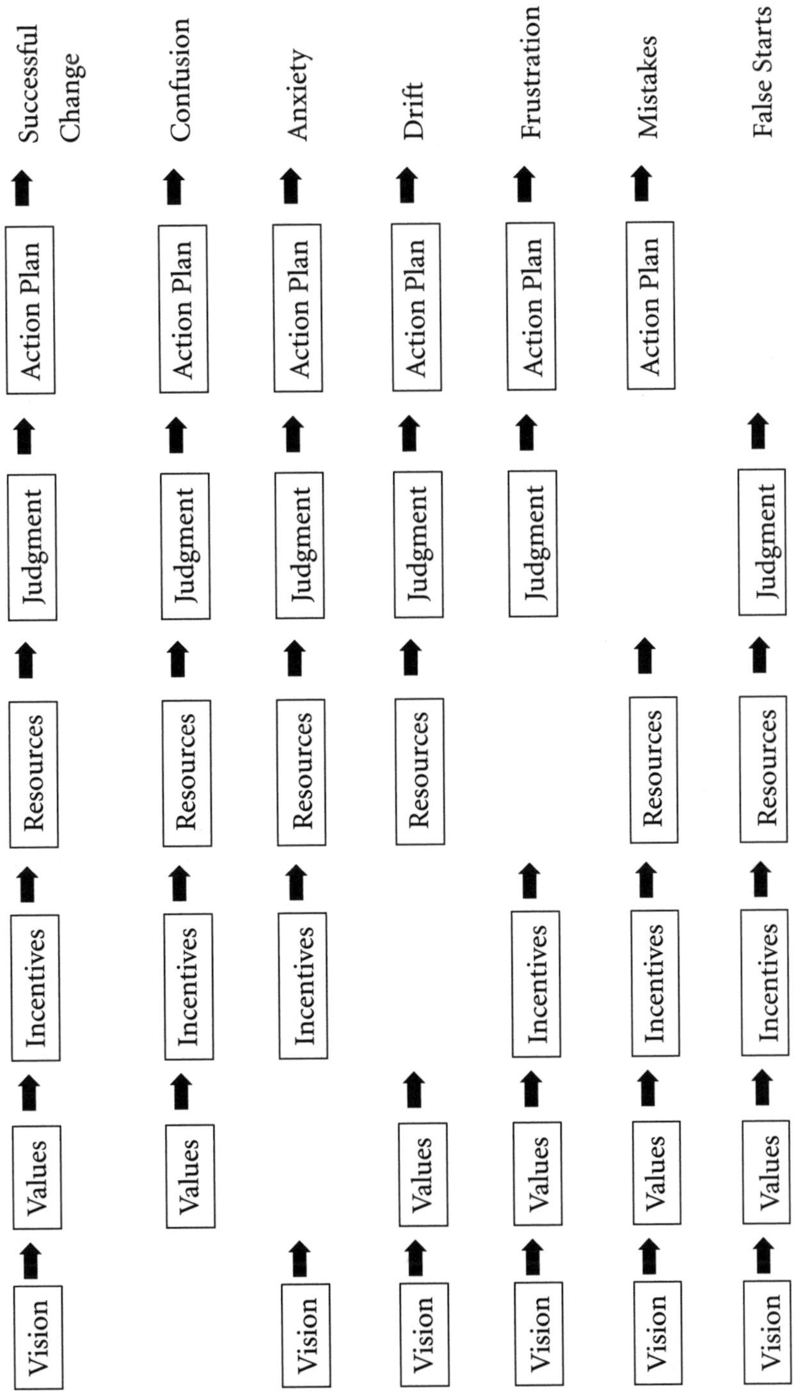

Vision	Values	Incentives	Resources	Judgment	Action Plan	→	Successful Change
	Values	Incentives	Resources	Judgment	Action Plan	→	Confusion
Vision		Incentives	Resources	Judgment	Action Plan	→	Anxiety
Vision	Values		Resources	Judgment	Action Plan	→	Drift
Vision	Values	Incentives		Judgment	Action Plan	→	Frustration
Vision	Values	Incentives	Resources		Action Plan	→	Mistakes
Vision	Values	Incentives	Resources	Judgment		→	False Starts

Without a vision or clear goals, there is confusion. Without values, there are no standards of right and wrong, and anxiety results. Without incentives, there is lack of energy and the individual drifts as the pawn of external forces. Without resources, there is lack of progress and frustration is experienced. Without judgment, poor choices are made and mistakes occur. Without an action plan and strategy for change, there are false starts.

In dealing with personal change, use this model and ask:

1. Do I have a clear, compelling vision; do I have a purpose in life with meaningful goals to achieve?

2. Do I have values and principles that anchor and guide me?

3. Do I have incentives and motivation to take responsibility for my own destiny?

4. What resources can I garner to achieve my goals?

5. Do I balance feelings with logic and let reason guide so that my judgments are sound?

6. What plan of action should I follow; what steps should I take for successful change?

In all walks and periods of life, we will be faced with the challenge of change. To the building blocks of vision, values, incentives, resources, judgment, and an action plan, add two essential elements: the *will to change* and *personal courage*. In the final analysis, the ability to change is less a function of capacity and more a function of determination and courage to live by one's convictions even in the face of adversity.

Change in the workplace

Generally, the biggest cause of stress in the workplace is change—change of people, change of products, change of place, change of pace. In America today, the average employee changes jobs seven times, a radical shift from a generation ago, when lifetime service was commonplace.[4]

A case in point
Over the years, I have had six occupational changes. The first was to work as a young professional in labor relations. Prior to this, I knew school, sports, and part-time jobs. To say the adjustment was a challenge is an understatement.

After four learning years on a factory floor, the second change was to enter the world of consulting. I did this reluctantly because (1) I didn't think I knew anything of special importance, and (2) I had a family to support and consulting sounded shaky to me. Fascinating assignments and excellent colleagues made the difference.

The third change was the shift from business to the university. The fact that I was new to teaching was overcome by the desire to teach and the support of caring leaders.

The fourth change was a shift from teaching to administration. I was pleased with the opportunity, but truly challenged to develop the attitude and skills of a coordinator versus individual practitioner.

The fifth shift was back into the classroom, which I saw as a step up. I thought administration was good, but I thought teaching was great.

The sixth shift required going back to school and studying humanistic psychology, in contrast to psychoanalysis and behaviorism. This proved to be just what the doctor ordered in terms of personal growth and satisfaction.

What is next, I'm not sure. But then, who is?— Author's file notes (G. M.)

Change is the label under which we put all of the things that we have to do differently in the future. In general, people dislike change. It makes a blank space of uncertainty between what is and what might be.

The four major types of change in the workplace are:[5]

1. **Structure.** Change in structure is often severely resisted by people. Mergers, acquisitions, right-sizing, and re-engineering activities typically involve tremendous change.

2. **Tasks.** Changes in the environment, including products and processes, require changes in tasks. Driving forces include customer needs, productivity improvement, and quality initiatives.

3. **Technology.** Innovations in this area have dramatically increased the rate of change. No industry, trade, or profession is immune to change caused by technological advancements.

4. **People.** Change in any of the above variables can result in changing relationships—change in managers, employees, coworkers, and customers—and change within a given person, such as change in knowledge, attitude, and skills.

A particularly stressful change in the American workplace is the downsizing and reorganization activities resulting from re-engineering business, reinventing government, and other management initiatives. Employees who are victims of job loss, particularly in their middle years, face enormous economic, social, and personal stress. Employees who remain with an organization often experience the "survivor syndrome." They are afraid they will be part of the next round of cuts, and they feel sadness and guilt over their coworkers' fate. In addition, they often have more work to do personally if production demands do not reflect the reduced number of people to do the job.

Many lessons have been learned from studying the downsizing of organizations, but four stand out: (1) People need to be flexible and willing to change in order to preserve superordinate values and goals. (2) People need a positive attitude toward lifelong learning to remain viable in the workplace. (3) Career education is a survival skill, since people must learn to manage their own careers. (4) Change can be expensive. Consider that if one hundred employees with an average annual salary of $24,000 go through a six-month change or transition resulting in two hours of distraction per day, the cost is $276,000.[6]

Coping with change taxes the resources of everyone involved—managers, nonmanagers, and customers—especially if the change is sudden or disagreeable. Some change is unavoidable, and change often results in worthwhile benefits, but too often the reverse is true, as the following example shows:

> One company had hardware and software products that were the biggest sellers in its particular market. Then it decided to re-engineer—because someone got the idea that re-engineering was a good thing to do. In the process, it cut its customer-service department by half. When the company completed its change effort six months later, it discovered it didn't have any customers left. It took both its eyes off the ball by cutting back on customer service and ignoring its business so that it could follow the newest business craze. The company is now in Chapter 11.[7]

How prevalent is change in the workplace? A recent study found that 42 percent of the North American companies surveyed engaged in eleven or more change initiatives in a five-year period. In essence, the report describes a "change frenzy" that is creating cynical, demoralized employees and failing to produce meaningful improvements. The result is front-line workers who are overstressed by all of the changes created by managers frantically searching for the next formula for success. Consider the following letter from an apologetic and enlightened management.[8]

Dear Employees:

For the last decade, we have been trying to change our organization. Because we are frightened for our economic future, we kept looking for—and finding—another program du jour. We've dragged you through quality circles, excellence, total-quality management, self-directed work teams, re-engineering, and God knows what else. Desperate to find some way to improve our profitability, we switched from change to change almost as fast as we could read about them in business magazines.

All of this bounding from one panacea to the next gave birth to rampant bandwagonism. We forgot to consider each change carefully, implement it thoughtfully, and wait patiently for results. Instead, we just kept on changing while you progressed from skepticism to cynicism to downright intransigence because you realized that all of these changes were just creating the illusion of movement toward some ill-defined goal.

Now we've got a lot of burned-out workers and managers, tired of the change-of-the-month club and unlikely to listen to our next idea, no matter how good it might be. For our complicity in this dismal state of affairs, we are sincerely sorry.

The Management

Managing people through change

Figure 6.2 shows a picture of all-too-common responses to change at various organizational levels.

Figure 6.2 Organizational Response to Change[9]

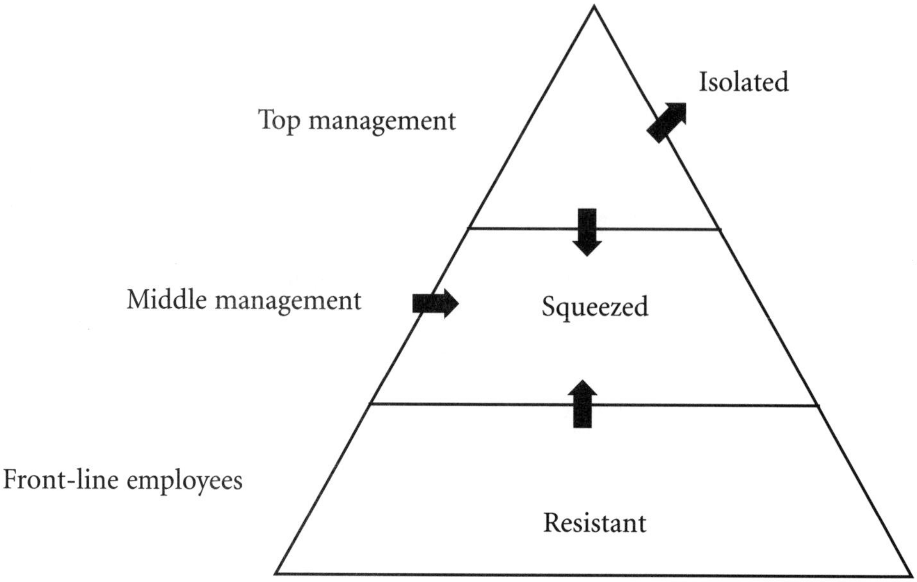

Top management

Isolated

Middle management

Squeezed

Front-line employees

Resistant

Top management: Top leaders may underestimate the impact of change on lower levels of the organization. They expect employees to "go along" when a change is announced and blame middle managers if people resist or complain. They may be so insulated that they truly don't know the results of their decisions and programs.

Middle management: Managers in the middle feel pressure to implement organizational change, but often lack information and top leadership direction to be successful. They feel squeezed between resistant or withdrawn subordinates and demanding but out-of-touch superiors.

Front-line employees: Front-line people may feel threatened by changes announced by management and may respond with denial and resistance, leading eventually to anger and worry. At this point, employees may shut down and be morale casualties.

Loss of control is one of the things people dislike most about change. Out of a need for control, they may choose dysfunction over uncertainty. Often, the only way to get people to say good-bye to the past is to convince them that the price of holding onto it is too high and that change is the only way to survive.

Rules to guide leaders in implementing change

When organizations have the right goals in mind—they want to be customer-focused, quality-conscious, empowered, and profitable—and the reason for change is accounted for by market competition, customer demands, and other forces, the question of how to implement or manage change should be addressed. Seven rules should guide leaders in all change efforts:

1. **Have a good reason for making a change.** Consider each change carefully against the following criteria: Will it support the organization's mission, purpose, and goals; does it reflect the organization's basic principles and core values?

2. **Personalize change.** Let people know where you stand. Why is the change important to you? How will you be affected if the change is successful or if it fails? Why is this change important to them? What do they stand to gain or lose?

3. **Implement change thoughtfully.** Follow four proven principles: Involve the people who are affected by the change; go slow, giving people time to adjust; keep people informed through constant personal communication; be available.

4. **Put a respected person in charge of coordinating change.** Select someone who is trusted by all. Then tap the constructive power of the group through transition teams to plan, coordinate, and communicate change efforts. Provide training in new knowledge, attitudes, and skills to support change.

5. **Tell the truth.** When change is necessary, give the facts and rationale, not sugar-coated pep talks. Trust goes up when the truth is shared. Only after people know the truth and come to terms with negative feelings can they focus effectively on the future.

6. **Wait patiently for results.** It takes time for a seed to grow, and it takes time to realize benefits from change. Change that is too rapid can be destructive. Rush the process and reduce the results.

7. **Acknowledge and reward people.** As change is made, take time to recognize people and show appreciation. Acknowledge the struggles, sacrifices, and contributions people have made. A word of thanks goes a long way.

Social psychologist Kurt Lewin identified a three-step process for managing people through change. First, unfreeze the status quo. Second, move to the desired state. Third, live by conditions that become the new, but not rigid, status quo.[10]

- **Unfreezing** involves reducing or eliminating resistance to change. As long as people drag their heels about a change, it will never be implemented effectively. To accept change, people must first deal with and resolve feelings about letting go of the old. Only after people have dealt successfully with endings are they ready to make transitions.

- **Moving to the desired state** usually involves considerable two-way communication, including group discussion. Lewin advised that the person managing change should make suggestions and encourage discussion. Brainstorming, benchmarking, field study, and library research are good techniques for channeling the energies of the group. The best way to overcome resistance to change is to involve people in the changes that will affect them.

- **Living by new conditions** involves such factors as pointing out the successes of the change and finding ways to reward the people involved in implementing the change. This shows appreciation for their efforts and increases their willingness to participate in future change efforts.

Understanding complex organizational change

There are many models for understanding organizational change. One of the best is an eight-stage process provided by John Kotter of Harvard University. Kotter's model summarizes the steps necessary to produce successful change. The first four steps unfreeze the status quo and energize the organization around a new vision. The second four steps help move the organization to the desired state, including implementing new practices and reinforcing changes in the organizational culture.[11] See Figure 6.3.

Figure 6.3 The Eight-Stage Process of Creating Major Change

1 Establishing a Sense of Urgency
- Examining the market and competitive realities
- Identifying and discussing crises, potential crises, or major opportunities

2 Creating the Guiding Coalition
- Putting together a group with enough power to lead the change
- Getting the group to work together like a team

3 Developing a Vision and Strategy
- Creating a vision to help direct the change effort
- Developing strategies for achieving that vision

4 Communicating the Change Vision
- Using every vehicle possible to constantly communicate the new vision and strategies
- Having the guiding coalition role model the behavior expected of employees

5 Empowering Broad-Based Action
- Getting rid of obstacles
- Changing systems or structures that undermine the change vision
- Encouraging risk taking and nontraditional ideas, activities, and actions

6 Generating Short-Term Wins
- Planning for visible improvements in performance, or "wins"
- Creating those wins
- Visibly recognizing and rewarding people who made the wins possible

7 Consolidating Gains and Producing More Change
- Using increased credibility to change all systems, structures, and policies that don't fit together and don't fit the transformation vision
- Hiring, promoting, and developing people who can implement the change vision
- Reinvigorating the process with new projects, themes, and change agents

8 Anchoring New Approaches in the Culture
- Creating better performance through customer- and productivity-oriented behavior, more and better leadership, and more effective management
- Articulating the connections between new behaviors and organizational success
- Developing means to ensure leadership development and succession

Source: Reprinted by permission of Harvard Business School Press. John P. Kotter, Leading Change, *(Harvard Business School Press, 1996): 21. Copyright © 1996 by John P. Kotter, all rights reserved.*

Kotter has identified common errors and their consequences in creating organizational change. These are presented in Figure 6.4.[12]

Figure 6.4 Eight Errors Common to Organizational Change Efforts and Their Consequences

Common errors
- Allowing too much complacency
- Failing to create a sufficiently powerful guiding coalition
- Underestimating the power of vision
- Undercommunicating the vision by a factor of 10 (or 100 or even 1,000)
- Permitting obstacles to block the new vision
- Failing to create short-term wins
- Declaring victory too soon
- Neglecting to anchor changes firmly in the corporate culture

Consequences
- New strategies aren't implemented well
- Acquisitions don't achieve expected synergies
- Re-engineering takes too long and costs too much
- Downsizing doesn't get costs under control
- Quality programs don't deliver hoped-for results

The empowerment of people is a key element for successful organizational change. Figure 6.5 presents five principles leaders should follow for tapping the constructive power of all employees.[13]

Figure 6.5 Empowering People to Effect Change

- **Communicate a clear, compelling vision to employees:** If employees have a shared sense of purpose, it will be easier to initiate actions to achieve that purpose.

- **Make structures compatible with the vision:** Unaligned structures block needed action.

- **Provide the training employees need:** Without the right skills and attitudes, people feel disempowered.

- **Align information and personnel systems to the vision:** Unaligned systems block needed action.

- **Confront supervisors who undercut needed change:** Nothing disempowers people the way a bad boss can.

Myths and realities in dealing with change

Historians have identified ages or periods of history—the Dark Ages, the Renaissance, the Age of Reason, and so on. An argument can be made that the current period is the Age of Change; and, further, the rate of change keeps picking up speed.

Figure 6.6 shows the broad changes that are occurring in U.S. society today. These are drivers or themes that can result in significant pressure, conflict, and frustration. To personalize the subject, put a check mark next to those changes that impact your own level of stress.

Figure 6.6 Changes in Today's World

Technology is becoming a major influence at work and at home.
- ____ All forms of work are affected by computerized systems.
- ____ New technology puts a premium on technical knowledge.

The pace of technological and social change is rapid and accelerating.
- ____ We expect things to change; some like it, but some resist.
- ____ It is often easier to throw away objects and relationships than to repair them.

The speed of communication and access to information is increasing.
- ____ People are bombarded daily by information from a myriad of sources—print, electronic, etc.
- ____ More available information poses more choices.

There is increasing reliance on self-help versus institutional help.
- ____ There is a trend toward empowering individuals.
- ____ There is greater need for continued lifelong learning.

A dominant trend is greater diversity in the workplace.
____ Increasing numbers of women in the work force means systemic change in family life.
____ Issues like human dignity, mutual respect, and inclusion are important social concerns.

There is a greater variety of living arrangments.
____ More people are living in nontraditional families.
____ Young people are increasingly raised by nonrelated adults as less and less time is spent with natural parents and legal guardians.

There is growth in population including cultural and ethnic diversity.
____ The population of our planet didn't reach one billion until the 1860s, about the time of the Civil War; the U.S. Census Bureau predicts it will reach ten billion by the year 2040.
____ Minority groups are affirming themselves as well as their rights to mainstream entitlements. Differing beliefs make it more difficult to know how to live.

There is globalization of world economies.
____ International competition in goods and services impacts the workplace and marketplace.
____ Globalization brings opportunities to exchange ideas and customs.

There is a trend toward breakdown of traditional values and social order.
____ Parents, teachers, and other leaders increasingly fail to live by high ethical standards.
____ People are increasingly exposed to crime and violence, both in person and through the media.

Source: J. Naisbitt, Megatrends: Ten New Directions Transforming Our Lives *(New York: Warner Books, 1984); and* Future Work: Seven Critical Forces Reshaping Work and the Work Force in North America *(San Francisco: Jossey-Bass Publishers, 1990).*

There are a number of myths and realities in dealing with change.[14] One myth is that *change will go away*, when the reality is *change is here to stay*. If you have lived long enough, you have witnessed first hand the truth of this statement as you have seen your own body change, family change, work change, and even your mind change.

Another common myth is that *I can just keep on doing things the way I have been*, when the reality is *if your world is changing—home, work, and society—then you may have to change as well*. For example, if the marketplace or technology or other external forces require doing business differently, can we as individuals expect to succeed if we are unwilling to make adjustments? Sometimes, in order to protect family, health, and other high-priority values, people have to make changes.

It is not the strongest of the species that survive, nor the most intelligent, but the one most responsive to change.—Charles Darwin

The importance of attitude

What a person does when change occurs depends upon his or her attitude. At one extreme, the individual may shut down and declare, "I will never change." A more effective approach is to keep an open mind and say, "Let's consider the possibilities."

In all areas of life, attitude affects our happiness, effectiveness, and general well-being. Attitude can make or break your career, your relationships, and even your health. We have all known someone with an *attitude problem.*

Some people take the attitude of the victim when change occurs. This robs them of personal energy and makes them less appealing to others. In contrast, other people view change as a challenge and focus on the opportunities and benefits that change can bring.

The power of attitude to change people's lives is reflected in the statement, "If you change your attitude, your attitude will change you." Figure 6.7 shows an attitude curve in response to change.

Figure 6.7 Attitude Curve in Response to Change[15]

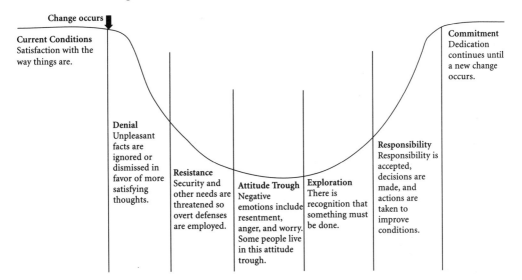

Change occurs

Current Conditions
Satisfaction with the way things are.

Commitment
Dedication continues until a new change occurs.

Denial
Unpleasant facts are ignored or dismissed in favor of more satisfying thoughts.

Resistance
Security and other needs are threatened so overt defenses are employed.

Attitude Trough
Negative emotions include resentment, anger, and worry. Some people live in this attitude trough.

Exploration
There is recognition that something must be done.

Responsibility
Responsibility is accepted, decisions are made, and actions are taken to improve conditions.

The following is a description of each phase of the attitude curve.[16]

Current conditions. Conditions are the way one likes them. There is a feeling of satisfaction and well-being. Events appear stable and manageable.

Change occurs. Caused by self or caused by others, something changes. On the job, in the home, or in society at large, change occurs that impacts the person.

Denial. Unpleasant facts and circumstances are mentally and emotionally denied. Avoidance behavior is shown and silence is evident as people don't want to face the reality of change. People don't want to know about, talk about, or otherwise deal with change in their lives.

Resistance. The fact is accepted that a change has occurred, but resistance develops as personal needs are threatened. Resistance is intensified if change is seen as unnecessary or if people don't like the way it is introduced. During resistance, forces are garnered to combat change. Energy is dissipated and people have difficulty concentrating as they complain about conditions and mourn for the past.

Attitude trough. Negative emotions are experienced, including resentment, anger, and worry as well as fear and guilt. Joy and enthusiasm are missing. There is loss of vitality and a feeling of resignation. Physical and emotional signs of stress are common. Some people live their lives in this attitude trough.

Exploration. When conditions are intolerable and the pain becomes too great, exploration begins. The individual goes from a closed and defensive state to a condition of awareness. Alternative ways of thinking, feeling, and behaving are considered. There is new interest and a sense of hope for the future.

Responsibility. Personal responsibility is accepted to improve conditions. Decisions are made and acted upon. Energy builds as the individual takes control of his or her own life. There is coordinated effort and a feeling of enthusiasm. Creativity characterizes behavior.

Commitment. The highest level of the attitude curve is achieved. It is characterized by a sense of purpose, emotional strength, and personal mastery. There is an overall feeling of satisfaction and well-being. You see high performance and personal pride.

Figure 6.8 shows effective responses in dealing with change. Denial, resistance, and negative attitudes are avoided in favor of proceeding directly to states of exploration, personal responsibility, and commitment. This is most likely to happen when people:

- believe the change is the right thing to do;

- have influence on the nature and process of change;

- respect the person who is championing the change;

- expect the change will result in personal gain; and

- believe this is the right time for change.[17]

Figure 6.8 Effective Responses in Dealing with Change

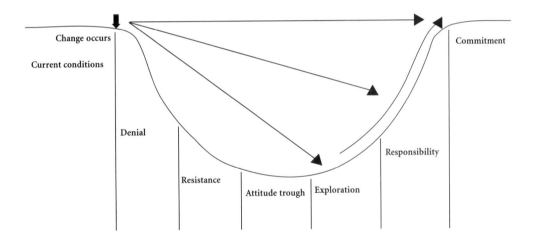

Strategies for dealing with change

Change often means loss, and this can be difficult to deal with. Loss may include loss of security, confidence, relationships, direction, or possessions or territory. Healthy coping means dealing with loss realistically and letting go of what must be given up in order to move on. You must adopt the belief that it is never too late to change your attitudes and set your life on a new and positive course.

At each phase of the attitude curve, there are strategies that can be taken to help one deal successfully with change.

Denial

What the individual can do
Don't put your head in the sand like an ostrich. Remember the adage "He who drinks from the cup of denial will sleep in the inn of defeat." Know the truth and it will set you free.

What others can do
Provide information; answer questions; communicate, communicate, communicate, ideally in person.

Resistance

What the individual can do
State how you feel; get it off your chest.

What others can do
Listen and acknowledge feelings; show understanding. This shows respect for others and may yield important and otherwise unknown information.

Attitude trough

What the individual can do
Say this is intolerable—enough is enough. Resolve to improve. Say good-bye to the past. Be willing to alter techniques.

What others can do
Model and reinforce positive actions; be patient.

Exploration

What the individual can do
Have an open mind; consider the possibilities. Coping includes fact finding and visioning an ideal future.

What others can do
Focus on priorities; channel energy in a helpful way. Brainstorm ideas and alternatives; provide helpful training; set short-term goals.

Responsibility
What the individual can do

Have courage; take action; accept the consequences.

What others can do

Encourage and expect the best. Help with planning and goal setting. Show support when decisions are made.

Commitment
What the individual can do

Learn from the past; enjoy the present; plan for the future.

What others can do

Acknowledge accomplishments and show appreciation. Help prepare for future challenges.

Initiating change

Thus far, our discussion about change has dealt with reacting healthfully and effectively to a changing world. What about initiating change? What if one's goal is to change others or improve conditions? This is an admirable ambition, but a word of advice from an old and wise source is worth remembering.[18]

> **It starts with you**
> When I was young and free and my imagination had no limits, I dreamed of changing the world. As I grew older and wiser, I discovered the world would not change, so I shortened my sights somewhat and decided to change only my country.
>
> But it, too, seemed immovable.
>
> As I grew into my twilight years, in one last desperate attempt, I settled for changing only my family, those closest to me, but alas, they would have none of it.
>
> And now as I lie on my deathbed, I suddenly realize: *If I had only changed myself first,* then by example I would have changed my family.
>
> From their inspiration and encouragement, I would then have been able to better my country and, who knows, I may have even changed the world.— Anglican bishop, name unknown, Westminster Abbey, 1100 A.D..

More modern but similar advice on this question is provided by the Indian political and spiritual leader Mahatma Mohandas Gandhi, who said:

> If you would change the world, then you must be the way you want the world to be.

Chapter Six References

[1] Daryl R. Conner, *Managing at the Speed of Change* (New York: Villand Books, 1993), 38.

[2] Conner, *Managing at the Speed of Change*, 223.

[3] William Stavropolus, CEO, The Dow Chemical Company, 1997.

[4] Mortimer B. Zuckerman, "America's Silent Revolution," *U.S. News & World Report,* July 18, 1994, p. 90.

[5] Harold J. Leavitt, *Corporate Pathfinders* (Homewood, Ill.: Dow Jones-Irwin, 1986); and Harold J. Leavitt, *Managerial Psychology* (Chicago: University of Chicago Press, 1964).

[6] Price Pritchett, *Business as Unusual: The Handbook for Managing and Supervising Organizational Change* (Dallas: Pritchett and Associates, 1994).

[7] Bob Filipczak, "Weathering Change: Enough Already," *Training* 31, no. 9 (Sept. 1994): 23.

[8] Filipczak, "Weathering Change: Enough Already," 23.

[9] Cynthia D. Scott and Dennis T. Jaffe, *Managing Organizational Change: A Practical Guide for Managers* (Los Altos, Calif.: Crisp Publications, 1989).

[10] Kurt Lewin, *A Dynamic Theory of Personality* (New York: McGraw-Hill, 1935).

[11] John P. Kotter, *Leading Change* (Boston: Harvard Business School Press, 1996): 21.

[12] Kotter, *Leading Change*, 16.

[13] Kotter, *Leading Change*, 115.

[14] Price Pritchett, *Team Reconstruction* (Dallas: Pritchett Publishing, 1992); and *High-Velocity Culture Change: Creating a Change-Adaptive Culture (Participant's Guide)* (Dallas: Pritchett & Associates, 1994).

[15] Scott and Jaffe, *Managing Organizational Change;* and Scott and Jaffe, *Managing Personal Change.*

[16] Scott and Jaffe, *Managing Organizational Change;* Cynthia D. Scott and Dennis T. Jaffe, *Managing Personal Change: Self-Management Skills for Work and Life Transitions* (Los Altos, Calif.: Crisp Publications, 1989); and Don Osgood, *Breaking Through* (Old Tappan, N.J.: Fleming Revell Co., 1986).

[17] Brian L. Davis, et al., *Successful Manager's Handbook: Development Suggestions for Today's Managers* (Minneapolis, Minn.: Personal Decisions International, 1996), 426-27.

[18] Jack Canfield and Mark Hansen, *Chicken Soup for the Soul: 101 Stories to Open the Heart and Rekindle the Spirit* (Deerfield Beach, Fla.: Health Communications, 1993), 72.

Chapter Seven
Lives in Progress

Every life is worth a novel

Charles Dickens wrote in *A Tale of Two Cities*: "It was the best of times, it was the worst of times, it was the age of wisdom, it was the age of foolishness, it was the epoch of belief, it was the epoch of incredulity, it was the season of light, it was the season of darkness, it was the spring of hope, it was the winter of despair, we had everything before us, we had nothing before us . . . in short, the period was . . . like the present period."[1] This condition describes most people's lives today.

No one is stress-free. At every age of life there are certain stresses we all must face—the frustrations of childhood, the conflicts of adulthood, and the pressures of advancing old age. These are challenges that result in stress across the life span.

Why are some people happy and fulfilled, while others are sad and depressed? Psychology provides an answer with Erik Erikson's model of life span development. Erikson described life as a journey with predictable challenges at different ages. If we meet these tests successfully, our self-image goes up. We have a sense of worth and well-being. With strength, skill, and an optimistic attitude, we are more likely to accomplish the tasks of the next period of life.

The opposite can happen too. If a person fails to make progress and feels inadequate, it is depressing and de-energizing for future tasks. Each person's life is like a novel, with each chapter building on the past, but capable of change for better or for worse.[2]

The importance of self-concept should not be underestimated. What a person thinks and feels about her- or himself influences every aspect of life. It affects how they treat themselves and how they treat others. It is singularly the most important determinant of the stress and overall quality of a person's life. Magazines and newspapers are full of accounts of famous people who have made a shambles of their lives and are miserable, proving that nothing—not money, prestige, or the attention of others—can make up for not liking oneself.[3]

Stages and tasks of lives in progress

Erikson, in his influential book *Childhood and Society*, identified eight stages of development from birth to old age. During each stage, the individual is challenged to accomplish certain tasks—physical, psychological, and social tasks of life. The successful completion of these tasks results in happiness and a positive self-concept. The failure to meet the tasks of any of life's stages can lead to low self-esteem and difficulty with later development. Figure 7.1 shows the eight stages and tasks of lives in progress.

Figure 7.1 Stages and Tasks of Lives in Progress[4]

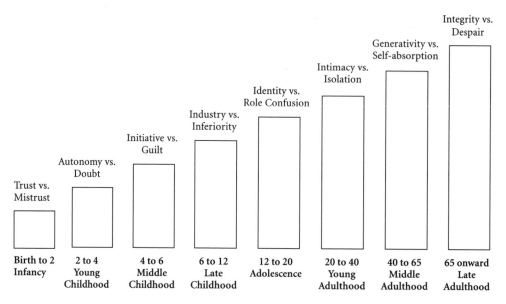

Developmental tasks arise from physical maturation, the influence of culture, and the desires and values of the emerging self. They arise in most cases from a combination of these factors acting together. At this point, the individual is at the optimum teachable moment. Important teachers and learning sites at each stage of development are as follows: Birth–6, *parents in the home*; 6–20, *teachers in the school*; 20–40, *leaders in the workplace*; 40 onward, *self in society*.

We are faced with three objectives at every stage of life: (1) resolve issues unsolved in previous stages; (2) accomplish the critical tasks of the present stage; and (3) prepare for the next stage. Just as constructing a solid base when building with blocks provides a firm foundation to support the structure, meeting the developmental tasks of each stage of life provides a foundation for further development. The eight stages and developmental tasks are as follows:[5]

Stage 1: Trust vs. mistrust—can I trust the world?

The first stage of development occurs during infancy (the first one or two years of life). A baby in Chicago, Zamboango, Amsterdam, or Rangoon has the same pitch and key, each saying, "I am! I have come through! I belong! I am a member of the human family."[6] A newborn needs stimulation and affection. If these needs are satisfied, the infant will develop *trust*—a sense that the world is a safe and secure place and that other people (particularly parents) will provide protection. On the other hand, if a baby's needs for stimulation and affection are not satisfied and the child is ignored or abused, *mistrust* will result. The baby will learn to view the world as a hostile place, requiring self-protective behavior rather than openness toward others. Basic mistrust may become the core of later insecurity, suspiciousness, or inability to relate to others.

Challenges: The major developmental tasks of infancy are (1) giving and receiving affection; and (2) achieving a loving, reliable relationship with the mother and other primary caretakers.

Benefits: Successful completion of these tasks results in feelings of security and well-being.

Possible crisis events: Disruption in feeding; physical illness or injury; rejection by primary caregiver.

Stage 2: Autonomy vs. doubt—can I control my behavior?

The second stage of development usually occurs during young childhood (from about 2 to 4 years of age). If a young child learns to explore and to do things independently during this period, self-confidence and a sense of *autonomy* will develop—the sense that "I can do it myself." On the other hand, if the child does not succeed at such tasks as eating or controlling body functions and is continually criticized for making mistakes, shame and *doubt* will result. Patience and persistence are important attributes for parents and other caretakers during this developmental period.

Challenges: The major developmental tasks of this period are (1) achieving physical self-control; and (2) viewing oneself as an independent and worthy person.

Benefits: The young child who has learned trust and autonomy is better prepared for all subsequent stages of life.

Possible crisis events: Physical illness or injury; conflict with primary caregivers over increased assertiveness; difficulty with toilet training; etc.

Stage 3: Initiative vs. guilt—can I become an independent person?

The third stage of development is associated with the preschool years (from about 4 to 6 years of age). Language develops and motor skills and physical coordination improve during this stage. It is an extension of the previous stage, when autonomy can develop into *initiative* or doubt can deteriorate into *guilt* and fearfulness. If a 5-year-old proclaims, "I am going to climb that tree," and succeeds in this initiative, self-confidence and mastery of the environment are reinforced. In contrast, if the child is discouraged from trying, or is ridiculed for failing, the child may feel guilt and may be reluctant to attempt anything new or difficult again. The small child has dreams of being a giant and a tiger, but may, in these same dreams, run in terror for dear life.

Also, the young child must learn the concept of right and wrong. The rest of one's life is spent distinguishing what falls into each category. These lessons are learned primarily from parents and mainly by example.

Challenges: Important developmental tasks of this period include (1) learning personal care; (2) learning to be a member of a family or social group; and (3) beginning to distinguish right from wrong.

Benefits: The favorable outcomes of satisfying these tasks are constructive personal habits and self-approval.

Possible crisis events: Physical injury; conflict with teachers/parents/peers; difficulty with preschool or kindergarten adjustment; loss of friends through moving/migration.

Stage 4: Industry vs. inferiority—can I master skills to succeed?

The fourth stage of development usually occurs during later childhood (from about 6 to 12 years of age). If scholarship, craftsmanship, and social skills are learned successfully during this period, a child develops a sense of *industry* and feelings of accomplishment. Tremendous self-worth can be created by succeeding in schoolwork, animal care, athletics, music, hobbies, and other activities. On the other hand, feelings of *inferiority* (the feeling that "I can't do anything right") can result from failure. This is why it is important for every child to be encouraged and receive recognition in the areas of his or her interests and aptitudes during this period of life.

Feelings of industry or inferiority formed during this period represent either an advantage or a handicap for all subsequent growth. The sphere of activity during this stage of development usually extends beyond the family and includes the neighborhood, school, and other social institutions. Scouting, sports, and hobby clubs are examples of important childhood activities. Caring teachers, coaches, and other youth leaders can be highly important to the developing child during these formative years.

Challenges: The major developmental tasks of this period include (1) developing a conscience and a system of values; (2) learning mental, physical, and interpersonal skills; (3) learning to compete and cooperate with age-mates; and (4) learning how to win and lose gracefully.

Benefits: Satisfying these tasks successfully results in personal competence and effective work and social habits.

Possible crisis events: Learning difficulties; conflict with teachers/parents/peers; change in schools.

Stage 5: Identity vs. role confusion—do I know and like who I am?

The fifth stage of development usually occurs during adolescence (from about 12 to 20 years of age). The greatest task of this period is to develop a sense of personal *identity*. The feeling that "I know and like who I am" is the goal. Included in the definition of "self" is a healthy sexual identity (There are boys and girls, and I am glad I am a girl), a personal moral code (There are right and wrong, and I believe I know what is right), and an initial life plan (I want to work with my hands, have a family, and live in the country). The concern with discovering and being oneself occurs concurrently with the concern for establishing satisfying human relationships and sharing with others. Belonging to a peer group and giving and receiving affection are important to the adolescent.

The young person who suffers from either *role confusion* or a lack of love wanders through the teen years without self-understanding, without clear goals, and in an unhappy state. Adolescence is a critical period of life and is often filled with stress, not only for the individual, but for family and friends as well. This is due primarily to the teenager's natural efforts to escape from parental dominance and to establish an independent identity. Guidance and encouragement from teachers and other adult advisors can be very helpful to the adolescent youth.

Many young people yield to pressures to decide too early what they will do in life and what serious commitments they will make. Thus, they may never realize the range of possibilities open to them. To deal with this problem, Erikson suggested a *psychological moratorium*—a period of time during which society would give permission to adolescents to experiment with different roles and values so that they could sample life before making major commitments. Going to college, joining the military, and serving in the Peace Corps are all effective ways to see the world and broaden one's view.

Challenges: Important developmental tasks of this stage include (1) adjusting to body changes; (2) achieving emotional independence from parents; (3) making new friends of both sexes; (4) developing intellectual skills; and (5) selecting and preparing for an occupation.

Benefits: The satisfactory completion of these tasks results in feelings of self-esteem, fidelity in human relations, and optimism toward life.

Possible crisis events: Sexual problems; unwanted pregnancy; conflict with parents over habits and lifestyle; breakup with girlfriend/boyfriend; acceptance of peers; career indecision; difficulty on first job; difficulty in school/college.

Stage 6: Intimacy vs. isolation—can I give fully of myself to others?

The sixth stage of development is usually associated with young adulthood and includes the ages from about 20 to 40. During the twenties, the individual typically begins to develop a dream—a vision of what she or he would like to achieve as an adult. Men's dreams tend to center on occupational goals. They may want to be a builder, farmer, discoverer, and so on. Women historically have been more likely to have split dreams, including both career and family goals.

During this period, the individual typically "leaves the family nest" psychologically and economically. During this stage, balance must be found between two opposing challenges. The many possibilities of adult life must be explored, keeping options open, while at the same time the young adult must achieve basic occupational success.

Meaningful relationships are sought with people outside the family during this period. A major goal of these relationships is to establish a sense of *intimacy*, a feeling of closeness and commitment with another person. A relationship in which one can be oneself and can experience unconditional love is what is meant by intimacy. For most young people, establishing intimacy through a loving relationship is a vital concern.

Economically, the young adult begins earning a livelihood. Assets developed during earlier periods (autonomy, initiative, industry, and identity) will be of immense help, while doubt, guilt, inferiority, and role confusion will be liabilities as a career is pursued. Without a loving relationship and meaningful work, the young adult typically experiences a sense of *isolation* and feelings of being unimportant. Sigmund Freud identified the central issues of this stage of development to be "love and work." Leo Tolstoy wrote in 1856, "One can live magnificently in this world, if one knows how to work and how to love."

Also, during the period of young adulthood, important personal and social values solidify as the individual considers the purpose of existence and the meaning of life. Finally, young adulthood is usually a period of starting a family and nurturing children. Concern for an independent self expands to include concern for dependent others. During this period, commitments are typically made to a life structure and to significant others.

The challenges of young adulthood can be highly stressful, as Gail Sheehy describes in *Passages*:

> Who's afraid of growing up? Who isn't? . . . There is a moment—an intense and precarious moment—of stark terror. And in that moment most of us want to retreat as fast as possible because to go forward means facing a truth we have suspected all along: We stand alone.[7]

Older and more experienced adults can be helpful teachers to the young person who is trying to solve the developmental tasks of early adulthood. Particularly important can be the leader in the workplace who is willing to give time and attention to developing others.

Challenges: Important developmental tasks of this stage include (1) finding a satisfactory social group; (2) selecting and learning to live with a mate; (3) starting a family and meeting the physical and psychological needs of young children; (4) getting started in an occupation; and (5) defining personal and social values.

Benefits: Successfully meeting these challenges results in loving relationships, economic independence, and social responsibility.

Possible crisis events: Rejection by potential partner; extramarital affairs; separation, divorce; unwanted pregnancy; inability to bear children; birth of a child; discipline problems with children; illness of sons or daughters; inability to manage the various demands of parenthood; military service; academic difficulties; failure to graduate from high school/college; inability to find a satisfactory career; poor performance in chosen career; purchase of home; financial difficulties; conflict between career and family goals.

Stage 7: Generativity vs. self-absorption—what can I do for succeeding generations?

The seventh stage of development is associated with middle adulthood, approximately 40 to 65 years of age. Gray hair, wrinkles, and reading glasses are physical signals that this stage has been reached. Not too long ago, this period was thought of as the beginning of the end, but for most people today it is merely the end of the beginning. When you reach the half-century mark, you can look forward to about another quarter century of living, and much longer in many cases.

With personal affairs in order, the adult who achieves *generativity* directs attention toward other people—family and friends, as well as the larger community. The person becomes concerned about the state of the world and the well-being of future generations. There is the need to be needed and the desire to contribute to the welfare of others. As Carl Jung explains, we reach backward to our parents and forward to our children, and through their children to a future which we will never see but about which we care very much. Productivity, creativity, and responsibility are important values for the person who exhibits generativity during middle adulthood.

In contrast, a person who has not developed generativity experiences *self-absorption*, the feeling that "I come first before anyone or anything else." Oscar Wilde portrayed such self-absorption in *The Picture of Dorian Gray*, a story about a vain young man who received his wish to remain young forever. He used other people and was cruel to those who loved him. A self-portrait reflected all of his misdeeds, and this evil image haunted him. In the end, he stabbed the picture, then died. Wilde's story is a parable that illustrates the disaster of self-absorption.[8]

More and more people are living longer and longer, and this impacts the stresses of middle adulthood. In addition to raising children, many are caring for aging parents. On top of this is the added demand of preparing for one's own old age. This three-front struggle can be an enormous task that is highly stressful. A common situation is the midlife adult who has too much to do and not enough time to do it. If youth's theme is potential, midlife's is reality, as the focus is on coming to terms with facts and finite resources.

The midlife period sometimes involves a painful struggle as people appraise their values and talents and the extent to which they have lived up to them. A reckoning occurs. According to Jung, one must live long enough to experience such a crisis before the public self and the private self can be reconciled and the full flowering of the human personality can be achieved. The term he uses for this process is *individuation*. A key characteristic of this process is that it must be accomplished by the individual her- or himself. Others may care and others may share, but true individuation is ultimately a personal challenge.

Completing unfinished tasks and resolving old business is a common theme for people in midlife. Finishing one's education, healing old relationships, and fulfilling one's dreams are recurring stories. Although the challenges of midlife are great and although there are plenty of exceptions, the data show that the middle years are considered the best time in life for most people, says Ronald Kessler of the University of Michigan's Institute for Social Research.

Challenges: The developmental tasks of middle adulthood include (1) making productive contributions; (2) relating to other people as people; (3) helping young people become happy and self-sufficient; (4) adjusting to aging family members; (5) establishing economic security for one's remaining years; (6) developing leisure-time activities; (7) providing leadership in social, economic, religious, and other institutions; and (8) adjusting to the physical changes of aging.

Benefits: The satisfactory resolution of these tasks leads to a sense of contribution, social stability, and peace of mind.

Possible crisis events: Awareness of physical decline; chronic illness (self or spouse); conflict with children; death or prolonged illness of parents; setback in career; conflict at work; financial problems; moving associated with career; awareness of discrepancy between life goals and achievements; regret over earlier decisions not to marry, not to have children, or vice versa; marital problems; death of family and friends.

Stage 8: Integrity vs. despair—have I found contentment and inner peace?

The last stage of development occurs during later adulthood, from about 65 years of age onward. This is the period of reflection and summing up. The central task of this stage is to achieve *integrity* and inner peace. The older person with integrity feels that life has been good and the years have been used well. There is a sense of fulfillment.

On the other hand, the elderly person who has not achieved integrity feels that life has been wasted, is filled with regret, and feels personal *despair*. The older person with integrity cares about future generations and seeks to help other people, while the older person with despair dwells on personal problems of the past, thinking, "If I could only live my life over, I would do things differently." Older people with integrity make wonderful teachers, because they have learned from life and because they care about those who are younger.

The secret to emotional well-being in old age seems to be not professional success or a blissful marriage, but an ability to cope with life's setbacks and shortfalls without blame or bitterness. The later years can be the happiest of one's life. Many of those who have achieved what others call old age have confessed to feeling embarrassingly young and unexpectedly fresh. It is the kind of freshness that the long-distance runner experiences when at the peak of fatigue he experiences a second wind that takes him on to the finish line.[9]

> **Retirement**
> One of the best bosses we ever had was Ralph Tesseneer. He understood people and he loved them. Because of this, he was a great teacher.
>
> After he was retired several years, we thought it would be good to ask what he had learned about retirement.
>
> From what he had observed and experienced, it seemed to him that the best predictor of a happy retirement was a happy work life. Similarly, the person who is miserable during the working years is most likely to remain so.
>
> What we got from this is the importance of personal qualities versus social circumstances. It is not age and employment that matter; it is health and attitude. Life is pretty much what a person makes it to be.—Authors' file notes (G. M. and K. C.)

Challenges: The developmental tasks of later adulthood include (1) adjusting to decreasing physical strength; (2) adjusting to retirement and reduced income; (3) maintaining interests beyond oneself; (4) adjusting to the deaths of family and friends; and (5) accepting one's own impending death.

Benefits: The satisfactory accomplishment of these tasks results in a sense of fulfillment and inner peace.

Possible crisis events: Health problems; change in physical living arrangements (farmhouse to city apartment, or home to retirement community); conflict with grown children/parents; "empty nest" (last child leaves home); death of spouse; divorce; resistance to retirement; separation or letting go of work roles/responsibilities; financial difficulties; death of family and friends.

Erikson's model of human development provides a review of past development, a diagnosis of present conditions, and a preview of future tasks. It identifies the special stresses of each period of life and helps explain why one person at any age may feel happy and fulfilled, while another person may feel adrift and depressed. An important point to remember is that although developmental tasks tend to be age-related, people can accomplish unfinished tasks of earlier periods at any point in time. The late bloomer is a phenomenon we all have witnessed. Also, a shooting star may fall and a person's life may diminish. A good way to view this is to see lives like books. Each is in the process of being written, and every life is worth a novel. Today is a new page and you are the writer of your own story. What will it be?

Figure 7.2 summarizes changes in seven domains of human functioning from young adulthood through late adulthood.

Figure 7.2 Changes in Seven Domains of Human Functioning Across the Adult Life Span

	Young Adulthood 20–30	Early Adulthood 30–40	Middle Adulthood 40–65	Older Adulthood 65–75	Late Adulthood 75+
Major tasks	Separate from childhood family; form partnership; begin new family; find job; create individual life pattern.	Raise family; establish personal work/family pattern; strive for success.	Redefine life goals achieve individuality; care for aging parents.	Adjust to retirement; cope with declining physical strength; redefine life goals and sense of self.	Come to terms with one's own life and with death.
Physical change	Peak functioning in most physical skills; maximum health; optimum childbearing time.	Good physical functioning and health in most areas; health habits established here create pattern of later risks.	Beginning signs of physical decline in some areas, e.g., strength, elasticity, height, cardiovascular functioning.	Physical decline continues. Risk of disability or disease increases; reaction time slows.	Acceleration of rate of physical and health decline.
Cognitive change	Cognitive skill high on most measures; maximum synaptic speed.	Peak period of cognitive skill on most measures at about age 30.	Some signs of loss of cognitive skill "fluid," timed, unexercised skills; high cognitive investment; little functional loss.	Small declines on "crystallized" and "exercised" skills; larger losses on "fluid" skills. Rate of loss has not yet accelerated.	Approximate point of acceleration of cognitive loss, including areas of memory and both fluid and crystallized abilities.
Family and sex roles	Major role acquisition; marriage and family formation; clarification of male and female roles.	Family roles dominant, with continued differentiation of sex roles; women do most family and home work.	Children leave home; post-parental phase; begin care of elderly parents.	Grandparent role; significantly less dominance of family and sex role.	Senior advisor and source of connection with past.
Relationships	Maximum emphasis on forming friends and friendships and partnership; usually high marital satisfaction at least until birth of first child.	Lower marital satisfaction; fewer new friends made and lower contact with friends; continued contact with parents.	Increased marital satisfaction; increase in the importance of friends.	High marital satisfaction for those not widowed; children, friends, and siblings are important.	Majority are widowed; siblings are important; relationships become less intense.
Work roles	Choose career; often several job changes; develop occupational skills.	Rising work satisfaction; major emphasis on work or career success; work responsibilities increase.	Plateau of career steps; high work satisfaction.	Retirement for vast majority.	Occupational roles unimportant for most.
Personality	Task of intimacy; formative period of meaning development.	Increasing individuality; increasing self-confidence; independence and autonomy.	Peak and then decline in desire for power; lower use of psychological defenses.	Task of ego integrity; contemplative and value-based reasoning.	Continuation of previous pattern.

Source: Adapted from Helen L. Bee, The Journey of Adulthood (New York: Macmillan, 1992), 436-37.

Life span development is a dynamic concept in that ages and tasks can change across cultures and time. Consider the observations of author Gail Sheehy in her book *New Passages*:

> There is a revolution going on in the adult life cycle. People today are leaving childhood sooner, but they are taking longer to grow up and much longer to die. That is shifting all the stages of adulthood ahead—by 10 years. Adolescence is now prolonged for the middle class until the end of the 20s. Today, our First Adulthood only begins at 30. Most baby boomers don't feel fully "grown up" until they are in their 40s. When our parents turned 50, we thought they were old! But today, women and men routinely feel they are five to 10 years younger than the age on their birth certificates. Fifty is what 40 used to be; 60 is what 50 used to be. Middle age has already been pushed far into the 50s. People are living increasingly longer and this amounts to a second adult lifetime.[10]

Personality consistency

Some aspects of personality change little over time and across life's eight stages. Researchers have identified five "robust" dimensions or traits, each of which shows considerable stability from one situation to another and over time: neuroticism, extroversion, openness to experience, agreeableness, and conscientiousness. These "big five" traits capture the bulk of variation in personality among individuals. See Figure 7.3.

Figure 7.3 The "Big Five" Personality Traits and Their Stability Over Time

Trait	Quality of individual high in that trait	Stability over six years
Neuroticism	Anxious, temperamental, self-conscious, worrying, emotional, vulnerable, highly strung	.83
Extroversion	Sociable, talkative, fun-loving, outgoing, active, people-oriented, affectionate	.82
Openness to experience	Imaginative, creative, original, curious, independent, adventurous, variety-loving	.83
Agreeableness	Soft-hearted, trusting, generous, lenient, good-natured, courteous, considerate	.63
Conscientiousness	careful, reliable, hard-working, well-organized, punctual, persevering, dependable	.79

Source: Robert R. McCrae and Paul T. Costa Jr., Personality in Adulthood *(New York: Guilford Press, 1990), adapted from Table 1, p. 3.*

It is believed that neuroticism and extroversion are more stongly influenced by heredity than environment, while the other three dimensions are thought to be determined more by environment, although they also have a genetic component. All five factors of personality have been consistently observed in both Eastern and Western cultures.[11]

An interesting example of personality consistency comes from David McClelland, who has been one of the major figures in personality research. McClelland describes his encounters over a period of years with a man originally known as Richard Alpert:

> In the early 1960s, Richard Alpert was a psychologist at Stanford and Harvard, very verbal, charming, successful. He could hold classes spellbound. Alpert was ambitious, interested in influencing others, and had a strong need for power accompanied by guilt about wanting such power.
>
> When he was a young faculty member, Alpert got involved with Timothy Leary, another Harvard professor who was experimenting with LSD and who advised young people of that time to "turn on, tune in, and drop out." Alpert did all three. He left Harvard, drifted about for a few years, then went to India, where he stayed at the ashram (study center) of a guru. Eventually Alpert came back to the United States with a new name—Ram Dass—and a new philosophy.
>
> When I first saw Ram Dass again in the early 1970s he seemed like a completely transformed person. His appearance was totally different from what it had been. He was wearing long Indian style clothes with beads around his neck; he was nearly bald but had grown a long bushy beard. He had given away all his possessions, refusing his father's inheritance, carried no money on his person, and for a time lived as a nomad in a van which was all he had in the world. He had given up drugs, abandoned his career as a psychologist, no longer wanted even to save the world, and talked all the time as if he were "nobody special," although previously it had been clear to himself and others that he was somebody special.
>
> Yet after spending some time with him, I found myself saying over and over again "It's the same old Dick." He was still very intelligent, he was still verbally fluent, and he was still charming. At a somewhat less obvious level, Alpert was very much involved in high drama, just as he had always been. I would certainly conclude that he continues to have a strong interest in power. Furthermore he still feels guilty about being so interested in power.[12]

The influence of age, gender, and other differences on happiness

Each of us is curious about what the best years of our life were or will be. That is, which age group is the happiest? Is it carefree, independent youth? Optimistic, energetic young adults? Successful, experienced adults? Or fulfilled, retired older people? When individuals report how happy and satisfied they are with their lives, no particular age group stands out.[13]

As Figure 7.4 shows, perceived well-being remains consistently high across all age groups. Since growing older is a certain outcome of living, we can take satisfaction in knowing that we are likely to be just as happy as older adults as we were when we were younger.[14]

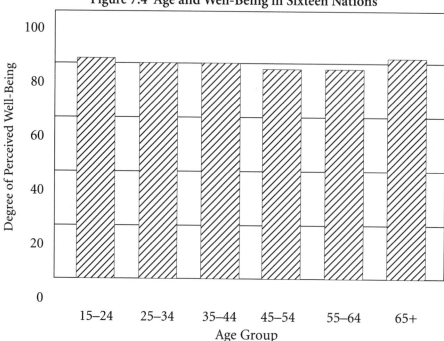

Figure 7.4 Age and Well-Being in Sixteen Nations

Source: Data from 169,776 people reported by Ronald Inglehart, Culture Shift in Advanced Industrial Society *(Princeton: Princeton University Press, 1990).*

The stability of well-being across the life span obscures some interesting age-related differences. As our years go by, our feelings tend to mellow. Our highs are less high, our lows less low. Successes provoke less elation and setbacks less despair. Adult moods tend to be moderate and enduring. Having survived past sufferings and enjoyed past pleasures, older people look beyond the moment.

In contrast, young people typically descend from elation or ascend from gloom in less than an hour. An argument with a friend, and it seems as if the world is going to end. But then comes a phone call and all is forgotten. Researchers report that ratings of parental warmth by adolescents living at home bear no relation to ratings made by the same adolescents six weeks earlier. When teenagers are down, their world, including their parents, seems inhuman; when their mood brightens, their parents' traits become admirable.[15]

Another much-studied predictor of well-being is gender. What does the research show? Men and women are equally likely to report being "satisfied" or "very happy" with life. See Figure 7.5.

Figure 7.5 Gender and Well-Being in Sixteen Nations

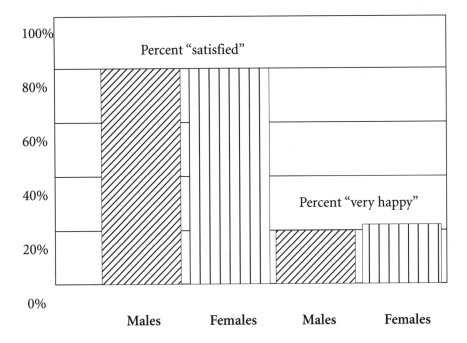

Source: Data from 169,776 people reported by Ronald Inglehart, Culture Shift in Advanced Industrial Society *(Princeton: Princeton University Press, 1990).*

What about money? Does wealth bring happiness? Large amounts of money are not the key to happiness for most people. What is important is having sufficient money to provide life's necessities—food, shelter, and the like. Extremely wealthy people on average are no happier than people who can purchase the necessities for living a safe and healthy existence. For example, people in wealthy countries do not rate themselves happier than people in poor countries, and the people in *Forbes* magazine's annual list of the richest Americans are no more or less happy than any other Americans.

In *The Pursuit of Happiness*, David Myers summarizes the findings of hundreds of studies of happiness. He dispels the following popular but *mistaken* ideas:

Myth	Fact
Few people are genuinely happy.	The majority are happy.
Wealth brings happiness.	Money is no guarantee of happiness.
Tragedies permanently erode happiness.	Time usually heals.
Teens and the elderly are the unhappiest people.	Happiness is consistent across the ages.
One gender is happier than the other.	Both are the same.
Religion suppresses happiness.	There is no relationship.
People more often feel low than high self-esteem.	The opposite is true.[16]

In contrast, a number of demographic and personal differences are linked to life satisfaction and happiness. Major findings are summarized in Figure 7.6.

Figure 7.6 Recipe for Happiness

Happiness is influenced by conditions in our lives. What factors are most closely associated with happiness in your life? Does your list correspond with the following recipe for happiness?

Most important ingredient
Good health

Other important ingredients
Stable marriage
Supportive spouse
Meaningful goals
Work involvement
Adequate income
High energy level
Supportive friendship
Positive self-concept
Personal autonomy

Sources: The most comprehensive source is Diener, 1984. More current sources for specific items included are: Costa and McCrae, 1984; Gibson, 1986; Koenig, Kvale, & Ferrell, 1988; Lee, 1988; Willits & Crider, 1988; Umberson & Gove, 1989; Gove, Style, & Hughes, 1990.

In concluding a discussion of happiness, we should revisit the characteristics of a hardy personality identified in Chapter 5. Happiness is less about what happens to a person and much more about qualities of the person her- or himself. For true happiness, one needs a purpose in life that focuses and energizes existence and needs freedom and acceptance of responsibility for his or her own actions; happiness comes from finding a positive for every negative, viewing a setback as a challenge, and enjoying what we have versus wishing for what we do not have; happiness requires perspective and balance, keeping little things little and first things first; and happiness requires love in all of its forms, both giving and receiving. These are the elements of true happiness.

Evaluating your life

Understanding the past can help one deal with the future. The following exercise provides this perspective.

Application: All Things Considered[17]

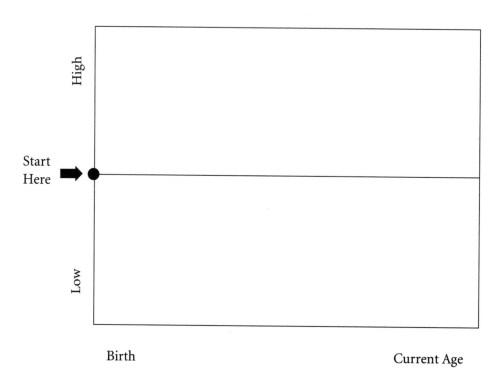

Start Here →

Birth   Current Age

The left-hand corner of the baseline represents your birth and the right-hand corner represents your current age. The vertical line represents how you feel about your life on a continuum from low (depressed) to high (excited). Halfway up the vertical line is the neutral point; here you feel neither low nor high, just content. From this neutral point, draw your personal lifeline across the page from birth to death.

Indicate by the configuration of your line how you feel about your life, through childhood (birth to 12), adolescence (12 to 20), young adulthood (20 to 40), middle adulthood (40 to 65), and late adulthood (65 onward). Your line may be slanted, jagged, straight, or curved. Number the high and low points on your line and describe the important people and events that have helped shape your life. See Figure 7.7 for an example.

Figure 7.7 Sample Lifeline[18]

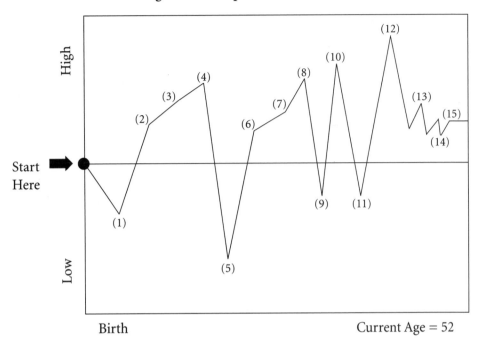

Birth to age 18 was a difficult time (1), because my parents were divorced and there were serious problems between me and my stepfather. In 1959 (2) I was crowned Honored Queen of Job's Daughters, with a white robe, a floor-length purple cape, and a crown. Lots of flowers and excitement—I felt like Queen of the World! In 1960 (3) I eloped because of no parental consent but was still married in church, two states away on a letter of recommendation from our preacher. I forfeited a four-year full scholarship to college. (4) In 1968 Jamie was born. The light of my life! (5) A year later an unexpected and unexplained divorce resulted in my total emotional collapse. Hospitalized for an extended period. (6) Had adjusted to divorce, so I moved from my birthplace to Cincinnati, Ohio. (7) In 1976, I began college. Completed my freshman and sophomore years. (8) Joseph was born. He felt like a miracle, since I went to have surgery for a tumor. (9) Jamie left my home to live with his dad so he could go to a county school. (10) I returned to college as a computer programming major. Two years later (11), my beloved 42-year-old brother died from diabetes. (12) Now I'm a senior in college. Joseph is in high school, going to Outward Bound this summer. Jamie and his wife Lisa are doing a good job raising my precious grandchildren, Joshua and Amanda. I realize it won't be a snap from here on out, there will be highs and lows every now and then, (13), (14), (15) . . . but that's LIFE!

Chapter Seven References

1. Charles Dickens, *A Tale of Two Cities* (London: Chapman and Hall, 1859).

2. Erik H. Erikson, *Childhood and Society*, 2nd ed. (New York: W. W. Norton, 1963); and Robert J. Havighurst, *Developmental Tasks and Education* (New York: Longman's, Green and Co., 1952).

3. Loren Ford, *Game Plan: A Guide for Improving Human Relations and Personal Adjustment* (Upper Saddle River, N.J.: Prentice-Hall, 1997).

4. Carl Sandburg, *The Family of Man* (New York: Museum of Modern Art, 1955).

5. James C. Coleman, *Personality Dynamics and Effective Behavior* (Glenview, Ill.: Scott, Foresman, 1960), 90; Erikson, *Childhood and Society;* and Havighurst, *Developmental Tasks and Education.*

6. Erikson, *Childhood and Society.*

7. Gail Sheehy, *Passages: Predictable Crises of Adult Life* (New York: Dutton, 1976), 355.

8. Oscar Wilde, *The Picture of Dorian Gray* (New York: Modern Library, 1985).

9. Ashley Montagu, *Growing Young*, 2nd ed. (New York: Bergin and Garvey Publishers, an imprint of Greenwood Press, 1989).

10. Gail Sheehy, *New Passages: Mapping Your Life Across Time* (New York: Merritt Corporation and Alfred K. Knopf, 1995).

11. Robert R. McCrae and Paul T. Costa, Jr., "The Stability of Personality: Observations and Evaluations," *Current Directions in Psychological Science*, December 1994. Cambridge University Press, 1994.

12. David McClelland, "Is Personality Consistent?" in A. I. Rabin, J. Aronoff, A. M. Barclay, and R. A. Zucker, eds., *Further Explorations in Personality* (New York: Wiley-Interscience, 1981), 87-113.

13. W. A. Stock, M. A. Okum, M. J. Haring, and R. A. Witter, "Age and Subjective Well-Being: A Meta-Analysis," in R. J. Light, ed., *Evaluation Studies: Review Annual,* vol. 8 (Beverly Hills, Calif., 1983).

14. David Myers, *The Pursuit of Happiness* (New York: Avon Books, 1992).

15. Myers, *The Pursuit of Happiness.*

16. Myers, *The Pursuit of Happiness.*

17. Walter H. Gmelch, *Beyond Stress to Effective Management* (New York: John Wiley and Sons, 1982), 187-88.

18. Judith Marksberry, "Sample Lifeline," Northern Kentucky University, 1996. Used by permission.

Chapter Eight

The Meaning of Wellness

Wellness defined

In 1947, the World Health Organization defined the meaning of health as "a state of complete physical, mental, and social well-being, and not merely the absence of disease or infirmity."

Today we add to this definition to describe wellness as:

1. being free from illness and disease;

2. having no physiological measures that indicate risk to health, such as high blood pressure;

3. having a healthy lifestyle that allows one to be active;

4. being in good spirits with a zest for life.

These characteristics indicate that wellness is not something that is suddenly achieved at a specific time. Rather, it is an ongoing process and commitment— indeed, a way of life. See Figure 8.1.

Figure 8.1 The Wellness-Illness Continuum

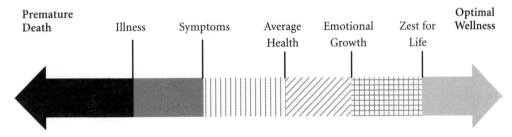

Health and wellness result from a complex interaction of biological, psychological, and social variables. See Figure 8.2.

Figure 8.2 Biological, Psychological, and Social Factors That Affect Health and Wellness

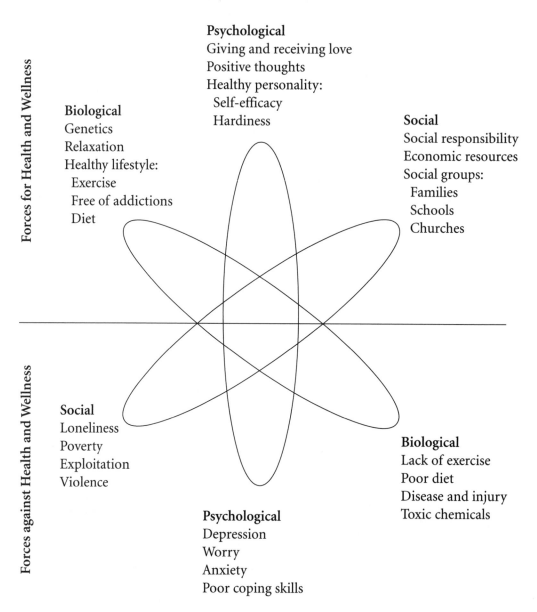

Psychological
Giving and receiving love
Positive thoughts
Healthy personality:
   Self-efficacy
   Hardiness

Biological
Genetics
Relaxation
Healthy lifestyle:
   Exercise
   Free of addictions
   Diet

Social
Social responsibility
Economic resources
Social groups:
   Families
   Schools
   Churches

Social
Loneliness
Poverty
Exploitation
Violence

Biological
Lack of exercise
Poor diet
Disease and injury
Toxic chemicals

Psychological
Depression
Worry
Anxiety
Poor coping skills

Forces for Health and Wellness

Forces against Health and Wellness

Source: Adapted from Judith Green and Robert Schellenberger, The Dynamics of Health and Wellness: A Biopsychosocial Approach *(Ft. Worth: Holt, Rinehart and Winston, 1991), 21. Reprinted with permission. Copyright © 1991 by Holt, Rinehart and Winston.*

Biological factors include "givens," such as inherited traits; environmental factors that affect physiological functioning, such as pesticides in the food chain that may cause birth defects and cancer; and behaviors that affect biological functions, such as smoking, diet, and exercise. *Psychological* factors include personality, stress management, life goals, perceptions, feelings, and health and sickness behaviors. *Social* factors include social systems such as the family, work, school, church, and government, and social values, customs, and social support.

Consider a person who has a long and healthy life. Biological factors might include "good" genes, a wholesome diet, and an unpolluted environment. Social factors might include a supportive family, a fulfilling job, and social status. Psychological factors might include an easygoing personality and high self-esteem. Individually, these variables promote health to some degree, but in combination they produce a stronger effect. They interact—the easygoing personality encourages family support and love, which in turn enhances self-esteem, which encourages risk-taking at work, which leads to advancement and social status; financial security reduces stress, which promotes health, and so on. If these variables were studied independently, the essential interaction would be overlooked.[1]

Dimensions of wellness

Wellness expert Wiley Piazza states that we tend to think of wellness as the number of times we exercise each week. While exercise is important, it is equally important to understand the true depth of personal wellness. The National Wellness Institute describes interacting dimensions that comprise the whole of ourselves. These areas of life are shown in Figure 8.3.

Figure 8.3: Dimensions of Wellnesss

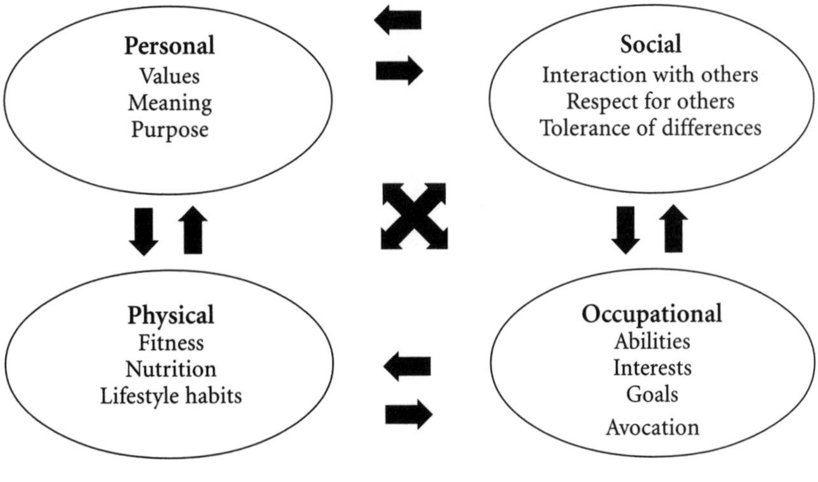

For each area, stress points or issues causing pressure, conflict, and frustration are as follows:

- Personal: Beliefs and Values—See Part Four *Personal Stress*

- Social: Love and Support—See Part Five *Interpersonal Stress*

- Occupational: Satisfaction and Success—See Part Six *Stress in the Workplace* and Part Seven *Peak Performance*

- Physical: Health and Fitness—See Part Eight *Stress Prevention*

Making choices

Every person who wishes to manage stress and cope with change must learn the art of saying *no* to some things in order to possess other things more fully. The young person may vacillate among a dozen different plans for the future, but the mature individual is willing to renounce many paths in order to follow a truly meaningful one.

The paired-comparison technique is a systematic method for making choices in life. It forces comparisons between all subjects being evaluated on common criteria. As the following quotation from Benjamin Franklin shows, the idea is not new:

Canceling out pros and cons
When confronted with two courses of action, I jot down on a piece of paper all the arguments in favor of each one—then, on the opposite side, I write the arguments against each one. Then, by weighing the arguments pro and con and canceling them out one against the other, I take the course indicated by what remains.—Benjamin Franklin

Application: The Paired-Comparison Technique for Making Life Choices

Step I
Identify a decision to be made—personal, social, occupational, or physical. Use a phrase or sentence to pose the question. For example, "What career would be most fulfilling?"

Step II
Make a list of individuals or options to be compared on the question. Assign a number to each one.

1 _____	2 _____
3 _____	4 _____
5 _____	6 _____
7 _____	8 _____
9 _____	10 _____

Step III
Look at the first line of the grid below. You will see a 1 and a 2. Compare options 1 and 2 on your list, using the question. Circle your choice. Then go to the next pair (1 and 3). Continue in this manner until you have compared every option with every other option. If you need to compare a list with more than ten items on it, add new rows to the bottom of the grid—1,11; 2,11; etc.—until you have all the numbers needed, arranged in pairs.

1 2

1 3   2 3

1 4   2 4   3 4

1 5   2 5   3 5   4 5

1 6   2 6   3 6   4 6   5 6

1 7   2 7   3 7   4 7   5 7   6 7

1 8   2 8   3 8   4 8   5 8   6 8   7 8

1 9   2 9   3 9   4 9   5 9   6 9   7 9   8 9

1 10   2 10   3 10   4 10   5 10   6 10   7 10   8 10   9 10

Step IV
Count the number of times each option was circled on the grid. Enter the totals in the appropriate spaces below.

1____ 2____ 3____ 4 ____ 5____ 6____ 7____ 8____ 9____ 10

Step V
Recopy the list, beginning with the option circled most often. You have determined this choice to be the best at this time, based on the criterion. The option circled next most often is the second best, and so on. In case of a tie (if two options receive the same number of circles), look back on the grid to see which one you circled when you were comparing the two. This means you prefer one over the other; thus you break the tie. The rank order of options is as follows:

1. _____

2. _____

3. _____

4. _____

5. _____

6. _____

7. _____

8. _____

9. _____

10. _____

Source: Gene Archbold, Northern Kentucky Area Development District, 1976. Revised 1997.

Life is a marathon
Like a marathon, there is a beginning, middle, and end to every life. The secret is to take "pause points" and think about where you have been, where you are now, and where you are going.

In the beginning, *pause to focus and plan your future.* Some people don't, and consequently they languish and drift, or they waste time and energy on false starts during young adulthood. The result of focus and planning is knowing what is important to you, setting goals, and taking action to achieve your dreams.

In the middle years, *pause occasionally to rest and regroup.* This involves reviewing past accomplishments and planning future challenges. Some people don't, so they become fatigued and burned out. The wise midlife traveler is guided by George Santayana's reminder, "Those who cannot remember the past are condemned to repeat its mistakes." The result of pausing to review one's life and plan for the future is renewed energy and a sense of purpose in life.

Toward the end of the race, *pause to celebrate victories, learn from past mistakes, and pass lessons on to future generations.* Some people don't, and as a result they fail to experience the full satisfaction of a completed life.

Søren Kierkegaard wrote, "Life can only be understood backward, but it must be lived forward." At any point in time, we have to take action. The wise person does so after reviewing past events, gathering present facts, and then weighing and deciding on a future course of action.

The following exercise is particularly useful at pause points in life. It helps people clarify what is important by incorporating the reality of death into understanding and living one's life. It can help in the process of managing stress in your own changing world.

@ Application: Life in Perspective[2]

On a blank sheet of paper, write your life expectancy age (see Life Expectancy Quiz in the Introduction, or see Appendix B). Then draw a line and a circle as shown.

Example
Life expectancy of 78.

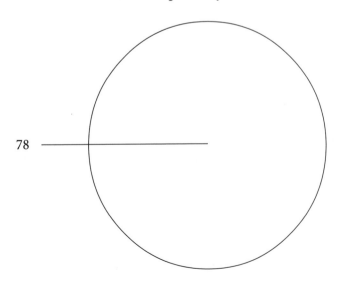

Now indicate your current age on an appropriate point on the circumference of the circle. Draw a line to it and shade in the percentage of the circle that represents the time that you have already lived. The unshaded area represents the time you have remaining.

Example
55-year-old with a life expectancy of 78.

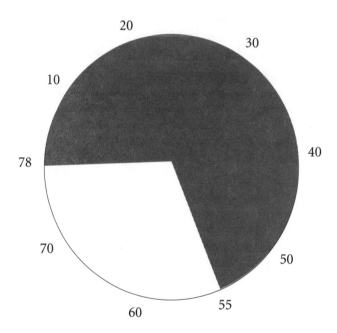

- Who and what are important to you in the days ahead?

- Based on this, what are your goals in life? What do you want to accomplish? What, for you, would be a life well lived?

- If you are currently in your later years, what have you learned that can help your children and future generations? What can you do to make your next years your best?

Personal Thoughts on Stress Across the Life Span

Answer the following questions to personalize the content of Part Three. Space is provided for writing your thoughts.

■ What has been the most difficult adjustment you have had to make in life? What has helped or hindered you in meeting this challenge?

■ What challenge(s) do you face at this point in time? What assets do you have to help you meet the task(s)?

■ What is your ideal future? Imagine what you want to do and with whom you want to be. What are your dreams and goals?

■ What changes in society have had impact on you—social, economic, political, etc.? Do you consider these changes to be favorable or not?

■ If there is one thing you could change about the world or about yourself, what would it be?

■ On a continuum of wellness from *illness* to *zest for life*, where are you now, if 1 is low and 10 is high? What actions should you take?

■ If you were beginning a self-improvement effort at this point in time, where should you start—physical health and fitness, social love and support, personal beliefs and values, occupational satisfaction and success? What actions should you take?

■ Use the paired-comparison technique to analyze alternatives and make a decision.

■ If you were to write your own life story, would it be a novel, a three-act play, an epic poem, or something different? What would be the title? Who are the heroes? Who are the villains? What is the quest, struggle, or defining event that gives meaning to your life?

Chapter Eight References

[1] Judith Green and Robert Shellenberger, *The Dynamics of Health and Wellness: A Biopsychosocial Approach* (Fort Worth: Holt, Rinehart, and Winston, 1991).

[2] Nancy Loving Tubesing and Donald A. Tubesing, eds., *Structured Exercises in Wellness Promotion*, vol. 2. (Duluth, Minn.: Whole Person Associates, 1994), 86, 88.

Part Four

Personal Stress

9. The Peaceful Mind

10. Know Thyself

11. Integrity

I am 78 years old today. At my age, I have found that I have taken in more than one thousand tons of water, food, and air, the chemistry of which has been temporarily employed for different lengths of time as my hair, my skin, my flesh, my bones and my blood, and then discarded. I weighed in when I was born at 7 pounds, and then I went on to 70 and 170—and at one time in my life, 207 pounds. Then I decided to go on a diet and I lost 70 pounds. After I lost it, I said "Bucky, who was that 70 pounds . . . because I am still here!" The 70 pounds I got rid of was ten times the flesh and blood inventory with which I was born in 1895. This loss of 70 pounds of organic chemistry obviously wasn't me, nor were any of the remaining presently associated atoms—ME! We make a great error in identifying you and me as these truly transient and sorely detected chemistries. We are more than that. Each life is an individual and unique pattern of integrity, and what matters in each is the high level of love and spirituality. You see this (body) is a vehicle.—Buckminster Fuller

What you will learn in Part Four

In Part Four you will learn:

- the need for having a purpose in life—something important yet to be done;

- the importance of values in managing stress and coping with change;

- the meaning of integrity or full-swing living.

Chapter Nine
The Peaceful Mind

The search for self

Managing stress and coping with change begins with knowing who you are and what is important to you. Answering these two questions and living your life accordingly results in inner peace and personal strength to overcome life's adversities. When there is inconsistency in one's thoughts, feelings, and actions, the body reacts with *dis-ease.*

The Dutch philosopher Baruch Spinoza wrote, "To be what we are and to become what we are capable of becoming is the ultimate end of life."[1] Psychologist Carl Rogers explains the importance of knowing who you are and becoming a person:

> As I follow the experience of my clients in the therapeutic relationship, it seems to me that each one has the same problem. Below the level of the problem situation about which the individual is complaining—behind the trouble with studies, or wife, or employer, or feelings, lies one central search. It seems to me that, at bottom, each person is asking: "Who am I, really? How can I get in touch with this real self, underlying all of my surface behavior? How can I become myself?" It appears that the goal the individual most wishes to achieve, the end that he knowingly or unknowingly pursues, is to become himself.[2]

More than a century ago, Søren Kierkegaard described this search for self. He emphasized that the most common despair is the unwillingness to be oneself, and that the deepest form of despair is choosing to be other than oneself. He wrote:

> Even the richest personality is nothing before he has chosen himself. On the other hand, even what one might call the poorest personality is everything when he has chosen himself; for the great thing is not to be this or that, but to *be oneself.*[3]

Sometimes people feel lost in life. They feel alone, with lack of direction. In times like these, good advice can be found in the *Official Boy Scout Handbook.*

What to do when you are lost
If you are on a hike and get lost in the woods, the main thing is to be calm. Take it easy. Sit down on a rock or under a tree. Then reason your way out.[4]

The philosopher's pie

An important concept in the search for self and peace of mind is the Philosopher's Pie, showing the central themes or questions of philosophy (see Figure 9.1).

Figure 9.1 Philosopher's Pie

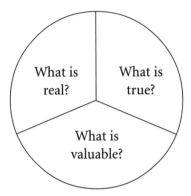

What is real is the concern of the branch of philosophy called metaphysics. It focuses on fundamental beliefs about the origin and nature of the universe, God, and humanity. A person with a theistic or religious orientation might say what is real is God and creation; a person with a nontheistic or secular orientation may say what is real is nature and evolution. Consider how your own view of reality influences you as you live your life and deal with stress.

What is true is the central concern of the branch of philosophy known as epistemology. It focuses on fundamental beliefs about knowledge and truth. The theistic or religious person may believe what is true is the Koran as conveyed to Muhammad; the nontheistic or secular person may believe truth is found in science and is discovered through rational inquiry. Consider your own view about what is true. Is your view based on religious faith or on scientific reason? How does this affect your behavior in stressful times?

Finally, *what is valuable* is the central issue in the branch of philosophy known as axiology. A theistic person may value the Ten Commandments and salvation of the soul; a nontheistic person may have essentially secular values—life, liberty, happiness, truth, beauty, and justice. You can see that the actions of each type of people are guided by different value perspectives. Although people may behave the same way in stressful situations, they may do so for different reasons. Are your own values primarily religious or secular in orientation?

See Figure 9.2 for an expanded picture of the Philosopher's Pie showing both theistic and nontheistic world views. Note that each question in the Philosopher's Pie (what is real, true, and valuable) is influenced by the answer to the other two questions as a general world view evolves.

Figure 9.2 Philospher's Pie: Sample Theistic and Nontheistic World Views

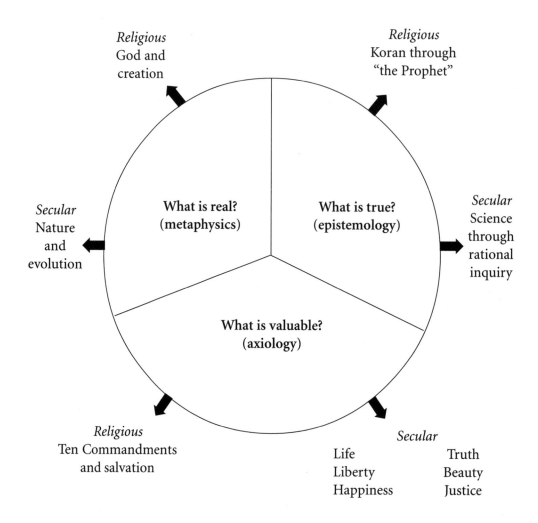

◎ Application: What Is Your World View?

Take time to create your own philosopher's pie. Consider what is real, true, and valuable to you. This process has three requirements:

1. **You should be in the mood.** Being in the mood means you feel doubt, curiosity, confusion, or a desire to know the meaning of life. Most people feel in the mood at key crossroads in their lives—when they leave home, when they choose a career, when they choose a mate, when they experience personal or emotional loss, when they face sickness or death.

2. **You should choose a good setting.** Many people use a sojourn, a journey in body and mind; many use a retreat, a private place. In either case, your mind and space should be free and uncluttered so that in this vacuum answers can form.

3. **You should write your thoughts.** The process of expressing your views with words that reflect your exact meaning results in clearer thinking and clearer personal understanding. Write your responses to the three central questions of philosophy:

   - What is real?

   - What is true?

   - What is valuable to you?

Everyone needs to consider life's basic questions at some point in time. When this is done, it can be an important source of strength in dealing with stress.

Personal sojourn
The fall semester was almost over. As a young philosophy student, I found myself questioning the beliefs of a lifetime when I realized I hadn't actually read the book on which these beliefs were based.

When winter break came, I set out for Israel by way of Greece, Turkey, and the Mediterranean Sea—arriving at Kibbutz Kfar Menachem early in January. During this journey, I read the Bible from beginning to end. The place and the process seemed to fit.

On my last day in Israel at the port city of Haifa, I closed the completed book and thought, *I still feel the same.* Then I looked out the window and saw Mt. Carmel rising over the city. I remembered this to be the place where the prophet Micah was said to have proven that Yahweh was the one true God of all people everywhere.

There were four hours remaining before sunset, so I decided to climb Mt. Carmel *just in case*. When I reached the top, I stood quietly and waited for a sign. I waited with hope. Finally I thought, *OK, fifteen more minutes.*

When the time passed and I walked back down the mountain, my questions had been answered. The answers were not conventional but they served to anchor and guide my life.

By this process and at that time, I experienced the peace of mind that comes when one personally asks, *what is real, what is true,* and *what is valuable*—and then makes a commitment to live his or her life based on the answers.—Author's file notes (G. M.)

The importance of solitude

Occasionally, we must learn to do things, think things, and *become* someone, alone. We must withdraw from the world of others and find new experiences within ourselves. The introverted person does this naturally, but the extrovert too can benefit from time alone. The story, "Solo," on page 212 shows the importance of getting away and answering life's basic questions on a personal level.

People need periods of solitude in which to develop their individual selves. The group around the table in the evening is richer if its members have spent some part of the day by themselves.

Some things can only be experienced alone. A picture is painted personally, and no amount of public approval can capture its full value. And the song of a bird will lack full meaning unless we at some time go alone to hear it.[5]

Everyone needs something important yet to be done

In the search for purpose, people inevitably face the meaning of their own existence. The path their reasoning follows is "How can I know what is the right thing to do unless I know why I am here?" This question, so basic for humankind, is unique among all animal species. This is because human beings are the only animals who try to discover what sort of creatures they are. They are the only beings who consciously wonder, "Who am I, and why am I here?"

> I am a human being, whatever that may be. I speak for all of us who move and think and feel and whom time consumes. I am like a man journeying through a forest, aware of occasional glints of light overhead, with recollections of the long trail I have already traveled, and conscious of wider spaces ahead. I want to see more clearly where I have been and where I am going, and above all, I want to know why I am where I am, and why I am traveling at all.[6]

Aristotle began his *Metaphysics* with the statement, "All men by nature desire to see [understand]." In contrast, the behavior of other animals is determined primarily by the struggle for survival. Lacking the ability to think in abstractions and to reason, they do not face the problem of choosing real from false values, and they have no concern about the moral consequences of their behavior.[7] As social philosopher Erich Fromm states, "Man is the only animal who finds his own existence a problem that he has to solve and from which he cannot escape."[8]

Viktor Frankl, author of *Man's Search for Meaning*, writes that *everyone needs something important yet to be done*. This simple and powerful statement is the foundation for preserving mental health and living a life with no regrets. At every crossroads and in every moment, the wise person asks what is important and then acts accordingly, knowing that what is done or is not done will go down in history, and in this sense be irretrievable.[9]

Having a purpose in life helped Frankl survive the stress of his own death-camp experiences during World War II. He writes that when he was disgusted and overwhelmed:

> I forced my thoughts to turn to another subject. Suddenly I saw myself standing on the platform of a well-lit warm and pleasant lecture room. . . . I was giving a lecture on the psychology of the concentration camp. . . . All that oppressed me at that moment became objective, seen and described from the remote viewpoint of science. By this method I succeeded somehow in rising above the situation, above the sufferings of the moment, and I observed them as if they already had become a part of the past.[10]

On the basis of his experiences in the Nazi camps, Frankl concluded that the need for meaning in one's life is the fundamental motive for human existence.

Frankl's ideas are basic to managing stress and coping with change. He explains that we each need a unifying purpose in our life that transcends the self and extends to other people and ideals. Just as an airplane is most like an airplane when it rises from the runway and flies, so are we most human when we exercise free will, seek meaning in our lives, and commit to a purpose that transcends the self. The more our activities and relationships have meaning, the more alive we feel. There is inner joy, peace of mind, and a sense of being in the right place at the right time.[11]

The search for meaning is common to all people, but what each person finds is unique to that person. One person may define meaning in a social sense—having children and raising a family. Another may define meaning in religious terms—to do one's part in God's divine plan. Still another may view meaning on a personal plane—to know oneself and one's place in the universe. Consider the ideas of English philosopher Bertrand Russell in his short essay:

What I have lived for

Three passions, simple but overwhelmingly strong, have governed my life: the longing for love, the search for knowledge, and unbearable pity for the suffering of mankind. These passions, like great winds, have blown me hither and thither, in a wayward course, over a deep ocean of anguish, reaching to the very verge of despair.

I have sought love, first, because it brings ecstasy— ecstasy so great that I would often have sacrificed all the rest of life for a few hours of this joy. I have sought it, next, because it relieves loneliness—that terrible loneliness in which one in shivering consciousness, looks over the rim of the world into the cold, unfathomable, lifeless abyss. I have sought it, finally, because in the union of love I have seen, in a mystic miniature, the prefiguring vision of the heaven that saints and poets have imagined. This is what I sought, and though it might seem too good for human life, this is what—at last—I have found.

With equal passion I have sought knowledge. I have wished to understand the hearts of men. I have wished to know why the stars shine. . . . A little of this, but not much, I have achieved.

Love and knowledge, so far as they were possible, led upward toward the heavens. But always pity brought me back to earth. Echoes of cries of pain reverberate in my heart. Children in famine, victims of torture by oppressors, helpless old people a hated burden to their sons, and the whole world of loneliness, poverty, and pain make a mockery of what human life should be. I long to alleviate the evil, but I cannot, and I too suffer.

This has been my life. I have found it worth living, and would gladly live it again if the chance were offered me.[12]

Personal responsibility

Increasingly, people as individuals versus people as a group have become the basis of moral judgments and right and wrong conduct. The sentiment that "just because the majority of a group or society judge an act to be right or wrong does not make it so" reflects an orientation toward individual conscience and personal conviction, as opposed to collective thought based on community pressure or self-service reflecting egocentric living.[13]

At this level of development, a person's actions are based on the meaning attached to personal existence, and this meaning is based on self-discovered and self-accepted values.

This is the orientation of German writer Hermann Hesse's young Siddhartha, even after he had heard the teachings of Buddha Gautama:

"Do not be angry with me, O Illustrious One," said the young man. "I have not spoken to you thus to quarrel with you about words. You are right when you say that opinions mean little, but may I say one thing more? I did not doubt you for one moment. Not for one moment did I doubt that you were the Buddha, that you have reached the highest goal that so many thousands of Brahmins and Brahmins' sons are striving to reach.

"You have done so by your own seeking, in your own way, through thought, through meditation, through knowledge, through enlightenment. You have learned nothing through teachings, and so I think, O Illustrious One, that nobody finds salvation through teachings. To nobody, O Illustrious One, can you communicate in words and teachings what happened to you in the hour of your enlightenment.

"The teachings of the enlightened Buddha embrace much, they teach much—how to live righteously, how to avoid evil. But there is one thing that this clear, worthy instruction does not contain; it does not contain the secret of what the Illustrious One himself experienced—he alone among hundreds of thousands.

"That is what I thought and realized when I heard your teachings. That is why I am going on my way—not to seek another and better doctrine, for I know there is none, but to leave all doctrines and all teachers and to reach my goal alone—or die. But I will often remember this day, O Illustrious One, and this hour when my eyes beheld a holy man."[14]

The philosopher Jean-Paul Sartre identifies the central task or *project* of every person's life to be as follows: Be aware of who you are and take personal responsibility for your own existence. He states: "The freedom to choose is the only freedom one does not have the freedom to renounce."[15] This is what Frankl observed and wrote based on his own experiences:

> We who lived in concentration camps can remember the men who walked through the huts comforting others, giving away their last piece of bread. They may have been few in number, but they offer sufficient proof that everything can be taken from a man but one thing: the last of the human freedoms—to choose one's attitude in any given set of circumstances, to choose one's own way.[16]

Two important concepts in stress management, the value of self-awareness and the importance of being responsible for your own life, are the themes of the following poem:

Mirrors

When humans found the mirror
They began to lose their souls.
The point of course is that
They began to concern themselves
With their images,
Rather than their selves.

Other people's eyes are mirrors,
But the most distorting kind;
For if you look to them,
You can only see
Reflections of your reflections;
Your warpings of their warpings.

What then instead?

Do not look at yourself,
Except perhaps with amusement.
Feel yourself instead,
As we did before mirrors
When we were young
And did not feel the need to please,
But only to be.
Experience how it is to be
Now.

Where are your passions and desires?
Your knots and pains and anxious
Unattended muscles?
Where are your laughter and your tears
That are deeper than your throat?

What is what you want?
Who do you love and hate?
How do you reach and push away?
Why do you waste your strength
In self-holding constriction,
Keeping yourself against reaching
And pushing away?

Be
And you will be involved in life;
So involved in life
That you will afford no time
Or inclination
For staring with bulging
Or squinting eyes
At mirrors.[17]

Creating a personal vision

Living a fulfilled life entails having a bold and uplifting dream, not settling for minor accomplishments when major ones are possible. People too often fill their minds and hours with trifling matters and pursue insignificant tasks when fully in their capacity is the accomplishment of something great, something meaningful.

Thomas Carlisle, the Scottish philosopher, believed that people do not fear death. We know we have to die. What we fear is death without meaning. We want to leave our mark and make a difference. This is what is meant by living a big life. A big life begins with a vision.

The proverb "Where there is no vision, the people perish" shows that our very existence depends on a positive and future-focused role image. A personal vision provides direction, generates energy, and creates commitment in your life. Such a vision must be:

1. self-developed—others can't do it;

2. true to one's nature, and thereby false to no other;

3. clear and compelling, neither vague nor boring;

4. important to do, making life worth living;

5. currently needed with opportunity to succeed;

6. multidimensional—written, visible, stated, concrete, and lived; and

7. a full-body experience—created by the mind, accepted in the heart, and acted upon with deeds.

The application Quo Vadis—Where Are You Going? can be used to create a personal vision for your life. After considering the forces and impactors that have shaped your past and evaluating the prouds and sorries that describe your present, you can develop a positive and future-focused vision that gives meaning to your life. Consider the following story and the power of vision.

> I was fourteen years old the night my daddy died. He had holes in his shoes, but two children out of college, one in college, another in divinity school, and a vision he was able to convey to me as he lay dying in an ambulance, that I, a young Black girl, could be and do anything; that race and gender are shadows; and that character, self-discipline, determination, attitude, and service are the substance to life.[18]

⊙ Application: Quo Vadis—Where Are You Going?

Complete the following questions. Do this when you are rested; do it alone. Then share with others who care. Note that "Quo Vadis" means "Where are you going?" It is a Latin phrase that alludes to a New Testament verse (John 13:36): Peter asks Jesus where he is going; Jesus replies, "Where I am going you cannot follow now."

Past—Forces and Impactors
What people and events have helped shape your life?

Significant people
(Indicate as primarily positive or negative influences: + or -)

Critical events
(Indicate as primarily positive or negative influence: + or -)

Top 10 list

Top 10 list

_____

_____

_____

_____

_____

_____

_____

_____

_____

_____

Star or circle the 5 people who have influenced you the most.

Star or circle the 5 events that have influenced you the most.

Present—Prouds and Sorries
What is the current status or condition of your life?

What is going right? (prouds)   What is going wrong? (sorries)

Top 10 list   **Top 10 list**

_____   _____

_____   _____

_____   _____

_____   _____

_____   _____

_____   _____

_____   _____

_____   _____

Star or circle your top 5 prouds (assets, strengths, and uplifters)   Star or circle your top 5 sorries (liabilities, setbacks, and areas for improvement)

Future—The Power of Vision
What positive and future-focused vision gives meaning to your life?

Purpose

What is important, yet to be done?

_____

_____

_____

_____

_____

_____

_____

_____

Goals

What goals must be accomplished to fulfill your purpose?

-
-
-

Values

What core values guide your life—on what basis do you decide what is right and wrong?

-
-
-

Stakeholders

Who cares about your vision and what will it mean to them when you are successful?

- family _____

- friends _____

- others _____

- self _____

Elements of a vision—definition of terms

Purpose (reason for existence). This is a clear, compelling statement of purpose that provides focus and direction for your life. It is your personal answer to the question, "Why do I exist?"

Goals (enduring intentions to act). These are accomplishments that must be attained to support and fulfill your purpose. Goals guide daily behavior and stimulate action.

Values (hills worth dying on). Values are used to measure the rightness and wrongness of all that you do. Sometimes called basic principles, the values you live by define your personal character. Examples include responsibility, love, and freedom.

Stakeholders (the human element). These are the people who will be directly affected by your vision. What will the fulfillment of your vision mean to them?

Strategy to succeed

Consider action steps to fulfill your vision

What is needed to achieve your vision?

-
-
-
-

What should you *continue doing* because it is working well?

-
-
-
-

What should you *start doing* if you are going to be successful?

-
-
-
-

What should you *stop doing* because it harms your vision?

-
-
-
-

How should you *monitor progress?*

-
-
-
-

Action steps, including who should do what by when, are as follows:

_____

_____

_____

_____

_____

_____

Three time-tested tips for making visions come true are *first*, picture the world of your dreams. Imagine what it would be like to live in that world. Read, go to lectures, and talk to people who are in that world. *Second*, seek advice and encouragement from people who believe in you and your dreams, but who are still willing and able to be objective. *Third*, be prepared to go the distance. The difference between people who have dreams and those who achieve them is usually a matter of hard work and dogged persistence. Remember:

A vision without a task is a dream,
A task without a vision is a drudgery,
A vision with a task is the hope of the world.

Church window in Sussex, England, c. 1730

Chapter Nine References

1 Will Forpe and John McCollister, *The Sunshine Book: Expressions of Love, Hope and Inspiration* (Middle Village, N.Y.: Jonathan David Publishers, 1979), 41.

2 Carl Rogers, *On Becoming a Person* (Austin, Tex: University of Texas, Hogg Foundation for Mental Hygiene, 1958), 5-10.

3 Søren Kierkegaard, *Either/Or*, vol. 2 (Princeton, N.J.: Princeton University Press, 1974), 181.

4 William Hillcourt, *Official Boy Scout Handbook*, 9th ed. (1986). Original source: Ernest Thompson Seton and Sir Robert Baden-Powell (New York: Doubleday, Page & Company, 1910).

5 Mary Ellen Chase, "You Become Someone ALONE," *The Yale Review*.

6 Norman John Berrill, *Man's Emerging Mind: Man's Progress Through Time* (New York: Dodd, Mead, 1955).

7 Aristotle, *Metaphysics*, book 1, ch. 1.

8 Eric Fromm, *The Art of Loving* (New York: Bantam Books, 1963).

9 Viktor E. Frankl, *Man's Search for Meaning: An Introduction to Logotherapy* (New York: Simon & Schuster, 1963).

10 Frankl, *Man's Search for Meaning*, 117.

11 "Viktor Frankl and Man's Search for Meaning," *Notable Contributors to the Psychology of Personality Series*. The University of Pennsylvania Audio-Visual Department, 1986.

12 Bertrand Russell, *The Autobiography of Bertrand Russell: 1872–1914* (Boston: Little, Brown, 1967), 3-4.

13 Harold Titus and Morton Keeton, *Ethics for Today*, 5th ed. (New York: Van Nostrand, 1975), 42.

14 Hermann Hesse, *Siddhartha* (New York: Macmillan, 1962).

15 Jean-Paul Sartre, *Being and Nothingness*, trans. Hazel E. Barnes (Secaucus, N.J.: Citadel Press, 1974).

16 Frankl, *Man's Search for Meaning*.

17 S. Herman and N. Korenick, *Authentic Management* (Reading, Mass.: Addison-Wesley, 1977), 72. Copyright ©1977, Addison-Wesley Publishing Company, Inc., Reading, Mass. Reprinted with permission.

18 Marian Wright Edelman, *The Meaning of Our Success: A Letter to My Children and Yours* (Boston: Beacon Press, 1994).

Chapter Ten

Know Thyself

Values and stress

Values are the first line of defense in managing stress. A strong value system is the foundation for taking control of your life. Unless your values are clear, you cannot have a firm sense of direction. Values are the compass, the navigational system, and the beacon of light to guide decision making and give order to your life. Morris Schectman explains in *Working Without a Net*, "We must create value-driven personal and professional lives."[1]

Values are important because they affect everything a person does or is. Before we fully value something, certain criteria must be met. What we value must be freely chosen, personally cherished, publicly affirmed, overtly demonstrated, and worthy of sacrifice. The more you understand your values, the clearer you can be in your ideas about life and the more confident you will be in your actions.

> Religion is a basic value in my life. It focuses and calms me, and gives me strength. Going to church renews my faith and gives me energy to keep going when it would be easier to shut down.—Author's file notes (K. C.)

Personal values

Author Maury Smith describes how our values unfold as our lives unfold.

> We are not born with values, but we are born into cultures and societies that promote, teach, and impart their values to us. The process of acquiring values begins at birth. But it is not a static process. Our values change continually throughout our lives. For example, as children, our highest value might have been play; as adolescents, perhaps it was peer relationships; as young adults, our highest value may be the care of our families and the work we do. For many older people, service to others is the highest value. We are formed largely by the experiences we have, and our values form, grow, and change accordingly.[2]

In a sense, values are the glasses through which we view the world. People are always making decisions based on their personal values.

The foxhole

A sergeant said of a soldier in a foxhole: "Never mind him, as long as we can save the squad."

The lieutenant said of the squad: "Never mind them, as long as we can save the platoon."

The captain said of the platoon: "The platoon doesn't matter, as long as we can save the company."

The colonel said of the company: "Never mind the company, as long as we can save the regiment."

The brigadier was interested only in saving the brigade, while the general wanted only to save the army.

"The army doesn't matter," said the leader of the nation, "as long as we can save the country."

"The country doesn't matter," said the mother of the soldier in the foxhole, "as long as my son comes home safely."[3]

The following questionnaire can be used to understand your values. It is particularly useful at stress points in life and can be helpful in personal counseling, marriage counseling, and career guidance during times of change.

⊙ Application: Personal Values—What is Important to You?

Each of the following questions has six possible responses. Rank these responses by assigning a 6 to the one you prefer the most, a 5 to the next, and so on, to 1, the least preferred of the alternatives. Sometimes you may have trouble making choices, but there should be no ties; you should make a choice.

1. Which of the following branches of study do you consider to be most important?
   _____ a. philosophy
   _____ b. political science
   _____ c. psychology
   _____ d. theology
   _____ e. business
   _____ f. art

2. Which of the following qualities is most descriptive of you?
   _____ a. religious
   _____ b. unselfish
   _____ c. artistic
   _____ d. persuasive
   _____ e. practical
   _____ f. intelligent

3. Of the following famous people, who is most interesting to you?
   _____ a. Albert Einstein—discoverer of the theory of relativity
   _____ b. Henry Ford—automobile entrepreneur
   _____ c. Napoleon Bonaparte—political leader and military strategist
   _____ d. Martin Luther—leader of the Protestant Reformation
   _____ e. Michelangelo—sculptor and painter
   _____ f. Albert Schweitzer—missionary and humanitarian

4. What kind of person do you prefer to be? One who:
   _____ a. is industrious and economically self-sufficient
   _____ b. has leadership qualities and organizing ability
   _____ c. has spiritual or religious values
   _____ d. is philosophical and interested in knowledge
   _____ e. is compassionate and understanding toward others
   _____ f. has artistic sensitivity and skill

5. Which of the following is most interesting to you?
   _____ a. artistic experiences
   _____ b. thinking about life
   _____ c. accumulation of wealth
   _____ d. religious faith
   _____ e. leading others
   _____ f. helping others

6. In which of the following would you prefer to participate?
   _____ a. business venture
   _____ b. artistic performance
   _____ c. religious activity
   _____ d. project to help the poor
   _____ e. scientific study
   _____ f. political campaign

7. Which publication would you prefer to read?
   _____ a. *History of the Arts*
   _____ b. *Psychology Today*
   _____ c. *Power Politics*
   _____ d. *Scientific American*
   _____ e. *Religions Today*
   _____ f. *Wall Street Journal*

8. In choosing a spouse, who would you prefer? One who:
   _____ a. likes to help people
   _____ b. is a leader in his or her field
   _____ c. is practical and enterprising
   _____ d. is artistically gifted
   _____ e. has a deep spiritual belief
   _____ f. is interested in philosophy and learning

9. Which activity do you consider to be more important for children?
   _____ a. scouting
   _____ b. junior achievement
   _____ c. religious training
   _____ d. creative arts
   _____ e. student government
   _____ f. science club

10. What should be the goal of government leaders?
    _____ a. promoting creative and aesthetic interests
    _____ b. establishing a position of power and respect in the world
    _____ c. developing commerce and industry
    _____ d. supporting education and learning
    _____ e. providing a supportive climate for spiritual growth and development
    _____ f. promoting the social welfare of citizens

11. Which of the following courses would you prefer to teach?
    _____ a. anthropology
    _____ b. religions of the world
    _____ c. philosophy
    _____ d. political science
    _____ e. poetry
    _____ f. business administration

12. What would you do if you had sufficient time and money?
    _____ a. go on a retreat for spiritual renewal
    _____ b. increase your money-making ability
    _____ c. develop leadership skills
    _____ d. help those who are disadvantaged
    _____ e. study the fine arts such as theater, music, and painting
    _____ f. write an original essay, article, or book

13. Which courses would you promote if you were able to influence educational policies?
    _____ a. political and governmental studies
    _____ b. philosophy and science
    _____ c. economics and occupational skills
    _____ d. social problems and issues
    _____ e. spiritual and religious studies
    _____ f. music and art

14. Which of the following news items would be most interesting to you?
    _____ a. "Business Conditions Favorable"
    _____ b. "Relief Arrives for Poor"
    _____ c. "Religious Leaders Meet"
    _____ d. "President Addresses the Nation"
    _____ e. "What's New in the Arts"
    _____ f. "Scientific Breakthrough Revealed"

15. Which subject would you prefer to discuss?
    _____ a. music, film, and theater
    _____ b. the meaning of human existence
    _____ c. spiritual experiences
    _____ d. wars in history
    _____ e. business opportunities
    _____ f. social conditions

16. What do you think the purpose should be for space exploration?
    _____   a. to unify people around the world
    _____   b. to gain knowledge of our universe
    _____   c. to reveal the beauty of our world
    _____   d. to discover answers to spiritual questions
    _____   e. to control world affairs
    _____   f. to develop trade and business opportunities

17. Which profession would you enter if all salaries were equal and you felt you had equal aptitude to succeed in any one of the six?
    _____   a. counseling
    _____   b. fine arts
    _____   c. science
    _____   d. politics
    _____   e. business
    _____   f. ministry

18. Whose life and works are most interesting to you?
    _____   a. Madame Curie—discoverer of radium
    _____   b. Gloria Vanderbilt—business woman
    _____   c. Elizabeth I—British monarch
    _____   d. Mother Teresa—religious leader
    _____   e. Martha Graham—ballerina and choreographer
    _____   f. Harriet Beecher Stowe—author of *Uncle Tom's Cabin*

19. Which television program would you prefer to watch?
    _____   a. "Art Appreciation"
    _____   b. "Spiritual Values"
    _____   c. "Investment Opportunities"
    _____   d. "Marriage and the Family"
    _____   e. "Political Power and Social Persuasion"
    _____   f. "The Origins of Intelligence"

20. Which of the following positions would you like to have?
    _____   a. political leader
    _____   b. artist
    _____   c. teacher
    _____   d. theologian
    _____   e. writer
    _____   f. business entrepreneur

Source: Jim McCue and Marianne Bailey, Northern Kentucky University, 1979–1983 (rev. 1997); based on Gordon Allport, Phillip E. Vernon, and Gardner Lindzey, The Study of Values: Grade 10–Adult, *3d ed. (New York: Houghton Mifflin, 1970).*

Scoring

Step 1

For each question, insert your score in the appropriate space in Figure 10.1. Note that the letters are not always in the same column.

Example: a <u>2</u>   b <u>6</u>   c <u>4</u>   d <u>5</u>   e <u>3</u>   f <u>1</u>

Figure 10.1 Scoring

Question	I	II	III	IV	V	VI
1.	a___	e___	f___	c___	b___	d___
2.	f___	e___	c___	b___	d___	a___
3.	a___	b___	e___	f___	c___	d___
4.	d___	a___	f___	e___	b___	c___
5.	b___	c___	a___	f___	e___	d___
6.	e___	a___	b___	d___	f___	c___
7.	d___	f___	a___	b___	c___	e___
8.	f___	c___	d___	a___	b___	e___
9.	f___	b___	d___	a___	e___	c___
10.	d___	c___	a___	f___	b___	e___
11.	c___	f___	e___	a___	d___	b___
12.	f___	b___	e___	d___	c___	a___
13.	b___	c___	f___	a___	a___	e___
14.	f___	a___	e___	b___	d___	c___
15.	b___	e___	a___	f___	d___	c___
16.	b___	f___	c___	a___	e___	d___
17.	c___	e___	b___	a___	d___	f___
18.	a___	b___	e___	f___	c___	d___
19.	f___	c___	a___	d___	e___	b___
20.	e___	f___	b___	c___	a___	d___

Totals   _____   _____   _____   _____   _____   _____

Step 2
Total the six columns.

Step 3
Place the total for each personal value in the appropriate place in Figure 10.2. Connect the scores with a straight line to form a profile of your overall value orientation. See the example in Figure 10.3.

Figure 10.2 Your Personal Value Orientation

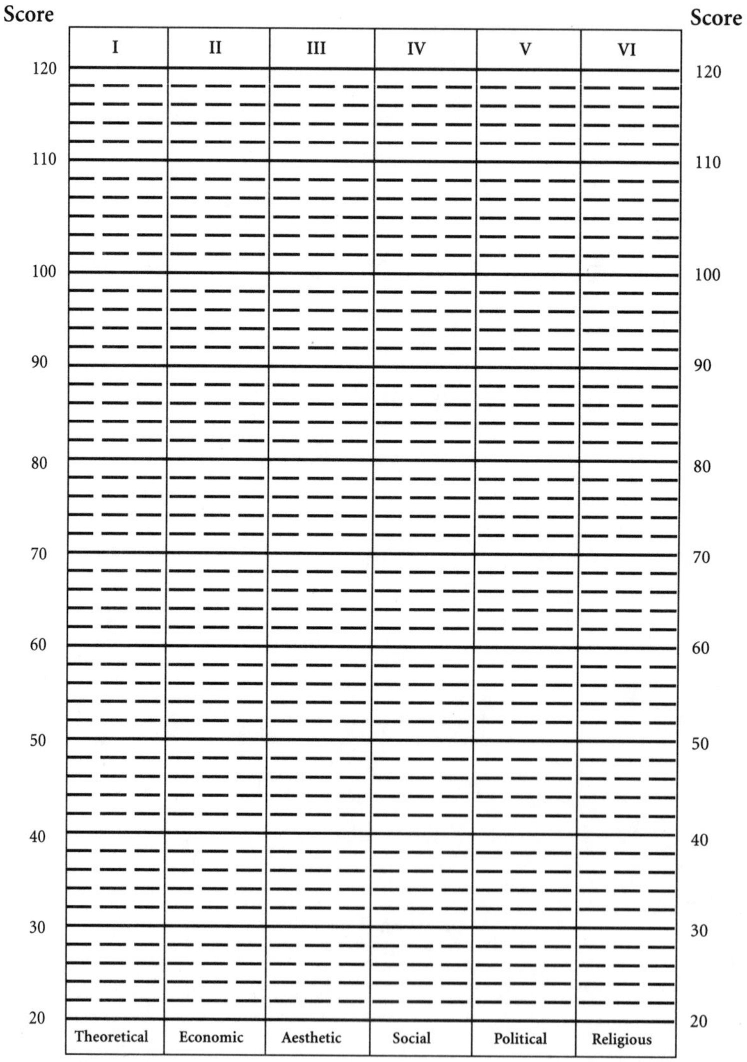

Figure 10.3 Example: Personal Value Orientation

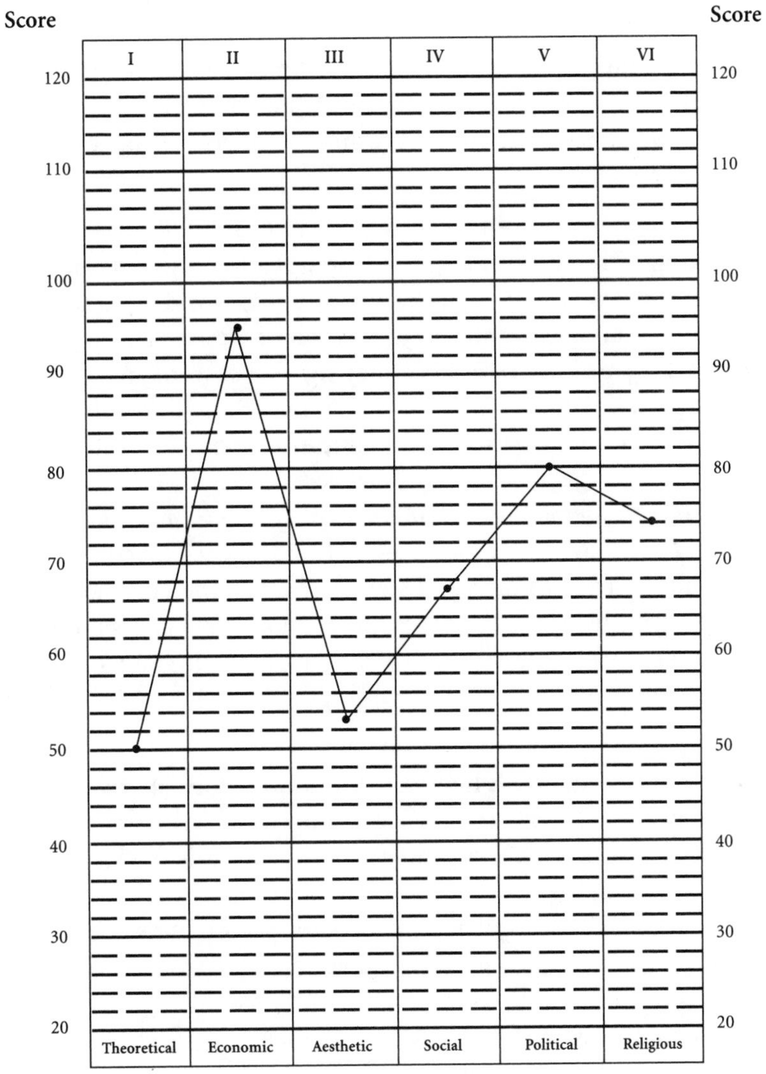
Score
Score
I
II
III
IV
V
VI
120
110
100
90
80
70
60
50
40
30
20
Theoretical
Economic
Aesthetic
Social
Political
Religious

Interpretation

A description of each personal value is as follows:

Theoretical

The primary interest of the theoretical person is the discovery of truth. In the lab, field, and library, and in personal affairs, the purpose of the theoretical person is to know the truth above all other goals. In the pursuit of truth, the theoretical person prefers a cognitive approach, one that looks for identities and differences, as opposed to the beauty or utility of objects. This person's needs are to observe, reason, and understand. Because the theoretical person's values are empirical, critical, and rational, this person is an intellectual and frequently is a scientist or philosopher. Major concerns of such a person are to order and systematize knowledge and to understand the meaning of life.

Economic

The economic person is interested in what is useful. Based originally on the satisfaction of bodily needs and self-preservation, the interest in usefulness extends to the practical affairs of the business world—the production and marketing of goods, and the accumulation of wealth. This type of person is enterprising and efficient, reflecting the stereotype of the average businessperson. Economic values sometimes come into conflict with other values. The economic person wants education to be practical and regards un-applied knowledge as wasteful. Great feats of engineering and application result from the demands economic people make on people in science. Economic values may conflict with aesthetic values, such as in the advertising and promotion of products and services, except when art meets commercial ends. In relationships with people, the economic person is more likely to be interested in surpassing others in wealth than in dominating them politically or in serving them socially.

Aesthetic

The aesthetic person finds highest satisfaction in form, harmony, and beauty. The value of each single experience is judged from the standpoint of grace, symmetry, and fitness. The aesthetic person regards life as a procession of events, with each impression to be enjoyed for its own sake. An aesthetic person may not be a creative artist; the aesthetic person finds chief interest in the artistic episodes of life. Unlike the theoretical person, the aesthetic person usually chooses, with the poet John Keats, to consider truth as equivalent to beauty, or agrees with H. L. Mencken, "To make a thing charming is a million times more important than to make it true." In the economic sphere, the aesthetic often sees the process of manufacturing, advertising, and trade as a destruction of important aesthetic values. In social affairs, the aesthetic may be said to be interested in people, but not necessarily in their welfare. The aesthetic person tends toward individualism, self-sufficiency, and idealism in personal relations.

Social

The highest value for this type of person is love. The altruistic or philanthropic aspect of love is the interest of the social person. Humanistic by nature, the social person prizes other people as ends in and of themselves, and not as tools or means to other goals. Therefore, the social person is kind, sympathetic, and helpful toward others. Such a person may find the economic and political values to be cold and inhuman. In contrast to the political type, the social person regards love instead of power as the most suitable form of human relationship. In purest form, social values are totally unselfish.

Political
The political person is interested in power and influence, although the person's activities may not fall within the narrow field of politics. Whatever the vocation, the political person seeks to be a "Machtmensch," an individual who is powerful. Leaders in any field usually will have a high interest in power and status. Because competition and struggle play a large part in all of life—between the sexes, between groups, between nations, and between individuals—many philosophers have viewed power as the most universal and most fundamental of human motives. In certain people, however, the desire for direct expression of power is uppermost, and their primary values are social influence and the exercise of authority.

Religious
The highest value of this type of person is spiritual peace. A religious person may or may not belong to an organized religion; people are religious if they but seek to comprehend the cosmos as a whole and to relate themselves to its embracing totality. Religious people have as their goal the creation of the highest and most satisfying value experience. Some people who are religious focus on events, people, and experiences in this world; that is, they experience meaning in the affirmation of life and active participation therein. With zest and enthusiasm, they see something divine in every event. On the other hand, some religious people are transcendental mystics, seeking to unite themselves with a higher reality by withdrawing from life. This type is ascetic and, like the holy men of India, finds inner peace and unity through self-denial and meditation. In many individuals, the affirmation and negation of human existence alternate to yield the greatest value satisfaction.

In evaluating your personal values, you should remember the following points:

- All six values on the questionnaire are positive. The questions do not measure negative values, such as greed or violence.

- Culture influences personal values. Through the processes of bonding, imprinting, modeling, and socialization, people learn to place higher importance on some values over others. Thus, the prestige afforded the monarch, priest, businessperson, scientist, artist, and teacher depends on the values promoted by each society. In the Pygmy culture, for example, the male with the greatest social esteem usually is not the strongest, wealthiest, most spiritual, most artistic, or most intelligent; rather, he is the one who shares most generously. Consider American society: What are the primary values for people in the United States today? Are they the same for men and women? Do they reflect your personal values?

- By forcing choices among six personal values, the questionnaire gives an overall value orientation. This means that your lowest personal value may be more important to you than the highest personal value of another individual. Similarly, your highest may be less important to you than the lowest of another individual. The questionnaire measures the relative strength of six personal values, so that you obtain a picture of *your* overall value orientation, or an understanding of what is most important to you.

- Ideally, a person's life will allow maximum expression of personal values. This helps explain the achievement and satisfaction of "theoretical" Albert Einstein, "economic" John D. Rockefeller, "aesthetic" Leonardo da Vinci, "social" Jane Addams, "political" Elizabeth I, and "religious" Martin Luther.

Basic value systems are fairly firm by the time most people reach adulthood. Ideas about what is right and wrong and good and bad are well established and are unlikely to change unless a *significant emotional event* takes place, an experience so emotional and so dramatic that it changes one's life.[4]

For most people, few experiences are significant or emotional enough to disrupt basic values formed during childhood and adolescence. Typically, values and beliefs solidify sometime during the twenties, and when you are thirty, fifty, seventy, and ninety years of age, you will be doing what you do largely because of the forces and events that occurred during your youth. As a rule, if a person changes basic values during the adult years, it is only because a situation is experienced that previous values cannot resolve.

Think of your own life and consider: Have you ever had a significant emotional experience that has changed your values? It may have been a brush with death or a loss of someone or something important to you; it may have been a book you read or a film you saw; it may have been a person you met or an adventure you had. Any of these experiences can have an effect on you that is so significant and so emotional that it will change your value system.

Different work and social organizations reflect different values, and each organization's success depends on having people in it, especially leaders, who promote its value system. Some people may be ideally suited for *theoretical* organizations such as universities, *economic* organizations such as corporations, *aesthetic* organizations such as performing groups, *social* organizations such as human service agencies, *political* organizations such as political parties, or *religious* organizations such as churches, synagogues, and mosques.

Mismatches can be stressful for the individual and the organization. Examples include the social person who gives away the store, the individual who uses religious position for personal power, and the art curator whose priority is profit. Consider your own values. What type of organization, if any, would be most appropriate for you?

Values conflict can be an important cause of stress, both on the job and in the home. Consider how similarities and differences in values affect your relations with others. Consider whether each person honors and allows the full expression of the values that are important to the other and how points of agreement as well as differences can be used to benefit all parties. Remember, the Personal Values questionnaire does not measure other important factors, such as interpersonal sensitivity, personal interests, and individual temperament, nor does it measure levels of morality, a critical element in human relationships. Finally, remember that different values can actually enrich a relationship. In this spirit, use the following thought as a guide: "Our errors and our controversies in the sphere of human relations often arise from looking on people as though they could be altogether bad, or altogether good."[5]

Motivation, growth, and the power of goals

The word *motivation* comes from the Latin term meaning "to move." Ancient scholars were fascinated by the fact that some objects in the world seem to be *self-movers*, while other objects remain stationary unless *acted upon* by some outside force. They assumed that self-initiated proactive motion was caused by a *spirit* inside the object—a "little man" of some kind—that pushed or impelled the object into action. Whenever the "spirit was moved," so was the object or body that the spirit inhabited.[6]

The motivation to grow and achieve one's full potential is an important subject in stress and change. Psychologist Gordon Lippitt has identified six points to remember about the positive stress of personal growth:[7]

1. Growth is improvement in attitudes and behaviors that are related to self-concept.

2. Growth is not always possible in all areas of life. Heredity or strong environmental forces may prevent even desirable changes.

3. Negative attitudes and opinions may discourage growth because they reduce receptiveness to alternative ways of thinking and acting.

4. Defensive behavior may interfere with growth by distorting reality.

5. Growth is accelerated by openness, curiosity, eagerness to learn, and lack of fear.

6. Generally, we have more ability and potential for personal and interpersonal growth than we realize.

To be motivated and grow, we should begin with the end in mind. This is where goals are helpful. They focus and energize behavior. While values define what is important, goals move us to act and make progress. Without goals, daily activities seem meaningless and decision making is difficult. Happiness comes to those who have goals and pursue their dreams.[8]

The psychologist William Menninger wrote, for the best mental health and emotional balance, the individual needs a course or goal in life that is constructive and so big that his faculties are challenged and he has to keep working on it.[9]

What do goals do for us?

- They help us persevere despite discomfort and criticism.

- They help us live our lives in line with our values.

- They help us accomplish our purpose and provide a sense of a life worth living.

Goals can come in three varieties: (1) what you want to *be*—what qualities you want to develop; (2) what you want to *do*—what experiences you want to have or contributions you want to make; (3) what you want to *have*—what tangible and intangible possessions you want.[10]

To personalize the subject of goals, consider what you enjoy doing, what you don't like to do, and what you wish you could do. Then, write your goals down. Goals can be long-term—to graduate, get married, and have a family; and they can be short-term—to pass an exam, lose weight, or buy a car. When setting goals, be as specific as possible so you can actually picture yourself attaining them.

Prioritize your goals based on your value system. Trouble here is a major source of stress. While it is natural to have more than one goal at any given time, having too many goals, or conflicting goals, is certain to lead to pressure and frustration. Be selective and keep your goals in perspective. Remember the adage, put first things first.

The following is a goal-setting exercise that can help focus and energize your life.

⊘ Application: How Will You Spend Your Life?

The areas of life that concern most people are family and friends; work and career; personal development (mental, physical, and spiritual); civic and community; and economic well-being.

What would you like to accomplish in each area? Think both long-range and short-term. Write the goals you would like to achieve in each box. Write rapidly; don't evaluate; don't think about whether or not you can accomplish the goals. If you think of something you would like to do, write it down.

I. Family and Friends

Long-range goals   Short-term goals

1. _____   1. _____

2. _____   2. _____

3. _____   3. _____

II. Work and Career

Long-range goals   Short-term goals

1. _____   1. _____

2. _____   2. _____

3. _____   3. _____

III. Personal Development (Mental, Physical, and Spiritual)

Long-range goals   Short-term goals

1. _____   1. _____

2. _____   2. _____

3. _____   3. _____

IV. Civic and Community

Long-range goals   Short-term goals

1. _____   1. _____

2. _____   2. _____

3. _____   3. _____

V. Economic Well-Being

Long-range goals	Short-term goals
1. _____	1. _____
_____	_____
2. _____	2. _____
_____	_____
3. _____	3. _____
_____	_____

After you have listed your goals, review them, based on your values and priorities in life. Some goals may be more important than others. Rate each goal using a 1, 2, 3 method: number 1's are most important, then number 2's, and then number 3's.

Rank all of your 1's in order of importance, and assign a due date for accomplishing them using Figure 10.4.

Figure 10.4 Prioritized Goals

	Most Important Goals	Target Dates
1		
2		
3		
4		
5		

Allocate time and resources to your most important goals first. At least once a year, repeat this exercise. Your birthday or New Year's Day is an excellent time to think about who you are, what is important, and where you are going.

A goal without action is insufficient, even when it is based on one's values. A helpful bridge to turn words into deeds is the goal-action strategy in Figure 10.5.[11]

Figure 10.5 Goal-Action Strategy

Choose a goal in your life and develop an action strategy.
My goal is: (Write in a single sentence what you intend to accomplish.)

Benefit/cost analysis: (What are the postives and negatives of accomplishing this goal?)

Personal, social, and economic benefits (+'s)	Personal, social, and economic costs (-'s)
a.	a.
b.	b.
c.	c.

Action strategy: (What steps should be taken to accomplish this goal?)

1.   Due Date:

2.   Due Date:

3.   Due Date:

4.   Due Date:

5.   Due Date:

6.   Due Date:

7.   Due Date:

8.   Due Date:

9.   Due Date:

10.   Due Date:

Source: Naomi Miller, Northern Kentucky University, 1982. Based on David A. Kolb, Irwin M. Rubin, and James M. McIntyre, Organizational Psychology, *3rd ed. (Englewood Cliffs, N.J.: Prentice-Hall, Inc., 1979), 423-67.*

Chapter Ten References

1   Morris Shectman, *Working Without a Net: How to Survive in Today's High Risk Business World* (New York: Prentice-Hall, 1994).

2   Maury Smith, *A Practical Guide to Value Clarification* (La Jolla, Calif.: University Associates, 1977).

3   Alfred Polgar, in Will Forpe and John McCollister, *The Sunshine Book: Expressions of Love, Hope and Inspiration* (Middle Village, N.Y.: Jonathan David Publishers, 1979), 57.

4   Morris Massey, *The People Puzzle: Understanding Yourself and Others* (Reston, Va.: Reston Publishing, 1979).

5   S. G. Stevens, trans., *The Reflections and Maxims of Vauvenargues* (London: Humphrey Milford, 1940).

6   J. A. Simpson and E. S. C. Weiner, eds., *The Oxford English Dictionary*, 2nd ed, vol. 9 (Oxford: Clarendon Press, 1989), 1131.

7   Gordon Lippitt, *Implementing Organizational Change* (San Francisco: Jossey-Bass, 1985).

8   Donald A. Tubesing, *Kicking Your Stress Habit: A Do-It-Yourself Guide for Coping with Stress* (Duluth, Minn.: Whole Person Associates, 1981).

9   William Menninger, *The Problem of Our Age* (Philadelphia: National Mental Health Foundation, 1948).

10   Stephen R. Covey, *The Seven Habits of Highly Effective People* (New York: Simon & Schuster, 1989).

11   Richard Leider, *Life Skills: Taking Charge of Your Personal and Professional Growth* (San Diego: Pfeiffer, 1994).

Chapter Eleven

Integrity

Full-swing living

In its highest form, character is based on a value system that is known, cherished, stated, lived, and lived habitually. These are the layers of character development, the highest being integrity. Integrity is a key concept in managing personal stress. Boris Pasternak, author of *Doctor Zhivago*, explains:

> Your health is bound to be affected if day after day you say the opposite of what you feel, or do the opposite of what you say.[1]

The idea of full-swing living can be used to understand integrity. Think for a moment about the game of baseball, in which a full swing is needed to hit a home run. An arrested swing will result in less success—a triple, double, single, or a foul ball. The same is true in life; a home run, or integrity, results only when one completes a full swing and does not suffer axiological, or values, arrest.[2]

A full swing comprises five points, beginning through completion:

- Point 1 is to *know* one's values.

- Point 2 is to *cherish* one's values.

- Point 3 is to *declare* one's values.

- Point 4 is to *act* on one's values.

- Point 5 is to *act habitually* on one's values.

Arrested development occurs if a person fails to complete all five points on the integrity swing. Consider the case of Bill, Donna, Phil, Karen, and David, each facing a personal or professional dilemma.

- Bill knows what he values but has not examined other alternatives. His is an unthinking stance with little or no personal commitment. *He hits a foul.*

- Donna knows what she values and cherishes this personally. She experiences self-satisfaction with her value system. *She hits a single.*

- Phil knows what he values, cherishes this personally, and declares his values. He publicly states his value system. *He hits a double.*

- Karen knows what she values, cherishes this personally, declares this publicly, and acts on her values. She takes action and accepts the consequences. *Karen hits a triple.*

- David knows what he values, cherishes this personally, declares this publicly, acts upon his values, and does this habitually. David exhibits full-swing living with no axiological arrest and *hits a home run.*

See Figure 11.1 for a picture description of full-swing living. Note that there is an invisible but real line separating Bill, Donna, and Phil, from Karen and David. This is a line of integrity that makes Karen and David worthy of special respect. We may love Bill, Donna, and Phil—they may even be family members—but we give special respect to those individuals who demonstrate courage of conviction and live their lives based on their value system.

Figure 11.1 Full-Swing Living

Personal or Professional Dilemma

Points on the Swing	Bill	Donna	Phil	Karen	David
Knows values	✓	✓	✓	✓	✓
Cherishes values		✓	✓	✓	✓
Declares values			✓	✓	✓
Acts on values				✓	✓
Acts habitually on value system					✓

Each person experiences arrested development at some point on the integrity swing, except David, who shows maximum strength of conviction and personal character.

The importance of courage

Integrity, or full character development, includes both knowledge and courage. One without the other is insufficient, as Rebecca McCann's poem "Inconsistency" implies:

> I'm sure I have a noble mind,
> And honesty and tact;
> And no one's more surprised than I,
> To see the way I act![3]

It is a difficult challenge to live life full swing in accord with your value system. There are many temptations, and it can involve personal risk. To do so requires courage. In *Love and Will*, Rollo May writes:

> Courage is not a virtue or value among other personal values like love or fidelity. It is the foundation that underlies and gives reality to all other virtues and personal values. Without courage our love pales into mere dependency. Without courage our fidelity becomes conformism.

> The word courage comes from the same stem as the French word *coeur*, meaning "heart." Thus just as one's heart, by pumping blood to one's arms, legs, and brain enables all the other physical organs to function, so does courage make possible all the psychological virtues. Without courage, other values wither away into mere facsimiles of virtue.

> An assertion of the self, a commitment, is essential if the self is to have any reality. This is the distinction between human beings and the rest of nature. The acorn becomes an oak tree by means of automatic growth; no courage is necessary. The kitten similarly becomes a cat on the basis of instinct. Nature and being are identical in creatures like them. But a man or woman becomes fully human only by his or her choices and his or her commitment to them. People attain worth and dignity by the multitude of decisions they make from day to day. These decisions require courage.[4]

As people grow in awareness and establish individual identities, commitments are made to important values. With commitment comes inner strength to "choose one's self." This strange-sounding phrase of Kierkegaard's means to be responsible for oneself and one's own existence. Choosing one's self is the opposite of blind momentum or routine; it is an attitude of decisiveness, meaning one accepts personal responsibility for one's own conduct and choices. This is the essential element of character formation.[5]

Nietzsche wrote that character is not given to us by nature, but is given or assigned as a task that we ourselves must solve.[6] This is supported by Paul Tillich's belief that courage opens the way to being: If we do not have the courage to form and be true to our own character, we lose our very being.[7] Jean-Paul Sartre contended that human beings, in final analysis, are creatures of their own choices. In this way, each person defines and determines his or her own existence.[8]

To personalize the subjects of identity, values, and strength of character, evaluate your own values—honesty, responsibility, love, freedom, and so forth. Consider a dilemma in which your values play a part. Ask yourself, are you living life *full swing?* Do you demonstrate personal integrity and strength of character? See Figure 11.2.

Figure 11.2 Personal Integrity—Strength of Character

Sample dilemma: How much to charge; how much to pay; what to do about safety; what to do about discrimination—sex, race, religion.

Points on the swing	Check (✓) if appropriate
Do you *know* what you value?	_____
Do you *cherish* your values privately?	_____
Do you *declare* your values publicly?	_____
Do you *act* on your values and accept the consequences?	_____
Do you *act habitually* on your values and accept the conseequences?	_____

Qualities of the fully functioning person

Along with knowledge and courage, there are additional qualities of the fully functioning person. These are detailed by Abraham Maslow in the body of his writings, especially the classic *Toward a Psychology of Being*.[9]

In studying the characteristics of the healthy personality, Maslow identified people he believed were living or had lived rich, fulfilled lives. Included were Albert Einstein, Eleanor Roosevelt, Ludwig van Beethoven, and Albert Schweitzer. Maslow found that these people shared fifteen characteristics:

1. **Acceptance of self and others.** Self-fulfilled people accept themselves and others as they are. They place a high value on every person as a unique individual and accept individual differences as normal and even desirable.

2. **Accurate perception of reality.** Self-fulfilled people have the ability to see events and conditions as they actually are, without denying painful or unpleasant information. Their assessments and judgments are realistic.

3. **Intimacy.** Self-fulfilled people are able to have close, intimate friendships in which they reveal themselves fully. They are easily able to express and receive affection.

4. **Personal autonomy.** Self-fulfilled people are self-sufficient, with the strength to stand alone when necessary. They will stick by their personal convictions, even when others disagree. This strength helps them to survive crises and losses.

5. **Goal-directedness.** Self-fulfilled people have a sense of purpose in life. They make decisions based on life goals, even if this means temporary sacrifice and frustration.

6. **Spontaneity.** Self-fulfilled people are spontaneous and natural. They respond to life in an effortless way and are not bound by social convention.

The nine remaining characteristics of the fully functioning person are as follows: a need for privacy; an appreciation for new experiences; a sense of unity with nature; a sense of brotherhood with all people; the ability to relate to others without consideration of race, religion, or creed; distinct ideas of what is right and wrong; a sense of humor; creativity; and the ability to resist cultural influences that run counter to personal principles.[10]

In summary, Maslow writes about the self-fulfilled person:

> I have found none of my subjects to be chronically unsure about the difference between right and wrong in his actual living. Whether or not they could verbalize the matter, they rarely showed in their day-to-day living the chaos, confusion, inconsistency, or conflict that are so common in the average person's ethical dealings. Further, the self-fulfilled person practically never allows convention to hamper him or inhibit him from doing anything that he considers very important or basic.[11]

To evaluate your development as a fully functioning person, complete the following questionnaire.

⊚ Application: Characteristics of the Fully Functioning Person

Rate yourself on the following characteristics. Circle the number that best represents your current status (1 is low; 10 is high).

Acceptance of self and others
| 1 | 2 | 3 | 4 | 5 | 6 | 7 | 8 | 9 | 10 |

Accurate perception of reality
| 1 | 2 | 3 | 4 | 5 | 6 | 7 | 8 | 9 | 10 |

Close relationships
| 1 | 2 | 3 | 4 | 5 | 6 | 7 | 8 | 9 | 10 |

Personal autonomy (independence)
| 1 | 2 | 3 | 4 | 5 | 6 | 7 | 8 | 9 | 10 |

Goal-directedness; achievement orientation
| 1 | 2 | 3 | 4 | 5 | 6 | 7 | 8 | 9 | 10 |

Naturalness (spontaneity)
| 1 | 2 | 3 | 4 | 5 | 6 | 7 | 8 | 9 | 10 |

Need for privacy
| 1 | 2 | 3 | 4 | 5 | 6 | 7 | 8 | 9 | 10 |

Orientation toward growth and new experience
| 1 | 2 | 3 | 4 | 5 | 6 | 7 | 8 | 9 | 10 |

Sense of unity with nature
| 1 | 2 | 3 | 4 | 5 | 6 | 7 | 8 | 9 | 10 |

Sense of brotherhood with all people
| 1 | 2 | 3 | 4 | 5 | 6 | 7 | 8 | 9 | 10 |

Democratic character
| 1 | 2 | 3 | 4 | 5 | 6 | 7 | 8 | 9 | 10 |

Sense of justice
| 1 | 2 | 3 | 4 | 5 | 6 | 7 | 8 | 9 | 10 |

Sense of humor

1   2   3   4   5   6   7   8   9   10

Creativity

1   2   3   4   5   6   7   8   9   10

Personal integrity (high principles)

1   2   3   4   5   6   7   8   9   10

Scoring and interpretation

How did you do on the Characteristics of a Fully Functioning Person questionnaire? Add the numbers you circled to find your total, then compare it with the following scale:

If your score is:	Your progress is:
15–45	Not great—much work is needed
46–120	Just OK—some work is needed
121–150	Very good—characteristic of the fully functioning person

Character development

The books of Stephen Covey, author and educator, have had tremendous influence on American audiences in recent years, especially *The Seven Habits of Highly Effective People,* published in 1989.[12] This well-written and instructive book can help focus and energize the reader in the area of principles for living, so important for managing stress and coping with change.

In a 1976 research project, Covey reviewed the success literature of the United States. He found that the first 150 years focused almost exclusively on character, meaning such subjects as loyalty, hard work, persistence, kindness, honesty, and courage. Character was understood as having principles that you adhere to even when it is difficult.

Then, a marked shift occurred during the next 50 years, away from character and toward technique. Skill mastery, including everything from time management to effective speaking to remembering names, was seen as the key to success. Although useful tools, these skills rarely addressed the important questions of philosophy—what is real, what is true, and what is good? Nor did the literature concentrate on the key concerns of ethics—personal values and levels of morality.

This shift was analogous to another period in history, when the ancient Greeks began to focus less on the concepts of virtue and reason characteristic of the Golden Age of Pericles (c. 495–429 B.C.), and more on the Sophist skills of argument and manipulation that Socrates criticized when he committed suicide in 399 B.C. The term "Sophist" came from the Greek words for "expert" and "clever."

The decline of Greek culture can be a lesson for other cultures: skill, yes; but for what good purpose, by what good means, and with what good result? These are the questions that are basic to character development for both the individual and society.

Covey concluded that efforts to develop social skills and techniques are neither good nor bad in theory. The main factor is whether they are firmly rooted in a character base. If not, people will become effective only at manipulating others. The premise is that, in the course of human development, some things must come before others. Just as we must walk before we run and shouldn't get the cart before the horse, each person should strive to develop seven important habits that are basic ingredients for character development.

Habit 1: Be proactive.

Take personal responsibility for your life. Be a driver, not a drifter. View yourself as the master of your own destiny.

Habit 2: Begin with the end in mind.

Everything is created twice—first in the mind, then in the deed. Beginning with the end in mind means having a clear picture of what you want to accomplish before you act.

Habit 3: Put first things first.

To gain control of your time and your life, prioritize your activities in line with your value system. Then work on first things first.

Habit 4: Think win-win.

Helping another person can help both parties succeed. Thinking win-win can be traced to caring about others and treating others as one would like to be treated, two basic pillars of human development.

Habit 5: Seek first to understand, then to be understood.

This principle shows humility, which is an endearing human quality. Also, it shows respect, which meets a universal human need. Finally, it yields more truth and multiplies knowledge, two requirements for human advancement.

Habit 6: Synergize.

This is the principle behind the concept that together everyone accomplishes more. It means that one plus one can equal more than two. Synergy is the process that reveals a third and otherwise undiscovered alternative. Synergy requires an openness to change and appreciation of diversity.

Habit 7: Sharpen the saw.

Even if one develops principles for good living and applies these to achieve personal, social, occupational, and physical well-being, there will be inevitable need for renewal and reinforcement. This is where continuing education, sabbaticals, foreign exchange, and good books can be used to keep one fresh and effective. Also, this is where doing the right things in private helps produce public victories.

A useful exercise is to overlay these seven habits on yourself as a measure of personal character development. Which are high; which are low? Which need attention at this point in time? Remember Thomas Jefferson's words:

> In matters of style,
> swim with the currents;
> in matters of principle,
> stand like a rock.
> Character is what you are.
> It is different than reputation,
> which is from other people.
> Character is in you.

We end this chapter with two powerful ideas, one to instruct and the other to motivate. In his famous book *The Principles of Psychology*, William James wrote, "Sow an action and reap a habit; sow a habit and reap a character; sow a character and reap a destiny."[13] Addressing the American people of his times, William Jennings Bryan (1860–1925) said, "Destiny is not a matter of chance, it is a matter of choice. It is not something to be wished for; it is something to be attained."

Personal Thoughts on Personal Stress

Answer the following questions to personalize the content of Part Four. Space is provided for writing your thoughts.

- Do you feel satisfied with your life at this point in time? What is working? What is not working?

- Personal development writer Richard Leider states, "The most fortunate people are those who have found an idea that is bigger than they are, a vision that moves them and fills their lives with interest and energy." What is your vision in life? What is important to you that is yet to be done? In a single paragraph, write clearly your purpose in life.

- Imagine yourself as a very old person, talking with your grandchildren. When asked, "What was most important in your life?" what would you say?

- What values are important to you—theoretical, economic, aesthetic, social, political, religious?

- Are your values compatible with those of your family and friends? Can you generally accept and support the values of others?

- How strong is your value system? Do you exhibit full-swing living or experience axiological arrest?

- Think of a time in your life when you have followed Mark Twain's advice, "Always do what is right. It will please most of the people, and astound the rest." What was the result?[14]

- A simple but powerful exercise can be used to clarify what is important in your life at any point in time. First, divide a piece of paper into four quadrants. Next, put the name or symbol of the four most important values in your life—people, possessions, ideals, goals, experiences, etc. Next, cut or tear the paper into fourths. Now throw away the least important of these fourths. Look at the three remaining fourths, and throw away the least important of these. Consider the two remaining fourths, and throw away the least important of these. In your hand you have what you consider to be the most important value in your life. Now ask: Are you living your life in line with this most important value?

Chapter Eleven References

1. Boris L. Pasternak, *Doctor Zhivago* (New York: Pantheon, 1958).

2. Louis E. Raths, Merrill Harmin, and Sidney Simon, *Values and Teaching* (Columbus, Ohio: Merrill Publishing, 1966), 27-36.

3. Rebecca McCann, "Inconsistency," in *Complete Cheerful Cherub* (New York: Covice, Friede/Crown, 1932), 224.

4. Rollo May, *The Courage to Create* (New York: W.W. Norton, 1975), 3-5.

5. Raymond F. Gale, *Developmental Behavior* (New York: Macmillan, 1969), 25, 563.

6. Gale, *Developmental Behavior*, 563-64; and Walter A. Kaufman, *Nietzsche: Philosopher, Psychologist, Anti-Christ* (Princeton, N.J.: Princeton University Press, 1979), 136.

7. Paul Tillich, *The Courage to Be* (New Haven, Conn.: Yale University Press, 1952).

8. Gale, *Developmental Behavior*, 5, 564

9. Abraham Maslow, *Motivation and Personality*, 2nd ed. (New York: Harper and Row, 1970); Abraham Maslow, *Toward a Psychology of Being* (New York: Van Nostrand Reinhold, 1982); and James F. Calhoun and Joan Ross Acocella, *Psychology of Adjustments and Human Relationships* (New York: Random House, 1978), 35.

10. Maslow, *Motivation and Personality;* Maslow, *Toward a Psychology of Being;* and Calhoun and Ross, *Psychology of Adjustments and Human Relationships*, 35.

11. Maslow, *Motivation and Personality*, 220-21.

12. Stephen R. Covey, *The Seven Habits of Highly Effective People* (New York: Simon & Schuster, 1989).

13. William James, *The Principles of Psychology* (New York: H. Holt, 1950).

14. Mark Twain, as found in John Bartlett, *Familiar Quotations,* 16th ed. (Boston: Little, Brown, & Co., 1992), 528.

Part Four Reading

Solo

Most of us yearn at times to be alone in the wilderness, contemplating creation undisturbed. Only a few ever make that dream a reality.

One bright April morning, a young man named Tom Brown stood at the edge of the New Jersey Pine Barrens, a thousand square miles of oaks and pines. He removed his clothing. Then he walked into the wilderness, naked and alone.

He was 20 years old, healthy, fit. It was his intention to live by himself in the forest one entire year, the Barrens providing all his shelter, clothing, and food. For twelve months he wanted to see no human face. And he wanted to hear no human voice, except his own exuberant shout as he dove into a forest pond in the misty dawn.

Brown's urge to be alone in the wilderness seems extreme, even reckless. Yet it was hardly unprecedented. He conceived the idea as a child, when he learned that among certain Indian tribes it was a rite of passage for youths to live four seasons alone in the wilderness. He had been preparing for the epic adventure since he was a toddler, mastering outdoor skills as assiduously as any medical student memorizes his anatomy text. And within days of entering the Barrens, he was comfortably settled in a Neolithic hut, clothed in skins and woven plant fibers, and well fed on rabbit and wild salads.

"I went to the woods because I wished to live deliberately, to front only the essential facts of life, and see if I could not learn what it had to teach, and not, when I came to die, discover that I had not lived. " Thus did Henry David Thoreau explain *his* reasons for living alone in the woods, in a cabin he built beside Walden Pond. Tom Brown's motivations were the same. He also wanted, he says, to certify his mastery of wilderness skills. And he wanted, too, to find a vocation, for he was unsure of what to do with his life.

The idea was still alluring and frightening. "Will the loneliness drive me mad?"he found himself wondering. "Will I lose the ability to speak?"

He was never lonely, as it turned out, as he wandered through the forest and through the seasons. "I was as much a part of it as the deer," he says. "I was at peace. I was time-rich." One morning, like Thoreau, he decided to be the " self-appointed inspector of snowstorms." He walked into a field as a blizzard began, wrapped himself in a robe, and sat watching all through the day as the flakes slowly mounded over him.

Source: Richard Wolkomir, "Solo" Outward Bound, *1985, pp. 16-17. Reprinted with permission.*

Deer wandered by, and patrolling foxes. He watched the oaks standing firm against the storm, dead branches cracking off under the snow's weight. And he watched the pines, the alternate lesson on how to withstand life's buffering, gracefully bending their branches until the mounded snow avalanched off. Entranced, he stayed the night, buried under a drift, listening to the storm and the forest. Sometimes his meditation became a prayer.

Most of us, regardless of creed or lack of creed, experience flashes of the anchorite. Like Paul of Thebes, the second-century Egyptian hermit, we yearn to be alone in the wilderness, contemplating creation undisturbed.

Primarily, of course, we are creatures of the pack, requiring the animal heat of our own kind. Like wolves, with their elaborate language of grimaces and tail wags, we live in a haze of signs and signals—our shirt pockets flaunting their stitched alligators, a raised eyebrow fraught with significance. Not for nothing are our national sports baseball and football, games for teams.

Yet Tom Brown's yearning to test his performance alone was not unique. Every pilot is a rookie until the ultimate test, the solo. And we may instinctively feel that, to become fully human, we must for a time soar entirely on our own, checking ourselves out at the controls.

In 1933, Admiral Richard E. Byrd decided to spend the fierce Antarctic winter-seven months of darkness-alone at a weather station deep in the continent's interior. "I wanted to sink roots into some replenishing philosophy," he said. "Perhaps the desire was also in my mind to try a more rigorous existence than any I had known." Byrd found the rigor he sought out on the south polar plain, where the silence was broken only by the roaring wind and the aurora crackling in the black sky overhead. A few months into his sojourn, his malfunctioning heater filled his cabin with carbon monoxide, leaving him seriously ill and so weak that the working of a can opener exhausted him for the day.

With temperatures dropping to eighty-four degrees below zero, Byrd faced months alone buried under the snow in a tiny cabin that, as he put it, "I could span in four strides going one way and in three strides going the other." Outside, the frozen winds shrieked like ghouls.

Yet it was not all misery. Surveying his little realm, Byrd realized that "half the confusion in the world comes from not knowing how little we need." And watching the polar night come on, with curtains of auroral light undulating overhead and a mirage of mountains crystal clear on the horizon, he thought, "These are the best times, the times when neglected senses expand to an exquisite sensitivity." In his diary he noted, "I wish very much that I didn't have the radio. It connects me with the places where speeches are made." He discovered "the sheer excitement of silence." And out there alone on the polar plateau, inside himself, the explorer discovered an anchorite.

"For all my realism and skepticism there came over me, too powerfully to be denied, that exalted sense of identification—of oneness—with the outer world which is partly mystical but also certainty," Byrd wrote. "There were moments when I felt more *alive* than at any other time in my life."

Everyone's solo is his own. Byrd, finally rescued, came away convinced that only two things matter to a person: "They are the affection and understanding of his family. Everything else he creates is insubstantial," he said. And out on the ice he came to one more certainty: "The universe is not dead."

Forty years later, soloing on the Pine Barrens, Tom Brown discovered his own truths. One day, like Robinson Crusoe spying the electrifying footprint of Friday, he tracked a lost child, finding the terrified boy just in time to chase off a pack of the feral dogs that infested the Barrens. He led the child to his parents, slipping back into the woods before they saw him. The experience verified that, even in mid-solo, we have unbreakable ties to our kind.

That was fourteen years ago. Today Tom Brown has a wife and family. He operates a school in Asbury, New Jersey, where each year he teaches tracking and woodcraft to two thousand people from all walks of life and parts of the country. He has found the vocation he sought.

Pack creatures though we are, something draws us to the solo experience, as if we know instincively that it is nourishing. When Tom Brown emerged from the Barrens after twelve months alone, his first encounter with civilization was a busy highway, with evil-smelling diesel trucks rushing by. For a moment he watched in dismay. Then he wheeled and walked back into the woods.

"I stayed there three more months," he says. "And then I came out."

Question

1. Have you ever experienced a sojourn, quo vadis, or other "solo" activity? If so, describe your experience, including all the lessons you learned.

Part Five

Interpersonal Stress

12. Our Social Nature

13. Healthy Relationships

14. No One is an Island

The best marriages, like the best lives, are both happy and unhappy. There is even a kind of necessary tension, a certain tautness between the partners that gives the marriage strength. Like the tautness of a full sail, you go forward in it.—Anne Morrow Lindbergh

What you will learn in Part Five

In Part Five you will learn:

- the importance of human relationships;

- the characteristics of a healthy relationship;

- how to build relationships based on trust and respect.

Chapter Twelve

♥

Our Social Nature

Social interaction

Hans Selye, after years of research on the causes and consequences of stress, was often asked about the implications of his work on how to live a healthy and worthwhile life. His view is captured in the expression *altruistic egoism*—"to earn thy neighbor's love."[1]

Selye drew on basic biology to arrive at his conclusions. People are essentially self-serving. That is, there is a fundamental force in all living creatures that ensures survival and growth. Yet, human beings have survived and grown as a species only through cooperation and commitment to the welfare of others. Thus it is biologically natural to balance concern for self with consideration for others.

> I expect to pass through life but once. If, therefore, there be any kindness I can show, or any good I can do for any fellow human being, let me do it now, for I shall not pass this way again.—William Penn

People need to be needed—it gives purpose to life and a reason to live. Caring for and protecting others—children, pets, and other loved ones—is a powerful motivator that allows one to persevere against adversity and overcome obstacles.

A case from history shows that social interaction is necessary for the very survival of the young human being. In the thirteenth century, Emperor Frederick II conducted an experiment recorded by a medieval historian in these terms:

> His folly was that he wanted to find out what kind and manner of speech children would have when they grew up if they spoke to no person beforehand. So he bade foster mothers and nurses to suckle the children, to bathe and wash them, but in no way to play with them or to speak to them; for he wanted to learn whether they would speak the Hebrew language, which was the oldest; or Greek, Latin, or Arabic; or perhaps the language of their parents, of whom they had been born. But he labored in vain, because all of the children died. They could not live without the petting and the joyful faces and loving words of their foster mothers.[2]

This example, as well as results from modern studies, shows that life itself depends on social relationships. Evidence of the importance of human interaction comes from studies of children who have been deliberately isolated from human contact by their own families. Usually, they have been locked in an attic room or cellar. In all of these cases, the children are underdeveloped in the areas of motor skills, speech, and socialization. Attempts to socialize them usually result in extremely slow progress, and death often occurs at a very early age. Consider the case of Anna:

> Anna was discovered at the age of six. She had been born illegitimate, and her grandfather had insisted that she be hidden from the world in an attic room. Anna received a bare minimum of physical care and attention and had virtually no opportunities for social interaction. When she was found, she could not talk, walk, keep herself clean, or feed herself; she was totally apathetic, expressionless, and indifferent to human beings. In fact, those who worked with her believed at first that she was deaf and possibly blind as well.

> Attempts to socialize Anna had only limited success. The girl died four and a half years later, but during that time, she was able to learn some words and phrases, although she could never speak complete sentences. She also learned to use building blocks, string beads, wash her hands, brush her teeth, follow directions, and treat a doll with affection. She learned to walk, but could run only clumsily. By the time of her death at almost eleven, Anna had reached the level of socialization of a child of two or three.

> Kingsley Davis (1948) comments: "Here was a human organism who had missed nearly six years of socialization. Her condition shows how little her purely biological resources, when acting alone, could contribute to making her a complete person."[3]

The importance of touch on the development of a healthy brain and well-adjusted child has been well-documented by neuroscientists. The denial of a caregiver's touch has serious biochemical consequences on the baby, affecting reaction to stress and lowering the level of mental and motor ability.

Social support and health

People need people, especially in times of stress.

> The cardiac care nurse called at 3:30 A.M. One of Mary's bypasses broke, and she was being rushed back to surgery. The surgeon told me that her heart stopped three times—in the recovery room, on the way to surgery, and on the operating table. A staff member who resuscitated Mary was recognized for her life-saving action. However, Mary went into a coma for six weeks following the emergency surgery. During this period, they attempted to take her off the ventilator. When it was discovered that she could not breathe on her own, I received another 3:00 A.M. call requesting permission to put her back on the ventilator. Obviously, I

wanted to know her condition since she did not want to just exist; she wanted to live. With the assurance of a truly caring surgeon, I gave permission for the ventilator hook-up and Mary is alive and well. The stress of this situation was greatly lessened by a competent, caring, and understanding medical team.— Author's file note (K. C.)

Many argue that the Western world, the United States in particular, is too much into *acquiring objects and getting things done*, and not enough into *caring about people and relating with others*. In *The Different Drum*, Scott Peck writes:

> We are all, in reality, interdependent. Throughout the ages, the greatest leaders of all of the religions have taught us that the journey of growth is the path out of and away from narcissism, toward a state of being in which our identity merges with that of humanity.[4]

The health consequences of social support have been well documented. The bulk of evidence shows that individuals with high levels of social support live longer, even when other potential causal factors such as initial health status, social class, smoking, alcohol consumption, level of physical activity, weight, and race have been controlled or matched.[5] Also, they are less likely to be depressed and more likely to report high levels of life satisfaction or happiness.[6] Finally, they are less likely to respond to stressful experiences with either physical illness or emotional disturbance.[7]

In a major research project, L. F. Berkman followed the health histories of seven thousand residents of Alameda County, California, for nine years. She gathered statistics on factors such as contacts with friends and relatives, marital status, group membership, and attendance at religious services. Berkman found that those with the fewest social connections faced the greatest risk of dying, with mortality rates two to three times higher than those individuals who maintained high levels of social connectedness.[8] See Figure 12.1.

Social intimacy

Studies of social support in stressful conditions show that the intimacy of relationships is a key variable. Adults with emotionally supportive relationships are less likely to respond to stress with illness than are adults without such support. Dean Ornish, author of *Programs for Reversing Heart Disease*, writes:

> Anything that promotes a sense of isolation leads to chronic stress and, often, to illnesses. . . . Conversely, anything that leads to . . . intimacy and feelings of connection can be healing in the real sense of the word: to bring together, to make whole. The ability to be intimate . . . [is] a key to emotional health . . . [and is] essential to the health of our hearts as well.[9]

Figure 12.1 Predictability of Death Risk Based on Social Network

A person's social network is predictive of the risk of death over the next decade, an example of the potency of the impact of social support on health.

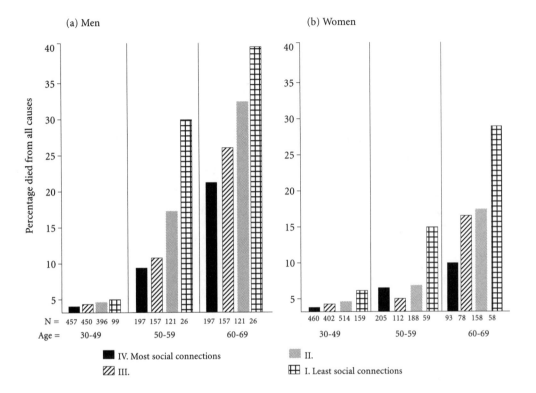

(a) Men

(b) Women

N = 457 450 396 99   197 157 121 26   197 157 121 26   460 402 514 159   205 112 188 59   93 78 158 58

Age = 30-49   50-59   60-69

■ IV. Most social connections   ▨ II.

▨ III.   ⊞ I. Least social connections

An important report published in Science reviewed the mounting evidence that social intimacy helps people deal with illness. According to James House, one of the authors of this article, "It's the 10 to 20 percent of people who say they have nobody with whom they can share their private feelings, or who have close contact with others less than once a week, who are at most risk."[10]

The report states that social isolation is as significant to mortality rates as smoking, high blood pressure, high cholesterol, obesity, and lack of physical exercise. In fact, when age is adjusted for, social isolation is as great a mortality risk as, or even a greater one than, smoking. The evidence linking social support to health is roughly as strong as the evidence linking smoking to cancer.[11]

Duke University researchers have confirmed the importance of social intimacy on health. In a nine-year follow-up study of 1,368 patients initially admitted for cardiac catheterization to diagnose heart disease, they found that those patients with neither a spouse nor a friend were three times more likely to die than those involved in a caring, communicative relationship.

What is important is having a relationship in which you can communicate and share your feelings. Although there is evidence that simply having a number of social contacts can be good for one's health, a close, intimate relationship has the most powerful healing effect.[12]

The role of the family

George Burns once said, "Happiness is having a large, close-knit family in another city." On a serious note, in different shapes and sizes, still the number-one source of satisfaction worldwide is having a family.[13]

As society has changed over time, so has the family. Fewer than 10 percent of the population now live in traditional families with a working husband, home-maker wife, and two children. More than half of the children born in 1990 will spend at least one year living in a single-parent household before they reach age 18. Three of every ten households consist of "blended" families formed by two divorced people who remarry.[14]

Of all the social variables, the single most potent in predicting overall life satisfaction is a person's satisfaction with family relationships. National surveys show the correlation between satisfaction with family life and overall life satisfaction is in the range of .40 to .45, which means that as much as 15 to 20 percent of the variation in happiness is attributable to this feature of life.[15]

Satisfaction with family relationships is a better predictor of overall life satisfaction than other key aspects of adult life, such as one's work. This is true even among highly educated people, for whom work commitment is typically high. In his autobiography, former Chrysler chairman Lee Iacocca makes this point: "Yes, I've had a wonderful and successful career. But next to my family, it really hasn't mattered at all."[16]

It is interesting to note that 10 percent of Americans say they frequently feel lonely. As antidote to this, 64 percent talk to family members first when they have a problem.[17]

What does a family need to be effective? What qualities help its members deal with the stress of the external world as well as the demands of family life—disputes, disagreements, foibles, and finances? Author Jane Howard identifies eleven characteristics of effective families.[18]

Application: Family Report Card

Evaluate a *real-life* family on eleven key characteristics using the following guide: A = excellent; B = very good; C = average; D = needs improvement; F = dysfunctional.

1. *There is love;* that is, members show love and affection for one another. _____

2. *There is authority;* that is, there are parents who make final decisions. _____

3. *There is an anchor;* that is, there is someone who keeps track of what the others are doing. _____

4. *There is a place;* that is, there is a house or a town or some other place to which members feel connected. _____

5. *There is ritual;* that is, members celebrate holidays, grieve at funerals, and in other ways experience a sense of tradition. _____

6. *There is safety;* that is, members are secure in the knowledge others will provide comfort and protection. _____

7. *There is competence;* that is, when problems arise, they are dealt with quickly and effectively. _____

8. *There is continuity;* that is, members feel as though something came before them and something will continue after them to which they are linked. _____

9. *There is honor;* that is, all members are valued and cared for. Their experience and wisdom are respected. _____

10. *There is work;* that is, all lend a hand to do household chores, make a pleasant home, and provide economic security. _____

11. *There is talk;* that is, conversation is rich as members say what they think and listen to each other. _____

Scoring and interpretation
To determine a grade point, use the following code: A = 4; B = 3; C = 2; D = 1; F = 0. Add the points for the eleven items and divide by 11. The interpretation is: 3.5–4.0 = A, excellent; 2.5–3.4 = B, very good; 1.5–2.4 = C, average; 0.5–1.4 = D, needs improvement; 0.0–0.4 = F, dysfunctional.

Discussion
If improvement is needed for family effectiveness, time should be taken to have a family conversation around six key questions: (1) What are the positive forces that are helping the family? (2) What are the negative forces that are hindering the

family? (3) What should be done to reinforce family strengths? (4) What should be done to correct low areas? (5) What action steps should the family take? (6) How should we monitor progress? All family members should participate—as the saying goes, the person in the boat with you never bores a hole in it.

The need for love

The fundamental truth about our individual lives is the indispensability of love to every human being. Love is relatedness to some treasured person or group, the feeling of belonging to a larger whole or being of value to others. In *The Ways and Power of Love*, Pitirim Sorokin describes the importance of love:

> Love has enormous creative and therapeutic potentialities, far greater than most people think. Love is a life-giving force, necessary for mental, moral, and even physical health.[19]

Erich Fromm wrote that love develops from our awareness of separateness and the need to overcome anxiety that this separateness brings. He stressed the point that the only healthy union is one in which the integrity of the individual is not threatened. Although one can achieve a feeling of belonging through dependence upon others or through conformity to the group, in so doing individuality is surrendered. Only in mature love can the sense of relatedness be achieved without the loss of individuality and integrity of either person. Immature love says, "I love you because I need you." Mature love says, "I need you because I love you."

In his classic book *The Art of Loving*, Fromm writes:

> Beyond the element of giving, the active character of love becomes evident in the fact that it always implies certain basic elements. . . . These are care, responsibility, respect, and knowledge. . . . [And] love is union with somebody, or something, outside oneself, under the condition of retaining the separateness and integrity of one's own self. It is an experience of sharing, of communion, that permits the full unfolding of one's inner activity. . . . [Finally,] love is one aspect of what I have called the productive orientation: the active and creative relatedness of man to his fellow man, to himself, and to nature.[20]

Tender loving care

The following discussion concerns an important concept in managing stress. "Tender loving care" (TLC) must be developed for the good of children, older people, and mates. It is important for everyone to have a high-quality relationship with at least one or two people who are nonjudgmental and who demonstrate nonpossessive caring.

Children

Children are the lifeline of a healthy society, and they must be nurtured with large doses of discipline and affection if they are to deal successfully with the stresses of growing up. In the words of Socrates (400 B.C.), raising children has never been an easy task:

> Our youths love luxury. They have bad manners and contempt for authority; they show disrespect for their elders, and love to chatter in place of exercise. Children are now tyrants, not the servants of their households. They no longer rise when their elders enter the room. They contradict their parents, chatter before company, gobble up their food, and tyrannize their teachers.[21]

Yet the joy of children is irrefutable, as seen in the following:

In the End It's Worth It
"Don't wake up the baby.
Come gently, my dear."

"O, mother. I've torn my new dress;
Just look here."
"I'm sorry.
I only was climbing the wall."

"And Nelly, in spelling, went up to the head."
"O, say. Can I go on the hill with my sled?"

"I've got such a toothache."
"The teacher's unfair."
"Is dinner almost ready?
I'm just like a bear."
Be patient worn mother;
They're growing up fast;
These nursery whirlwinds, not long do they last;

A still, lonely house
Would be far worse than noise;
Rejoice and be glad
In your brave girls and boys.[22]

Meeting a child's need for love can be as important as meeting more obvious needs for food and water. Rejection during infancy can result in a lasting inability to form deep emotional attachments to others. An important developmental task for the first year of life is creation of a bond of trust and affection between the infant and at least one other person. Parents are sometimes afraid of "spoiling" a baby with too much attention, but for the first year or two this is practically impossible. As a matter of fact, a later capacity to experience warm and loving relationships may depend on it.

A child's need to give love can be as powerful a motivator as the need to receive love, as the following story shows:

> Martha was eleven years old when it was learned that her father was dying of kidney disease. There was only one way to save his life. The situation was explained to everyone—mother, father, and Martha—and the little girl's answer was yes, she would give her kidney to her father.
>
> On the day of the operation, Martha was placed on one table, her father on the table next to her, and anesthesia was administered. Eight hours later, the little girl opened her eyes, looked at her mother, and asked, "Mommy, am I dead yet?"... Martha had misunderstood. She thought that in order to save her father's life, she must give up her own. What motivated Martha to do this? Martha was motivated by the need to give love to her father.

In *The Prophet*, Kahlil Gibran describes the relationship between parent and child:

> Your children are not your children
> They are the sons and daughters of
> Life's longing for itself.
> They come through you but not from you,
> And though they are with you yet they belong not to you.[23]

Parents are the protectors and teachers of children, for they are who children love as only innocents can love—with all of their hearts. The German writer Goethe once said, children learn from those they love, and what is taught is taught by example. Consider Dorothy Law Nolte's Children's Creed, found on most pediatricians' walls:

The Children's Creed[24]
If a child lives with criticism,
He learns to condemn.

If a child lives with hostility,
He learns to fight.

If a child lives with ridicule,
He learns to be shy.

If a child lives with shame,
He learns to feel guilty.

If a child lives with encouragement,
He learns confidence.

If a child lives with praise,
He learns to appreciate.

If a child lives with fairness,
He learns justice.

If a child lives with security,
He learns to have faith.

If a child lives with approval,
He learns to like himself.

If a child lives with acceptance and friendship,
He learns to find love in the world.

The family is a training ground for living. We use our experience in the family to learn how to behave in other groups and with other individuals. If parents are loving and show respect toward each other, their children will learn how to have loving and healthy relationships. Nobel Prize–winning poet Gabriela Mistral writes:

Many of the things we need can wait. The child cannot.

Right now is the time bones are being formed blood

is being made senses are being developed.

To the child we cannot answer "Tomorrow."

The child's name is "Today."[25]

Working parents spend an average of 84 hours a week on combined work and family responsibilities (15–25 hours more than people without children who work). Increasingly, they are having difficulty meeting the demands of work and the demands of raising children. In a recent survey of one thousand families, most parents said they felt overwhelmed and guilty. Eighty percent of mothers and 40 percent of fathers said they would quit working if they could to be home with their children.[26]

The challenges of parenting include tangible needs for food, shelter, and protection, as well as psychological and emotional needs that must be met. A child's greatest emotional need is for love—the feeling of being wanted and cared for, of being special, and of realizing that parents like the child for him- or herself. Children have needs for security as well—the assurance that their parents will be there when needed. Finally, children need a set of standards and values, role models to learn from, with a sense of clearly defined limits and controls.

The following are six time-tested rules for raising children with TLC.[27]

- Make raising your children your number-one priority.

- Set aside time for one-to-one interaction with each child every day.

- Hug your children. Show them you love them and are happy to see them.

- Remember, it's not just little kids who need to be "tucked in." Although they protest, children of all ages need signs of love and affection.

- Provide learning opportunities. Take them to the library; let them bake cookies; teach them to care about others.

- Teach morality. Set standards and limits for behavior that all family members follow.

Regarding the quality of time spent with children, consider the following advice from the *Old Farmer's Almanac*, 1982 edition:

> Why should we not try to make our children enjoy their home? They will not, unless they are made happy there. Try to avoid all unnecessary fault-finding, and especially abstain from it at mealtimes. It tends to destroy the appetite, not only of the poor offender, but the rest of the family as well. Give a pleasant greeting to all in the morning, and at night, and when meeting at the table. Do not be stingy of kisses. It is better to put them at interest than to hoard them.[28]

Our own small child
The first time I saw Heather, I could only marvel at this pink and precious person who would change our lives forever, and for whom I felt instant love.—Author's file notes (G. M.)

What are the main sources of stress for children? John and Katerina Digman have identified three main areas: (1) Low educational achievement as evidenced by poor grades and lack of interest in school. *Coaching, encouragement, and affirmation by parents and teachers are interventions that work.* (2) Problems with peers, including physical conflict and lack of acceptance. *Youth groups and activities that build character, raise self-esteem, and develop friendships with age-mates can be helpful.* (3) Problems with parents, including rejection or low emotional involvement.

The child must feel loved and cherished unconditionally. Parental action that demonstrates the importance of the child and emotional involvement are required.[29]

What works and doesn't work in terms of parental support? Parental behavior that is either overly authoritarian and controlling or overly permissive and indulgent should be avoided. The most consistently positive outcomes are achieved by parents who uphold high standards of conduct and simultaneously demonstrate unconditional love for the child.[30]

For many parents, the teenage years are the most stressful years of raising children. Every morning mirror reveals another wrinkle and gray hair traced to the stress of raising teenagers. Some comfort can be drawn from George Burns's observation—"Children resist and despise their parents until age forty, when they suddenly become just like them—thus preserving the system."

Older people

In 1776, 2 percent of the American population was sixty-five or older; in 1900, 4 percent. Today, the elderly are more than 11 percent of the population and will represent 12 percent by the year 2000. Somewhere around 2030, when the peak of the postwar baby boom hits the age of 65, one American in five will be elderly.[31]

Older people are faced with many types of stressors—physical, economic, and social. With advanced age, many experience failing health and reduced income that pose direct threats to survival and independence. Statistics show that one out of every four Americans over the age of 65 lives below the poverty level.[32]

Another stressor of older age is loneliness. Many older people miss the day-to-day contacts provided by employment. Many also lose touch with their children and relatives, who may live thousands of miles away. Finally, many older people face the prospect of living the rest of their lives alone as family and friends die before they do.

Old age is a time of life filled with change. There may be physical, social, and financial changes that create the need for adjustment. These may be stressful and a threat to health and happiness.

On the other hand, old age can be described as a "state of mind." We are old when we allow ourselves to feel old. This can occur at age 30 for some, at age 65 for others, or may never arrive for those who remain "young at heart."

We can focus on the negative side of old age or focus on the positive aspects. We can feel sorry for ourselves because of retirement or can welcome the time to spend with family and the challenge of new activities. The choice is up to each individual. When we recognize that we are not immortal, the fact of death can help us live more fully by setting priorities.

Older people need the support and love of others in order to cope with the stressors of aging. The importance of TLC to the individual is obvious, and the fact that older people have much to offer society is shown in the following:

- Winston Churchill served as prime minister of Great Britain during his 60s and 70s, and then only after a lifetime of defeats and setbacks.

- Laura Ingalls Wilder is best known for her *Little House Books.* She was 65 years old when she published her first book, and she wrote some of her best children's stories during her 70s.

- Golda Meir was named prime minister of Israel when she was 71 and held that office for 5 years.

- Michelangelo, who created the sculptures *David, Moses*, and *The Pietà* and who painted the Sistine Chapel, continued to produce his masterpieces years after he was 70.

- Anna Mary "Grandma" Moses, best known for her realistic scenes of rural life, was 76 when she began painting.

- Mahatma Gandhi led India's opposition to British rule when he was 77.

- Benjamin Franklin helped write the Declaration of Independence when he was 70 and participated in drafting the United States Consitiution when he was 81.

- Sophocles wrote *Oedipus at Colonus*, one of the greatest Greek tragedies, at 70 and *Electra* when he was nearly 90.[33]

The Roman philosopher Cicero (age 62) explains why older people have so much to offer:

It is not by muscle, speed, or physical dexterity that great things are achieved, but by reflection, force of character, and judgment; in these qualities, old age is usually not only not poorer, but is even richer.[34]

Author Pearl Buck, at age 79, wrote:

Would I wish to be "young" again? No, for I have learned too much to wish to lose it. It would be like failing to pass a grade in school. I have reached an honorable position in life because I am old and no longer young. I am a far more valuable person today than I was 50 years ago, or 40 years ago, or 30, 20, or even 10. I have learned so much since I was 70! I believe that I can honestly say that I have learned more in the last 10 years than I have learned in any previous decade. This, I suppose, is because I have perfected my techniques, so that I no longer waste time in learning how to do what I have to do.[35]

One important way people generate TLC during their later years is to guide and develop young people.

Pass it on
I was a big man on campus—popular with the girls, lettered in three sports. I was important. Then I got involved with the wrong crowd, and was adrift and sinking. That's when she found me. Like a grandmother, Dr. Dotson took an interest and reached out to help. But she said I must repay her.

It wasn't until I finished my education and was teaching others that I understood this debt. She meant . . . I must *pass it on* and do for others what she had done for me. It was a powerful message—each generation must care about and help the next.—Author's file notes (S. M.)

Mates

The importance of helping your mate should not be underestimated, if he or she is to live a long and happy life. This message is particularly true for couples locked in a daily struggle to meet the responsibilities of a home and the responsibilities of a job. Many partners join each other at the end of pressure-filled, conflict-ridden, and frustrating days and give each other additional stress. What is missing is TLC, and the result is distress, with accompanying physical and emotional problems. Even premature aging and death can result. The major deficiencies are:

- Insensitivity to the other person's problems—pressures, conflicts, and frustrations.

- Lack of awareness of the impact of your own behavior—your moods and actions.

- The idea that your mate must be perfect, so that you are intolerant of his or her shortcomings and idiosyncrasies. The importance of tolerance and keeping small differences in perspective is perfectly illustrated by the following story:

The grapefruit syndrome
My husband and I had been married about two years—just long enough for me to realize that he was a normal man rather than a knight on a white charger—when I read an article recommending that couples regularly discuss the habits they find annoying in each other. I talked to my husband about the idea, and he agreed to give it a try.

As I recall, we were to name five things we found irritating, and I started off. After more than fifty years, I remember only my first complaint: grapefruit. I told him that I didn't like the way he ate grapefruit. He peeled it and ate it like an orange. Could a woman be expected to spend a lifetime watching her husband eat a grapefruit like that? Although I've forgotten them, I'm sure the rest of my complaints were similar.

After I finished, it was his turn. I still carry a mental image of his handsome young face as he gathered his brows together in a thoughtful, puzzled frown and then looked at me with his large, blue-gray eyes. "Well, to tell the truth," he said, "I can't think of anything I don't like about you, honey."

Tears ran down my face. I had found fault with him over such trivial things as the way he ate grapefruit, while he hadn't noticed any of my own annoying habits.

I wish I could say that this cured me of fault-finding. It didn't. But it did make me aware early in my marriage that husbands and wives need to keep in perspective the small differences in their habits and personalities. Whenever I hear of couples being incompatible, I always wonder if they are suffering from the grapefruit syndrome.—Lola B. Walters

- The misconception that you can or should control the life and feelings of your partner. The most satisfying relationships allow each person to be what they are and become what they can be. The words of the Lebanese poet Kahlil Gibran make this point:

> But let there be spaces in your togetherness,
> And let the winds of the heavens dance
> between you.
> Love one another, but make not a bond of
> love:
> Let it rather be a moving sea between the
> shores of your souls.
> Fill each other's cup but drink not from
> one cup.
> Give one another of your bread but eat
> not from the same loaf.
> Sing and dance together and be joyous,
> but let each one of you be alone,
> Even as the strings of a lute are alone
> though they quiver with the same music.

*Give your hearts, but not into each
other's keeping.*

*For only the hand of Life can contain
your hearts.*

*And stand together yet not too near
together:*

*For the pillars of the temple stand
apart,*

*And the oak tree and the cypress grow not
in each other's shadow.*[36]

■ Lack of physical contact. Remember the importance of regular doses of physical affection. Research shows what common sense has always known: mates need to be touched. As the humanist Leo Buscaglia states, "Hugging can lift depression, enabling the body's immune system to become tuned up. Hugging breathes fresh life into tired bodies and makes people feel younger and more vibrant. The husband who kisses his wife before leaving in the morning lives up to five years longer than the man who does not. He has fifty percent less illness and [even] fewer car accidents." Buscaglia concludes, "For goodness' sake, do it."[37]

Psychologist Virginia Satir, author of *PeopleMaking*, is famous for saying, "People need 4 hugs a day for survival, 8 hugs a day for maintenance, and 12 hugs a day for growth." Jack Canfield, author of *Chicken Soup for the Soul*, explains the importance of physical affection:

Hugging is healthy. It helps the body's immune system, it keeps you healthier, it cures depression, it reduces stress, it induces sleep, it's invigorating, it's rejuvenating, it has no unpleasant side effects, and hugging is nothing less than a miracle drug.

Hugging is all natural. It is organic, naturally sweet, no pesticides, no preservatives, no artificial ingredients, and 100 percent wholesome.

Hugging is practically perfect. There are no movable parts, no batteries to wear out, no periodic check-ups, low energy consumption, high energy yield, inflation proof, nonfattening, no monthly payments, no insurance requirements, theft-proof, nontaxable, nonpolluting, and, of course, fully returnable.[38]

The U.S. Bureau of the Census reported 2,344,000 marriages and 1,150,000 divorces for 1996. In an era when almost half the marriages end in divorce, it would be good to know the answer to the question, what do people look for in a mate? Figure 12.2 summarizes the results of cross-cultural studies conducted in thirty-seven countries on the characteristics most sought in a mate.

Both sexes rank kindness-understanding and intelligence higher than physical attractiveness. Statistically significant gender differences in rankings are found for two characteristics, which are shown in italics. Men rank physical attractiveness higher than women do, and women rank earning capacity higher than men do.

Figure 12.2 Characteristics Commonly Sought in a Mate[39]

Rank	Characteristics preferred by men	Characteristics preferred by women
1	Kindness and understanding	Kindness and understanding
2	Intelligence	Intelligence
3	*Physical attractiveness*	Exciting personality
4	Exciting personality	Good health
5	Good health	Adaptability
6	Adaptability	*Physical attractiveness*
7	Creativity	Creativity
8	Desire for children	*Good earning capacity*
9	College graduate	College graduate
10	Good heredity	Desire for children
11	*Good earning capacity*	Good heredity
12	Good housekeeper	Good housekeeper
13	Religious orientation	Religious orientation

Success in a relationship is much more than finding the right person. To no small degree, it is a matter of being the right person. Many important influences on marital success are factors of the individual partners and exist before a marriage even begins. Statistical analysis shows factors that help in weathering the stresses of marriage are:[40]

- good health (including lower rate of alcoholism)

- positive self-esteem

- good problem-solving ability

- low level of neuroticisn or "difficult temperament"

- more religious or of the same religious background

- parents less likely to have divorced

- married after age twenty, but before age thirty

- have not cohabited before marriage or have lived together only a short time

- higher education level and middle-class background

The relationship between mates is more than the sum of the characteristics of two individuals. Equally important is the quality of the interactions between the partners. People in successful relationships:[41]

- like each other and consider their partner to be their best friend;

- agree on roles and like the way their partner is filling his or her role;

- are sensitive to and accommodating of each other's needs and moods;

- have high levels of positive or supportive interaction;

- are good at resolving conflict and confronting problems directly, but avoid personal criticism or blame;

- are willing to change in response to each other;

- are committed to each other—they love each other and want to live their lives together.

In contrast to successful relationships, people in poor relationships are plagued by four horsemen that increase stress and lower the quality of life for both partners.[42]

The First Horseman: Criticism
A pattern of constant criticism, especially about the nature, character, or personality of one's partner, will wear down and ultimately destroy a relationship.

The Second Horseman: Contempt
Criticism can escalate to contempt. At this level of negativity a relationship can become toxic to the physical and emotional health of one or both partners.

The Third Horseman: Defensiveness
If partners engage in defensive behaviors and self-protection, attitudes typically harden, almost assuring breakdown of the relationship.

The Fourth Horseman: Stonewalling
This behavior is characterized by disapproval, icy distance, and rigidity. The psychological stonewall prevents trust and respect, the essential elements of any healthy relationship.

In 1991, 1,500 married couples came together in Chicago to celebrate their fiftieth wedding anniversaries. There were many reasons cited for their long marriages, but the words of one couple reflect the most-mentioned requirements—love, respect, and consideration.

> Be considerate. Be patient. Always ask; try not to command. Say "please" and "thank you." Work together and talk things over often. Love each other with all of your hearts.

To summarize the role of TLC in relationships, it can be said that *the exchange of simple affection is the true secret of success.* When we are accepted and valued by those who know all about us and like us anyway, we know the happiness involved in a deep and satisfying relationship. To personalize the subject, is there someone in your world who believes that you are a special person and who loves you with all of his or her heart? For a picture of a stressful relationship, see page 265, "What We Have Here Is a Failure to Communicate."

Pets and tender loving care

People and pets are important to each other. There are about 49 million dogs and 42 million cats living as pets in the United States; together they far exceed the number of children under 18. This reflects, among other things, our continuing need for belonging and affection.[43]

Pets can help improve the quality of life and even the length of life. Studies show that after returning home from hospitalization for a heart attack, patients who have pets live longer than those who do not. Patients who have pets have half the mortality rate of those without. The very act of stroking a pet can lower heart rate and blood pressure of both the pet and the person.[44]

The importance of responsibility

The subject of our social nature is incomplete without a discussion of the importance of responsibility. Scott Peck, author of *The Road Less Traveled*, puts responsibility center stage as the key ingredient for a successful life. He identifies disorders of responsibility that are particularly distressful in human relationships—neuroticism and character deficiency.[45]

The *neurotic* person feels overly responsible, even for people and events beyond his or her control. In contrast, the person with *character deficiency* lacks responsibility. This is shown in low concern for the needs and interests of others. Either disorder spells trouble for the individual and can be stressful for the people in his or her world.

People in our lives—especially our families and friends—can have profound influence on our health and happiness. Responsibility is the distinguishing feature between toxic and nourishing people. Toxic people are irresponsible individuals who harm relationships and deplete resources for coping. Nourishing people are responsible and supportive. They are rational copers who lift human spirits and are a joy to others. The challenge to every person is to be nourishing and responsible in all relationships, and in so doing add to love, add to health, and add to life.

Chapter Twelve References

[1] Hans Selye, *Stress without Distress* (Philadelphia: J. B. Lippincott, 1974), 5.

[2] Peter Farb, *Humankind* (Boston: Houghton-Mifflin, 1978), 7.

[3] Kingsley Davis, *Human Society* (New York: Macmillan, 1947), 204-6.

[4] M. Scott Peck, *The Different Drum* (New York: Simon & Schuster, 1987), 288.

[5] L. F. Berkman, "The Relationship of Social Networks and Social Support to Morbidity and Mortality," in S. Cohen and S. L. Syme, eds., *Social Support and Health* (Orlando, Fla.: Academic Press, 1985).

[6] S. Cohen and T. S. Wills, "Stress, Social Support, and the Buffering Hypothesis," *Psychological Bulletin*, 98(1985): 310-57.

[7] Cohen and Wills, "Stress, Social Support, and the Buffering Hypothesis,": 310-57.

[8] L. F. Berkman and S. L. Syme, "Social Networks, Host Resistence and Mortality: A Nine-Year Follow-Up Study of Alameda County Residents," *American Journal of Epidemiology* 109 (1979): 186-204.

[9] Dean Ornish, *Dr. Dean Ornish's Program for Reversing Heart Disease* (New York: Ballentine, 1990).

[10] J. S. House, K. R. Landis, and D. Unberson, "Social Relationships and Health," *Science* 241 (1988): 540-45.

[11] House, Landis, and Unberson, "Social Relationships and Health": 540-45.

[12] Redford Williams and Virginia Williams, *Anger Kills: Seventeen Strategies for Controlling the Hostility that Can Harm Your Heart* (New York: Times Books, 1993).

[13] "Happiness is a Family," *Psychology Today,* March, 1989, p. 10.

[14] Mark Toeger, "Work and Family Issues: A New Frontier in Health Practice," *American Journal of Health Practice* (Jan./Feb. 1990).

[15] A. Campbell, *The Sense of Well-Being in America* (New York: McGraw-Hill, 1981); and N. D. Glenn and C. N. Weaver, "The Contribution of Marital Happiness to Global Happiness," *Journal of Marriage the Family* 43 (1981): 161-68.

[16] Lee Iacocca, *Iacocca: An Autobiography,* (Toronto: Bantam, 1984), 289.

[17] Linda DeStefano, "All the Lonely People," *San Francisco Chronicle,* March 7, 1990.

[18] Jane Howard, *Families* (New York: Simon & Schuster, 1978), 350.

[19] Pitirim A. Sorokin, *The Ways and Power of Love: Types, Factors, and Techniques of Moral Transformation* (Boston: Beacon, 1954).

[20] Erich Fromm, *The Art of Loving* (New York: Bantam, 1963), 20-21, 26-27, 30-31.

[21] *Some Favorite Quotations*, http://www.best.com/~dolphin/quotes.shtml.

[22] L. D. Nichols, in Will Forpe and John McCollister, *The Sunshine Book: Expressions of Love, Hope and Inspiration* (Middle Village, N.Y.: Jonathan David, 1979), 232.

[23] Kahlil Gibran, *The Prophet* (New York: Knopf, 1976), 16-17.

[24] Dorothy Law Nolte, "The Children's Creed" (physician's wall plaque, source unknown).

[25] Doris Dana, ed., *Selected Poems of Gabriela Mistral* (Baltimore, Md.: Johns Hopkins Press, 1971), dedication page.

[26] Diane Hales, *An Invitation to Health* (Redwood City, Calif.: Benjamin/Cummings, 1992), 227.

[27] Michael K. Meyerhoff and Burton L. White, "Making the Grade as Parents," *Psychology Today,* September 1986,: pp. 38-45.

[28] Forpe and McCollister, *The Sunshine Book,* 227.

[29] John M. Digman and Katarina C. Digman, "Stress and Competence in Longitudinal Perspective," in *Human Functioning in Longitudinal Perspective,* ed. S. B. Sells, Rick Crandall, Merrill Roff, John S. Strauss, and William Pollin (Baltimore, Md.: The Williams and Wilkins Company, 1980).

[30] E. E. Maccoby and J. A. Martin, "Socialization in the Context of the Family: Parent-Child Interaction," in E. M. Hethrington, ed., *Handbook of Child Psychology* (New York: Wiley, 1983).

[31] *Centerscope: A Report to Friends of the Washington Hospital Center* (Washington, D.C.: The Washington Center, Spring/Summer, 1981), 6.

[32] Robert N. Butler and Myrna Lewis, *Aging and Mental Health: Positive Psychosocial Approaches* (St. Louis: C. V. Mosby, 1973), 10.

[33] *The World Book Encyclopedia,* 1981.

[34] *Centerscope,* 3.

[35] *Centerscope,* 3.

[36] Kahlil Gibran, "On Marriage," in *The Prophet* (New York: Knopf, 1976), 16-17.

[37] From "Together with Leo," a public lecture by Leo Buscaglia.

[38] Jack Canfield and Mark V. Hansen, *Chicken Soup for the Soul* (Deerfield Beach, Fla.: Health Communications, 1993), 227-28.

[39] D. M. Buss, "Human Mate Selection," *American Scientist* 73 (1985): 47-51.

[40] A. Booth and J. N. Edwards, "Age at Marriage and Marriage Instability," *Journal of Marriage and the Family* 47 (1985): 65-67; G. L. Bowen and D. K. Orthner, "Sex Role Congruency and Marital Quality," *Journal of Marriage and the Family* 45 (1983): 223-30; E. E. Filsinger and S. J. Thoma, "Behavioral Antecedents of Relationship Stability and Adjustment: A Five-Year Longitudinal Study," *Journal of Marriage and the Family* 50 (1988): 785-95; J. M. Gottman R. W. Levenson, "Why Marriages Fail: Affective and Physiological Patterns in Marital Interaction," in J. C. Masters and K. Yarkin-Levin, eds., *Boundary Areas in Social and Developmental Psychology* (New York: Academic Press, 1984); J. M. Gottman and A. L. Porterfield, "Communicative Competence in the Non-Verbal Behavior of Married Couples," *Journal of Marriage and the Family* 43 (1981): 817-24; W. K. Halford, K. Hahlweg, and M. Dunne, "The Cross-Cultural Consistency of Marital Communication Associated with Marital Distress," *Journal of Marriage and the Family* 57 (1990): 487-500; T. B. Heaton and E. L. Pratt, "The Effects of Religious Homogamy on Marital Satisfaction and Stability," *Journal of Family Issues* 11 (1990): 191-207; J. Lauer and R. Lauer, "Marriage Made to Last," *Psychology Today* 19 (1985): 22-26; R. B. Schafer and P. M. Keith, "A Causal Analysis of the Relationship between the Self-Concept and Marital Quality," *Journal of Marriage and the Family* 46 (1984): 909-14; and M. R. Wilson and E. E. Filsinger, "Religiosity and Marital Adjustment: Multidimensional Interralationships," *Journal of Marriage and the Family* 48 (1986): 147-51.

[41] Booth and Edwards, "Age at Marriage and Marriage Instability" 65-67; Bowen and Orthner, "Sex Role Congruency and Marital Quality," 223-30; Filsinger and Thoma, "Behavioral Antecedents of Relationship Stability and Adjustment: A Five-Year Longitudinal Study," 785-95; Gottman and Levenson, "Why Marriages Fail: Affective and Physiological Patterns in Marital Interaction"; Gottman and Porterfield, "Communicative Competence in the Non-Verbal Behavior of Married Couples," 817-24; Halford, Hahlweg, and Dunne, "The Cross-Cultural Consistency of Marital Communication Associated with Marital Distress," 487-500; Heaton and Pratt, "The Effects of Religious Homogamy on Marital Satisfaction and Stability," 191-209; Lauer and Lauer, "Marriage Made to Last," 22-26; Schafer and Keith, "A Causal Analysis of the Relationship between the Self-Concept and Marital Quality," 904-14; and Wilson and Filsinger, "Religiosity and Marital Adjustment: Multidimensional Interrelationships," 147-51.

[42] John Gottman, "What Makes Marriage Work?" in *Why Marriages Succeed or Fail* (New York: Simon & Schuster, 1994).

[43] B. Robey, "The Two-Cat Family," *American Demographics*, May 1983.

[44] E. Friedman, A. H. Katcher, J. J. Lynch, and S. A. Thomas, "Animal Companions and One-Year Survival of Patients after Discharge from a Coronary Care Unit," *Public Health Reports* 95 (1980): 307-12.

[45] M. Scott Peck, *The Road Less Traveled* (New York: Simon & Schuster, 1978).

Chapter Thirteen
♥
Healthy Relationships

Truth in relationships

Honesty is the best policy in human relationships. It is the foundation of trust, without which there is insecurity, pain, and, ultimately, death of a relationship. Martin Buber wrote, "What is real is you and what is real is me, but what is really real is we." For this to be so, people must shed their masks and pretenses and be their true selves. True love loves truth.[1]

There are two kinds of truth—*value-free* and *value-full.* With value-free truth, people say and do what they believe to be true without regard for the consequences. So to speak, they let the chips fall where they may. By itself, this type of truth is good, but it can be harmful in human relationships. Far better is value-full truth. This is truth combined with kindness and consideration. With value-full truth, the welfare of others is as important as truth itself.

This is where experience and wisdom enter the picture. The honest and kind person asks, "What will help everyone in this situation?" If truth will, as it almost always does, "How can it be conveyed in a helpful and constructive way?" Because the answers to these questions vary so much, there is truth to the saying, "If this experience doesn't kill us, it can make us stronger."

The prescription is to be both honest *and* kind. Since this is not always easy and there are no simple formulas that apply in every situation, dealing with people requires patience and understanding. This also explains why so much stress can be traced to interpersonal relationships.

Your true personality

If "Who are you?" and "Where are you going?" are the two most important questions in your life, then "Who will go with you?" is the third. Problems occur if these questions are answered in the wrong order. This is the case for many people who love each other but are incompatible. To prevent this from happening, the solution is to follow Socrates' dictum to *know thyself* and Shakespeare's advice to *be true to yourself and you will be false to no other.* This brings us to the subject of personality.

The term *personality* comes from the Latin word *persona,* meaning "mask." Actors in the plays of ancient Greece and Rome wore masks to indicate whether they were happy or sad. Unlike a mask that one can put on or take off, the term personality implies something stable. Personality consists of all the consistent ways in which the behavior of one person differs from that of others.

Years ago, Gordon Allport of Harvard University analyzed the English language and found 18,000 traitlike terms used to designate distinctive patterns of behavior. Allport believed that this rich collection of words provided a way to capture the uniqueness of each individual and that this uniqueness could be described in terms of personality. He identified three levels of strength or dominance of personality: cardinal dispositions, central tendencies, and secondary traits.

When an individual has a cardinal disposition, almost every aspect of his or her life is influenced by it. The person's entire identity is shaped by this powerful disposition. People who have a cardinal disposition are often labeled with names or adjectives derived from historical or fictional characters, such as Christlike, Machiavellian, Quixotic, Scrooge, or Don Juan.

Few people have one cardinal disposition. Ordinarily, the personality develops around several outstanding central tendencies. These central tendencies form the basic characteristics of the person. Allport believed that the central tendencies of a personality were likely to be those traits you would mention in writing a letter of recommendation—dependable, intelligent, kindhearted, and resourceful are examples. Examples of negative central tendencies are lazy, incompetent, dishonest, and cowardly.

A third level of personality is that of secondary traits. Secondary traits function more on the periphery of the personality. They are less significant, less conspicuous, and less consistent than cardinal dispositions or central tendencies, but they still are important in understanding why people do what they do. "Likes sports," "likes to travel," and "prefers brunettes" are examples of secondary traits.[2]

To personalize the subject of personality, complete the following exercise.

❂ Application: Cardinal, Central, and Secondary Traits—Personal Evaluation

Answer the following questions.

Cardinal disposition: Briefly describe your cardinal disposition. For example, are you an "optimist"? Are you a "scientist"? Are you a "mystic"? Are you an "animal person"? What are you more like than anyone else you know? If your life is not dominated by a "ruling passion" or cardinal disposition, describe the cardinal disposition of a family member, friend, or acquaintance.

Central tendencies: Think about your central tendencies. Identify the most important central tendencies in your personality, and give examples of how these characteristics affect your life. For example, are you dominant or accommodating? Are you introverted or extroverted? Do you love variety or routine? Are you high strung or calm? Are you liberal or conservative?

Secondary traits: Identify your secondary traits—what is important to you? Do you enjoy music, do you like the outdoors, do you like sports, do you like to read? What interests you?

Going from me to we

Nothing is more stressful than a miserable relationship. Ask anyone who has one. On the other hand, nothing is more satisfying than a loving relationship.

An unhappy relationship is double trouble. You lose a major source of support and replace it with a major source of stress. When couples fight, they activate the *general adaptation syndrome* (GAS) that can suppress their immune systems. The result is that both unhappy people may become ill.

Occasional arguments are usually not the problem. It is chronic disagreement that overstimulates the physical system and can lead to negative stress effects. Studies show that people in troubled relationships have poorer health than people in satisfying relationships. A prescription for good health is to keep relationships happy.

More than twenty years ago, psychologist Carl Rogers identified the characteristics of a healthy relationship. To some degree, these characteristics are present in all successful relationships.

- **Honesty:** Even though it is difficult to achieve, the strongest bond between people is a large component of self-disclosure. We are able to say with honesty what we want and those emotions we feel, such as fear, guilt, resentment, anger, and worry, without worrying about the impression we are making. We are willing to be ourselves.

- **Sensitivity:** A satisfying relationship depends on the willingness of each party to understand the other's emotions and experiences. This takes time, energy, and, most important, the desire to know how the other person feels and to understand that person's needs.

- **Open communication:** Thoughts and feelings, including negative ones, are expressed, so they do not block closeness and so each person has an opportunity to decide whether he or she wishes to change.

- **Respect for autonomy:** While the relationship is characterized by openness on both sides, there is acceptance of the rights of each individual to believe and behave according to his or her own standards. We do not require that the other person, in order to be valued, must meet our conditions for thoughts, feelings, and actions. In this sense, positive regard is unconditional.

- **Rhythm:** Relationships have a rhythmic variation to them, an ebb and flow. There is openness and sharing of feelings and then a period of assimilation of these experiences. Intense discussion, with anxiety and change, are followed by a secure time of no change and quiet.[3]

Think of a relationship that is important to you and ask, "Are you doing all you can to demonstrate sensitivity, are you open in communication, are you honest with your feelings, do you show respect for the other person, is there rhythm in the relationship?" People grow within a healthy relationship. In a true sense, they develop into better human beings.

To have a healthy relationship, you have to follow the law of nature. Just as the farmer sows seed to reap a harvest, you must be loving to be loved, and you must be respectful to be respected. Some people live their entire lives without applying this simple message, and they suffer. It isn't a case of not growing up. The smallest child can love and respect. Rather, it is a case of not growing out.

At any point, this can be changed if one wants to. It is a matter of giving for the well-being of others versus taking in self-absorption. Other people can help through example and encouragement, but essentially it is a personal choice.

In developing a relationship, it is important to know what makes a person easy to live with. The following are nine basic principles:

1. **Seek to love, not to change.** Care about your partner and his or her activities, but never let interest become interference. Letting people be free to be themselves is a healthy tonic that nurtures and enhances the relationship.

2. **Avoid being judgmental and fault-finding.** Instead, praise your partner for his or her good qualities. This is pleasing and makes a long and happy relationship. As Benjamin Franklin said regarding a good marriage: Keep your eyes wide open before you marry, and half shut afterward.

3. **Lighten up and let it be.** When minor disagreements occur, keep things in perspective. Realize that most matters are minor in the big picture of life. Don't get angry and don't hold a grudge; let it go. Choose to laugh and build a future together.

4. **Make peace, not war.** By all means, have opinions, and express your ideas readily. But keep the emphasis on sharing, not winning. If life is a struggle and a contest, don't let it be with your partner.

5. **Seek never to harm.** Be pure of heart. This builds trust and creates a sense of security that is the foundation for happiness.

6. **Help your partner.** Try to solve problems, not make problems. This is a basic ingredient of being a *helpmate* and a basic requirement for a productive relationship.

7. **Tell truth with kindness.** This is a core characteristic of a healthy relationship. Be honest *and* considerate in all matters.

8. **Love on all planes.** Show love emotionally and physically. Make love the single most descriptive word for your relationship.

9. **Communicate.** Be open to discuss all subjects, from dollars to dogs. Don't blow up, don't shut down, just talk, fairly and frankly. Say what you think and listen to understand. Communication is the heart of a healthy love.[4]

Dealing with difficult people

Human relationships are not always easy. When someone is being difficult, remember the acronym HALT. People often behave badly when they are hurt, angry, lonely, or tired. Usually they will respond positively if you are patient and understanding. Think of yourself and times when you may have been difficult; think of your own needs for patience and understanding.

Difficult behavior is ingrained in some people, and the best answer may be to avoid them. If this is not possible, or desirable, there is only one alternative, and that is to endure with grace just as you would the weather. Sometimes it can help if you reframe the situation. Instead of focusing on the negative aspects of the person, find the good. Consider the positive qualities the person possesses.

Most difficult behavior is situational, which means that something can be done about it. The solutions are to (1) change the situation, (2) help the person change, (3) change yourself, or (4) leave. Every effect has a cause, and if the cause can be discovered, the problem behavior can often be corrected. Specific causes of difficult behavior are (a) bad habits developed from bad role models, (b) feelings of insecurity and inadequacy, (c) feelings of being unappreciated and unloved, (d) a lack of learning to be nice or considerate of others, and (e) displacement of personal frustrations onto safe and convenient targets.[5]

Robert Bramson, in *Coping with Difficult People*, has identified types of people who can be highly stressful:

Hostile-Aggressives: These are people who bully and overwhelm others by making cutting remarks or throwing tantrums when things don't go their way.

Complainers: These are people who never try to improve what they complain about, either because they feel powerless to do so or because they refuse to bear the responsibility.

Silent-Unresponsives: These are people who respond to every question or request with a yep, a hmmm, a no, or a grunt.

Super-Agreeables: These are personable individuals who are supportive in your presence, but don't produce what they say they will.

Negativists: These are pessimists who respond to every idea with "It won't work" or "It's impossible." They deflate and depress other people.

Know-It-Alls: These are people who act like they know everything there is to know about anything worth knowing. They are condescending toward others and strive to inflate their own importance.

Indecisives: These are people who put off decisions until the decisions are finally made for them. Indecisives can be immobilized by fear, perfectionism, and procrastination.[6]

A difficult person may need help from others to correct the problem. Heavy doses of education, encouragement, and patience can be helpful as the individual attempts to replace negative patterns of behavior with healthy and effective ways of living.

An important point to remember is that the difficult person must want to change. If not, the problem behavior will continue. As an old adage goes, "You can lead a horse to water, but you can't make him drink." Of course, all behavior has consequences, as the difficult person will learn.

You can tell if you are dealing with a difficult person if:

- You think about him or her often.

- You tense up at the mention of his or her name.

- Ordinary coping techniques have failed.

- Your emotional health is deteriorating.

- Your job or personal performance is suffering.

- You are entertaining bizarre thoughts about the person.

So how do you deal with difficult people? There are ten steps or principles to follow.[7]

1. Be sure the best person available addresses the problem. Difficult people won't listen to everyone, and you may not be able to help them. Someone else may have more influence.

2. Choose battles carefully. People have just so much accommodation and flexibility in their makeup. Be sure the desired behavior change will be worth your effort.

3. Pick the right place. Address problems in private so that all parties can share thoughts and feelings in an uncensored way. Only when people are *fully* honest can problems be *truly* solved.

4. Pick the right time. Deal with problem behavior as soon as possible. Otherwise memories fade and the impact of actions will be filtered by time. One note: Balance timeliness with being calm. Overly emotional people can give and receive the wrong message.

5. Be constructive with feedback. Focus on the behavior, not the person. Discuss what the person has done and the impact as you see it. Be specific, but nonthreatening.

6. Tell and show how you feel. If the person knows you care, your criticism will get a better hearing. Think of a time when you have been corrected. You *really* listened when you knew the other person *truly* cared.

7. Manage your emotions. If you find yourself losing control, try biting your lip, counting to ten, taking "time out," or imagining yourself in a pleasant environment. Keeping a sense of humor will be an asset in this department.

8. Stop talking. Let the person vent. It is only natural to want to respond when someone gives criticism. There may be good reasons for the person's behavior, and these can be learned only when you listen. By listening carefully, you can understand underlying causes and feelings behind the facts.

9. Take the time to talk things over until there is agreement on appropriate future behavior. It is important to focus on creating a better future instead of reliving a negative past. In reaching agreement, be sure the person knows that, although the behavior may have been unacceptable, the person as an individual is valued. There are two important corollaries to gaining agreement on future behavior: (a) don't block all exits; allow face-saving behavior; (b) ask for changes that are possible to achieve.

10. When the person takes steps to change or improve, reinforce this with honest appreciation and sincere encouragement. Even small steps in the right direction should be recognized.

People can change by following this ten-point plan. As a last important point, remember that difficult behavior is in the eye of the beholder, and unless a person understands how his behavior harms others, he will not change happily or wholeheartedly. Any change will be accompanied by resentment that at some point and in some way may present a problem.

Three faces of love

The Greeks distinguished the various aspects of love with different words: *Eros* is romance, *philia* is friendship, *lude* is playfulness, *mania* is passion, and *agape* is altruism. Yale psychologist Robert Sternberg has developed a contemporary model of love based on three components—intimacy, passion, and commitment.[8]

- **Intimacy** is the emotional aspect of love and includes closeness, sharing, and understanding.

- **Passion** involves physical attraction and intense longing to be united.

- **Commitment** involves unwavering loyalty and personal sacrifice for the partner or the relationship.

These three components are the emotional, physical, and mental sides of a love triangle. Alone and in combination, they translate into eight possible kinds of relationships that have consequences in the subject of stress. See Figure 13.1.

1. **Nonlove:** When none of the three components is present, there is no love. This describes the majority of personal relationships, which are simply casual interactions.

2. **Friendship:** Intimacy is present, but passion and commitment are not. People share experiences, feel closeness, and like each other. Warmth and consideration characterize the relationship.

3. **Infatuation:** Passion is present, but intimacy and commitment are not. This involves a high degree of physical arousal and the desire for sexual contact.

4. **Mental love:** Commitment is present, but intimacy and passion are not. Intimacy is absent because partners do not share things. Passion may have been present, but it is now dormant.

5. **Romantic love:** Both passion and intimacy are present, but there is no long-term commitment. This describes many new relationships and short-term affairs.

6. **Fatuous love:** Commitment and passion are present, but there is no true intimacy. This describes stormy relationships that lack emotional support to make them comfortable.

7. **Companionate love:** Both intimacy and commitment are present, but there is no passion. This describes many long-term relationships in which physical attraction is absent or passion has waned.

8. **Consummate love:** When all three sides of the triangle are present, there is consummate or complete love. It is not automatic or permanent, but takes attention to develop and sustain. Consummate love describes the highest and most satisfying type of relationship.

Figure 13.1 Types of Love

This model describes eight variations of love, each of which is defined in terms of a balance of passion (physical attraction), intimacy (affection and sharing), and commitment (conscious decision to stay together).

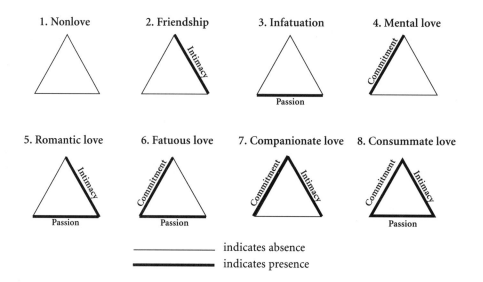

There is a pattern to the development of many relationships. Two individuals may begin with nonlove—no passion, commitment, or intimacy. In time, intimacy may grow and a friendship may develop. Then, passion may be added and romantic love may result. Eventually, consummate love may evolve as commitments are made. The end result may be marriage or some other long-term relationship. Such a relationship can be a great asset in managing stress, resulting in optimum health and happiness for both partners.

It usually takes time for consummate love to develop. High divorce rates can be the result of rushing events. Just as it takes time to grow a garden or make a good stew, it takes time for two people to get to know each other fully and care about each other with all of their hearts.

True love

Many people have the desire for love, but few are determined. This is why good relationships are as rare as they are. Determination requires effort and commitment. What is more, both partners must have these. When these elements are present and are seasoned with honesty, consideration, and patience, the result is true love.

A basic principle for a happy life is, don't settle. If you do, you will be doomed to be unhappy. Even if you hide the truth from others, you cannot hide it from yourself. Why do people settle for less when the result is so bad? They do so because, like children, they lack self-discipline to postpone gratification; or they do so because they feel unworthy of anything better; or they do so because they lack commitment to live at the level or standard of conduct of a more developed person.

Some people settle for less to please others, some settle for less to please themselves. Either way, their lives are diminished, and they never fulfill their full potential. Also, their partners are harmed because the relationship is either dishonest or selfish.

Poor choices

It is amazing to see how otherwise intelligent people spend more time shopping for a house or a car than they do for a partner for life. If a car isn't safe or a house isn't sound, they continue their search until they find one that is. But when it comes to a mate, they hurry the choice.

Some people rush because they fear losing out. They will accept almost anyone rather than risk being alone. Some people rush because they feel a void within themselves. Both of these reasons are prescriptions for disaster, because they are basically selfish.

Partners are *right* only when they are loved for themselves and not for oneself. This is the distinction between mature and immature love. The mature woman marries her hero, and the mature man marries his woman ideal, even if they have to wait to meet them.

While you wait, the answer is to be or become the person you yourself would love. This may involve reading, travel, education, service to others, and a myriad of other developmental activities. In doing so, you will be love-worthy rather than love-needy, and you will be ready to fulfill your part in a healthy relationship based on truth, trust, respect, and devotion to each other.

Chapter Thirteen References

[1] Martin Buber, *I and Thou*, trans. Gregory Smith (New York: Scribner, 1958).

[2] Gordon Allport, *Personality: A Psychological Interpretation* (New York: Henry Holt, 1937); and Gordon Allport, *Patterns and Growth in Personality* (New York: Holt, Rinehart, and Winston, 1961).

[3] Carl Rogers, *A Way of Being* (Boston: Houghton-Mifflin, 1980); and Carl Rogers, "The Necessity of Sufficient Conditions of Therapeutic Personality Change," *Journal of Consulting Psychology* 21 (1957): 95-103.

[4] Wendy Leebov, *Positive Co-Worker Relationships in Health Care* (Chicago: American Hospital Publishing, 1990).

[5] Raymond K. Tucker, *Fighting It Out with Difficult—If Not Impossible—People* (Dubuque: Kendall/Hunt, 1987), 5-6.

[6] Robert M. Bramson, *Coping with Difficult People* (New York: Simon & Schuster, 1986).

[7] Tucker, *Fighting It Out with Difficult People*, 5-6.

[8] R. J. Sternberg and S. Grajek, "The Nature of Love," *Journal of Personality and Social Psychology* 47, no. 1 (1984): 115-26; and R. J. Sternberg and J. L. Barnes, eds., *The Psychology of Love* (New Haven, Conn.: Yale University Press, 1988).

Chapter Fourteen
♥
No One is an Island

Human relations

Relationships are necessary for human survival and evolution. In the primate species, group life is required for protection from predators and for social learning. Although a solitary bear, elk, or bird can survive on its own, a solitary primate usually cannot. Only through cooperation have human beings come to dominate the world. Our early ancestors could no more have survived on the African savanna without working together than could a troop of baboons today.[1]

Human relations are important to the individual and the society. John Donne, the seventeenth-century English poet, wrote in the language of his time:

No man is an Iland, intire of it selfe;
Every man is a peece of the Continent,
A part of the maine;
If a Clod be washed away by the Sea, Europe is the lesse,
As well as if a Promontorie were,
As well as if a Mannor of thy friends, or of thine owne were;
Any man's death diminishes me,
Because I am involved in Mankinde;
And therefore;
Never send to know for whom the bell tolls;
It tolls for thee.[2]

Consider the parable of the good Samaritan, which makes a timeless point:

A certain man went down from Jerusalem to Jericho, and fell among thieves, who stripped him of his raiment, and wounded him, and departed, leaving him half dead. And by chance, there came down a certain priest that way: and when he saw him, he passed by on the other side. And likewise, a Levite, when he was at that place, came and looked on him and passed by on the other side. But a certain Samaritan, as he journeyed, came where he was: and when he saw him, he had compassion on him and went to him, and bound up his wounds, pouring in oil and wine, and set him on his own beast, and brought him to an inn, and took care of him. And on the morrow when he departed, he took out two pence, and gave them to the host, and said unto him, "Take care of him;

and whatsoever thou spendest more, when I come again, I will repay thee." Which now of these three, thinkest thou, was neighbor unto him that fell among the thieves? . . . Go, and do thou likewise.[3]

These messages have never been more important than in today's world. Most people live and work with others; therefore relationships are important in both our personal and our public lives.

Supportive relationships

The psychologist Karen Horney believed that all individuals naturally seek affection and approval. Where relationships are not warm and supportive, anxiety develops, and this interferes with the growth of a healthy personality. In such cases, people tend to respond in three basic ways: (1) by "moving toward people"— feeling inadequate, they become attached and dependent; (2) by "moving against people"—rejected, they become rebellious and aggressive; or (3) by "moving away from people"—they seek comfort for rejection in symbolic substitutes and fantasy. Neurotic behavior occurs when there is conflict over which response pattern to adopt in a given situation.[4]

Horney did not view people as doomed by predetermined instincts or trapped in patterns of behavior eternally established by early life experiences. Her concept of human existence is cheerful and optimistic. She saw the human being as a pilot, not a robot. She believed a person is born neither a devil nor a saint, but simply reflects the nature of relationships developed since the time of birth with significant people in the person's environment.

Horney believed that people have enormous potential to grow and develop. What is needed is not a method of controlling innately selfish or even predatory drives, but a means of tapping the human potential for growth by joining in supportive and productive relationships with others.[5]

Scott Peck, author of *The Road Less Traveled*, describes the character of supportive relationships. Such a relationship is safe precisely because no one is attempting to heal or convert you, to fix you, to change you. Instead, you are accepted as you are. You are tolerated and your foibles are accepted. You are valued, not as an object or means to other ends, but as a precious thing in your own right. In a supportive relationship, you are free to be you. You are free to discard defenses, masks, and disguises; free to grow and achieve your full potential; free to become your whole and true self.[6]

The importance of friendship

Friendship is affection and a bond that ties people together. It has a mental component based on shared values, an emotional component based on compatible personalities, and a behavioral component based on helpful actions. From Aristotle to the present, friendship has been constantly acknowledged for its contribution to the quality of living. The true friend is a life enhancer in good times and a life saver in bad times.

Best friends
On a rainy day long ago, a tall, skinny girl with an open smile walked up to me during recess and asked me to play. Her invitation marked the beginning of a friendship that has spanned four states, three marriages, and 30 years. Although we have been separated for most of those years, when we're reunited we can talk for five days straight. Kindred spirits, she called us when we were 11, using our favorite heroine's phrase from *Anne of Green Gables*, and kindred spirits we have remained.[7]—L. L.

In *Friends for Life*, Susan Wehrspann writes, "Friendship intensifies our consciousness and appreciation of life. It is the manifestation of the concept that one plus one can equal more than two. In our fast paced and increasingly isolated society, the importance of friendship cannot be denied. The affection and support of friends is imperative to our health and well-being."

According to Lillian Rubin, author of *Just Friends: The Role of Friendships in Our Lives*, kinship falls into the realm of the sacred, while friendship remains in the secular. Still, for many people—especially for young people who are exploring the world extending beyond the family and for older people whose family may be distant or even deceased—friendships can be extremely important.

What is a friend? A friend is someone you know, respect, trust, and like, and the feeling is mutual. The presence of these in a relationship determines whether a person is a best friend, close friend, good friend, or just a friend. What is the ideal friendship? It is based on mutual understanding, consideration, honesty, and, not least of all, compatibility of temperament and habits. Three key qualities that are valuable in a friend and helpful in a friendship are: (1) a cheerful disposition; (2) emotional stability; and (3) sensitivity to others' needs.[8]

How are women and men different in our society regarding friendship? In general, women compared to men:

- Believe it is more important to have a close friend,

- Feel more fulfilled in their friendships and are less lonely,

- Are more intimate with and feel closer to their friends,

- Are more open and self-disclosing in their relationships,

- Feel more affectionate and loving toward their friends,

- Feel more comfortable sharing personal problems and insecurities.

Communication problems and interpersonal conflicts are typically highly stressful for women.[9]

Men value friendship, but it is generally less personal and emotion-based. A minority of men report having a close friend. When asked what a "close friend" means, men typically say sharing similar activities such as participating in sports, playing cards, drinking, and working together. When men talk with friends, the topics most discussed are personal successes, current events, sports, women, and children. Topics rarely discussed are personal failures, insecurities, and financial problems, except between the closest of friends.[10] Pressure to communicate and intimate discussions can be uncomfortable and stressful for most men.

From the earliest days, American society has put relatively less value on enduring adult friendships, especially among males. Alexis de Tocqueville described the character of early-nineteenth-century American men as "always considering themselves as standing alone, and they are apt to imagine that their whole destiny is in their own hands."[11] The rugged individual—strong, alone, self-contained, and resourceful—continues as a heroic ideal for American men. Consider a ten-year-old boy's fourth-grade poem that begins, "I'm a space man, a great man, a high paid man, and alone." One can see that a strong male-image can be helpful in a hostile and competitive world but that an additional repertoire of attitudes and interpersonal skills is necessary to achieve one's full potential in life.[12]

Building relationships

Trust and respect are the key elements of a supportive relationship and true friendship. Trust is expressed by one's openness in sharing ideas and feelings. Respect is demonstrated by the willingness to listen to the ideas and feelings of others. The importance of trust is shown in the following story.

> **Trust in me**
> Three turtles went for a walk, and one said to the others, "Let's go have a cup of coffee."
>
> They entered a restaurant, and soon thereafter it began to rain.
>
> The oldest turtle said to the youngest, "Son, would you mind running home for my umbrella?"
>
> Whereupon, the young turtle replied skeptically, "I'll go get your umbrella if you promise not to drink my coffee."
>
> The old turtle promised, and the young turtle left to perform his mission.

Two years passed, when the old turtle said: "You know, I don't think Harry's coming back. We might as well drink his coffee."

Just then, a tiny voice was heard from behind the door: "If you do, I won't go get your umbrella."[13]

People can't learn trust and respect from listening to a lecture or reading a book; some concepts must be learned through firsthand experience. The following exercise allows you to build a relationship as well as review stress and change concepts in a two-way conversation with another person. It is ideally suited for a quiet environment, free from distractions.

Ⓔ Application: The Stress Encounter[14]

A theme frequently thought and occasionally voiced when people meet or work together is, "I'd like to get to know you, but I don't know how." This sentiment often is expressed in work groups and emerges in marriage and other one-on-one relationships. Getting to know another person involves a learnable set of skills and attitudes — self-disclosure, trust, listening, acceptance, and nonpossessive caring.

The conversation that you are about to have is intended to result in more effective human relations. Tasks are accomplished more effectively if people have the capacity to exchange ideas, feelings, and opinions freely. You will also review stress and change concepts and principles as they apply in your life.

In an understanding, nonjudgmental manner, one person shares information with another, who reciprocates. This results in a greater feeling of trust, understanding, and acceptance, and the relationship becomes closer.

The following ground rules should govern this experience:

- Each person responds to each statement before continuing to the next statement.

- Complete the statements in the order they appear, first one person responding and then the other.

- Do not write your responses.

- Questions and discussion are permitted, but always return to the questionnaire until all topics are covered (approximate time, one to two hours).

If your partner has finished reading, begin the exercise.

Introduction

My name is _____

My hometown is _____

What I do best is _____

My most unusual characteristic is _____

My favorite possession is _____

Understanding Stress

The biggest stress in my life is _____

My pressures are_____

My conflicts are _____

My frustrations are _____

My signs of stress are _____

My most healthful habit is _____

My least healthful habit is _____

I am aging at a rate that is _____

My hassles are _____

My uplifts are _____

What makes me laugh is _____

Personality and Stress

My best coping technique is_____

Commitment means _____

Control is _____

My attitude is _____

Keeping life in perspective means _____

Good relationships are_____

Stress Across the Life Span

Change is _____

My experience with change is _____

What I would like to change about myself is _____

My biggest adjustment has been _____

Changes at work_____

My current challenge is _____

The future appears _____

Personal Stress

I believe in _____

Reality is _____

Truth is _____

What I value most is _____

Peace of mind means _____

Misery is _____

Happiness is _____

My dream is _____

My fear is _____

Courage means _____

Character development _____

Interpersonal Stress

I like people who _____

To me, a relationship should _____

Love is _____

My family is _____

Men and women should _____

The ideal mate/partner for me is _____

The most difficult person in my life is _____

My best friend is_____

The person I trust most is _____

The person I respect most is _____

My biggest interpersonal stress is_____

Job Stress

For me, work means _____

My job is _____

The people I work with _____

My company/organization is _____

Money makes me _____

My biggest source of stress at work is _____

Peak Performance

My best talent is _____

I would like to _____

My biggest time waster is _____

My best time management technique is _____

My "personal best" has been _____

My next goal in life is _____

Stress Prevention

Tobacco, alcohol, and other drugs _____

I am thankful for _____

My physical exercise is _____

My rest habits are _____

My eating habits are _____

My fitness goal is _____

The Partnership

My first impression of you was _____

Now I think _____

Right now, I am feeling _____

If I were you, _____

You and I could _____

Have a brief discussion of your reactions to this conversation. Time permitting, you may wish to discuss other topics. Several possibilities are: projects at work, projects at home, and plans for the future.

Proven principles for good human relations

There is a well-known book that teaches universal principles for good human relations. Dale Carnegie's *How to Win Friends and Influence People*, first published in 1936, belongs in every personal development and stress management library. The following are five guidelines for good human relations drawn from this tried-and-true source.[15]

1. **Don't argue.** A good way to reduce stress and improve relationships is to be less judgmental, and a good way to handle an argument is to avoid it. Most of the time, an argument ends with each person more firmly convinced than ever that he or she is absolutely right. You can't win an argument. You can't win, because even if you win, you lose, for you will never get the other person's good will.

   In his biography, Benjamin Franklin tells how he conquered the habit of argument. One day, when Franklin was a youth, an old friend took him aside and said, "Ben, your opinions have a slap in them for everyone who differs with you. Your friends find they enjoy themselves better when you are not around. You know so much that no man can tell you anything. Indeed no man is going to try, for the effort would lead only to discomfort. So you are not likely ever to know any more than you do now, which is very little." Franklin was wise enough to realize that this was true, and he changed immediately.

   > I made it a rule," said Franklin, "to forbear all contradiction to the sentiments of others, and all assertions of my own. I even forbade myself the use of every expression that imported a fix'd opinion, such as 'undoubtedly,' and adopted, instead, 'I conceive a thing to be so'; or 'it so appears to me at present.' When another asserted something that I thought an error, I deny'd myself the pleasure of contradicting him abruptly, and in answering I began by observing that in certain cases or circumstances his opinion would be right, but in the present case there seem'd to me some difference. This became at length so habitual that perhaps for 50 years past no one has ever heard a dogmatical expression escape me. And to this habit I think it principally owing that I had early so much weight with my fellow citizens when I proposed new institutions, or alterations in the old, and so much influence in public councils."[16]

2. **Avoid complaining.** Complaining will not change things, and it doesn't make you feel better either. People don't like complainers and will avoid them if at all possible. Associating with complainers will bring you down in other peoples' minds and in your own as well. Negative thinking puts one in a negative mood and this can result in negative behavior. It is a destructive stress cycle that begins with complaining. Instead of complaining, look for the positive. Be an optimist.

As a practical matter, develop the habit of smiling. A smile shows interest and appreciation for others. It may interest efficiency experts and conservationists to know that it takes fewer muscles to smile than it does to frown. The adage "Smile and the world smiles with you; weep and you weep alone" has truth to it. Frowners go around complaining, looking for the negative, and putting people down. Don't be a frowner.

3. **Focus on others.** Be genuinely interested in their welfare. Think about the people you have liked in your life, and think about why. There is a good chance that they were genuinely interested in you as a person, not simply as a means of getting or accomplishing something. Think about good friends. One of the reasons you like them so much is because they show a genuine interest in you.

If you want good relations with others, forget yourself. People are interested in you, but they are interested in themselves as well. That is why you can make more friends in two months by becoming interested in other people than you can in two years by trying to get other people interested in you. If you want to improve your relations, do things for other people— things that require time, energy, and thoughtfulness. This is the secret of success in both personal and business dealings. Remember that the person you are talking to is usually more interested in himself than in any other subject. The ache in his tooth can mean more to him than a famine in China. If you want good human relations, be a good listener and encourage others to talk about themselves.

4. **Help people feel important.** The philosopher John Dewey believed the deepest urge in human nature is the desire to be important. Children cry for praise and men die for it. It was this recognition that led Abraham Lincoln to study law, that inspired Dickens to write his novels, and that makes people put their best foot forward in the presence of company. Because people want to feel important, you can achieve wonders by giving them honest appreciation. Every person feels special in some way, and a sure way to the heart is to let people know that you recognize their importance.

We should stop thinking of our own accomplishments and our own wants. Instead, focus on the other person's good points. Give honest and sincere appreciation, and people will cherish your words years after you have forgotten them. A word of thanks, a comment on how well a task is done, a handwritten note of sincere appreciation—these are thoughtful acts that satisfy everyone's natural need to feel important.

5. **Remember names.** One of the simplest, most obvious, and most effective ways of gaining good will and building relationships is to remember names. Yet so few people do it. Often we are introduced to a person, talk a few minutes, and can't even remember the person's name when we say goodbye. Many people fail to remember names because they don't expend the effort required to concentrate, repeat, and fix names indelibly in their minds. It takes effort, but "good manners," said Ralph Waldo Emerson, "are made up of small sacrifices." Remember that *a person's name is to him the sweetest and most important sound in the English language.*

As a review, if you want to prevent interpersonal stress and improve relationships, follow five proven principles: avoid arguments, don't be a complainer, show interest in others, help people feel important, and remember people's names.

Conclusion

For most people, the highs and lows of life involve others—children, parents, partners, and friends. In human relations, achieve the peaks of good stress and avoid the valleys of distress by knowing who you are, being true to your values, being honest and kind, considering others' needs, giving for giving's sake, and never doing harm.

As a practical application to end Chapter 14, do at least one of the following:

- Help someone with a problem.

- Write a thank-you letter to a person who has changed your life.

- Call a friend or family member you have not talked to for a long time.

- Do a great kindness for someone without that person knowing about it.

Emerson once wrote, "The only true gift is a portion of thyself." People have different things to give. Some have time. Others have talent. Everyone has love—which requires no expenditure at all unless for a postage stamp, or a telephone call, or a simple caring act.[17]

Personal Thoughts on Interpersonal Stress

Answer the following questions to personalize the content of Part Five. Space is provided for writing your thoughts.

- Have you ever had a relationship that made you sick physically or emotionally? Who was involved? What happened? What lessons were learned?

- Consider your family and its patterns of behavior. What can be done to improve family happiness and effectiveness?

- Martin Luther King Jr., spoke of the "web of mutuality" that connects human beings. List the people who have influenced your life the most. What specific advice or value has stuck with you?

  Person_____Value/advice_____

  Person_____Value/advice_____

  Person_____Value/advice_____

- What actions can you take to increase TLC in your world—with (a) children; (b) older people; (3) mates; (4) others?

- Evaluate a current relationship on the basis of intimacy, passion, and commitment. What type of love is this—mental love, romantic love, consummate love, etc.?

- Who can you turn to? Who listens to you when you need to talk? Who understands your innermost feelings? With whom can you be totally yourself? Who do you count on when you have problems to solve?

- Find a quiet place. Write a letter to someone out of your past who needs to hear from you. Show trust by sharing your feelings and ideas. Show respect by asking for the other person's advice or opinion. Mail your letter.

Chapter Fourteen References

[1]   Peter Farb, *Humanhind* (Boston: Houghton-Mifflin, 1978), 253.

[2]   John Donne and William Blake, *The Complete Poetry and Selected Prose of John Donne and the Complete Poetry of William Blake* (New York: Random House, 1941), 332.

[3]   *Holy Bible*, Luke 10: 30-37 King James version (Gordonsville, Tenn.: Dugan, 1988).

[4]   Karen Horney, *Neurosis and Human Growth: The Struggle Toward Self-Realization* (New York: W.W. Norton, 1950).

[5]   Horney, *Neurosis and Human Growth.*

[6]   M. Scott Peck, *The Road Less Traveled* (New York: Simon & Schuster, 1978).

[7]   Phillip Lopate, "What Friends are For," *Utne Reader*, September/October 1993. Originally from *Family Therapy Networker*, September/October 1990. Taken from *Against Joie de Vivre* (New York: Simon & Schuster, 1989).

[8]   Douglas Heath, *Fulfilling Lives: Paths to Maturity and Success* (San Francisco: Jossey-Bass Publishers, 1991), 165.

[9]   Heath, *Fulfilling Lives: Paths to Maturity and Success*, pp. 162-64.

[10]   Joel D. Block, *Friendship* (New York: Macmillan, 1980).

[11]   W. J. Schlaerth, ed., *A Symposium on Alexis de Tocqueville's Democracy in America* (New York: Fordham University Press, 1945).

[12]   Heath, *Fulfilling Lives: Paths to Maturity and Success*, p.163.

[13]   Will Forpe and John McCollister, *The Sunshine Book: Expressions of Love, Hope and Inspiration* (Middle Village, N.Y.: Jonathan David, 1979), 187.

[14]   Based on the work of John E. Jones and Johanna J. Jones in J. William Pfeiffer and John E. Jones, eds., *A Handbook of Structured Experiences for Human Relations Training* (San Diego: University Associates, 1974), 1.

[15]   Dale Carnegie, *How to Win Friends and Influence People* (New York: Simon & Schuster, 1936).

[16]   Benjamin Franklin, *Benjamin Franklin: An Autobiographical Portrait* (New York: Macmillan, 1969).

[17]   Ralph Waldo Emerson, "Gifts," in *The Collected Works of Ralph Waldo Emerson*, vol. 3, *Essays, Second Series* (Cambridge, Mass.: Belkap Press), 94.

Part Five Reading

What We Have Here is a Failure to Communicate

The following is the "anatomy of a marriage" from both the husband's and the wife's perspective. The picture painted is one couple's experience, occurring in a sequence of eleven stages. It rings of stress and pain, and illustrates the need for open and honest communication.

Wife's perspective	Husband's perspective
Stage 1	
The wife is in a state of emotional need. She is lonely, suffers from low self-esteem, and has had difficulty making female friends. She reaches for the romantic involvement of her husband, but he fails to notice. She resorts to nagging and complaining, which puts a greater wedge between them.	The husband has made business commitments that he must meet. He's in a highly competitive and satisfying position, and his emotional energies are drained by the time he comes home. He loves his wife, but he doesn't have much time to "carry her," psychologically.
Stage 2	
She experiences greater frustration and depression, which gradually gives way to anger. She begins to "attack" her bewildered husband for his failures in the home.	He makes some feeble attempts to relate to his wife, especially after emotional explosions have occurred between them. But this leopard finds it difficult to change his spots. He is still overcommitted at work, whether he likes it or not, and he constantly falls back into familiar patterns.
Stage 3	
This needy woman is now in a dangerous position. She is vulnerable to any attractive, available man who comes into her life. Inevitably, such an encounter occurs. A casual introduction to a flirtatious man sets the wheels in	The husband continues in ignorance of what his wife is experiencing. His mind is elsewhere. He wishes she would be happier because he loves her and the kids, but he has no idea how her unhappiness relates to him.

Source: Charles C. Dobson, Love Must Be Tough. *Copyright © 1994, Word Publishing, Nashville, Tenn. All rights reserved.*

motion, and he quickly becomes the object of her fantasies, hopes, and dreams. He appears to be so compassionate compared to her husband, so much more dignified, so much more in touch with her feelings, so much more worthy of respect. Nothing illicit has occurred at this point, but she is spending a great deal of time thinking about an affair with this specific man.

Stage 4

An extramarital relationship gradually begins to heat up. It is no sudden romp in the grass. Rather, the affair grows slowly, with more secret meetings and an escalating friendship. She feels guilty, of course, but the excitement is incredible. Anyway, her husband doesn't seem to care. Finally it happens; a sexual experience occurs.

The man of the house is still not aware of any unfaithfulness. He may notice some coolness and a lessened demand for his attention, but his suspicions are not aroused. Her hostility to him may increase during this time, but he has already become accustomed to that attitude in her.

Stage 5

More illicit sexual activity now transpires, with all the guilt, fear, and raw passions that accompany this way of life. Her spiritual life rapidly deteriorates, as she lies and rationalizes and lives a double standard. It is a tough assignment to play-act the role of a faithful wife when she's giving her all to someone else. Bible reading and church attendance become less frequent or even nonexistent. She loses all sexual interest in her husband.

The man may now begin to worry about the deteriorating relationship for the first time. He doesn't yet have much evidence on which to base his suspicions, but he knows intuitively that something has changed. His reaction is still one of confusion at this stage.

Stage 6

For the wife, the affair continues hot and heavy. Every minute that can be spent with her new lover is grabbed.

Somehow discovery occurs, usually by "accident." Perhaps a tiny lie is betrayed, or an anonymous phone call is received. His first reaction is one of utter shock! He can't believe what has happened. He confronts his wife in one of the most emotional and unpleasant encounters in their lives. It will be remembered forever.

Stage 7

Her feelings of guilt and embarrassment are concealed behind rationalizations and recriminations against her husband. She is going to admit nothing that she doesn't have to disclose. Depending on the quality of her husband's evidence, she may continue to lie and deny at this stage. On the other hand, some women will break emotionally, weeping profusely and begging for forgiveness. Either way, this stage is characterized by wildly fluctuating emotions from day to day.

For the first time, enormous pain is felt by the husband. Whereas he could hardly give his wife the time of day a few weeks before, his unfaithful partner suddenly becomes the only important thing in his life. This guy who would rather go to a football game with his male friends than be with his wife—the man who hid behind the newspaper every night after work—now finds himself pleading for her favors.

Stage 8

We come now to a critical juncture. When confronted by the implications of their behavior, some women decide not to sacrifice their families, but to reconcile with their husbands. Others are determined to have their own way and go with the new lover, who is infinitely more exciting and alluring. Such a woman may pity her mate and desire not to hurt him, but she finds him boring and disdainful.

The pain experienced by the husband is intensified. He had never known such stress in his entire life. Jealousy burns through his mind as he imagines what his wife and her lover have done together. At alternating times, he feels rage, guilt, remorse, love, hate, and despair.

Stage 9

It has been said, "A woman wants a man she can look up to, but one who won't look down on her." It is true. Women need to hold their husbands in a certain awe, or at least in modest respect, if their relationship is to be healthy. Men are taught to love their wives, and women to respect their husbands. Those are the conditions needed by each sex. Nevertheless, this woman begins to experience a tug-of-war in her mind. The welfare of her children weighs heavily in her thoughts, and she knows they are hurting. She sees the flaws and faults of her new lover for the first time, and the romantic dream fades just a bit. Sex with him is still exciting, but it no longer thrills her as it did. All the ugly realities of divorce stare her in the face. Is that what she wants? Still, she remembers her prior state of loneliness and low self-esteem. "I can't go back to that!" she says to herself. It is this motivation, more than any other, that may push her over the edge.

The agitation of stage 8 continues unabated, especially as the husband contemplates the details of what his wife and her lover are experiencing together. He doesn't think he can stand it, and that sense of panic is evident in everything he does. His work suffers and his face reveals the strain he is under. Unfortunately, the behavior now being shown by the rejected lover serves to assassinate respect and put a severe strain on a relationship already stretched to the breaking point.

Stage 10

The decision to divorce is made; lawyers are consulted; papers are filed; hearings are held and property is divided. The children are caught between the parents and become the object of struggle and contest. A bloody custody battle is fought with numerous casualties on both sides. Harsh words are exchanged. Tears are shed. Then they are dried. Life goes on,

The human mind cannot tolerate agitated depression and grief indefinitely. The healthy personality will act to protect itself in time, throwing off the despair and groping for stability. One method by which this is accomplished is by turning pain into anger. Thus, the husband may harbor a deep hostility toward his wife —the one who betrayed his trust,

people learn to cope. But every now and then, just before the woman goes to sleep at night or perhaps in a moment of quietness, she asks herself, "What have I done?"

shattered his home, took half his money, and hurt his kids. He no longer accepts the blame for what has happened, feeling instead that he was betrayed. He would not take his wife back now under any circumstances. He begins to brace himself for whatever may come.

Stage 11

As events unfold, she weds her new lover and life is exciting for a time. But eventually, it becomes more like her first marriage. The great thrill is gone, and daily living is routine once more. The dating and laughter and the walks and talks give way to doing laundry and fixing meals and going to work. The marriage may be successful or it may not. The probabilities of another divorce are higher than for first marriages, perhaps because both partners have demonstrated a willingness to have an affair with married lovers. If there is no divorce, the new husband and wife plod on through the years. They have convinced themselves they did the right thing—except . . . when they think of the children . . . they feel guilty.

The man gradually works his way through bitterness to a state of apathy. Life returns to normal except that his wife is gone. He will probably remarry, since divorced men are in much greater demand than divorced women in our society. He again loses himself in work and slams the door on the past. Except . . . when he thinks of the kids . . . he feels guilty.

Questions

1. Contrast a happy marriage with an unhappy marriage. What are the qualities of the people and qualities of the relationship that make a difference?

2. Evaluate this case on the basis of intimacy, passion, and commitment. Which components of love appear to be present or missing?

3. Do you think the wife in this case did the right thing? What, if anything, should she have done differently? What is your opinion of the husband?

Part Six

Stress in the Workplace

15. Job Stress

16. The Job Burnout Phenomenon

17. Work Morale

The job was getting to the ambulance attendant. He felt disturbed by the recurring tragedy, isolated by the long shifts. His marriage was in trouble. He was drinking too much. One night it all blew up.

He rode in back that night. His partner drove. Their first call was for a man whose leg had been cut off by a train. His screaming and agony were horrifying, but the second call was worse. It was a child-beating. As the attendant treated the youngster's bruised body and snapped bones, he thought of his own child. His fury grew.

Immediately after leaving the child at the hospital, the attendants were sent out to help a heart attack victim seen lying in a street. When they arrived, however, they found not a cardiac patient but a drunk—a wino passed out. As they lifted the man into the ambulance, their frustration and anger came to a head. They decided to give the wino a ride he would remember.

The ambulance vaulted over railroad tracks at high speed. The driver took the corners as fast as he could, flinging the wino from side to side in the back. To the attendants, it was a joke. Suddenly, the man began having a real heart attack. The attendant in back leaned over the wino and started shouting. "Die, you . . . ," he yelled. "Die."

He watched as the wino shuddered. He watched as the wino died. By the time they reached the hospital, they had their stories straight. "Dead on arrival," they said. "Nothing we could do."—*Cincinnati Enquirer*, January 20, 1980, sec. F, p.10.

What you will learn in Part Six

In Part Six you will learn:

- the causes and consequences of stress in the workplace;
- the relationship between stress levels and job performance;
- job burnout prevention and wellness efforts.

Chapter Fifteen

Job Stress

Understanding the problem

The ambulance attendant is a tragic story about stress and burnout. It is extreme but instructive, because it shows the life-and-death consequences this subject can have.

Job-related stress is one of the most important issues of our time. The National Institute for Occupational Safety and Health reports that psychological disorders are among the ten leading work-related impairments in the United States, accounting for an estimated $15 billion in disability payments and lost wages. This is in addition to the debilitating toll that job stress takes on the mental and physical well-being of individual workers and their families.[1]

The modern workplace is an increasingly stressful place. If Ozzie and Harriet of the fifties were catapulted into the nineties, their stress levels would be high indeed. To begin with, Ozzie's salary alone wouldn't be enough to keep David in sports and Ricky in music, so Harriet would probably have to work outside the home, bringing a myriad of challenges to everyone in the family.

The 1964 World's Fair in New York promised a 20-hour workweek, time-saving conveniences in the home, and more leisure time than we would know what to do with. What happened instead? The pace and volume of work is relentless for increasing numbers of people. High profile cases of burnout are only the most visible, as more and more Americans feel stressed and stretched to exhaustion. Working parents in particular feel overloaded, sleep-deprived, and often guilty for not spending enough time with their children and each other. Add global competition, changing technology, and consumerism to our work ethic, and one sees a nation that is pushing too hard.[2]

Michael Losey, president of the Society for Human Resource Management, describes the impact of stress on the individual:

> The feverish pace most corporations have set for themselves is perhaps the largest contributor to workers' high stress levels. Facsimile machines, beepers, computers, cellular telephones, and other products of the modern workplace have fueled the problem. Automation has left many workers virtually on call twenty-four hours a day. They feel a sense of "never punching out" and "no down time for rest." Clients and bosses can and do contact employees at home, in the car, at restaurants, during family outings—basically anywhere, at any time. As Henry David Thoreau once said, men have become the tools of their tools.[3]

A 1997 Gallup/USA Today survey showed the average Fortune 1000 worker receives 83 messages a day—84 percent say they are interrupted three or more times an hour. The average day: regular phone messages 32; e-mail messages 14; voice mail messages 11; fax documents 9; Post-It notes 6; telephone message slips 5; paper messages 4; cellular phone messages 2. This excludes U.S. mail, overnight courier, and interoffice mail. Message overload has resulted in an unintended but real reduction in business civility as people are simply unable to respond to the volume of messages they receive.

Juliet Shor, Harvard economist and author of *The Overworked American: The Unexpected Decline of Leisure,* sheds light on historical forces and events that have helped create the overstressed American worker:

> It all began with the Pilgrims who reduced leisure by dropping from the calendar more than 50 holidays enjoyed by the English since medieval times. Sunday was declared to be the only toil-free day. By the time the Industrial Revolution arrived in America, the Pilgrims' work ethic was woven thoroughly into management's expectations; so much so that labor unions had to work for a century to secure eight-hour work days with at least one day of rest.

> With the end of World War II and the increased prosperity and leisure of the next thirty years, most unions reduced their vigilance. When the era of layoffs and vast cutbacks came to first one and then another industry and company during the '70s, '80s, and '90s, employees were unprepared to resist the side effects of "downsizing." Today companies routinely ask employees, including managers, to do the work of 1.3 people—for the same pay and with less time off. Overtime is at a modern-day high (an average of 4.7 hours a week) while in the last decade, the average yearly vacation and other paid absences decreased by 3.5 days. These are patterns that are expected to continue.[4]

More than 100 million Americans spend approximately one-third of their day on the job. Currently, five major forces or trends are sources of stress for increasing numbers of these people.

- **New technology.** Job skills and tasks are changing rapidly. No one can ignore the revolution in work caused by computer technology. Nearly every employee, from the front-line worker to the corporate executive, has been impacted by the introduction of the computer in the workplace[5]. No longer can a person just walk in the door and be a decent citizen. Now it's walk in the door, be a decent citizen, and know how to run several computer programs. More than fifty million workers use computers every day along with other products of modern technology—faxes, cellular phones, and e-mail. This creates "virtual offices" for workers on the go, accelerating information transfer and changing the way products are developed and services provided.[6] Check here if *new technology* affects you. _____

- **Workforce diversity.** New members of the workforce are increasingly diverse and possess skill sets and value systems that are different from those of earlier generations. Existing workers may have either obsolete or advanced skills; new employees may have either deficient or superior skills. These differences, along with differences in race, gender, nationality, and creed, can result in a social mix that is highly stressful.[7] Check here if *workforce diversity* affects you. _____

- **Global competition.** The intensification of international competition brings pressure to perform and fear of failure. This phenomenon has been studied extensively in the case of Japan and the manufacture of automobiles, but it involves many other countries and a multitude of industries.[8] In the relatively sheltered era of the 1960s, 7 percent of the U.S. economy was exposed to international competition. That number grew to 70 percent during the 1980s , and it is expected to climb higher with every passing year.[9] Check here if *global competition* affects you. _____

- **Organizational restructure.** The phenomenon of organizational restructuring—mergers, takeovers, re-engineering, and rightsizing—is a continuing drumbeat reported in newspapers, magazines, and television. For an enormous number of people, these developments are sources of uncertainty, worry, and stress.[10] Displaced workers typically experience pay cuts, as downward mobility is the norm more than the exception. The reality for most people caught in organization restructure is that spending power and standards of living decline.[11] Check here if *organization restructure* affects you. _____

- **Changing work systems.** There is an emerging redefinition of work itself, with a growing disappearance of the job as a fixed bundle of tasks. In its place is an emphasis on fluid and constantly changing work assignments required to fulfill ever-increasing demands of customers. Change in how work is accomplished has become a way of life in the workplace, as many new concepts are tried, adapted, and discarded, only to be replaced by newer approaches. Quality teams, process improvement, and semiautonomous work groups are examples of a trend in which traditional methods of hierarchical supervision are replaced by work teams and self-direction in a general shift from tier to peer.[12] Check here if you are affected by *changing work systems.* _____

Stress at work and public policy

The good news is that the majority of U.S. workers are psychologically sound and are coping relatively well with work and with life in general. The bad news is that substantial numbers of people do not enjoy this condition, but are afflicted by the job stress syndrome. Some of these people are struggling with personal or family problems that often have repercussions on the job. The good news is that in recent years the mental health community and some governmental agencies have focused attention and resources on the subject of work and well-being.[13]

One product of collaboration between the National Institute of Occupational Safety and Health, the Association of Schools for Public Health, and experts from the American Psychological Association, labor, and industry is agreement on a blueprint for protecting the health and well-being of American workers. The four cornerstones of this blueprint are:

- well-designed jobs;

- evaluation systems to detect psychological disorders and underlying risk factors;

- education of workers and managers on the signs, causes, effects, and control of work-related psychological disorders; and

- improved mental health service delivery for workers.[14]

Stress across cultures[15]

Occupational stress is not only an American issue. It is a concern in other industrial nations as well, for example, Japan. *Karoshi* is a Japanese word meaning "death (shi) from overwork (karo)." Officially defined as a fatal mix of apoplexy, high blood pressure, and stress, *karoshi* strikes primarily middle managers in their 40s and 50s who are characterized as being *moretsu sha-in* (fanatical workers) and *yoi kigyo sen-shi* (good corporate soldiers).

Karoshi is becoming more common in Japan as men and women struggle to meet the physical and emotional demands of modern Japanese life. Long working hours, little or no exercise, constant pressure to meet expectations, relentless traffic, little time for family, too much alcohol, too many cigarettes, increasing financial pressures, and a poor diet set the stage. The curtain comes down, not from an epidemic of some insidious virus, but from heart attacks, complications of high blood pressure, lung cancer, suicide, and the entire collection of degenerative diseases.[16]

Research conducted by Japan's Institute of Public Health identified five patterns of work behavior that lead to the fatal *karoshi* syndrome:

1. Extremely long hours that interfere with normal recovery and rest patterns

2. Night work that interferes with normal recovery and rest patterns

3. Work without holidays or breaks

4. High-pressure work without breaks

5. Extremely demanding physical labor and continuously stressful work without relief[17]

Assessing job stress

In this country, an important study of workplace stress conducted by Northwestern National Life Insurance Company (NWNL) revealed that 27 percent of American workers considered their jobs to be their greatest single source of stress. Additional results showed the following:[18]

- One in three Americans have thought seriously about quitting their jobs because of workplace stress.

- One in three expects to be "burned out" on the job in the near future.

- 14 percent quit or changed jobs in the past two years due to job stress.

- 46 percent of workers report job stress levels that are extremely or very high, twice as many as in 1985.

- Employees who are single or divorced report a higher likelihood of burnout.

- 70 percent of workers say job stress lowers their productivity and contributes to frequent health ailments.

- 91 percent say employers must act to reduce stress.

- 82 percent say victims of job stress deserve disability pay from their employers.

Figure 15.1 shows a positive correlation between the size of an organization, based on number of employees, and the likelihood that managers are working near burnout—the bigger the organization, the higher the burnout reported. NWNL discovered other factors, such as "working longer hours," "spending more time in the office on weekends," and "being less patient with subordinates," also tend to increase with organizational size.

Figure 15.1 Stress by Organization Size

Number of employees in organization	% reporting "managers working near burnout"
Fewer than 100	17
100 to 499	27
500 to 2,499	28
2,500+	33
Overall Average	**25**

Source: Northwestern Life Insurance Company, Fear and Violence in the Workplace, *1993.*

Figure 15.2 shows the perceived impact of organizational downsizing or consolidation on management-level employees.

Figure 15.2 Managers, Stress, and Downsizing

Managers in my organization	Respondents from organizations that *have* significantly downsized or consolidated	Respondents from organizations that *have not* significantly downsized or consolidated
Are preoccupied with their careers.	11%	5%
Are less patient with their subordinates.	16	9
Are treated less like members of the management "team" than they once were.	25	14
Are less decisive.	18	11
Act as if they are in less control of what goes on around them.	39	23
Appear more "stressed"; that is, under pressure and chafing at it.	58	35
Seem tired all the time.	18	12
Seem to be working close to "burnout."	35	22
Are more competitive and less cooperative with fellow managers.	15	10
Seem to be working longer hours.	56	39
Come into the office on weekends more frequently.	29	23

Source: Northwestern Life Insurance Company, Fear and Violence in the Workplace, *1993.*

Harold Kahler, president of the Wellness Councils of America, states, "The corporate culture of many workplaces makes unrealistic demands on employees. Organizations need to assess their environments, organization structures, and personnel policies to make stress-reducing changes." For example, family-friendly work policies such as emergency leave and flexible work schedules that help employees (especially lower-wage employees) cope with the demands of child care and caring for sick parents typically result in appreciation and tangible economic returns—decreased absenteeism, turnover, and waste; increased loyalty, productivity, and profits.

Complete the following questionnaire to assess the level of stress in your workplace. Managers and employees can use the results of this survey to work together in creating a high-morale and high-performance work environment.

Application: The NWNL Workplace Stress Test[19]

Thinking about your workplace, how strongly do you agree or disagree with the following statements? For each statement, mark the response that best describes conditions.

	Disagree Strongly	Disagree Somewhat	Neutral or Don't Know	Agree Somewhat	Agree Strongly
Section A					
1. Management is supportive of employees' efforts.	4 ❏	3 ❏	❏	2 ❏	1 ❏
2. Management encourages work and personal support groups.	4 ❏	3 ❏	❏	2 ❏	1 ❏
3. Management and employees talk openly.	4 ❏	3 ❏	❏	2 ❏	1 ❏
4. Employees receive training when assigned new tasks.	4 ❏	3 ❏	❏	2 ❏	1 ❏
5. Employees are recognized and rewarded for their contributions.	4 ❏	3 ❏	❏	2 ❏	1 ❏
6. Work rules are published and are the same for everyone.	4 ❏	3 ❏	❏	2 ❏	1 ❏
7. Employees have current and understandable job descriptions.	4 ❏	3 ❏	❏	2 ❏	1 ❏
8. Management appreciates humor in the workplace.	4 ❏	3 ❏	❏	2 ❏	1 ❏
9. Employees and management are trained in how to resolve conflicts.	4 ❏	3 ❏	❏	2 ❏	1 ❏
10. Employees are free to talk with one another.	4 ❏	3 ❏	❏	2 ❏	1 ❏

	Disagree Strongly	Disagree Somewhat	Neutral or Don't Know	Agree Somewhat	Agree Strongly
Section B					
11. Workloads vary greatly for individuals or between individuals.	1 ❑	2 ❑	❑	3 ❑	4 ❑
12. Employees have work spaces that are crowded.	1 ❑	2 ❑	❑	3 ❑	4 ❑
13. Employees do not have access to technology they need.	1 ❑	2 ❑	❑	3 ❑	4 ❑
14. Few opportunities for advancement are available.	1 ❑	2 ❑	❑	3 ❑	4 ❑
15. Employees are given little control in how they do their work.	1 ❑	2 ❑	❑	3 ❑	4 ❑
16. Employees generally are physically isolated.	1 ❑	2 ❑	❑	3 ❑	4 ❑
17. Mandatory overtime is frequently required.	1 ❑	2 ❑	❑	3 ❑	4 ❑
18. Employees have little or no privacy.	1 ❑	2 ❑	❑	3 ❑	4 ❑
19. Performance of work units generally is below average.	1 ❑	2 ❑	❑	3 ❑	4 ❑
20. Personal conflicts on the job are common.	1 ❑	2 ❑	❑	3 ❑	4 ❑
21. Consequences of making a mistake on the job are severe.	1 ❑	2 ❑	❑	3 ❑	4 ❑

	Disagree Strongly	Disagree Somewhat	Neutral or Don't Know	Agree Somewhat	Agree Strongly

Section C

	Disagree Strongly	Disagree Somewhat	Neutral or Don't Know	Agree Somewhat	Agree Strongly
22. Employees expect the organization will be sold or relocated.	1 ❏	2 ❏	❏	3 ❏	4 ❏
23. There has been a major reorganization in the past 12 months.	1 ❏	2 ❏	❏	3 ❏	4 ❏

	Disagree Strongly	Disagree Somewhat	Neutral or Don't Know	Agree Somewhat	Agree Strongly

Section D

	Disagree Strongly	Disagree Somewhat	Neutral or Don't Know	Agree Somewhat	Agree Strongly
24. Meal breaks are unpredictable.	1 ❏	2 ❏	❏	3 ❏	4 ❏
25. Medical and mental health benefits are provided by the employer.	4 ❏	3 ❏	❏	2 ❏	1 ❏
26. Employees are given information regularly on how to cope with stress.	4 ❏	3 ❏	❏	2 ❏	1 ❏
27. Sick and vacation benefits are below that of similar organizations.	1 ❏	2 ❏	❏	3 ❏	4 ❏
28. Employee benefits have been significantly cut in the past 12 months.	1 ❏	2 ❏	❏	3 ❏	4 ❏
29. An employee assistance program (EAP) is offered.	4 ❏	3 ❏	❏	2 ❏	1 ❏
30. Pay is below the going rate.	1 ❏	2 ❏	❏	3 ❏	4 ❏
31. Employees can work flexible hours.	4 ❏	3 ❏	❏	2 ❏	1 ❏
32. Employees have a place and time to relax during the workday.	4 ❏	3 ❏	❏	2 ❏	1 ❏

33. Employer has a formal employee communications program.

4 ❑   3 ❑   ❑   2 ❑   1 ❑

	Disagree Strongly	Disagree Somewhat	Neutral or Don't Know	Agree Somewhat	Agree Strongly

Section E

34. Child care programs or referral services are available.

4 ❑   3 ❑   ❑   2 ❑   1 ❑

35. Referral programs or day care for elderly relatives are offered.

4 ❑   3 ❑   ❑   2 ❑   1 ❑

36. Privileges are granted fairly, based on an employee's level of responsibility.

4 ❑   3 ❑   ❑   2 ❑   1 ❑

37. Better machines or ways of working were introduced in the past year.

4 ❑   3 ❑   ❑   2 ❑   1 ❑

38. Employer offers exercise or other stress-reduction programs.

4 ❑   3 ❑   ❑   2 ❑   1 ❑

	Disagree Strongly	Disagree Somewhat	Neutral or Don't Know	Agree Somewhat	Agree Strongly

Section F

39. Work is primarily sedentary or physically exhausting.

1 ❑   2 ❑   ❑   3 ❑   4 ❑

40. Most work is machine-paced or fast-paced.

1 ❑   2 ❑   ❑   3 ❑   4 ❑

41. Staffing or expense budgets are inadequate.

1 ❑   2 ❑   ❑   3 ❑   4 ❑

42. Noise or vibration is high, or temperatures are extreme or fluctuating.

1 ❑   2 ❑   ❑   3 ❑   4 ❑

43. Employees deal with a lot of red tape to get things done.
    1 ❑   2 ❑   ❑   3 ❑   4 ❑

44. Downsizing or layoffs have occurred in the past 12 months.
    1 ❑   2 ❑   ❑   3 ❑   4 ❑

45. Employees can display personal items in their work areas.
    4 ❑   3 ❑   ❑   2 ❑   1 ❑

46. The amount of change is too great or too rapid for employees to handle.
    1 ❑   2 ❑   ❑   3 ❑   4 ❑

Scoring

Add your scores for each section and insert your section totals below.

Section A. Employee Support and Training Total: _____

Low	Medium	High
0 .... 14.1	14.2 .... 19.6	19.7 40

The Employee Support and Training Scale is composed of ten measures of how well management communicates with employees and encourages a nonthreatening, comfortable work atmosphere. The scale also reflects the adequacy of training, clearness of direction, and fairness of management. *A low score on the scale indicates supportive behaviors that reduce workplace stress.*

Section B. Work Conditions Total: _____

Low	Medium	High
0 .... 17.8	17.9 .... 22.2	22.3 44

The Work Conditions Scale is composed of eleven items measuring how effectively work loads are managed. *A low score indicates management efforts to reduce stress by empowering employees, ensuring adequate resources are available, and allocating work effectively and equitably.*

Section C. Organizational Change Total: _____

Low	Medium	High
0 .... 2.3	2.4 .... 4.6	4.7 8

The Organizational Change Scale comprises two changes that significantly affect workplace stress: a major reorganization and the expectation that the company will be sold or relocated. *A low score indicates few stressors related to change.*

Section D. Employee Benefits Total: _____

Low	Medium	High
0 .... 18.3	18.4 .... 22.1	22.2 40

The Employee Benefits Scale is composed of ten items describing the employee benefits and workplace amenities that are offered by an organization. *Employers who provide a wide range of benefits and competitive compensation will record a lower organizational stress level.*

Section E. Progressive Programs Total: _____

Low	Medium	High
0 .... 12.9	13.0 .... 14.2	14.3 20

The Progressive Programs Scale is composed of five advanced programs or activities that help employees cope with job stress. *A low score indicates lower workplace stress.*

Section F. Job Design and Physical Environment Total: _____

Low	Medium	High
0 .... 15.9	16.0 .... 18.8	18.9 32

The Job Design and Physical Environment Scale uses eight characteristics of the organization's working environment that affect stress. The scale reflects type of work, staffing levels, and physical conditions. *A low score reflects a positive work environment.*

Grand Score, 1 to 184 Total: _____
	Low	Medium	High
	0 .... 81.1	81.2 .... 101.5	101.6 184

The Grand Score for the NWNL Workplace Stress Test reflects overall risk from the negative effects of job stress. Workplaces that record low stress scores are less likely to suffer the costs associated with high turnover and frequent stress-related illnesses among employees.

According to NWNL research director Peggy Lawless, the top ten ways organizations can reduce employee burnout are:[20]

- Allow employees to talk freely with one another.

- Reduce personal conflicts on the job.

- Give employees adequate control in how they do their work.

- Ensure adequate staffing and expense budgets.

- Talk openly with employees.

- Support employees' efforts.

- Provide competitive personal leave and vacation benefits.

- Maintain adequate levels of employee benefits.

- Reduce red tape and paperwork.

- Recognize and reward employees for their efforts and accomplishments.

Research shows that a higher percentage of employees report burnout in organizations that do not have programs or policies similar to the ten recommendations.

Additional surveys available to assess job stress include the Occupational Stress Inventory,[21] the Generic Job Stress Questionnaire,[22] and the Work Environment Scale.[23]

The Occupational Stress Inventory (OSI) measures a wide range of job stressors, employee resources for coping with stress, and mental and physical strains. The various subscales have demonstrated good test reliability, and occupational norms are available. Plotting standardized scores on each subscale provides a "stress profile" for workers.

The Generic Job Stress Questionnaire (GJSQ), developed by the National Institute of Occupational Safety and Health, assesses a variety of job stressors as well as stress reactions or strains. Most of the subscales were adapted from prior scales with known reliability and validity. The questionnaire is modular so that organizations can select individual scales, or the whole instrument can be used.

The Work Environment Scale (WES) is designed to assess the general work climate. It contains ninety items that compose ten subscales, and it uses a true-false response format. The subscales have demonstrated good reliability and validity and are used often by researchers. Also, occupational norms are available for this instrument.

Another excellent resource for information on job stress assessment is *Stress and Well-being at Work: Assessments and Interventions for Occupational Mental Health*, published by the American Psychological Association.[24]

The costs of work stress

Work stress is costly and is reflected in decreased productivity and low job satisfaction. Stress contributes to absenteeism, mistakes, turnover, and increased health costs.[25] The Aspen Institute for the Management of Stress reports that premature death of employees costs American industry more than $25 billion per year, and this amount is rising.[26] Paul Rosch of the American Institute of Stress Research reports that U.S. industry is spending more than $200 billion annually on job stress costs, a figure that continues to increase every year. This amount is more than ten times the cost of all combined strikes and more than the after-tax profits of all the Fortune 500 companies.[27]

The Metropolitan Life Insurance Company estimates that an average of one million workers are absent on any given day, largely due to stress disorders.[28] The National Council on Compensation Insurance reports that claim benefits paid for stress average $15,000, twice the amount paid for the average physical injury claim.[29] The *Wall Street Journal* reports that U.S. stress-related disability cases doubled in ten years, rising to cost employers an average of $73,720 each.[30] The yearly cost of U.S. workers' compensation payments due to stress is expected to exceed $90 billion by the turn of the century.[31]

Even minor stress-related illnesses can have a substantial impact on an organization. A study conducted by one insurance company showed that the annual cost of a single employee with anxiety headaches was almost $3,400. This included loss of productivity, visits to the company medical facility, and negative psychological effects on coworkers and subordinates. One employee under stress can cause stress in others.[32]

Causes of job stress

For many people, the workplace is becoming more and more stressful. The work*load* is increasing, work *standards* are being raised, and the work *pace* is relentless. The following are common causes of stress on the job.[33] Suggested solutions for leaders follow each (see Rx):

- **Job assignments.** Seventy-eight percent of American workers report that their jobs are often stressful. Findings indicate that the single greatest cause of job stress is dissatisfaction with job assignments. This includes lack of meaning, lack of challenge, and lack of participation in decision making, especially in how work is organized and paced.[34]

  Rx: The number-one strategy for preventing and reducing job stress is to assign the right person to the right job in the first place. This includes establishing meaningful and challenging goals and encouraging active involvement in decision-making activities.

- **Schedules, shift work, and deadlines.** Heavy workload and time pressure are increasingly common causes of stress in the workplace. Jobs can be categorized as easy jobs, middle jobs, and killer jobs. Have you ever had a killer job due to schedules and deadlines? If so, you know firsthand how stressful a job can be. The volume of work a person is expected to do, including travel, meetings, reports, and record keeping, can be highly stressful. Whether the workload is dictated by others or initiated by the individual, continually having too many things to do, and having to do many things almost simultaneously, can result in excessive wear and tear, fatigue, and breakdown.

  Rx: Leaders should distribute workloads evenly across the workforce. Overworking some people and underusing others results in high stress, low morale, and decreased productivity for all.

- **Fear of failure.** Have you ever felt over your head and afraid of failing? A major cause of stress at work is fear of failure, especially if an individual is the sole or primary provider for his or her family. Such worries as, "I won't be able to do what is expected," "I might let others down," and "I will probably look foolish" wear a person down emotionally and physically.

  Rx: Leaders should avoid assigning work that is beyond a person's current level of ability. This can be done by matching the person with the task according to interest and skill and by being sure that everyone is properly trained.

- **Inadequate support.** Have you ever had a tough assignment to do without the resources to do it? A common cause of stress at work is lack of support to do the job. If there are insufficient funds, inadequate supplies, improper tools, or too little teamwork, tension builds and energy is drained.[35]

   Rx: Leaders should not make work assignments without providing the support necessary to accomplish them. (Imagine a person given the task of cleaning a facility without the supplies and equipment to do the job.) Also, leaders should promote communication, teamwork, and a one-team attitude within the work group. Lack of coworker support creates stress, lowers morale, and reduces overall productivity.

- **Problems with the leader.** If you have ever been the victim of a bad boss or the beneficiary of a great boss, you know how important the leader can be in the stress equation. The inadequacies of another person can be particularly stressful, especially if the other person has power over you. Stress is created when people do not feel understood, appreciated, and supported. Also, if the leader is incompetent in administrative or technical duties, extra stress will be experienced when mistakes are made. If a leader is incompetent and also provides inadequate support, people may really have trouble, since the inadequate leader may blame others for personal failings when something goes wrong.

   Rx: Leaders should guard against being "stress carriers." Stress carriers don't feel pressure, conflict, and frustration personally; they pass these on to others. In contrast, a good leader embodies three virtues: (1) Integrity—The leader tells the truth as he or she believes it to be and has courage to live by convictions. (2) Job knowledge—This helps the leader solve problems and aids in teaching others. (3) Concern for others—The caring leader spends time and effort to understand others, shows appreciation for their work, and actively supports them. A good leader strives to be effective in technical and administrative duties so that unnecessary stress is not created.

- **Not knowing what is expected of you or where you stand.** Role ambiguity or lack of clarity about the job and criteria for performance is a common cause of stress in the workplace. Have you ever had a job, but you didn't know what your job was? Have you ever had a job and you didn't know how well you were doing? Both of these conditions can cause anxiety and result in unnecessary stress.

   For example, one university department head thought his job was first, to teach two courses each term; second, to advise students; and third, to develop new academic programs. After discussing his responsibilities with the dean, he learned he had the elements of the job correct, but in opposite priority order. His job was actually first, to create new academic programs; second, to advise students; and third, to teach a course every once in a while. The situation was stressful to both parties until they reached a common understanding about what was expected of the department head.

Rx: Leaders should communicate job duties in order of priority and should let people know how they are getting along. A good leader will point out in private ways to improve and will give credit in public for a job well done. Clarity of assignment and feedback on performance are especially important in today's rapidly changing organizations.

Besides these common causes of stress, each job has unique pressures, conflicts, and frustrations. What are the special problems of your industry, profession, or trade? Consider customers, work processes, safety, and other aspects of the work environment. See Figure 15.3.

Figure 15.3 Causes of Stress in the Work Setting

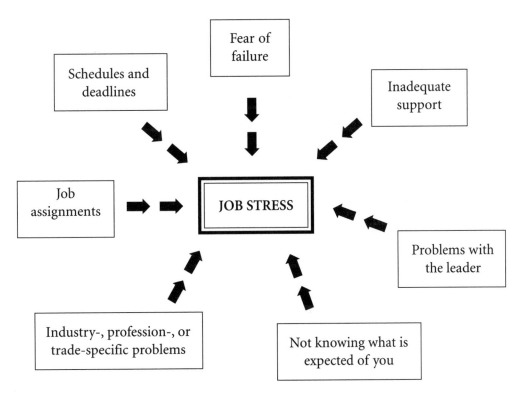

Stress levels and job performance—occupational overload and underload

In 1908, Robert Yerkes and J. D. Dodson of Yale University showed that stress improves performance up to a maximum point, after which efficiency decreases.[36] As seen in Figure 15.4, stress is necessary for optimum job performance. If stress levels are either too low or too high, job performance is reduced. The Yerkes-Dodson law can be illustrated in an athletic event, a college exam, or a business transaction. The lesson is the same: People perform best when mental and physical arousal are moderate rather than extreme. At the optimum performance zone, there is high physical energy, mental alertness, and personal motivation.

Figure 15.4: The Relationship between Stress Levels and Job Performance

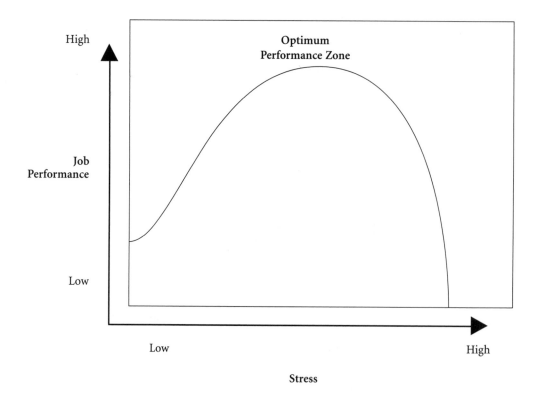

Source: Keith Davis, Human Behavior at Work, *8th ed. (New York: McGraw-Hill, Inc., 1989). Copyright © 1989, McGraw-Hill. Reprinted with permission.*

Some occupational stress comes from overload—too much pressure, conflict, and frustration; some comes from underload—boredom, lack of meaning, and low job satisfaction. Both overload and underload are likely to result in high levels of stress, poor health, and ultimately, poor job performance.

The following report on air traffic controllers shows the impact that occupational overloading can have on stress levels and health.

Tension in the tower

Air traffic controllers at Chicago's O'Hare International Airport are responsible for millions of passengers a year. About 666,560 takeoffs and landing occur—one every 20 seconds. Any letup from constant vigilance, a slight error in the instructions, or a switch missed can result in a fatal air crash. This intense stress is comparable to battle fatigue and has been labeled "collisionitis."

By the controllers' own estimates, there are two or three near-misses every day. These near-misses might be avoided if the controllers followed the FAA regulations that specify the minimum distance between landing aircraft: five miles apart for big jets and three miles apart for standard-sized planes. That is the theory. In practice, the controllers cannot "go by the book" because the volume of traffic is too great. The standards become the maximum, not the minimum. When peak traffic reached 220 takeoffs and landings in one hour, the controllers were commended by their supervisors, commended in part for violating the safety overload.

When the medical records of 4,000 flight controllers were compared to those of 8,000 second-class airmen, the results were startling. High blood pressure was four times as common and developed at an earlier age among the controllers. Twice as many controllers also suffered from peptic ulcers as did the airmen. These psychosomatic illnesses, as well as anxiety, insomnia, loss of appetite, irritability, and depression, were found to be greatest among controllers at the busiest airports. And O'Hare is the busiest one of all. [67.2 million passengers in 1996, according to Airports Council International][37]

When an individual is unable to handle all the work input, a state of overload occurs. Unlike an electrical system with a circuit breaker, people do not have an automatic safety device, and the overload condition can lead to physical, mental, and job performance problems.

Some occupations are by nature more stressful than others. Police officers, firefighters, and bus drivers hold relatively high-stress jobs because of the amount of pressure, conflict, and frustration inherent in the work. The National Institute for Occupational Safety and Health (NIOSH) reports that the highest-stress jobs are those that place the worker in contact with the public in situations over which the worker has little personal control.

Researchers from Cornell Medical College found that the most stressful jobs combine high demands with lack of autonomy. People in this double bind suffer three times the usual incidence of high blood pressure. Also, stress is compounded if the image of the job is negative in either the public or the employee's eye or if the employee perceives a lack of organizational support.[38]

In contrast to overloading, some employees are underloaded. They experience low challenge and little intrinsic satisfaction in their jobs. Their workdays are boring and dissatisfying. The following study shows the negative effect occupational underloading can have on stress levels and health.

Assembly-line hysteria

This strange malady affects women more than men and strikes suddenly, without warning. It spreads so quickly that an assembly line or an entire plant may have to shut down within days or even hours of the first appearance of the disorder.

Consider the experience of an electronics plant in Ohio. One morning a worker on the assembly line began to feel dizzy, light-headed, and nauseous. She complained of muscular weakness and difficulty in breathing. In a matter of minutes, some three dozen employees were being treated in the company's dispensary for the same symptoms. The illness spread. Shortly thereafter the plant had to be closed.

Investigators thought it was something in the air—some chemical, gas, virus, or other infectious agent. Physicians, toxicologists, and industrial hygienists conducted an intensive search and found nothing in the plant that could explain the disorder. The cause was assembly-line hysteria, a mass psychogenic illness that spreads by contagion and has no physical origin. It is not uncommon.

Typical symptoms of assembly-line hysteria are headaches, nausea, chills, blurred vision, muscular weakness, and difficulty in breathing. The condition seems to be related to physical and psychological stress on the job. Assembly-line hysteria is a psychological illness; there is nothing toxic in the air to produce the symptoms. Psychological stressors may be more important. Boredom seems to be the key. Monotonous, repetitive work can lead to muscle tension, job dissatisfaction, and depression.[39]

In general, the most stressed workers are those at the bottom of the job ladder—the bossed, rather than the bosses. One reason is that they typically have far less control over their work situations. People "on the front line" often have high pressure to perform but may have little authority to make decisions. In addition, they may receive low financial rewards combined with low job security and promotion prospects. In 1978, NIOSH commissioned a group of researchers to determine which occupations are associated with the highest incidence of stress-related disorders, such as hypertension and heart disease. The group studied 130 occupations and examined the health records of 22,000 people. Laborers had more stress-related illnesses than other occupations, and secretaries were second.[40]

The most stressful jobs have "high demand" tasks with little relief, power, or pay. Or they involve great responsibility and some control, but they do not meet the social esteem and self-actualization needs of the worker. The best jobs have a high salary to compensate for stress, involve the worker in making decisions, and are challenging for personal growth.

As you evaluate your own job, is yours a case of overload or underload, or is your stress level ideal for optimum job performance and personal satisfaction?

Women, work, and stress—desiring careers but loving families

Many women do not work for wages, yet the stress in their lives can be fully as great as for those who do. The duties required in maintaining a home and raising children may result in overload or underload, depending on the person and the situation.

For those who choose or are required to hold down a job and raise a family at the same time, significant levels of stress can result. The amount of pressure they face, conflict they experience, and frustration they feel can be enormous.

Sociologist Arlie Hochschild describes the working mother's plight in her book *The Second Shift:* After working a full day on the job, she then puts in a full shift at home. In fact, women work an average of fifteen hours a week more than their husbands do.[41]

The typical problem unfolds: Wanting to be a model mother and wonderful wife, as well as a perfect professional, the modern woman is increasingly over-committed and overstressed.

Everyone has heard the saying "Man must work from sun to sun, but a woman's work is never done." Consider that this phrase was coined before the current era when more and more women have the responsibility of a job outside the home in addition to the traditional roles of mother and homemaker. If you are this woman, or if you live with her, you know the syndrome firsthand—day after day of constant work morning until night. If you do not know such a person yourself, you can learn from reading the following description:

A day in the life of a working mother
She is up at 6:00 A.M., has a shower and her makeup on by 6:30, at which time she wakens her husband and kids. She makes breakfast and everyone eats by 7:15. Everyone needs something—lunch money, a doctor's note, or a newspaper tucked under the arm—on the way to the door.

As she drives to work, she makes three stops: drops off Jessie at day care, picks up dry cleaning, and buys donuts for the office monthly meeting. It is 7:55 when she swings into the parking lot. She grabs her high heel shoes (because she's supposed to dress great, too), and dashes across the drive and into the door at 8:00 sharp.

She no longer feels fresh as a daisy as she confronts her desk and the to-do list ahead. By 8:15 and with a kickoff coffee, she is focused and in the work groove. Her pace is steady as she moves efficiently through the day, from meeting to memo to meeting again. Her energy holds up as she maintains a high level of production, pausing just once for a personal break. She loves her work and is proud of her company, so her job is not a negative.

Lunch time is used for errands, the normal pattern for most workdays. She buys a card for her friend who has just had surgery and has lunch while she drives, including a soda from the cooler that she keeps in the car.

From 1:00 P.M. on, the day goes crazy. A supplier slips up, a customer complains, a coworker has problems, and then she gets the message she most hates to hear—"Your son's school called." She handles them all and still finishes the key account report by the end of the day.

As she straightens her office and prepares to go home, she thinks of the day and what it has meant. She is relieved that her son's school problem was easily handled, but she is also thankful that she could have called on her husband if the problem had required a trip to school. It was work as normal, but what does that mean? It was money for the family, but was it enough? It was time, which is life, and was it well spent?

These are good questions for the future, but more important is the flurry of activity that lies ahead. First is day-care pickup of little Jessie, then a swing by school for Billy. Both of these are must-hits and they are always eventful, with progress reports, funny stories, laughter, and sometimes tears.

She arrives home at 5:45 but can't sit down or even start dinner because Susie is standing in the driveway and needs to be at her dance lesson by 6:00.

While she waits for Susie, she uses the time productively to outline the talk she has to give the next day. The company believes in employee involvement and her team presentation has to go well.

She's off again by 7:30, but now it's so late she decides to zip by the fast-food drive-through rather than cooking the meal she had planned. At 8:00 she is ready to set the food out, talk with the kids, and meet her husband.

Dinner goes well, but as with most things, it seems a little late and a little rushed, plus dishes, homework, and laundry are yet to be done.

At 10:00 she has a choice: do the family bills, check the news, return her mom's call, sew Billy's pants, write her friend's card, or talk with her husband. She wants to talk with Fred, but he is concentrating on Billy's Cub Scout project. She does 1 through 5, and then it's time for bed.

She is too tired to fall asleep, plus she is waiting on Fred. She thinks about the family, each one in turn—their health, their happiness, and what they need. She then thinks about herself. She is tired but happy. She knows she is spending her chips, but she wouldn't change if she could. Her only question is, can I keep it up? And, how do others do it who don't have a husband?

The second half of the twentieth century has witnessed profound change in the lives of American women. In 1950 fewer than one-fourth of married women were in the workforce. Today more than 58 percent of married women work, and 75 percent of them are employed full time. The proportion of women who have young children and work has also risen. In 1950 only 12 percent of women with preschool children worked. Today, 60 percent are employed outside the home. For women with school-age children, the proportion is 75 percent who work, up from 28 percent in 1950.[42] As women have moved into paid employment, there has been little reduction in home responsibilities and duties, making them candidates for poor physical and mental health resulting from work-family role conflict, role strain, and fatigue from sheer overwork.[43]

Occupational boredom, satisfaction, and health

Hours worked and volume of workload often have less influence on job satisfaction than personal factors, such as having the opportunity to use one's skills and to participate in decision making. Also, as job satisfaction decreases, anxiety, depression, and psychosomatic illnesses increase. Thus, assembly-line workers typically report less satisfaction and experience greater stress-related disorders than do family physicians, who work an average of fifty-five hours per week, with many demands on their free time and great mental concentration required on the job. Figure 15.5 presents fifteen occupations and their rankings according to level of satisfaction and level of boredom.

Figure 15.5 Ranking of Occupational Satisfaction and Boredom
(Average Boredom: 100)

Level of satisfaction (highest to lowest)	Occupation	Level of boredom (lowest to highest)
1	Physician	48
2	Professor	49
3	Air traffic controller (large airport)	59
4	Police officer	63
5	Administrator	66
6	Scientist	66
7	White-collar supervisor	72
8	Electronics technician	87
9	Computer programmer	96
10	Engineer	100
11	Accountant	107
12	Monitor of continuous flow of goods	122
13	Assembler (working at own pace)	160
14	Forklift driver	170
15	Assembler (work paced by machine)	207

Source: R.D. Caplan, et al., Job Demands and Worker Health: Main Effects and Occupational Differences *(Washington, D.C.: National Institute for Occupational Safety and Health; University of Michigan, Institute for Social Research, 1980)*

Two points should be noted:

- this study reports statistical averages and not individual cases;

- occupational satisfaction is a function of both the specific job assignment and the nature of the individual worker.

Thus, a person employed as an assembly worker, forklift operator, or accountant may find the job to be stimulating and satisfying and not harmful to health, while another person employed as a physician, professor, or administrator may be unchallenged and dissatisfied with the job and suffer stress-related health problems. This is called the "job rust-out" phenomenon.

The executive monkey studies

Whether yours is a high-stress field, such as law enforcement, or a low-stress profession, such as library science, and regardless of whether you are satisfied or bored with your job, if you feel the responsibility of office yet feel out of control, then the case of the "executive monkey" and related research will be of interest to you.

"Executive monkeys develop ulcers" was the conclusion of a study Joseph Brady did in 1958.[44] In this study, Brady placed pairs of monkeys in an environment where both received electric shocks. A red light signaled the shock period. However, the monkeys were not shocked if one of them operated a lever that prevented the flow of electric current. See Figure 15.6.

In each pair of monkeys, the "executive monkey"—the one having access to an operational lever (so named because of the analogy to human executive situations)—was able to learn the relationship between the light, the lever, and the shocks. The other, "nonexecutive" monkey had a nonoperational lever and therefore was unable to learn any way to prevent the flow of electric current. The only thing this monkey knew was that every once in a while there was a shock, but the monkey didn't know why.

Figure 15.6

Which one is the executive? The executive monkey is the one that must keep pressing the key to keep from getting shocked; the other monkey just gets shocked without knowing anything about the responsibility placed on the one with the key. The executive monkey will develop ulcers and die, while the other moneky, though receiving the same shocks, will remain healthy.

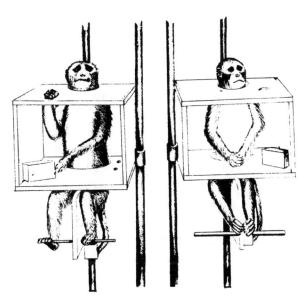

In this study, the executive monkeys, who were responsible for saving their partners and themselves, developed ulcers and died, while the uninformed, nonexecutive monkeys remained healthy. The results of the study suggested that the burden of responsibility, including the need to maintain a high degree of vigilance and pressure to make decisions, was the cause of the high level of stress resulting in death.

A follow-up study on rats conducted by Jay Weiss provided additional information as to the demise of the executive monkeys.[45] One primary difference between the Weiss study and the Brady study was that Weiss used a warning tone to signal the imminent onset of electric current. Weiss showed that the executive animals were much more able to cope with responsibility and avoid ulcers if they were given feedback on their behavior. He did this by arranging conditions so that the lever, when operated, would prevent shock *and* would also turn off the warning tone that preceded the shock. This provided clear evidence to the executive animal, in the form of tone cessation, that shock could be avoided, whereas Brady's executive monkeys received no such assurances.

Weiss's animals learned through feedback that they could control their situation, whereas Brady's monkeys felt less control. The conclusion was that pressure to perform without feeling in control can result in health problems and even death. Weiss found that the responsibility of office was not the cause of debilitating stress, but the feeling of frustration and being out of control was.

In light of the executive animal studies, you may decide against assuming significant responsibilities in life (such as becoming a parent or supervisor, or having a business of your own). On the other hand, you may recognize the penalties in wear and tear that may accompany responsible positions but decide that the price is justified by the personal, social, and economic rewards. In any case, the executive animal studies demonstrate the importance of having a sense of control when one assumes responsibility.

Robert Karasek of Columbia University has found that people with little control over their jobs, such as assembly-line workers and cooks, have higher rates of heart disease than people who can choose the pace and method of their work. People who deal with the public but have little opportunity for independent decision making are those most negatively affected. The combination of high psychological demands and low personal control appears to raise the risk of heart disease by "about the same order of magnitude as smoking or having a high cholesterol level.[46]

If you are in a position to accept responsibility, be sure you have adequate power to influence the events for which you will be held responsible. In addition, management should be sure to delegate to subordinates sufficient authority as well as responsibility to accomplish tasks. The following is a classic experiment demonstrating the importance of feeling in control—not only to manage stress, but to maximize job performance.

> Adult subjects were given complex puzzles to solve and a proofreading chore. In the background was a loud, randomly occurring distracting noise; to be specific, it was "a combination of two people speaking Spanish, one person speaking Armenian, a mimeograph machine running, a desk calculator, a typewriter, and street noise—producing a composite, nondistinguishable roar. The subjects were split into two groups. Individuals in one set were just told to work at the task. Individuals in the other were provided with a button to turn off the noise, a modern analog of control—the off switch." The group with the off switch solved five times the number of puzzles as their cohorts and made but a tiny fraction of the number of proofreading errors. Now for the kicker: " . . . none of the subjects in the off switch group ever used the switch. The mere knowledge that one can exert control made the difference."[47]

Chapter Fifteen References

[1]   Gwendolyn Puryea Keita and Joseph J. Hurrell Jr., *Job Stress in a Changing Workforce: Investigating Gender, Diversity, and Family Issues* (Washington, D.C.: American Psychological Association, 1994), xiii.

[2]   "A Nation of the Quick and the Dead-Tired," *Newsweek,* March 6, 1995.

[3]   Michael Losey, "Managing Stress in the Workplace," *Modern Office Technology,* February 1991.

[4]   "Breaking Point," *Newsweek* , March 6, 1995, pp. 56-61.

[5]   B. Garson, *The Electronic Sweatshop* (New York: Simon & Schuster, 1988); and S. Suboff, *In the Age of the Smart Machine: The Future of Work and Power* (New York: Basic Books, 1988).

[6]   Wayne F. Cascio, "Whither Industrial and Organizational Psychology in a Changing World of Work," *American Psychologist,* November 1995.

[7]   D. M. Herold, "Using Technology to Improve Management and Labor Trends," Journal *of Organizational Change Management* 3, no. 2: 44-57.

[8]   R. E. Walton, *Innovating to Compete* (San Francisco: Jossey-Bass, 1987).

[9]   S. C. Gwynne, "The Long Haul," *Time,* September 28, 1992,: pp. 34-38.

[10] P. R. Lawrence and D. Ryer, *Renewing American Industry* (New York: Free Press, 1983).

[11] Wayne F. Cascio, "What Do We Know? What Have We Learned?" *Academy of Management Executive* 7, no. 1 (February 1993): 95-104.

[12] Wayne F. Cascio, "Whither Industrial and Organizational Psychology in a Changing World of Work," *American Psychologist,* November 1995, and S. M. Dray, "From Tier to Peer: Organizational Adaptation to New Computing Architectures," *Ergonomics* 31, no. 5 (1988): 721-25.

[13] E. Carroll Curtis, Panel Comments, "Surveillance of Psychological Disorders in the Workplace," in *Work and Well-Being: An Agenda for the 1990s,* ed. Gwendolyn Puryear Keita and Steven L. Sauter, (Washington, D.C.: American Psychological Association, 1992): 97-99.

[14] Steven L. Sauter, "Introduction to the NIOSH National Strategy," in Keita and Sauter, *Work and Well-Being.*

[15] S. Glazer (in progress). *A Cross-Cultural Study of Job Stress Among Nurses.* Unpublished doctoral dissertation, Central Michigan University, Mt. Pleasant.

[16] Robert S. Eliot, *From Stress to Strength* (New York: Bantam, 1994), 13.

[17] James E. Loehr, *Toughness Training for Life* (New York: A Plume Book, 1994).

[18] Northwestern National Life Insurance Company, *Fear and Violence in the Workplace: A Survey Documenting the Experience of American Workers* (Minneapolis, Minn.: Northwestern National Life Insurance Company, 1993).

[19] "Employee Burnout: Causes and Cures" 1992, ReliaStar. Reprinted with permission.

[20] Peggy Lawless, Northwestern National Life Insurance Company.

[21] S. M. Osipow and A. R. Spokane, *A Manual for Measures of Occupational Stress, Strain, and Coping* (Columbus, Ohio: Marathon Consulting and Press, 1983).

[22] J. Hurrell Jr. and A.M. McLaney, "Exposure to Job Stress: A New Psychometric Instrument," *Scandinavian Journal of Work Environment and Health,* Suppl. 1, 14 (1988): 27-28.

[23] R. H. Moos, *Work Environment Scale Manual* (Palo Alto, Calif.: Consulting Psychologists Press, 1981).

[24] J. Quick, L. Murphy, and J. Hurrell, eds., *Stress and Well-Being at Work: Assessments and Interventions for Occupational Mental Health* (Washington, D.C.: American Psychological Association, 1992). For additional information on predictions and consequences of occupational stress, see T. A. Beehr, *Psychological stress in the workplace.* (London: Routledge, 1995) and T. H. Monk and D. I. Tepas Shiftwork (1985). In C. L. Cooper and M. J. Smith, eds., *Job stress and blue collar work* (Chichester, Great Britain: John Wiley & Sons Ltd) pp. 65-84.

[25] Claudia Wallis, Ruth Mehrtens Galvin, and Dick Thompson, "Stress: Can We Cope?" *Time,* June 6, 1983, pp. 48-54; and Virginia M. Gibson, "Stress in the Workplace: A Hidden Cost Factor," *HR Magazine,* January 1993.

[26] Linda Standke, "The Advantages of Training People to Handle Stress," *Training/HDR* 16 (February 1979): 24.

[27] Paul J. Rosch, "Job Stress: America's Leading Health Problem," *USA Magazine,* May 1991; and National Safety Council, *Stress Management* (Boston: Jones and Bartlett, 1995).

[28] Rosch and Pelletier, 1987.

[29] McCarty, 1988 ; and "Risk Management/Benefits," *National Underwriter* 98, no. 19 (May 9, 1994).

[30] *Wall Street Journal,* May 1991.

[31] *Statistical Abstracts of the United States,* 110th ed. (Washington, D.C.: U.S. Department of Commerce, 1990), 363.

[32] James S. Munuso, "Executive Stress Management," *Personnel Administrator* 24 (November 1979): 23-26.

[33] Munuso, "Executive Stress Management," 23-26; also Robert Pearse, *What Managers Think about Their Managerial Careers* (New York: AMACOM, 1977), as it appeared in Warren H. Schmidt, "Basic Concepts of Organization Stress—Causes and Problems," in *Occupational Stress: Proceedings of the Conference on Occupational Stress,* Los Angeles, 3 November 1977 (Cincinnati: U.S. Department of Health, Education and Welfare: National Institute of Occupational Safety and Health, 1978), 5. Also see T. A. Beehr and J. E. Newman. (1978). Job stress, employee health, and organizational effectivensss: A facet analysis, model, and literature review. *Personnel Psychology,* 31, 665-699. C. L. Cooper and J. Marshall (1978). Sources of managerial and white collar stress. In C. L. Cooper and R. Payne, eds., *Stress at work* (pp. 82-105). (Chichester, England: John Wiley & Sons Ltd.). J. Barton, E. Spelten, P. Totterdell, L. Smith, S. Folkard, and G. Costa (1995). The Stnadard Shiftwork Index: A battery of questionnaires for assessing shiftwork-related problems. *Work and Stress,* 9 (1), 4-30.

[34] *Fears and Fantasies of the American Worker* (New York: D'arcy, Masius, Benton and Bowles Advertising, May 1986).

[35] J. Chapman, "Collegial Support Linked to Reduction of Job Stress," *Nursing Management* 24, no. 5 (1993): 52-54.

[36] Wallis, "Stress: Can We Cope?" 54; and J.M. Aurelio, "An Organizational Culture that Optimizes Stress: Acceptable Stress in Nursing," *Nursing Adminstration Quarterly* 18 (Fall 1993): 1-10.

[37] Adapted from L. Martindale, "Torment in the Tower," *Chicago,* April 1976, pp. 96-101; also R. L. Repetti, "Short-term Effects of Occupational Stressors on Daily Mood and Health Complaints," *Health Psychology* 12, no. 2 (March 1993): 125-31; also H. Zeier, "Workload and Psychophysiological Stress Reactions in Air Traffic Controllers," *Ergonomics* 37, no. 3 (March 1994): 525-39.

[38] "Stress Producing Jobs," from the Editor's Notebook, *Nursing 82* 12, no. 1 (January 1982): 97; also B. Kirkcaldy, C. L. Cooper, P. Ruffalo, "Work Stress and Health in a Sample of U.S. Police," *Psychological Reports* 76, no. 2 (April 1995): 700-702.

[39] Michael J. Colligan and William Stockton, "The Mystery of Assembly-Line Hysteria," *Psychology Today* 12 (June 1978): 93-99, 114, 116.

[40] M. Smith, M. Collisan, and J. Hurrell, "A Review of NIOSH Psychological Stress Research," in *Occupational Stress*, NIOSH #78-156 (Washington, D.C.: Department of Health, Education, and Welfare); also J. Siegrist, "Emotions and Health in Occupational Life: New Scientific Findings and Policy Recommendations," *Patient Education and Counseling* 25, no. 3 (July 1995): 227-36.

[41] Arlie R. Hochschild, *The Second Shift: Working Parents and the Revolution at Home* (New York: Viking, 1989).

[42] U.S. Bureau of Labor Statistics, 1992.

[43] F. Crosby, *Spouse, Parent, Worker: On Gender and Multiple Roles* (New Haven, Conn.: Yale University Press, 1988).

[44] Joseph V. Brady, "Ulcers in Executive Monkeys," *Scientific American* 199, no. 4 (October 1958): 95-100.

[45] Jay M. Weiss, "Psychological Factors in Stress and Disease," *Scientific American* 226 (June 1972): 104-13.

[46] Geoffrey Cowley, "Dialing the Stress-Meter Down," *Newsweek,* March 6, 1995; and Wallis, "Stress: Can We Cope?" 52.

[47] Thomas J. Peters and Robert H. Waterman Jr., *In Search of Excellence* (New York: Harper & Row, Publishers, Inc., 1982), xxiii, xxiv.

Chapter Sixteen

🌾

The Job Burnout Phenomenon

Describing the problem

Danger lurks in modern society, and the victim is often the dedicated and talented person. This danger is called "burnout," and it can occur both on the job and in the home. The dictionary definition of burnout is "to fail, wear out, or become exhausted due to excessive demands on one's strength, resources, and energy."

In the human sphere, burnout is what happens when a person experiences physical, psychological, and spiritual fatigue and is unable to cope. Lack of energy and low vitality are characteristics of physical fatigue. Symptoms of psychological fatigue include depression and loss of sharpness in thinking and feeling. Spiritual fatigue is characterized by lack of interest and meaning in life, resulting in unhappiness and pessimism.[1]

Burnout can strike the businessperson with too many pressures and too little time, the homemaker with too much work and not enough appreciation, and the friend who is tired of being his or her "brother's keeper." The following are common types of burnout victims. Do any sound familiar to you?

- "Superpeople," who want to do everything themselves because no one else can or will, and they have never let anyone down

- "Workaholics," who are driven to meet unreasonable demands placed on them (either self-incurred or assigned by others)

- "Burned-out Samaritans," who are always giving to others while receiving little help or appreciation in return

- "Mismatched people," who do their jobs well but who do not like what they are doing

- "Midcareer coasters," who may once have been high performers but whose enthusiasm is gone

- "Overstressed students," holding down full-time jobs and full course loads[2]

Burnout was introduced to the scientific literature in the early 1970s by psychologists Herbert Freudenberger and Christina Maslach. The evocative image of their term has made it a popular topic in the print and electronic media since that time. Extensive research has also been carried out. One literature search of the *Psychological Abstracts* revealed more than one thousand research articles and nearly one hundred books on burnout.[3]

Burnout occurs frequently and to a wide range of individuals. It has been identified as a problem in the work of such professionals as physicians, nurses, managers, police officers, teachers, lawyers, and social workers.[4]

Burnout is a great equalizer. It is blind to age, sex, color, and creed. It is a condition that can affect both white- and blue-collar workers as well as those who work at home. Job burnout is widespread in modern society. It is hazardous, and it can be contagious. If left unchecked, it can harm individual health, human relationships, and organization effectiveness.

A study by the American Academy of Family Physicians reported the extent of job stress for five occupations. They surveyed 4,473 people working as business executives, teachers, secretaries, garment workers, and farmers, and found the number who usually or always work under stress to be high—80 percent of the business executives, 66 percent of the teachers and secretaries, 44 percent of the garment workers, and 35 percent of the farmers.[5]

Participants in this study identified the major sources of stress to be work overload, pressure from superiors, deadlines, and low salaries. Probably the most important finding was the relationship discovered between job stress and health. Individuals reporting high work stress had two to four times as many health problems, including allergies, migraines, backaches, depression, insomnia, and other classic signs of burnout.[6]

The end result of burnout is that a company loses its best people at a critical point in time, or it leaves them so stressed that their attitude sabotages projects. The end result for the individual can be even more tragic, as the following story shows.

We buried Joe today

People were surprised when Joe suffered a sudden fatal heart attack since he didn't seem ill or particularly out of condition. Joe was a salesman in his late fifties, who went into sales thirty years ago because he could sell anything. He was a great talker, people liked him, and he was known for his tremendous energy. One day, Joe accepted a position with a large corporation. He liked the idea of having a big product to push and wanted the security that working for a big company offered him.

Gradually, though, Joe found that what he had accomplished was under siege by younger men who had the kind of energy and enthusiasm that, after two decades on the job, Joe found hard to muster routinely. The facts before Joe were scary—his mortgage payments and living expenses were high, his children were in college, and the prospect of retirement loomed darkly before him. The benefits of his work—a larger home and more expensive toys—suddenly caused more worry than joy.

Joe became troubled over whether he could maintain the pace that he set for himself and his company expected him to meet. He began pushing himself harder and harder to perform, complaining almost daily that he was losing his touch, that his memory wasn't as sharp, that he couldn't make the number of sales calls he used to, and that he couldn't put in the hours he did twenty-five or thirty years ago.

Joe's fears led to increased irritability. He had trouble sleeping and found himself in a constant state of worry. He even began drinking to relax and to help him fall asleep. Trying to overcome his alcohol-induced sleep, he began drinking more and more coffee in the morning to lift the veil of drowsiness. Joe also kept his fears and concerns shielded from what was potentially his greatest support system—his wife and family.

Finally, Joe's boss called him into his office one day. Joe had been anticipating this particular call with extreme dread for weeks. He had seen the trend—his good accounts gradually were being siphoned to younger salesmen, he no longer was invited to management meetings, and he sensed that people were talking behind his back. Even as Joe became more frantic and desperate, working harder and longer, his territory was dwindling around him. Joe was at the wrong end of a dangerous game of burnout. When the call came, Joe knew exactly what it meant. He never made it to his boss's office.[7]

The following is a formula for the burnout process:

Too many demands on strength and resources
over a prolonged period of time

+

High expectations and deep personal involvement
in the work one does

+

Too few actions taken to replenish the energy consumed
in meeting these demands

=

BURNOUT

There are four steps in the typical path to burnout:

1. **Enthusiasm.** This is a time for high hopes and high energy as a task or job is begun.

2. **Slowdown.** At this stage, excitement fades and energy wanes.

3. **Stagnation.** Frustration begins with questions on the value of the task or work effectiveness.

4. **Apathy.** Physical and emotional exhaustion are felt, depression is common, and performance deteriorates.

Burnout prevention

Job burnout can be prevented and overcome. This requires self-understanding and the support of others. For a better understanding of the job burnout phenomenon, take the following test to evaluate your own status (homemakers should evaluate conditions at home).

Application: Up in Smoke—Are You Burned Out?

Rate each question on a scale of 1 to 5. (1 = never; 2 = rarely; 3 = sometimes; 4 = often; 5 = always)

Do you:	Never	Rarely	Sometimes	Often	Always
Feel less competent or effective than you used to feel in your work?	1	2	3	4	5
Consider yourself unappreciated or "used?"	1	2	3	4	5
Dread going to work?	1	2	3	4	5
Feel overwhelmed in your work?	1	2	3	4	5
Feel your job is pointless or unimportant?	1	2	3	4	5
Watch the clock?	1	2	3	4	5
Avoid conversations with others (coworkers, customers, and supervisors in the work setting; family members in the home)?	1	2	3	4	5
Rigidly apply rules without considering creative solutions?	1	2	3	4	5
Become frustrated by your work?	1	2	3	4	5
Miss work often?	1	2	3	4	5
Feel unchallenged by your job?	1	2	3	4	5

Does your work:					
Overload you?	1	2	3	4	5
Deny you rest periods—breaks, lunch time, sick leave, or vacation?	1	2	3	4	5
Pay too little?	1	2	3	4	5
Depend on uncertain funding sources?	1	2	3	4	5

Does your work:	Never	Rarely	Sometimes	Often	Always
Provide inadequate support to accomplish the job (budget, equipment, tools, people, etc.)?	1	2	3	4	5
Lack clear guidelines?	1	2	3	4	5
Entail so many different tasks that you feel fragmented?	1	2	3	4	5
Require you to deal with major or rapid changes?	1	2	3	4	5
Lack access to a social or professional support group?	1	2	3	4	5
Involve coping with a negative job image or angry people?	1	2	3	4	5
Depress you?	1	2	3	4	5

Source: Copyright © 1980, The Washington Post. Reprinted with permission. Adapted from Carol Krucoff, "Careers: Confronting On-the-Job Burnout," The Washington Post, August 5, 1980, Health section, p.5.

Scoring and interpretation
Add up your scores for the Up in Smoke test and insert your total: _____

Scores	Category
94–110	Burnout
76–93	Flame
58–75	Smoke
40–57	Sparks
22–39	No fire

- **Burnout.** If your score is 94 to 110, you are experiencing a very high level of stress in your work. Without some changes in yourself or your situation, your potential for stress-related illness is high. Consider seeking professional help for stress reduction and burnout prevention. Coping with stress at this level may also require help from others—supervisors, coworkers, and other associates at work, and spouse and other family members at home.

- **Flame.** If you scored from 76 to 93, you have a high amount of work-related stress and may have begun to burn out. Mark the questions on which you scored 4 or above, and rank them in order of their effect on you, beginning with the ones that bother you the most. For at least your top three, evaluate what you can do to reduce the stresses involved, and act to improve your attitude or situation. If your body is reflecting the stress, get a medical checkup.

- **Smoke.** Scores from 58 to 75 represent a certain amount of stress in your work and are a sign that you have a fair chance of burning out unless you take corrective measures. For each question on which you scored 4 or above, consider ways you can reduce the stresses involved. As soon as possible, take action to improve your attitude or the situation surrounding those things that trouble you most.

- **Sparks.** If your score is from 40 to 57, you have a low amount of work-related stress and are unlikely to burn out. Look over those questions on which you scored 3 or above, and think about what you can do to reduce the stresses involved.

- **No fire.** People with scores of 22 through 39 are mellow in their work, with almost no job-related stress. As long as they continue at this level, they are practically burnout-proof.

Although you may be in a state of burnout, the phoenix phenomenon can occur. You can rise from the ashes to a new level of energy and commitment, depending on your use of corrective strategies. Strategies for dealing with burnout include *emergency aid*, *short-term actions*, and *long-term solutions*.[8]

Examples of emergency aid:

1. Doing deep breathing

2. Engaging in positive self-talk

3. Taking a physical retreat

4. Talking with a friend

Sample short-term actions:

1. Reducing workload

2. Setting priorities

3. Taking care of your body

4. Accentuating the positive

Important long-term solutions:

1. Clarifying values

2. Renewing commitments

3. Making lifestyle changes

4. Developing personal competencies

For many people, both the job and the home represent potential sources for high stress and burnout. For this reason, having at least one "safe haven" is important. Ideally, if things are going badly on the job, rest and comfort can be found in the home. Similarly, if home conditions involve pressure, conflict, and frustration, having a satisfying work life helps. The person who faces stress on the job and stress in the home at the same time is waging a war on two fronts and is a prime candidate for burnout.

Management's role in burnout prevention

A major factor in overcoming burnout is personal power—the perceived ability to control one's time, resources, space, workload, pace, and destiny. According to Peggy Lawless, Northwestern National Life Insurance research director, "The biggest change that needs to take place is a reorientation of how management deals with employees. An atmosphere where employees are empowered—where they have more control over how they perform their work—reduces the risk of burnout and stress considerably."[9]

The following are ten practices executives can institute to prevent burnout in the workplace:

1. Clarify the mission, goals, and values of the organization, and *live* these personally.

2. Clearly communicate role expectations. People need to know their place in the plan.

3. Maintain a healthy work environment—meet physical, safety, and emotional health needs.

4. Manage work processes so that individuals and groups are neither overloaded nor underloaded.

5. Maintain an effective balance between continuity and change. While self-renewing change is vital for keeping up with shifting conditions, change should not occur at a pace so fast that it produces widespread stress.

6. Foster a spirit of belonging and teamwork throughout the organization through personal involvement, effective communication, and community-building activities.

7. To the degree possible, allow people flexibility to work at the pace and manner that will ensure personal satisfaction while maintaining needed productivity.

8. Provide people opportunity for ongoing involvement in decisions affecting them.

9. Have career development policies and activities that help people achieve their full potential.

10. Provide assistance in times of stress. Services ranging from fitness programs to counseling centers can be provided within the organization, or referral networks can be established.[10]

In *Managing Stress for Mental Fitness*, Merrill Raber and George Dyck list ten strategies for supervisors to follow in helping employees manage job stress:

1. Maintain a safe and organized work environment.

2. Clarify work unit goals and objectives.

3. Be sure individual job expectations and instructions are clear.

4. Evaluate workloads and deadlines; are they reasonable?

5. Have regular reviews to provide accurate and timely feedback; give assurance that good work is appreciated.

6. Show patience, understanding, and support in dealing with employee problems.

7. Deal with personality differences directly and constructively.

8. Coach and develop employees to their full potential.

9. Involve people, as much as possible, in decisions that affect them.

10. Keep communication lines open with an open-door policy.[11]

Job stress interventions

The workplace is a recognized breeding ground for stress and associated mental and physical health disorders. Historically, three distinct approaches have been used as strategies for reducing or controlling stress. These approaches can be classified as primary, secondary, and tertiary prevention.

Primary prevention seeks to correct the fundamental cause of stress by changing working conditions and the physical environment. Primary prevention strategies include occupational safety, physical work comfort, work design, and participative management initiatives.

Secondary prevention strives to reduce the severity of stress symptoms before they lead to serious health consequences. Stress education, health promotion, and wellness programs are examples of secondary prevention efforts.

Tertiary prevention involves the treatment of health conditions to lessen the impact on personal functioning, regardless of the source. Tertiary treatment is typically reactive to existing problems and is traditionally provided by medical personnel, often through an employee assistance program. An important example is post-traumatic stress syndrome.[12]

Wellness programs

The workplace has become the home of many stress management and wellness programs. A 1992 national survey of work sites with fifty or more employees revealed that 37 percent of the sites sponsored some form of stress management and wellness education.[13]

Wellness programs are implemented at three levels of intensity and depth.[14] *Level I* programs include newsletters, health fairs, screening sessions, posters, flyers, and classes. These activities are useful in making people aware of the specific consequences of poor health habits.

Level II programs bring about lifestyle modification by providing specific programs, such as physical conditioning and proper methods of performing physically demanding tasks. The programs may last several months or may be available on an ongoing basis. Level II programs are aimed at helping people develop lifelong healthy habits, and may use behavior modification to achieve this goal.

Level III programs attempt to create an environment that helps people sustain healthy lifestyles and behaviors. A Level III program fosters participation by providing fitness center memberships and making healthy food available. Although a Level III program could be conducted independently, it is usually an outgrowth of ongoing Level I and Level II activities. The following describes a Level III program and the results it achieved.[15]

Live for life

In 1979, Johnson & Johnson Company began its Live for Life program for 28,000 employees in fifty plants. The goal of the program was to provide the means for Johnson & Johnson employees to become the healthiest in the world and to control the increasing illness and accident costs of the corporation. The program is free for employees. Live for Life is a prototype of effective in-house wellness programs that reduce company costs by improving employee health. The Live for Life program incorporates the following basic elements of a wellness program:

1. Lifestyle assessment and health screening.

2. A lifestyle seminar that introduces employees to the basic concepts of wellness and the Live for Life program.

3. Classes for smoking cessation, weight control, good nutrition, and stress management. The program also includes yoga classes, alcohol education, physical fitness classes, and assertiveness training.

4. Alteration of the work environment; that is, nutritious food in the cafeteria, rewards for nonsmokers, exercise facilities, car pools, flexible scheduling of work time, and training programs to improve employee-manager relations.

5. Feedback and follow-up. Each employee receives a summary of lifestyle points earned during a three-month period for lifestyle improvement and fitness achievement. Participants are contacted by letter or telephone for their reactions and progress in the program.

Several studies have assessed the effectiveness of Johnson & Johnson's Live for Life program. One study compared employees (N = 1,272) at four Live for Life plants who had participated in the program for two years with employees at four non–Live for Life plants (N = 751). Both groups of employees received health screenings. Before and after comparisons were made between the two groups. See Figure 16.1.

Figure 16.1 Evaluation of Live for Life Program[16]

	Live for Life employees	Non-Live for Life employees
Smoking cessation	23%	17%
High risk of coronary heart disease	13%	32%
Exercise improvement (men)	29%	19%
Exercise improvement (women)	20%	7%
Fitness	significant improvement	minimal or no improvement
Stress	significant decrease	minimal or the same
Work satisfaction	significant improvement	minimal or the same

A second study compared medical costs of three groups of employees over a four-year period:

1. employees who participated in the Live for Life program for more than thirty months (N = 5,192)

2. employees who participated in the Live for Life program from eighteen to thirty months (N = 3,259)

3. employees who did not participate in the program (N = 2,955)

Employees in all three groups were similar in age, sex, stress levels, and health levels at the beginning of the study. The main saving was in hospitalization cost, which was two times higher for the control group employees than the employees in the Live for Life program. Overall, the employees in the Live for Life programs saved Johnson & Johnson $980,316 over a four-year period.[17]

Kenneth Pelletier of Stanford's Center for Research in Disease Prevention has reviewed forty-eight studies of work-site health-promotion programs published since 1980. The result: Every program but one has shown positive effects on workers' health, as measured by risk factors and by rates of actual illness. Of the thirty programs analyzed for cost-effectiveness, every one has saved money.[18]

Important keys for success in implementing work site health promotion programs include:

- long-term commitment,

- top management support,

- employee involvement,

- professional leadership,

- clearly defined objectives,

- careful planning, and

- family involvement.[19]

Chapter Sixteen References

1   Adapted from Patti Nickell, *Burnout: Could It Happen to You?* (East Jefferson, Mass.: East Jefferson General Hospital, 1983), 6-8, 24; and Herbert J. Freudenberger, "Burn-Out: The Organizational Menace," *Training and Development* 31, no. 7 (July 1977): 26-27.

2   Nickell, *Burnout: Could It Happen to You?* 6-8, 24; and Freudenberger, "Burn-Out: The Organizational Menace," 26-27.

3   Freudenberger, "Staff Burnout," *Journal of Social Issues* 30 (1974): 159-65; Herbert J. Freudenberger, *Burnout: The High Cost of Achievement* (Garden City, N.Y.: Doubleday, 1980); Christina Maslach, "Burned Out," *Human Behavior* 5 (1976): 16-22; and Christina Maslach, *Burnout: The Cost of Caring* (Englewood Cliffs, N.J.: Prentice-Hall, 1980).

4   Hosmar Mawardi, "Aspects of the Impaired Physician," in B. A. Farber, ed., *Stress and Burnout in the Human Service Professions* (New York: Pergamon Press, 1983); E. A. McConnell, ed., *Burnout in the Nursing Profession* (St. Louis: C. Mosby, 1982); S. Jayaratne and W. A. Chess, "Job Satisfaction and Job Burnout in Social Work," in Farber, *Stress and Burnout in the Human Service Professions*; J. W. Jones, ed., *Burnout in Policing* (Park Ridge, Ill.: London House Press, 1985); C. Maslach and S. E. Jackson, "Lawyer Burn-out," *Barrister* 5 (1978): 51-54; L. Hallsten, "From Burnout to Burning Out: Some Issues and Model" (paper presented at the first European Network of Organizational Psychologists conference on professional burnout, Cracow, Poland, September 24-27, 1990); and M. Sakharov and B. A. Farber, "A Critical Study of Burnout in Teachers," in Farber, *Stress and Burnout in the Human Service Professions*.

5   *Minneapolis Star*, July 23, 1979.

6   *Minneapolis Star*, July 23, 1979.

7   Murray H. Rosenthal, *USA Today*, January 1991.

8   Donald Tubesing, *Stress Overload*, (Duluth, Minn.: Whole Person Associates, 1992).

9   Paul Froiland, "What Cures Job Stress?" *Training Magazine* (December 1993).

10 S. L. Sauter, L. R. Murphy, and J. Hurrell Jr., "A National Strategy for the Prevention of Work-Related Psychological Disorders," *American Psychologist* 45 (1990): 1146-58; A. J. Elkin and P. J. Rosch, "Promoting Mental Health at the Workplace: The Prevention Side of Stress Management," *Occupational Medicine: State of the Art Review* 5, no. 4 (1990): 739-54; and David Lewin and Steven Schecter, "Four Factors in Lower Disability Rates," *Personnel Journal* 70, no. 5 (May 1991).

11 Merrill F. Raber and George Dyck, *Managing Stress for Mental Fitness* (Los Altos, Calif.: Crisp Publications, 1993).

12 Lawrence R. Murphy, Joseph J. Hurrell Jr., Steven L. Sauter, and Gwendolyn Puryear Keita, *Job Stress Interventions* (Washington, D.C.: American Psychological Association, 1995), xi-xiii.

13 U.S. Department of Health and Human Services, Public Health Service, "1992 National Survey of Worksite Health Promotion Activities," *American Journal of Health Promotion* 7 (1993): 452-64.

14 Judith Green and Robert Shellenberger, *The Dynamics of Health and Wellness: A Biopsychosocial Approach* (Ft. Worth: Holt, Rinehart and Winston, 1991).

15 J. Bly, R. Jones, and J. Richardson, "Impact of Worksite Health Promotion on Health Care Costs and Utilization," *Journal of the American Medical Association* 256, no. 23 (1986): 3235-40; and Green and Shellenberger, *The Dynamics of Health and Wellness*.

16 Bly, Jones, and Richardson, "Impact of Worksite Health Promotion on Health Care Costs and Utilization"; and Green and Shellenberger, *The Dynamics of Health and Wellness*.

[17]   Bly, Jones, and Richardson, "Impact of Worksite Health Promotion on Health Care Costs and Utilization"; and Green and Shellenberger, *The Dynamics of Health and Wellness.*

[18]   Kenneth R. Pelletier, *Sound Mind, Sound Body: A New Model for Lifelong Health* (New York: Fireside, 1995), 261-62.; also, T. Theorell, "Medical and Physiological Aspects of Job Interventions," in C. L Cooper and I. T. Robertson, eds., *International Review of Industrial and Organizational Psychology,* vol. 8 (Chichester, UK: Wiley, 1993): 173-92.

[19]   J. E. Fielding, "The Challenges of Workplace Health Promotion," in S. M. Weiss, J. E. Fielding, and A. Baun, eds., *Health at Work* (Hillsdale, N.J.: Lawrence Earlbaum Associates, 1990), 13-28.

Chapter Seventeen
🌾
Work Morale

The changing meaning of work

History has witnessed an evolving definition of the meaning of work. To the ancient Greeks, work was a curse. Their name for work was *ponos*, having the same root as the Latin *poeno*, meaning sorrow. Homer wrote that the gods hated mankind and, out of malice, condemned human beings to work. Thus, the Hellenes developed a slave-based economy and relegated labor to "inferior people." In general, the Greeks, and later the Romans, viewed work as a painful necessity.[1]

The Hebrews constitute the second pillar of Western culture, and they too viewed work as punishment. The Hebrews saw work as man's burden to pay for original sin. The Talmud states, "If man does not find his food like the animals and birds, but must earn it, that is due to sin." Work, to the Hebrews, was atonement and a way to regain lost spirituality. So any work, no matter how lowly, was preferred over idleness.[2]

The early Christians shared the Hebraic attitude toward work. Although they believed that it was better to work than to be idle, they placed relatively low value on productive enterprise and the accumulation of wealth. Consider the words of Jesus (Matthew 6:24, 19:24):

> No man can serve two masters. . . . Ye cannot serve God and mammon.

> It is easier for a camel to go through the eye of a needle, than for a rich man to enter into the kingdom of God.

Essentially, early Christianity taught that the best work is that which least fills men's minds with desire for profit and least distracts them from God. Work at its best would be pure spirituality—a loving gaze fixed on a better world after death. The only admission of virtue in work was that it could be a means of charity in providing for the needs of others. This view of work remained virtually unchanged for the first one thousand years A.D. The dominant attitude toward work during this period was one of disregard and disdain.[3]

Between the eleventh and fourteenth centuries, Christianity began to assign work a more important role in life. The teachings of Thomas Aquinas, the church philosopher, speak for this era:

Work is natural and a duty, an important basis of society, and it is the legitimate foundation of property and gain, and of guilds and crafts; but all of this
to a higher spiritual end; and all of this according to a divine plan.[4]

The next five hundred years included the Renaissance, the Reformation, and
the Industrial Revolution, and Western society's attitude toward work changed
significantly during this period. At the beginning of the sixteenth century, Martin
Luther proclaimed that all forms of labor have equal value in the eyes of God and
that to carry out God's will was to perform one's vocational duties to the best of
one's ability. Luther taught that idleness is an unnatural and evil aberration and
that to maintain oneself by work is a way of serving God. With this, the historical
split between religious piety and worldly activity was resolved as work came to be
defined as a "calling" and a religious duty for all men.[5] In 1536, John Calvin taught
a doctrine of predestination that placed only the industrious among the chosen
for Heaven's grace. According to Calvin, work during this life and for this life was
endowed with religious dignity. Calvin wrote:

> Work alone suffices, and to please God, work must not be casual—now this,
> now that, now prolonged for the whole day, tomorrow laid down after an hour.
> Intermittent, occasional work will not do. It must be methodical, disciplined,
> rational, uniform, and hence specialized, work. To select a calling, and follow it
> with all one's conscience, is a religious duty.[6]

With Luther and Calvin, Protestant theology gave sanction to worldly achievements, and the Protestant work ethic was born. Other doctrines of the period
joined this new religious ethic to help establish work as a central tenet of Western
society. The Renaissance mission to build, create, and so realize one's potential,
the mercantilistic disregard for unproductive citizens, the Age of Enlightenment
and the emergence of science, the survival-of-the-fittest beliefs of social Darwin-
ists, and the primacy of work in socialist societies—all served to elevate society's
attitude toward work.

By the twentieth century, Protestant ethics, freewheeling capitalism, and humanistic socialism had meshed to form an essentially multidisciplinary religion
of work. Each of these major currents of thought embraced the idea that it was
every person's right and duty to perform work that would bring the greatest good
to oneself and society. The good person was the one who did good work.[7] Consider the words of Karl Marx, father of socialism, who believed work to be the
sum total of human rights and duties and who viewed work as the moral ideal:

> Production for the purpose of meeting men's needs (as opposed to our present
> production for the purpose of making a profit) will free labor from egotism,
> avarice, and fraud. In such a regime, work will no longer be a painful expiation

or an abstract moral duty: it will be seen as the normal human way of living. The model man will no longer be the wise man, the ascetic, or the citizen, but the worker, understood as producer. An immense society of free workers, freely associated, administering in common the instruments of work and endlessly transforming the matter of the world for the greater good of the community—such is the Socialist ideal.[8]

Capitalism, too, taught the importance of productive labor as a moral duty. This can be seen in a letter Abraham Lincoln wrote to his brother, who had asked for a loan:

Dec. 24, 1848

Dear Johnston:

Your request for eighty dollars, I do not think it best to comply with now. At the various times when I have helped you a little, you have said to me, "We can get along very well now," but in a very short time I find you in the same difficulty again. Now this can only happen by some defect in your conduct. What that defect is, I think I know. You are not lazy, and still you are an idler. I doubt whether since I saw you, you have done a good whole day's work, in any one day. You do not very much dislike to work, and still you do not work much, merely because it does not seem to you that you could get much for it.

This habit of uselessly wasting time is the whole difficulty. It is vastly important to you, and still more so to your children, that you should break this habit. It is more important to them, because they have longer to live, and can keep out of an idle habit before they are in it, easier than they can get out after they are in.

You are now in need of some ready money; and what I propose is that you shall go to work, "tooth and nail," for somebody who will give you money for it.

Let Father and your boys take charge of your things at home—prepare for a crop, and make the crop, and you go to work for the best money wages, or in discharge of any debt you owe, that you can get. And to secure you a fair reward for your labor, I now promise you that for every dollar you will, between this and the first May, get for your own labor either in money or in your own indebtedness, I will then give you one other dollar.

By this, if you hire yourself at ten dollars a month, from me you will get ten more, making twenty dollars a month for your work. In this, I do not mean you shall go off to St. Louis, or the lead mines, or the gold mines in California, but I mean for you to go at it for the best wages you can get close to home—in Coles County.

Now if you will do this, you will soon be out of debt, and what is better, you will have a habit that will keep you from getting in debt again. But if I should now clear you out, next year you will be just as deep in as ever. You say you would almost give your place in Heaven for seventy or eighty dollars. Then you value your place in Heaven very cheaply, for I am sure you can, with the offer I make you, get the seventy or eighty dollars for four or five months' work. You say if I furnish you the money you will deed me the land, and if you don't pay the money back you will deliver possession—

Nonsense! If you can't now live with the land, how will you then live without it? You have always been kind to me, and I do not now mean to be unkind to you. On the contrary, if you will but follow my advice, you will find it worth more than eight times eighty dollars to you.

Affectionately,

Your brother,
A. Lincoln[9]

The meaning of work in America today

We have seen dramatic changes in the meaning of work in Western culture—from Greek scorn for labor, to Hebraic atonement for sin, to early Christian disregard and disdain, to later Christian calling to work, to socialist doctrines of work for joy, to the present day, when work represents for many a search for meaning and self-expression. The following passage reflects this attitude toward work.

Then a ploughman said, Speak to us of Work.

And he answered, saying:

You work that you may keep pace with the earth and the soul of the earth.

For to be idle is to become a stranger unto the seasons, and to step out of life's procession, that marches in majesty and proud submission towards the infinite.

When you work you are a flute through whose heart the whispering of the hours turns to music.

Which of you would be a reed, dumb and silent, when all else sings together in unison?

Always you have been told that work is a curse and labour a misfortune.

But I say to you that when you work you fulfill a part of earth's furthest dream, assigned to you when that dream was born,

And in keeping yourself with labour you are in truth loving life,

And to love life through labour is to be intimate with life's inmost secret. . . .

You have been told also that life is darkness, and in your weariness you echo what was said by the weary.

And I say that life is indeed darkness save when there is urge,

And all urge is blind save when there is knowledge,

And all knowledge is vain save when there is work,

And all work is empty save when there is love;

And when you work with love you bind yourself to yourself, and to one another, and to God.

And what is it to work with love?

It is to weave the cloth with threads drawn from your heart, even as if your beloved were to wear that cloth.

It is to build a house with affection, even as if your beloved were to dwell in that house.

It is to sow seeds with tenderness and reap the harvest with joy, even as if your beloved were to eat the fruit.

It is to charge all things you fashion with a breath of your own spirit,

And to know that all the blessed dead are standing about you and watching.

Often have I heard you say, as if speaking in sleep, "He who works in marble, and finds the shape of his own soul in the stone, is nobler than he who ploughs the soil.

And he who seizes the rainbow to lay it on a cloth in the likeness of man, is more than he who makes the sandals for our feet."

But I say, not in sleep but in the over-wakefulness of noontide, that the wind speaks not more sweetly to the giant oaks than to the least of all the blades of grass;

And he alone is great who turns the voice of the wind into a song made sweeter by his own loving.

Work is love made visible.[10]

To personalize the meaning of work, consider: What does work mean to you? What value do you attach to your job or career? See Figure 17.1.

Figure 17.1 The Changing Meaning of Work

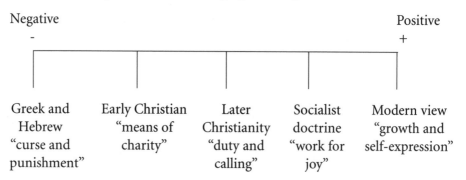

The value the individual attaches to the work experience is an important factor in the stress equation. It makes an enormous difference whether work is viewed as punishment or as an opportunity for fulfillment. Primarily because of the influence of culture, work has a positive value for large numbers of people in American society, who seek personal meaning and a sense of self-worth in the work experience. Consider the alcoholic who endures all loss until he loses his job, or the employee whose loss of her status at work results in the afflictions of self-doubt and depression.

Figure 17.2 shows that the majority of American workers attach a high degree of importance to the work experience. The data represent the responses of a cross section of people representing all levels of responsibility and all classifications of work.

Figure 17.2 The Importance of Work

If you had enough money to live as comfortably as you would like for the rest of your life, would you continue to work?

Worker would continue to work   71.5%

Worker would not continue to work   28.5%

71.5% of American workers would continue to work, even if they did not need the money.

Source: Robert P. Quinn and Graham L. Staines, Quality of Employment Survey (Ann Arbor, Mich.: The University of Michigan, Institute for Social Research, 1979); Gallup Report 288, "Political, Social, and Economic Trends, 1989."

Professionals are not the only ones who seek satisfaction from their work. The sentiment is found among factory workers and store clerks, as well as lawyers and nurses. The challenge to employers is how to create a work environment that encourages people in all fields and at all levels to view their jobs as important and rewarding.[11] The role and value of work is summarized by Bertrand Russell in his essay "Work":

> The habit of viewing life as a whole is an essential part both of wisdom and of true morality, and is one of the things which ought to be encouraged in education. Consistent purpose is not enough to make life happy, but it is an almost indispensable condition of a happy life. And consistent purpose embodies itself mainly in work.[12]

Work and psychological health

A satisfying work experience is important for emotional well-being. The Russian writer Fyodor Dostoevsky expressed this when he wrote, "If it were considered desirable to destroy a human being, the only thing necessary would be to give his work a climate of uselessness." The German writer Johann Goethe describes the importance of work in defining life's purpose and providing personal satisfaction: "Blessed is he who has found his work; let him ask no other blessedness. He has a work, a life-purpose; he has found it and will follow it." Sigmund Freud once said that to be mentally healthy, a person must be able to love and to work. He saw these as the central tasks of adulthood. Work, he pointed out, was a consistent and fundamental way of staying in touch with the world and of mastering it.[13]

> **What work has meant to me**
> For many years, the concept of work didn't play an important role in my life. As a student, I knew school and I knew part-time jobs, but I didn't know work. When graduation came, I had to decide what I was going to be. What *work* would I do in life?
>
> I knew I cared about people, but as to how I could help them, I had no idea. I loved children, but I didn't see myself as a teacher; and I cared about people's welfare, but I didn't see myself as a social worker.
>
> Then I had a course in industrial psychology. Like a lightening bolt, it dawned on me that the human condition is heavily influenced by what happens in the workplace. The job life affects the home life. Besides that, if jobs are done well, good products and services help society.
>
> I remember this revelation coming to me as I was driving down the interstate. At that time I chose a career path, and I would say, other than family and values, no other factor has been more important in my life.—Author's file notes (G. M.)

Loss of one's job, regardless of the cause, can result in severe emotional setback because of the psychological importance of work in American society. Self-confidence and self-esteem may deteriorate if joblessness continues for long. People who are unemployed for a prolonged period normally pass through four stages—denial, anger, depression, and finally, a sense of worthlessness. The words of one who lost her job summarize this feeling: "My job was my whole life. That's all I did. It's unbearable now . . . I can't go on like this."[14]

Findings from the Great Depression to the present, based on cross-sectional, longitudinal, and prospective research designs, have documented the psychological and social costs of job loss for the unemployed person and for the person's family as a whole. The research literature provides consistent evidence of the importance of meaningful work and the harmful effects of job loss.[15]

The emotional and physical consequences of job loss can be significant. A mere 1 percent increase in the national unemployment rate is associated with a 4.1 percent increase in suicides, a 3.4 percent increase in admissions to mental hospitals, a 4 percent increase in admissions to prisons, and a 5.7 percent increase in homicides.[16]

The concept of "flow"

Thomas Jefferson, in a letter to Mrs. A. S. Marks, wrote, "It is neither wealth nor splendor, but tranquility and occupation, which give happiness." Along these lines, University of Chicago psychologist Mihaly Csikszentmihalyi coined the term "flow" after studying artists who could spend hour after hour painting and sculpting with enormous concentration. The artists, immersed in a challenging project and exhibiting high levels of skill, worked as if nothing else mattered.

Flow is the confluence of challenge and skill and is what Joseph Campbell meant when he said, "Follow your bliss." In all fields of work from accounting to zookeeping, when we are challenged by something we are truly good at, we become so absorbed in the flow of the activity that we lose consciousness of self and time. We avoid states of anxiety, boredom, and apathy, and experience "flow." See Figure 17.3.[17]

Grant county flow

Barry has lived and worked in the same Kentucky county for 55 years, or should I say has *radiated* there, because that describes him better. From morning until night he is out there in his veterinarian's truck or on his farm tractor or with hammer and nails—healing something, growing something, or making something. Which it is doesn't matter to him, because it is all *good*. Barry knows flow; Barry *is* flow. When Barry moves, it is toward a thing and not away. He goes to bed to sleep. He goes to work to serve. For him, life is a full-body bear hug, an experience that can only be described as "flow."—Author's file notes (G. M.)

Figure 17.3 The Experience of Flow Combines Challenge and Skill

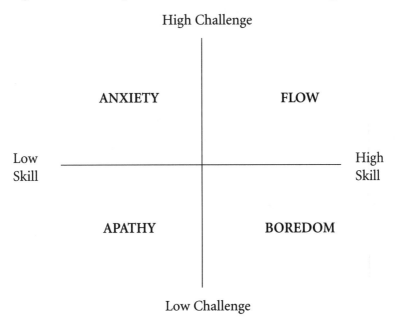

High Challenge

ANXIETY FLOW

Low Skill ——————————————— High Skill

APATHY BOREDOM

Low Challenge

What is it like to be in a state of flow? Csikszentmihalyi, in his book *The Evolving Self*, reports that over and over again, people describe the same dimensions of flow:

- a clear and present purpose distinctly known

- immediate feedback on how well one is doing

- supreme concentration on the task at hand as other concerns are temporarily suspended

- a sense of growth and being part of some greater endeavor as ego boundaries are transcended

- an altered sense of time that usually seems to go faster

In the zone
It was at a seminar on creativity that I experienced firsthand the concept of flow. Our group was involved in a culminating experience that included a thirty-six-hour creativity challenge. After about ten hours, our group became immensely productive and the ideas were flowing like a waterfall. This continued all night and into the next day. Time seemed to stand still, and to this day I can still recall the sights, sounds, and sensations. Totally throwing yourself into an activity is the key to experiencing the potential of flow.—Author's file notes (S. M.)

How much time is spent working?

Are you working more or less than your ancestors did? A comparison of annual work and leisure patterns shows that the average worker today spends roughly the same amount of time at work as did the average worker in the thirteenth century. Although innovations such as electricity, improved communications, and mass production have combined to allow a shorter workday, the average number of hours people work each year now, as then, remains around 1,900 to 2,500.[18] However, because people often live longer, retire later, and enter postretirement careers, modern workers may spend significantly more hours on the job over their lifetimes.

People in the upper strata of position and responsibility do not fit the norm, and the number of hours they spend at work can be extremely high. The following describes the dedication to work displayed by many of these individuals:

> The professional class has made work their duty, their reward, a joy in itself, and this is so much like their attitude toward sport that it is easy for them to pass from one to the other. Often they hardly know whether they are playing or working; often they seem to play at their work and to work at their games. Naturally enough. Once the result of the work is forgotten, once it is pursued as an end in itself, the difference between it and sport grows dim, and shrinks to a mere question of degree.[19]

Working evenings and weekends, people in higher levels of responsibility often amass enormous totals of time spent on the job. The top leaders of our economic, political, social, aesthetic, and religious institutions show a clear preference for work over leisure and appear to be truly absorbed by their work. Writer W. H. Whyte Jr. states:

> It seems clear that most executives work far more hours than they are required or asked to, not because of any compulsion, either internal or external, but simply because they are totally absorbed in their work. It is of interest to note that, despite a work week of from 67 to 112 hours, most executives do not complain.[20]

Mark Twain helps to explain some people's commitment to work and the long hours they spend on the job: "Work and play are words that can be used to describe the same thing under differing conditions."

As for people in the middle and lower economic strata, many must work long hours, and even at two jobs, to carve out a living and maintain self-sufficiency. This is an important distinction between feeling you *must* do something and *choosing* to do it.

Job satisfaction and stress

Job satisfaction is closely related to perceptions of stress. It is not necessarily high earners who are most satisfied with their jobs; it is those who are most comfortable with the total amount and type of stress they face.[21]

⊚ Application: How Satisfied Are You?

For a measure of your current job satisfaction, take the following *work, play, hell* test:

- What percentage of your job is *work?* (defined as drudgery, for the purpose of this test) _____ %

- What percentage of your job is *play?* (defined as enjoyment, as one's job can be enjoyable) _____ %

- What percentage of your job is *hell?* (defined as pain and torture, regardless of the source) _____ %

        Total   __100__ %

If you have less than 20 percent enjoyment, there is a problem; you currently experience less than one day of satisfaction per week. If you have more than 20 percent hell, there is a problem; either from people or events, there is too much pain and torture in your job. An acceptable drudgery score depends on how Calvin-trained or Luther-trained you are. Either due to Western world or Eastern world socialization, some people have a higher degree of self-discipline and tolerance for hard work.

What constitutes a good job? What are the stress points to consider? One of the best models of job design and satisfaction shows intrinsic and extrinsic factors that are necessary for a "rich" job.[22] Intrinsic factors are:

1. variety and challenge,

2. opportunity for decision making,

3. feedback and learning,

4. mutual support and respect,

5. wholeness and meaning,

6. room to grow.

The first three must be optimal—not too much, which can add anxiety, nor too little, which produces boredom. The second three are open-ended. No one can have too much respect, growing room, or "wholeness." Thus a rich job has optimal variety, responsibility, and feedback, and as much respect, growth, and wholeness as possible.

The rich job also includes extrinsic conditions of employment, including:

1. fair and adequate pay,

2. job security,

3. benefits,

4. safety,

5. health,

6. due process.

With this model as a basis, consider "The Price of Success" on page 338.

The importance of morale

> Napoleon once wrote: "An army's success depends on its size, equipment, experience, and morale . . . and morale is worth more than all of the other elements combined."

Studies have confirmed the economic importance of morale. Soon after the publication of The 100 *Best Companies to Work for in America* in 1984, stock analyst Patrick McVeigh compared the 100 Best Companies with a broad sampling of other companies from the Standard and Poor 500. McVeigh measured the two groups of companies using two conventional financial yardsticks—growth in profits over time (in terms of earnings per share) and increase in the price of stock (stock appreciation). The results were spectacular. Over the previous decade, the 100 Best Companies were more than twice as profitable as the average for the S & P 500. During the same period (1975–1984), the stock price of the 100 Best Companies grew at nearly three times the rate of the others.[23]

Robert Levering, in his best-selling book *A Great Place to Work*, describes high morale as having pride in what you do (the job itself), enjoying the people you are working with (the work group), trusting the people you work for (management practices), and gaining economic rewards (wages and benefits).[24] One of the best ways to understand stress at work is to evaluate your own level of morale in these four key areas. Complete the following exercise.

◎ Application: Morale Survey—What is your level of morale?

The following survey addresses a number of work-related issues. Answer each question as it relates to your own experience. Circle the appropriate response.

Job

1. At this point in my job, I am doing the things I feel are important.

Strongly Disagree	Disagree	Undecided	Agree	Strongly Agree

2. When it comes to challenge, the job I am doing is demanding.

Strongly Disagree	Disagree	Undecided	Agree	Strongly Agree

3. As things are now, I have a sense of accomplishment in the work I am doing.

Strongly Disagree	Disagree	Undecided	Agree	Strongly Agree

Group

4. When it comes to pride in the work of my coworkers, it is high.

Strongly Disagree	Disagree	Undecided	Agree	Strongly Agree

5. I like the people with whom I work.

Strongly Disagree	Disagree	Undecided	Agree	Strongly Agree

6. There is teamwork between my coworkers and me.

Strongly Disagree	Disagree	Undecided	Agree	Strongly Agree

Management

7. Management strives to be fair.

Strongly Disagree	Disagree	Undecided	Agree	Strongly Agree

8. I understand and agree with the goals of management.

Strongly Disagree	Disagree	Undecided	Agree	Strongly Agree

9. Management shows concern for employees.

Strongly Disagree	Disagree	Undecided	Agree	Strongly Agree

Economics

10. My wages are satisfactory.

Strongly Disagree	Disagree	Undecided	Agree	Strongly Agree

11. My fringe benefits are satisfactory.

Strongly Disagree	Disagree	Undecided	Agree	Strongly Agree

12. The opportunity for advancement is satisfactory — if I desire to pursue it.

Strongly Disagree	Disagree	Undecided	Agree	Strongly Agree

Scoring

What does the Morale Survey tell you about your own work situation? To find your level of satisfaction in four important areas—the job itself, relations with coworkers, practices of management, and economic rewards—complete the following three steps.

Step One

For each question, score 1 for Strongly Disagree, 2 for Disagree, 3 for Undecided, 4 for Agree, and 5 for Strongly Agree.

Step Two

Add the total scores for each section of the questionnaire, divide by 3, and enter the averages in the following spaces.

Job	Group	Management	Economics
_____	_____	_____	_____
Average for items 1, 2, and 3	Average for items 4, 5, and 6	Average for items 7, 8, and 9	Average for items 10, 11, and 12

Step Three

Make a three-dimensional picture of your morale at work, using Figure 17.4. Circle the appropriate number on each edge of the box, and connect the circles with straight and dotted lines as shown in the example (Figure 17.5).

Figure 17.4 Your Levels of Morale

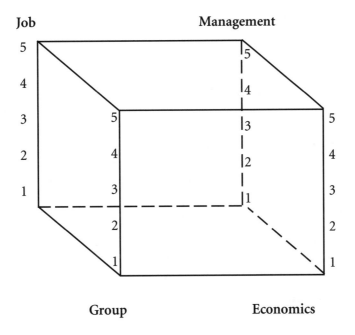

Figure 17.5 Example

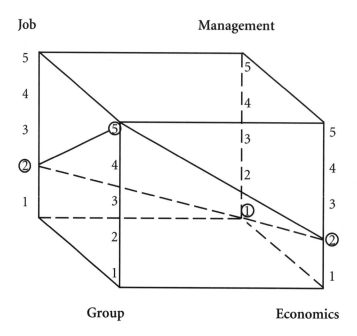

Interpretation

This exercise shows the importance of morale, both for personal satisfaction and for job performance. Assuming that a person has the basic skills and knowledge to perform a job, the quality of work and the quality of work life depend on commitment to do a good job. Regardless of the field—transportation, manufacturing, or medicine—and regardless of the level of responsibility—front-line employee, manager, or president—commitment results from positive attitudes (high morale) in four key areas: the job itself, the work group, management practices, and economic rewards.

The following is a description of what your scores mean.

Low morale

Scores from 1.0 to 2.5 on any one or a combination of the four edges of the box—job, group, management, and economics—indicate a low level of morale. If you are doing a good job, you are doing so because of personal qualities, not because of environmental support. Scores at this level reflect enormous stress on the individual.

Wait-and-see attitude

Scores between 2.6 and 3.4 on any one or a combination of the four edges indicate a wait-and-see attitude. It is likely that your morale is neither helping nor hurting your job performance at this point. However, you lack a sense of full satisfaction and do not feel complete commitment to your work. Your current condition can be likened to running in place or treading water.

High morale

Scores between 3.5 and 5.0 on all four edges indicate a high level of morale. You are fortunate in that you receive much satisfaction from your work. You are striving to do the best job possible, and with training and practice your level of performance could be expected to be high. Scores at this level reflect an optimum amount of good stress.

Employee morale and the role of management

Managing morale is the task of management. Meeting this responsibility requires a willingness to listen to employees and the ability to "read between the lines" of what they say and do. In this process, the morale of each person should be considered individually. Although the elements of morale are the same for everyone—job, group, management, and economic rewards—each element may be more or less important to different people at different times:[25]

- The nature of the job itself may not be as important to the individual who views work as a temporary source of income while going to school as it is to the person in midcareer who foresees 25 more years in the same line of work.

- Typically, wages and the opportunity for advancement are of primary importance to younger workers, while older employees are more interested in fringe benefits for their retirement years. All three—wages, benefits, and advancement—are usually important to workers in their middle years, when the financial demands of raising a family must be met, security for sickness and retirement must be considered, and social needs for status and responsibility can be great.

- Relations with coworkers and practices of management probably would be less important to the inventor, who works alone, than to factory and office employees, who spend a significant amount of time in the company of coworkers and who are subject to a supervisor's orders.

Some policies and techniques for maximizing morale seem to work with the majority of employees in most cases. A review of 550 studies published since 1959 shows nine areas in which management can take action that will have positive effects on employee satisfaction and job performance. These are:

- **Pay and reward systems.** Introduce a group bonus.

- **Job autonomy and discretion.** Allow workers to determine their own work methods.

- **Support services.** Provide service on demand from technical support groups.

- **Training.** Provide training and development for all employees.

- **Organizational structure.** Reduce the number of hierarchical levels.

- **Technical and physical aspects.** Break long production and assembly lines into smaller work units.

- **Task assignments.** Assign whole tasks, including preparatory and finishing work.

- **Information and feedback.** Solicit and utilize direct feedback from users—clients, customers, other departments.

- **Interpersonal and group processes.** Increase the amount and types of group interaction.

Research shows that positive results can be obtained by using one or more of these techniques. Costs go down, and the quality of work and quality of work life improve.[26]

In summary, when an employee has an attitude problem that is work related, stress levels rise. It may be discovered that management is part of the problem. Occasionally, the problem is caused by other employees. Often, the problem is caused by the employee her- or himself. In any case, management's potential to help is enormous. If you are a manager and have an employee attitude problem, you should be concerned for the sake of the individual and the good of the organization.

Part Six ends with a story to show that job stress applies in all types of work and levels of responsibility.

> The pope was scheduled to make an address at the United Nations, but his plane arrived late. Hurrying from the terminal, he hailed a taxi and asked the young man to please drive as fast as he could. The young man said he would, but he couldn't drive over the speed limit because he had a wife and two children who depended on him for all they had.

Being the man he was, the pope said, "I understand, my son. Would it be OK if you got in the back and let me drive?" "Of course," said the young man, and he hopped in the rear. The pope slid behind the wheel and stepped on the gas. In a minute the car was streaking and swerving down the freeway.

That's when a young police officer pulled them over. When he got out of the cruiser and saw who it was, he thought, "Whoa! I'd better call for instructions." "Sarge," he said to the desk officer, "I pulled this fellow over for speeding and reckless operation, and I don't know what to do."

"Of course you know what to do," said the sergeant. "You're a well-trained officer. Give him a ticket." "You don't understand," said the young officer. "This isn't just anybody. In fact this person is more important than the mayor."

"More important than the mayor? Who could be more important than the mayor?" "Well, let's put it this way," said the officer. "This person is more important than the governor."

"There's no one more important than the governor," said the sergeant. "Who could possibly be more important than the governor?" "Well, let's put it this way, Sarge: This person is more important than the president."

"Listen, officer, there's no one more important than the president. Who is this guy?" "Well, Sarge," said the officer, "I don't know exactly, but whoever he is, he's got the pope driving for him!"

Personal Thoughts on Job Stress

Answer the following questions to personalize the content of Part Six. Space is provided for writing your thoughts.

- What are the major problems facing people in your workplace? Are these primarily pressures, conflicts, or frustrations?

- What can the individual do to prevent the job burnout phenomenon? What works for you? What have you seen work for others?

- What does *work* mean to you? What value do you attach to your job or career? Are you one who lives to work, or are you one who works to live?

- How have family, education, and work experience influenced your attitude toward work?

- What is your level of morale? Do you experience good stress or distress in each sub-area—the job itself, the work group, management practices, economic factors?

- What is the single most important factor that would raise or reinforce your morale at this time?

Chapter Seventeen References

1   Adriano Tilgher, *Work: What It Has Meant to Men through the Ages* (New York: Harcourt Brace Jovanovich, Inc., 1930), 3.

2   Tilgher, *Work,* 11-12, 29-37.

3   Tilgher, *Work,* 29-37.

4   Tilgher, *Work,* 38-46.

5   C. Wright Mills, "The Meaning of Work Throughout History," in Fred Best, ed., *The Future of Work* (Englewood Cliffs, N.J.: Prentice-Hall, 1973), 7.

6   Tilgher, *Work,* 59-60.

7   Tilgher, *Work,* 137.

8   Tilgher, *Work,* 111.

9   Abraham Lincoln, letter to John D. Johnston, 24 December 1848, *A Treasury of the World's Great Letters* (New York: Simon & Schuster, 1940), 311-13.

10 Reprinted from *The Prophet,* by Kahlil Gibran, by permission of Alfred A. Knopf, Inc. Copyright © 1923 by Kahlil Gibran and renewed 1951 by Administrators C.T.A. of the Kahlil Gibran Estate and Mary G. Gibran.

11 Robert P. Quinn and Graham L. Staines, *Quality of Employment Survey* (Ann Arbor, Mich.: The University of Michigan, Institute for Social Research, 1979); Gallup Report #288, "Political, Social, and Economic Trends," 1989.

12 Bertrand Russell, *The Conquest of Happiness* (New York: Liveright Publishing Company, 1958).

13 Harry Levinson, *Executive* (Cambridge, Mass.: Harvard University Press, 1981), 28.

14 Frank Trippett, "The Anguish of the Jobless," *Time,* January 18, 1982, p. 90.

15 M. A. Dew, L. Penkower, and E. J. Bromet, "Effects of Unemployment on Mental Health in the Contemporary Family," *Behavior Modification* 15 (1991): 501-44.

16 Trippett, "The Anguish of the Jobless," 90.

17 Mihaly Csikszentmihalyi and Isabella Selega Csikszentmihalyi, *Optimal Experience: Psychological Studies of Flow in Consciousness* (New York: Cambridge University Press, 1988), 261.

18 Quinn and Staines, *Quality of Employment Survey,* 78-79.

19 Tilgher, *Work,* 189-90.

20 William H. Whyte Jr., *The Organization Man* (New York: Simon & Schuster, Inc., 1956), 142-50.

21 Quinn and Staines, *Quality of Employment Survey.*

22 F. E. Emery, "Characteristics of Socio-Technical Systems" (London: Tavistock Documents #527). Abridged in F.E. Emery, *The Emergence of a New Paradigm of Work* (Canberra: Centre for Continuing Education, 1959).

23 William Lindsay, George Manning, and Joseph Petrick, "Work Morale in the 1990s," *S.A.M. Advanced Management Journal* (Summer 1992).

24 Robert Levering, *A Great Place to Work* (New York: Random House, 1988).

25 See Chapter 7 of Levinson, *Executive,* and Chapter 5 of Ivancevich, et al., *Organizational Behavior and Performance.*

26 Based on T. G. Cumming's analysis of job satisfaction studies, Case Western Reserve University, Cleveland, Ohio.

Part Six Reading

The Price of Success

"Kevin, what has happened to that unswerving drive of yours toward working your way to the top of the company?" asked his boss. "You are almost there. We have offered you a division presidency. Three years of success in that job and we might be able to bring you back to the corporate office as Senior Vice-President of Marketing. You are big league timber, Kevin. You are destined for greatness in our company.

"Ten years ago you came to us as an eager young business administration major just out of college. What an impression you created! Eager, intelligent, and, even at age 21, with an executive aplomb about you. We grabbed you right away for our executive training program. After two years in the field as a territory salesman, you moved effortlessly into a marketing research assignment. Within one year, you became a senior market analyst. After two years of brilliance in that position, we made you a branch manager. Again, after several years of sterling performance you then became the youngest regional manager in the history of our company. We figure you are now ready for the big jump—a general management assignment where you will be operating a profit center of your own. What more can a young executive want?

"We are sticking our necks out for you. Should you fail as a 31-year-old division president, the company could look foolish. Our offer is real. You can become President of the Cosmetics Division if you will just accept the position. I hear the excuses you are making about not being experienced enough for the job, and that other people in the company are more deserving of the position, but I don't buy them. Something else is holding you back, Kevin. What is it?"

"Fred, you're pushing for a rapid answer to a major life decision. Becoming a company president isn't like buying a cabin cruiser or going on a two-week vacation to Bermuda. It's more like getting married or having triplets. It's a helluva change in your lifestyle. An impulsive person shouldn't even be in such an assignment."

"Am I really talking to ambitious Kevin Brady, that hard charging, good-looking Irishman who hates to lose at anything? Two years ago, if I asked you to tackle a special assignment in Venezuela, you would have been on your way to the airport before we went over all the details of the job. I always had the impression that if you weren't in business you would be an automobile racing driver.

"Could it be that you are acting coy because you want us to up the ante a little? As I said, the job should pay about $100,000 a year in salary plus a healthy

Source: Reprinted with permission from Andrew J. DuBrin, "The Price of Success," Casebook of Organizational Behavior (Elmsford, N.Y.: Pergamon Press, Inc., 1977), 58–63.

executive bonus, depending upon the profit of your division. In a boom year you could increase your salary by one third with your bonus. Besides that, being a division president would give you a fast track to perhaps a bigger division presidency or the Senior Vice-President of Marketing slot. It is conceivable that you could be set for life financially if you accept this assignment now."

"Fred, believe me. I'm not being an ingrate. I haven't turned down this magnificent offer. Yes, the challenge of a division presidency excites me. I believe in the product line of that division. For instance, my 14-year-old niece used that facial blemish cream and it really works. The improvement in her appearance actually raised her level of self-confidence. We are marketing something solid. Our cosmetic line does contribute something aesthetic to society in its own way. I think our company performs a lot of social good, considering its record on environmental safety and equal employment opportunity.

"Yet a man contemplating becoming a president has to carefully evaluate what becoming a president will do to his lifestyle. In other words, what am I really letting myself in for?"

"Kevin, you're speaking in generalities. Let's get down to the specifics of what's really holding you back from jumping at this once-in-a-lifetime opportunity. Be candid with me. I'm both your boss and your friend."

"A good way to begin, Fred, is to tell you about a recent experience my wife and I had at the Sales Executive Club. An industrial psychologist was giving a talk about the problems created by successful husbands. He wasn't putting down success, and he wasn't putting down husbands. What he seemed to be saying was that being a successful career person can create a lot of problems in your personal life, particularly with your wife and children. When he finished his talk there was tension in the air. Husbands were grinning sheepishly at their wives. Most wives had a surprised expression as if this man was revealing their personal case history. One skeptic said the psychologist was way off base, that he was dramatizing a few isolated case histories of obsessed executives and their neurotic wives. That was hardly the reaction my wife or I had to the theme of the talk.

"As an aftermath to the talk, my wife and I began some serious dialogue about our relationship. She has some real concerns that if I become any more successful as an executive I might flop as a husband. A woman quoted at the talk said something that really hit home with my wife. Something to the effect, 'I think the husbands with the least success in their careers make the best husbands, because their wives and families are all they have.'

"Noreen thinks that I have paid progressively less attention to her as I have advanced in my career. She told me that I'm so preoccupied with business problems that I only pay surface attention to her problems. One night she told me that her gynecologist said she would need a hysterectomy. I expressed my sympathy. She retorted that this was the second time she told me about the pending hysterectomy.

"That conversation served as a springboard for an examination of many other things about our family life. Out of nowhere, she asked me to name the teachers of our three children. I struck a blank on all three. She then asked me what grade our daughter Tricia was enrolled in. I told her I thought the third grade. I was off by one grade, which she used as evidence that I'm not really participating in our children's worlds.

"Worse than that, Noreen then pointed out that I have been out of town on her last three birthdays. I feebly pointed out to her that her birthday just happens to take place during the time of our annual sales convention. My opinion is that a good many husbands who are going nowhere in their careers—even a few unemployed husbands—forget their wives' birthdays. We can't attribute all of my shortcomings to my business success. But it did make me wonder if a company president can ever remember his wife's birthday, or maybe even his own."

"Okay, Kevin, you have the standard problems at home that an executive can anticipate. Just pay a little more attention to your wife and things will straighten out on that front."

"Fred, the problem of success interfering with my personal life goes beyond my relationship with my wife. I'm also worried about my physical health. I'm not a candidate for an ulcer or a heart attack, but the attention I have been paying to my career lately has taken its toll on my physical condition. I've gained a lot of weight owing to the amount of time I spend in bars and restaurants with customers and colleagues. Those hefty business lunches add more calories than most people realize. Not only am I gaining weight, but I don't look as sharp as I did when I devoted less time to the job.

"Part of the problem, of course, is that you have less time to exercise when you're immersing yourself in your job. When I am home on weekends, I have so much catching up to do on household tasks that I get less physical exercise. I wouldn't worry so much about having gained a few pounds and looking a little pale, if I didn't see a steady deterioration of my golf game. A few years ago, I heard a statement about golf and business that passed by me at the time, but now it makes a good deal of sense. According to the fellow making this statement, if your golf score gets under 75, you have no business.

"Now I know what that character was talking about. As my income and level of responsibility have increased, so has my golf score. When I do play, I'm more erratic. My putting is ragged, I slice more than ever, and I've added about 10 points to my average score. I used to pride myself on my golf. Now I'm just a duffer who plays recreational golf. To get my game back in shape, I'll either have to sacrifice my job or my family. I know that the stereotype of a golfer as an affluent executive fits the stereotype of a duffer. My career is very important to me, but so is my golf game. It would seem unfeeling on my part to chip away at my time with my family in order to bring my game back to snuff."

"Of course, Kevin, if you don't keep raising your income you soon will not be able to afford golf. A person needs a lot of money to keep a golf game going, perhaps a few thousand a year, depending upon the particular club. If we give you a job as a clerk, your game might return to its former level, but you would have to play in public parks. You'd spend so much time waiting to tee off, golf would then interfere with your personal life."

"Fred, I'm glad you brought up the topic of money. So far, the ever-increasing amount of money I've earned hasn't had an overwhelming impact on my standard of living. In the 10 years I've been working for the company my income has tripled, but my standard of living has hardly tripled. My cost of living creeps up every year, and I need that big 10 to 15 percent salary increase just to stay even. Taxes go up at a much steeper rate than your income does.

"At times I find it both disturbing and embarrassing when I realize how little real financial security my ever-increasing income has brought me. People think that as a regional manager for a large corporation, I have no financial worries. My in-laws think I'm stashing away about $2,000 per month for the kids' college and our retirement. The truth is that except for programmed saving like the company retirement system and a mutual fund plan I'm enrolled in, many months go by without my saving any cash.

"What eats away at my insides the most is that some people grossing half as much money as I do seem to live about the same. Maybe they drive an inexpensive car instead of an expensive car, but their vehicle still performs the same function. Noreen, the children, and I took a week's vacation to the Poconos last fall. We met loads of people there, such as foremen and school teachers, who make less than half my income and they had more dough to spend at the nightclub than I did. I'm beginning to wonder if the financial rewards associated with moving up in the executive ranks are real or illusory. Most of the bankruptcies I read about involve executives. Maybe there is something wrong with our system that subtly pushes up your expenses to meet your income."

"Kevin, maybe you're just having a bad day. Most of the problems you allude to are not as serious as you make them out to be. Perhaps you're over-reacting."

"I don't entirely discount that possibility, Fred, but before I take the big plunge to a presidency, there are certain things that would have to be ironed out in advance. Most important of all, what would be expected of a division president in this company? Who takes priority in my life, my company or my family? Do I get paid the same if I work 70 or 40 hours per week? What certainty do I have of that executive bonus? And how much of it will you guarantee?"

"Kevin, get hold of yourself. To succeed at the top you have to love every minute of the job. Digging in to the corporate problems should be your biggest source of kicks in life. All the concerns about the job and the little inconveniences at home are not the central issue. They are simply part of the 'price of success.'"

Questions

1. If you were Fred, how would you handle Kevin's reluctance to accept a division presidency?

2. If you were Kevin, what would you do?

3. What guarantees about income and working conditions do you think a company should give to upper-level managers?

Part Seven

Peak Performance

18. Be All You Can Be

19. Personal Performance

20. Time Management

> A master in the art of living
> draws no sharp distinction
> between work and play,
> labor and leisure,
> mind and body,
> education and recreation.
>
> He hardly knows which is which,
> He simply pursues his vision
> through whatever
> he is going and leaves
> others to determine
> whether he is working or playing.
>
> To himself he always seems to be doing both.
>
> —John McCollister

What you will learn in Part Seven

In Part Seven you will learn:

- the uncommon qualities of peak performers;

- ways to use stress to fulfill your potential;

- effective time management as a stress-coping technique.

Chapter Eighteen

Be All You Can Be

The beautiful laundress

Peak performance is hard to describe, but you know it when you see it.

A perfectly beautiful laundress

When I was very young—five years old, as I remember it—I heard my mother say that she had engaged a perfectly beautiful laundress, and being by endowment curious of feminine charm, I hid behind the kitchen sink to have my first look at beauty—my first look and my first disenchantment. The face of my mother's laundress was less beautiful than the soap that she exercised on my jumpers and my stockings, and her figure was, like that of her tub, round, stable, and very wide.

My mother had spoken in a metaphor, inaccessible to my understanding. She had used the word beauty to signify not an attribute of the laundress, but a quality of workmanship for which the laundress, irrespective of her appearance, had become an embodiment.

That which was called beautiful was neither the laundress nor the objects of her laundering, but the performance to which these were machine and medium, a performance made express and visible in the comforting, crisp cleanliness of linens, pajamas, towels, and pillowcases.

The work done was well done; the task and the process were perfectly mastered; the end was well attained, completely and without excess; and my mother, perceiving this unity of intention, method, and product, cast over all of these the aureole of beauty.[1]

The moral of this story is that whatever you are called to be in life, you should perform your tasks, even as Michelangelo painted or Beethoven composed music or Shakespeare wrote poetry. You should do your work so well that all the hosts of heaven will pause to say, here is a great baker, machinist, farmer, or chief, who does the work well.

To personalize the concept of peak performance, complete the following exercise.

@ **Application: Personal Best and Lessons Learned**

Personal best
Describe a time in your life when you performed at your personal best. When was it? Who was involved? What happened? What were the results?

Lessons learned
As a result of your personal best, what did you learn about yourself? About other people? About excellence?

The road ahead
Based on your personal best and lessons learned, what are your plans for the road ahead? What goals do you have? What steps can you take to perform (again) at a peak-performance level?

The peak performance process

Achieving peak performance requires three basic steps: setting goals, visualizing success, taking action.

Step 1 is to decide what is important to you. After studying the lives of highly successful people, Napoleon Hill presented his conclusions in *Think and Grow Rich*. Hill's analysis showed that the starting point of success is "definiteness of purpose." To achieve definiteness of purpose you must have a goal.[2] As the saying goes, if you aim at nothing, you are sure to hit it. This points to the importance of having a dream which will guide you and against which you can measure success. Miserable is the person who has no goal. In support of this view, Abraham Maslow wrote: "If you purposefully set out to be less than you can be, you are guaranteed to be miserable for the rest of your life."[3]

Step 2 is to "picture the completed thing." Success is visualized, and the steps to it are rehearsed in the mind. Top performers across all fields attribute success to some form of purposeful daydreaming that focuses and energizes their efforts. Henry David Thoreau wrote in *Walden*, "If one advances in the direction of his dreams and endeavors to live a life which he has imagined, he will meet success and fulfill his destiny."[4] In all areas of life—professional and personal—the visualization process is the same:

1. Relax mentally and physically.

2. Let the image of the situation come to mind.

3. Visualize handling the situation in precisely the manner desired.

4. Visualize handling one or two unexpected aspects of the situation.

5. Visualize a positive outcome.

For example, you may be asked to speak in public. The process is to visualize yourself at the beginning, middle, and end of the presentation. See yourself starting to speak confidently and clearly. See yourself speaking fluidly and effectively. See the audience responding positively. See yourself answering questions thoughtfully and thoroughly. See yourself ending successfully.

Step 3 is to "take action." This doesn't require setting records or even winning first place in a contest. What it means is performing at your full potential in a given endeavor at a certain point in time. The effect of this is exhilaration, a little-used term. The exhilaration of the professional is no more than that of the amateur when each performs at his or her personal best.

Peak experience

I will never forget a personal experience on a mountain top more than thirty years ago. It had taken all day to climb Hafelekar, and by the time I neared the top I thought I must be one of the few people in the world to achieve such a feat.

Then I saw the hat and heard the yodel. A young hiker and his dog appeared at the peak, and then passed me with a wave and a whistle on their way back down the mountain trail.

I waited until they were gone, and then humbled, but still with awe, I put one foot on each side of the topmost point. In exhilaration I surveyed the craggy range that stretched below the Austrian clouds.—Author's file notes (G. M.)

The power of self-image

What you think about yourself is more important than what others say about you in fulfilling your potential in life. In fact, a positive self-image is an important defense against public detractors, as the following examples illustrate:[5]

- Thomas Edison's teachers said he was too stupid to learn anything.

- Albert Einstein's teacher described him as "mentally slow, unsociable, and adrift forever in his foolish dreams."

- Walt Disney was fired by his newspaper for lack of ideas.

- The sculptor Rodin's father said, "I have an idiot for a son."

- Leo Tolstoy, author of *War and Peace*, was described as "both unable and unwilling to learn."

- An expert said of Vince Lombardi: "He possesses minimal football knowledge and he lacks motivation."

Peak performance requires, in addition to a belief in oneself, determination and perseverance, as both the story and the author of *Jonathan Livingston Seagull* show. Eighteen publishers turned down Richard Bach's ten-thousand-word story about a "soaring" seagull before MacMillan finally published it in 1970. By 1975, it had sold more than seven million copies in the United States alone.[6]

The intrinsic satisfaction of peak performance

Peak performance is intrinsically satisfying. The process itself is motivating over and above wages and work environment. Writer Studs Terkel explains:

It's about a search, too, for daily meaning as well as for daily bread, for recognition as well as cash, for astonishment rather than torpor; in short, for a sort of life rather than a Monday through Friday sort of dying.

There are, of course, the happy few who find a savor in their daily job: The Indiana stonemason who looks upon his work and sees it is good; the Chicago piano tuner who seeks and finds a sound that delights; the bookbinder who saves a piece of history; the Brooklyn fireman who saves a piece of life.

But don't these satisfactions, like Jude's hunger for knowledge, tell us more about the person than about the task? Perhaps. Nonetheless, there is a common attribute here: a meaning to their task well over and beyond the reward of the paycheck.[7]

As the following story shows, peak performance transcends all ages and occupations.

A friend asked Michelangelo:
"How's the work going at the Sistine Chapel?"

Michelangelo answered:
"About the same. You know, I really never should have started this thing. Four years, on and off, I've been at it. What I really wanted to do was a tomb for Julius II. But they made a decision, and I'm stuck with it. The worst thing is that I had to start at the entrance of the chapel first, which I thought was a stupid idea. But they wanted to keep the chapel open as long as possible while I was working."

His friend inquired:
"What's the difference?"

Michelangelo replied:
"What's the difference? Here I am trying to do a ceiling mural on the creation of man, right? But I have to start with the end of the whole scheme, and then finish with the beginning. Besides, I never painted a ceiling before, and I'm not very experienced at murals either."

The friend sympathized:
"Boy, that's tough."

Michelangelo went on:
"And on top of that, the scaffolding material I have to use is dangerous. The whole thing shakes and wiggles every time I climb up there. One day it's boiling hot, and the next day it's freezing. It's dark most of the time. Working on my back, I swallow as much paint as I put on the ceiling. I can't get any decent help.

The long climb up and down the ladders will kill me yet. And to top everything, they are going to let the public in and show the thing off before it's even finished. It won't be finished for another year at least. And that's another thing, they are always nagging me to finish. And when I'm finished, what then? I've got no security. And if they don't like it, I may be out of work permanently."

The friend responded:
"Gee, Michelangelo, that's tough. With no job security, such poor working conditions, irritating company policies, and inadequate subordinates, you must really be dissatisfied with your job. Are you ready to quit?"

Michelangelo replied:
"What? Quit? Are you crazy? It's a fascinating challenge. And I'm learning more and more every day about murals and ceilings. I've been experimenting and changing my style for these last few years, and I'm, starting to get a lot of recognition from some very important people. You can see for yourself that it's going to be one of the finest achievements of all time. I'm the only one responsible for the design, and I'm making all of the basic decisions. It may bring me other opportunities to do even more difficult things. Quit? Never. This is a terrific job."[8]

Peak performance profile

Do peak performers have a profile of shared characteristics? Psychologist Charles Garfield identifies six qualities or traits of top-performing people. Complete the following questionnaire to see how you measure up.

⊙ Application: Uncommon Qualities of Peak Performers[9]

Evaluate yourself on six qualities of peak performers. For each quality, circle the number on the scale—1 is low; 10 is high.

1. Challenge

   Peak performers resist the tendency to fall into a rut or zone of complacency. Instead, they seek "missions that motivate" and challenge their abilities.

   1   2   3   4   5   6   7   8   9   10

2. Continuous improvement

   Peak performers are dedicated to transcending their previous levels of accomplishment. They embody the spirit of the childhood rhyme: "Good, better, best. Never let it rest until the good gets better and the better is the best."

   1   2   3   4   5   6   7   8   9   10

3. Intrinsic reward

   Peak performers do what they do for the joy of doing it, and are guided by compelling internal goals and feelings as opposed to external standards.

   1   2   3   4   5   6   7   8   9   10

4. Problem solving

   Peak performers love to solve problems. They are energized by difficult tasks. In solving problems, they focus on possibilities and results, rather than problems and blame.

   1   2   3   4   5   6   7   8   9   10

5. Risk taking

   Peak performers readily take risks. They consider the worst possible consequences beforehand, and judge if they can live with the outcome. Then, they take action with focus and full commitment.

   1   2   3   4   5   6   7   8   9   10

6. Positive visualization

   Peak performers picture success in their minds and visualize doing the tasks needed to accomplish their goals.

   1   2   3   4   5   6   7   8   9   10

Interpretation

Using sports as a metaphor, your scores and their meanings are as follows:

Score	Meaning
9 or higher on all six qualities	You embody the qualities of the peak performer. Like Michael, Magic, Billie Jean, and Babe, your attitude and actions set the standard for others to follow.
7 or higher on all six qualities	You are on the floor and on the field with the first team. Your fundamentals are good and you have flashes of excellence.
5 or higher on all six qualities	You are in the league but on the bench. You travel with the club, and they know your name, but you need to practice more to start the game.
3 or higher on all six qualities	You know the sport and have basic talent, but serious performance will require focus and hard work.
2 or below in any quality	You have potential of course, but at the moment it is underdeveloped.

The new workplace

Lance Morrow writes in *The Temping of America* that today's workforce must be fluid and flexible, always learning and growing. His message is that each person is on his own. For good or ill, today's employees have to continually develop and market themselves in an ever-changing work environment.[10] Robert Schaen, former controller of Ameritech and currently a publisher of children's books, writes:

> The days of the mammoth corporations and lifetime work contracts are coming to an end. People are going to have to create their own lives, their own careers, and their own successes. Some people may go kicking and screaming into the new world, but there is only one message there: You're now in business for yourself.[11]

Job families

Managing your career requires knowing your strengths. The concept of job families can help in this area. One of the best models comes from John Holland, who identifies six personality or occupational types. See Figure 18.1.[12]

Figure 18.1 Holland's Model of Personality and Occupational Types

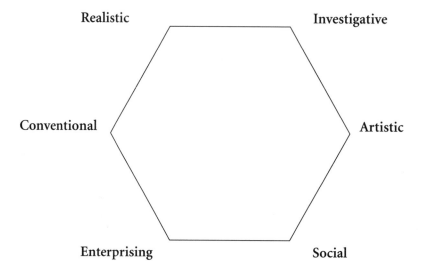

Types most similar to each other are arranged next to each other, while those most dissimilar fall directly across the hexagon. No person is a pure type, and most people have a pattern of interests combining all six. The following are descriptions of each personality-occupational type, including general characteristics, personality traits, sample occupations, and a typical high-stress activity or situation.

Realistic people like working outdoors and working with their hands. They prefer to deal with concrete physical tasks rather than with people. They are described as:

honest	natural	modest	strong
frank	practical	robust	rugged
humble	competent	stable	self-reliant

Sample occupations: engineer, surveyor, farmer, electrician, mechanic
Typical high-stress activity: making a speech

Investigative people enjoy the research and discovery process. They are task-oriented and prefer working alone. They are described as:

analytical	independent	introverted	scientific
critical	intellectual	rational	scholarly
curious	methodical	reserved	cautious

Sample occupations: biologist, chemist, physicist, anthropologist, geologist
Typical high-stress situation: parties and small talk

Artistic individuals thrive in artistic settings that offer opportunities for self-expression. They are described as:

creative	imaginative	intuitive	unique
emotional	impractical	nonconforming	idealistic
expressive	impulsive	original	aesthetic

Sample occupations: artist, writer, decorator, actor, composer
Typical high-stress activity: following rules and regulations

Social people like to work with people and are concerned with their welfare. They have little interest in machinery or physical exertion. They are described as:

friendly	helpful	responsible	tactful
generous	insightful	caring	concerned
kind	tolerant	understanding	supportive

Sample occupations: teacher, counselor, social worker, advisor, therapist
Typical high-stress activity: performing maintenance and repairs

Enterprising people enjoy leading, speaking, and convincing others. They are impatient with routine and detail work. They are described as:

adventurous	energetic	self-confident	enthusiastic
ambitious	optimistic	sociable	charismatic
variety-loving	pleasure-seeking	outgoing	dominant

Sample occupations: salesperson, business executive, producer, promoter, lawyer
Typical high-stress situation: restricted freedom of action

Conventional people prefer highly ordered activities, both verbal and numerical, that characterize detail work. They have little interest in artistic or physical skills. They are described as:

conscientious	dependable	organized	calm
careful	orderly	self-controlled	structured
conservative	neat	efficient	accurate

Sample occupations: accountant, assembler, banker, cost estimator, tax expert
Typical high-stress situation: ambiguity and clutter

There are many hundreds of professions and specialties in the world of work, and these are constantly changing. Holland's model of basic personality and occupational types is useful in considering avenues for peak performance throughout one's career. The best approach is to be what you are and do what you love. Success will follow.

The following exercise is based on Richard Bolles's excellent book *What Color Is Your Parachute*. It provides a useful way to evaluate your own personality based on Holland's model of job families.

⊚ Application: Understanding Personality and Occupational Types[13]

Presented below is a room in which a party is taking place. People with same or similar interests have gathered in the corners of the room as described.

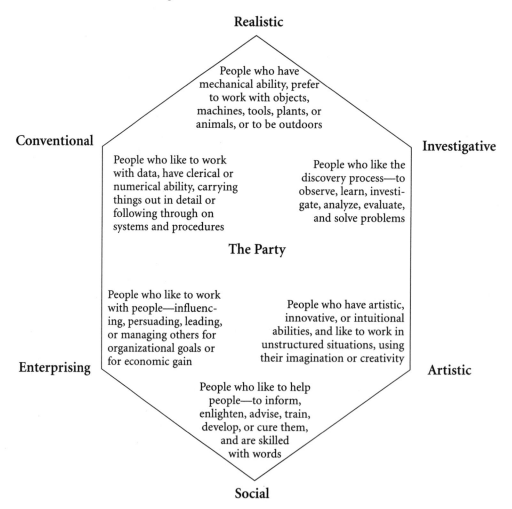

Realistic

People who have mechanical ability, prefer to work with objects, machines, tools, plants, or animals, or to be outdoors

Conventional

People who like to work with data, have clerical or numerical ability, carrying things out in detail or following through on systems and procedures

Investigative

People who like the discovery process—to observe, learn, investigate, analyze, evaluate, and solve problems

The Party

People who like to work with people—influencing, persuading, leading, or managing others for organizational goals or for economic gain

People who have artistic, innovative, or intuitional abilities, and like to work in unstructured situations, using their imagination or creativity

Enterprising

Artistic

People who like to help people—to inform, enlighten, advise, train, develop, or cure them, and are skilled with words

Social

1. Which corner of the room would you be drawn toward; which group of people would you most enjoy being with for the longest time?

2. After a period of time, everyone in the corner you have chosen leaves the room. Of the groups that remain, which one would you most enjoy being with for the longest time?

3. After a period of time, everyone in the corner you have chosen leaves the room. Of the groups that remain, which one would you most enjoy being with for the longest time?

Action steps

Consider the skills and activities of the people in each corner that you have chosen. Do further research on vocations and work opportunities that require these skills and activities. Read the *Occupational Outlook Handbook*, available at all libraries, and interview successful people who are engaged in your areas of interest.

Using stress as a growth technique

The Outward Bound movement, founded by educator Kurt Hahn, is an example of growth through challenge.[14]

In 1940, Hahn noted that younger crew members of sunken convoy ships did not survive as well as their older mates in the icy waters of the North Atlantic. They were more likely to see their ship as a symbol of safety, and once it was gone, they were more likely to give up hope of survival. Older crew members seemed to have greater inner strength to draw upon, and thus had a better chance for survival in the face of danger.

Based on these observations, Hahn founded the first Outward Bound school in Wales in 1941. The principle of using stress to improve survival skills has continued to prove its worth in over thirty schools around the world.

Outward Bound, in addition to teaching young people, has become a popular vehicle for helping adults develop their full potential. The various options include the Mountain School, the Sea School, and the Wilderness School. The stresses involved include rock climbing, digging snow caves for a night's shelter, surviving in wilderness and ocean settings, and kayaking down white-water rapids.

A personal account

Although I had sponsored independent studies and had for years believed in the value of challenge-and-initiative activities, I had never actually participated in one. Then a university management team invited me to join the group to observe events and debrief the experience from a social-psychological perspective.

Three dynamics marked the day: (1) The fellowship and team spirit that evolved out of the morning "low course" activities were excellent. (2) The anxiety and response experienced in the afternoon "high course" initiatives were specific to each person. (3) The attitude expressed by many members was, "The low course was fine, but I didn't really need to risk my neck and overcome fear in order to 'grow' in an artificial setting when I was not actually protecting my family, defending my country, or otherwise saving a life. For young people, it's okay, but not for most adults and definitely not for me."

The next morning in a conference room setting the full story came out. To the surprise of all, myself included, the dominant interest of the group was to discuss again the events of the previous day. With energy and animation every participant went on and on about what he had accomplished. One could see pride levels rise as basically cerebral and social individuals discussed the conquest of fear and the physical feats they had performed.

The experience left me with several opinions about using stress as a growth technique in Outward-Bound type activities. Is it safe? Semi. Is it for everyone? No. Is it effective? Generally. Was it good for the people I observed? Yes.—Author's file notes (G. M.)

Outward Bound has spawned many challenge-and-initiative programs that teach powerful lessons about the strengths that lie in comradeship and teamwork and about the untapped potential that lives within the individual. These are valuable lessons that can be applied back at home and back at work.

For example, if you have learned interdependence in a wilderness survival activity, it may be an easier matter to cooperate with work colleagues in solving a production problem; and if you have learned to climb a mountain, dealing with a business deadline may be viewed as a much smaller problem than you once thought it was.

It is important to note that field learning activities must be judged on a case-by-case basis against two key criteria—safety and growth. Such programs are not *automatically* safe, and a person may or may not be ready to grow.

For people who choose growth through challenge, the Outward Bound motto rings true: "To serve, to strive, and not to yield." It is reminiscent of another well-known quote that encourages individuals to get involved in life and be all they can be:

The credit goes to the one
who is actually in the arena,
whose face is marred by dust and sweat and blood;
who errs and comes short again and again,
who knows the great enthusiasms, the great devotions,
and spends himself in a worthy cause;
who at the best knows the triumph of high achievement;
and who, at the worst, if he fails,
at least fails while daring greatly,
so that his place shall never be
with those cold and timid souls
who know neither victory nor defeat.[15]

—Theodore Roosevelt

Chapter Eighteen References

[1] Joseph Hudnut, *Architecture and the Spirit of Man* (New York: Greenwood Press, 1949), 3.

[2] Napoleon Hill, *Think and Grow Rich* (Hollywood, Calif.: Powers/Wilshire Book Co., 1966).

[3] Duane Schultz, *Growth Psychology: Models of the Healthy Personality* (New York: Van Nostrand Reinhold, 1977).

[4] Henry David Thoreau, *Walden, or Life in the Woods* (New York: Vintage Books, 1991).

[5] Jack Canfield and Mark V. Hansen, *Chicken Soup for the Soul* (Deerfield Beach, Fla.: Health Communications, 1993), 227-28.

[6] Canfield and Hansen, *Chicken Soup for the Soul*, 228-30.

[7] Studs Terkel, *Working* (New York: Pantheon Books, 1974), xi.

[8] B. J. Cummings, Organizational Psychology, Northern Kentucky University, 1978.

[9] Charles Garfield, *Peak Performers: The New Heroes of American Business* (New York: Avon Books, 1986).

[10] William Bridges, *Job Shift: How to Prosper in a Workplace without Jobs* (Reading, Mass.: Addison-Wesley Publishing Company, 1994), 1.

[11] Bridges, *Job Shift: How to Prosper in a Workplace without Jobs*, 100.

[12] John L. Holland, *Making Vocational Choices: A Theory of Vocational Personalities and Work Environments*, 2nd ed. (Odessa, Fla.: Psychological Assessment Resources, 1992).

[13] Richard Bolles, *What Color Is Your Parachute: A Practical Manual for Job Hunters and Career Changers* (Berkeley, Calif.: Ten Speed Press, 1994), 225.

[14] Joshua L. Miner and Joe Boldt, *Outward Bound U.S.A.: Learning through Experience in Adventure Based Education* (New York: Morrow, 1981).

[15] Address at the Sorbonne in Paris, France, April 23, 1910; see *Works of Theodore Roosevelt*, vol. 13, "Strenuous Life," ch. 21, p. 510.

Chapter Nineteen

Personal Performance

The importance of performance

Performance, as the following story shows, is important in all fields of work:

> A mother was having a hard time getting her son to go to school one morning.
>
> "Nobody likes me at school," said the son. "The teachers don't and the kids don't. The superintendent wants to transfer me, the bus drivers hate me, the school board wants me to drop out, and the custodians have it in for me."
>
> "You've got to go," insisted the mother. "You're healthy. You have a lot to learn. You've got something to offer others. You're a leader. Besides, you're forty-nine years old, you're the principal, and you've got to go to school."[1]

Setting the stage

One of the most important stress management principles is to master your work, and the sooner you do this, the better. Although late bloomers and later-life success stories are not uncommon, showing personal performance to be a lifelong concern, for most people the early career sets the stage for all that follows. No matter what field or profession you pursue, the following guide will be of help.[2] Before your middle years, do these things:

1. **Know yourself.** Know who you are and what is important to you. This will anchor you and make you efficient. The time and energy required to do this can be substantial, and these are best spent in your youth, not in midlife when the needs of others should be the focus of your attention.

2. **Become an expert.** Develop a body of knowledge and skills that people need and will pay you to do. Examples are carpentry, nursing, accounting, cooking, singing, writing, typing, and plumbing. In the final analysis, your ability to perform a wanted service is the best insurance you can have.

3. **Establish your style.** Whatever methods or tools you use—early riser, suit and tie, fresh flowers, thank-you cards, pickup truck—be sure they are both productive and comfortable for you. Do this when you are young. Nothing

is more disconcerting than to see a midcareer professional still trying to find his or her style.

4. **Build a network.** This is usually done through personal interactions on the job, in the neighborhood, and in the family. It is best done by generous and gracious service to others—paid or unpaid. A web of trust, respect, and mutual support will result that will build relationships and benefit all parties for years to come.

5. **Focus.** Cherish the past, plan for the future, but live in the moment. Only then will all of your faculties be functioning on the task at hand. By living life fully in the moment, you maximize all you have been and realize the full potential of which you are capable.

6. **Create a cushion.** Ideally, you don't want to be in your midlife years and unable to say, I quit. By this time you will know in your heart the hills worth dying on versus minor matters of opinion or style. When faced with such a hill, your conscience will cry out for expression, and it will help if you have economic strength to support it.

7. **Be true to your values.** Yogi Berra once said, "Everything is easy until it becomes difficult." This is where integrity comes in. Integrity requires honest assessment and action, and it requires courage to live by your convictions even at self-risk or sacrifice. Integrity is the foremost requirement for a successful career and life.

To help this list be more than words, heed the words of Winston Churchill, a peak performer on a worldwide stage:

> Upon the plains of hesitation bleach the bones of
> countless millions, who on the threshold of victory,
> sat down to wait; and awaiting they died.

A Latin phrase conveys this thought well—"Carpe diem," seize the day!

What is your level of job performance?

The following questionnaire evaluates job performance in three important areas—statesmanship, entrepreneurship, and innovation. Complete the Performance Pyramid alone or with others, such as a coworker or supervisor. Points to remember are:

- Job mastery is an important component in stress management.

- Factors measured by the Performance Pyramid are important for success in every field of work, from steel fabrication to public service. Every industry and profession requires *statesmanship*—the ability to work with and through other people; *entrepreneurship*—the ability to achieve results; and *innovation*—the ability to generate new and usable ideas.

- The Performance Pyramid measures job behavior, not personal qualities. To increase objectivity, evaluation is based on actual rather than potential performance.

- Results on the Performance Pyramid are based on a normative group. Scores show how you compare with individuals considered to be top producers and those considered to be poor producers in U.S. business and industry.

- Attitudes influence job performance. Scores on the Performance Pyramid may be raised or lowered by changes in your level of morale.

- How high you score on the Performance Pyramid is less important than what you do about it. It is important to know where you stand in order to capitalize on strengths and improve weaknesses.

⊜ Application: The Performance Pyramid

Read the following sets of statements. For each set, make a check mark next to the statement that is most like your behavior on the job at this time. It may be difficult to select one statement over the others, but force a choice.

1. _____ a. You are interested in what will work, not what might work.
   _____ b. You are willing to listen to anyone's ideas.
   _____ c. You seek out the ideas and opinions of others.
   _____ d. You are tolerant of those whose ideas differ from yours.

2. _____ a. You rarely get worked up about things.
   _____ b. You measure up to what is expected of you in output.
   _____ c. You are one of the top producers of results.
   _____ d. You are busy with so many things that your output is affected.

3. _____ a. You avoid changing existing methods and procedures.
   _____ b. You continually search for better ways to do things.
   _____ c. Sometimes you think of things that could be improved.
   _____ d. You often make suggestions to improve things.

4. _____ a. You go out of your way to help others.
   _____ b. You rarely spend time on other people's problems.
   _____ c. Other people often come to you for help.
   _____ d. You lend a hand if others request your assistance.

5. _____ a. You have selected assignments that have had a good future.
   _____ b. Most jobs you have worked on have resulted in significant contributions.
   _____ c. You would be much farther ahead if you had not been assigned so many things that turned out to be unimportant.
   _____ d. Some of your time has been wasted on things that you never should have undertaken.

6. _____ a. You have changed the whole approach to your work.
   _____ b. You have initiated many changes in the work you are doing.
   _____ c. From time to time, you have made a change in the way you do your work.
   _____ d. You go along with established ways of working, without upsetting things.

7.   ____   a. You seek consensus in settling disagreements.
     ____   b. You do not concern yourself with the affairs of others.
     ____   c. You will yield a point rather than displease someone.
     ____   d. Once your mind is made up, you prefer not to change it.

8.   ____   a. You follow the motto, better safe than sorry.
     ____   b. You avoid taking risks except under rare circumstances.
     ____   c. You will gamble on good odds any time.
     ____   d. You sometimes take risks when the odds are favorable.

9.   ____   a. You are well known for your creativity.
     ____   b. You often think of new ways of doing things.
     ____   c. You are conservative and rarely experiment with new ideas.
     ____   d. From time to time, you introduce new ideas.

10. ____   a. You sometimes trust the wrong people.
     ____   b. Your judgment about people is usually correct.
     ____   c. You have as little to do with others as possible.
     ____   d. Your ability to work with people is excellent.

11. ____   a. You prefer doing work yourself rather than planning work for others.
     ____   b. You plan work and hold performance to schedule.
     ____   c. You make plans, but adjust to day-to-day changes.
     ____   d. You rarely make plans.

12. ____   a. Your ideas are almost always used.
     ____   b. You frequently say to yourself, "I wish I had thought of that."
     ____   c. Your ideas are sometimes put into practice.
     ____   d. Your ideas are often adopted.

13. ____   a. You consider alternatives before making decisions.
     ____   b. You wait as long as possible before making decisions.
     ____   c. You make decisions before weighing the consequences.
     ____   d. You involve others in decisions that affect them.

14. ____   a. You rarely push to have your plans adopted.
     ____   b. Inevitable roadblocks prevent you from accomplishing your goals.
     ____   c. You are known for getting difficult jobs done.
     ____   d. If you want something done, you find a way to get it done.

15. _____ a. You believe change should be gradual, if at all.
     _____ b. You are open to change and new methods.
     _____ c. You prefer traditional and established ways.
     _____ d. You are innovative in your ideas and approach to work.

Source: Adapted from Philip Marvin, Management Goals: Guidelines and Accountability. *(Homewood, Ill.:Dow Jones-Irwin Inc., 1980), 95-113. Used with permission.*

Scoring

Step One

Using the score matrix that follows, circle the score you gave yourself for each item under Self-Evaluation. (For item 1, if you checked (c), your score would be 7).

Step Two

If another person evaluated you, circle the score for each item under Partner's Evaluation. (For item 1, if your partner checked (b), your score would be 5.)

Step Three

Add each column of the score matrix to find your total scores on (A) statesmanship; (B) entrepreneurship; and (C) innovation.

Step Four

Plot your results on the Performance Pyramid in Figure 19.1. (See sample in Figure 19.2.) If there is disagreement between your self-evaluation and your partner's evaluation, use either the self-evaluation or an average of the two. In general, you know your own performance best. Discuss points of agreement and disagreement; you may be doing an exceptional job and not communicating this to your partner.

Score Matrix

Statesmanship		Entrepreneurship		Innovation	
Self-evaluation	*Partner's evaluation*	*Self-evaluation*	*Partner's evaluation*	*Self-evaluation*	*Partner's evaluation*
1. a. 1	1	2. a. 1	1	3. a. 1	1
b. 5	5	b. 5	5	b. 7	7
c. 7	7	c. 7	7	c. 3	3
d. 3	3	d. 3	3	d. 5	5
4. a. 7	7	5. a. 5	5	6. a. 7	7
b. 1	1	b. 7	7	b. 5	5
c. 5	5	c. 1	1	c. 3	3
d. 3	3	d. 3	3	d. 1	1
7. a. 7	7	8. a. 1	1	9. a. 7	7
b. 1	1	b. 3	3	b. 5	5
c. 3	3	c. 7	7	c. 1	1
d. 5	5	d. 5	5	d. 3	3
10. a. 3	3	11. a. 3	3	12. a. 7	7
b. 5	5	b. 7	7	b. 1	1
c. 1	1	c. 5	5	c. 3	3
d. 7	7	d. 1	1	d. 5	5
13. a. 5	5	14.. a. 3	3	15. a. 3	3
b. 1	1	b. 1	1	b. 5	5
c. 3	3	c. 5	5	c. 1	1
d. 7	7	d. 7	7	d. 7	7
A_____	A_____	B_____	B_____	C_____	C_____

Figure 19.1 Your Performance Pyramid

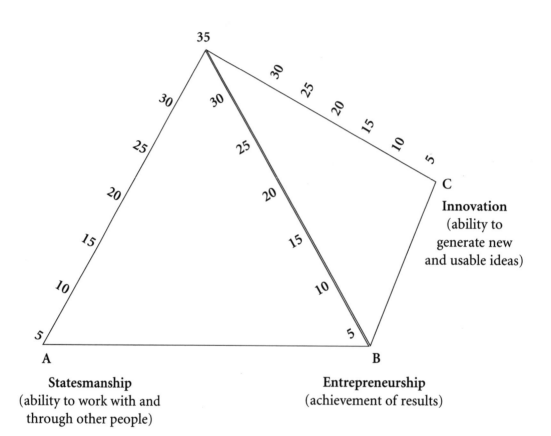

Figure 19.2 Sample Performance Pyramid

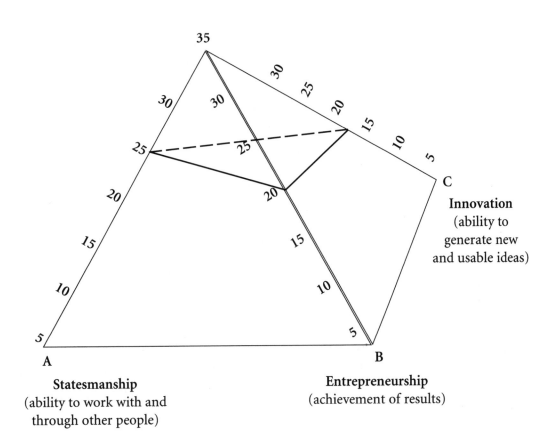

Statesmanship
(ability to work with and
through other people)

Entrepreneurship
(achievement of results)

Innovation
(ability to
generate new
and usable ideas)

Interpretation

High scores represent strengths on the job at this time; low scores represent areas you should strive to improve. Use the following formula to evaluate your scores:

Scores	Discussion
30–35	Extremely high performers receive these scores. As a result of ability, experience, motivation, and attitude, these individuals produce top results. If such a person were to leave, it is likely that the organization would suffer significantly.
20–29	Good performers receive these scores. They are pivotal people in their organizations and are solid producers. In college, these scores represent very good work.
15–19	People who receive these scores are "doing their jobs." They are doing what is expected of personnel in their positions—no more and no less. Although these scores are acceptable, they are nothing to write home about.
14 and lower	People whose performance needs improvement receive these scores. Such scores reflect problems in ability, experience, motivation, or attitude. Counseling and training should be considered.

Improving job performance

What can you do to maintain high performance or improve in the areas of statesmanship, entrepreneurship, and innovation?

- First, you have to want to perform at your best; you must not be complacent.

- Second, you have to know the essential behaviors that represent statesmanship, entrepreneurship, and innovation.

- Third, you have to apply principles and practices to perform these behaviors.

The following is a discussion of each performance area, including behaviors that reflect high performance and principles and techniques that can be used to improve performance.

Statesmanship

Statesmanship is the ability to work with and through other people. Such a person is skillful in human relations and is able to multiply personal accomplishments through the efforts of others. The following describes this role:

> A statesman is not a dictator, but rather a developer of effective relationships. The statesman is one who guides rather than leads, helping others to make decisions rather than making decisions alone. The statesman believes that if everyone works together, more can be accomplished.[3]

Consider the case of Abraham Lincoln. Throughout his life, Lincoln was always willing to teach others what he had learned himself. From childhood onward, he was the statesman—storyteller, speechmaker, and always the ringleader. One boyhood comrade relates:

> When he [Lincoln] appeared, the boys would gather and cluster around him to hear him talk. . . . He argued much from analogy and explained things hard for us to understand by stories, maxims, tales, and figures. He would almost always paint his lesson or idea by some story that was plain and near to us, that we might instantly see the force and bearing of what he said.[4]

Examine the following behaviors that represent a high level of statesmanship:

- You seek out the ideas and opinions of others.

- You go out of your way to help others.

- You seek consensus in settling disagreements.

- Your ability to work with people is excellent.

- You involve others in decisions that affect them.

As statesmanship goes up, stress levels go down. If you would like to increase your ability to work with and through others, develop good human relations skills and use four steps to solve problems.

Develop good human relations skills. The following principles will help you accomplish this goal:

1. **Let people know where they stand.** You should communicate expectations, then keep people informed on how they are doing. If criticism is necessary, do it in private; if praise is in order, give it in public.

2. **Give credit where due.** Look for extra or unusual performance, and share appreciation as soon as possible. You should not wait until December to say thank you for something done in July. If you do, for six months the

person probably will be thinking, "If she doesn't care, why should I?" In addition, you will have missed the opportunity to reinforce good performance. Psychologist Gordon Allport writes:

Not only does human learning proceed best when the incentive of praise and recognition is used, but the individual's capacity for learning actually seems to expand under this condition.[5]

3. **Tell people as soon as possible about changes that will affect them.** Keep people informed, and tell them why change is necessary. Many people dislike change, and they especially dislike sudden changes. Therefore, new ideas and methods are more easily accepted when introduced gradually.

4. **Make best use of each person's ability.** No two people are exactly alike, so let each person shine as only that person can. Take the time to look for potential not now being used. Also, never stand in a person's way. To do so creates resentment, reduces morale, and ultimately results in reduced performance.

5. **Lend a hand.** This shows that you care about others. The following story helps make the point:

A painter asked Albert Einstein if he would sit for a portrait. The famous mathematician replied, "No, no. I do not have the time." "But I desperately need the money," the painter pleaded. "Well, that's another story," Einstein replied. "Of course I will sit."[6]

6. **Involve people in decisions that affect them.** Whenever possible, tap the constructive power of the group to develop plans and procedures and to solve common problems. There is truth in the saying, "If you want people in the landing, include them in the takeoff."

Use four steps to solve problems. Statesmanship requires problem-solving ability. The following is a four-step method for solving any problem.

1. **Get the facts.** As Mark Twain said, "Get the facts first; then you can distort them as much as you please." You simply cannot solve a problem without first knowing the facts, so (a) review all records; (b) talk with the people concerned; (c) consider opinions and feelings (people act on their feelings); and (d) look at all sides. Seeing things from more than one point of view can help in the problem-solving process.

2. **Weigh and decide.** After getting all of the facts, you must weigh each fact against the others, fit the pieces together, and consider alternatives. Consider

the effects that different courses of action will have on individuals and groups. Sometimes it is a good idea to sleep on a problem so that you do not jump to conclusions or overreact. It is easy to rush the thinking step of the problem-solving process and forget critical details. Benjamin Franklin emphasized the importance of considering details when he wrote, "A little neglect may breed mischief; for want of a nail, the shoe was lost; for want of a shoe, the horse was lost; for want of a horse, the rider was lost; for want of a rider, the war was lost."[7]

3. **Take action.** After you have gathered the facts and determined a course of action, carry out your plan. Harry Truman realized the importance of this step in the problem-solving process. He believed that statesmanship required taking action; this was why he said, "The buck stops here" and "If you can't stand the heat, get out of the kitchen."

   Many people occupy positions requiring statesmanship but are indecisive and fail to act. Have you ever been affected by someone in authority—supervisor, parent, or public official—who could not, or would not, take action? William James wrote, "There is no more miserable human being than one in whom nothing is habitual but indecision."[8]

4. **Follow up.** Follow-up is an essential, but often neglected, step in the problem-solving process. Some people say "I'm so busy taking action that I don't have time to follow up." With this attitude, the same mistakes may be made over and over. At the least, people are not learning from experience.

   Statesmanship requires asking, "Did my action(s) help the quality of work or the quality of work life?" If not, admit this fact and try to find a better solution. Contrast the willingness to admit mistakes with the approach taken by many people: "Right or wrong, that is my decision." By taking time to follow up on actions and being willing to admit mistakes, the statesman achieves three important goals: (a) the respect of all who are watching; (b) another chance to solve the problem; and (c) the opportunity to set an example of honesty and thoroughness in problem solving.

Entrepreneurship

Entrepreneurship is the ability to achieve results, regardless of obstacles. It takes entrepreneurship to build a plant on time, to produce a quality product, and to close a sale successfully. Although an entrepreneur is action-oriented, such an individual knows that it is not just action, but achievement, that counts. Effective performance in any field requires entrepreneurship. Consider the entrepreneur Henry Ford, who founded and built the Ford Motor Company. Ford believed in honesty and hard work and often asked, "Did you ever see dishonest calluses on a man's hands?" Ford's story follows:

Profile of an entrepreneur

How it began

...But in the month of April, there came a burst of strenuous effort; the inventor worked two days and nights without rest or sleep, and at two o'clock in the morning came in to tell his wife that the machine was ready, and he was about to make a test. It was raining, and she came out under an umbrella to see what happened.

There was a crank in front, and you had to turn it over to start the engine. It made a mighty sputtering, then a roaring, and shook the vehicle most alarmingly; but it held together, and Mr. Ford got in and started. He had a kerosene lamp in front, and by this dim light went down the street paved with cobblestones. Mrs. Ford stood in the rain for a long time, wondering if she would ever see her husband again.

The young inventor was gone a long time, and came back pushing the contraption. A nut had come loose, with all the shaking. But he was exultant; in spite of bumpy cobblestones and muddy ruts, he had gone where he wished to go. "You're wet clear through," said his wife, as he let her lead him into the kitchen, take off his wet things, hang them up, and give him hot coffee. He was talking excitedly all the time. "I've got a horseless carriage that runs," said Henry Ford.

The early years

...He observed when they [the cars] bumped into each other, and devised plans to keep them from doing so. He examined materials, read contracts, discussed selling campaigns, and prepared advertisements shrewdly addressed to the mind of the average American, which he knew perfectly, because he had been one for forty years. It was his doctrine that any man who wanted to succeed in business should never let it out of his mind; and he had practiced this half a lifetime before he began to preach it.

In the first year the sales of the Ford Motor Company brought Ford a million and a half dollars, nearly one-fourth of which was profit. From then on, all his life, Henry Ford had all the money he needed to carry out his ideas. He took care of his money, and used it for that purpose.

The drive to succeed

...Henry Ford went on expanding his business. There was nobody to stop him now; he was master of his own house. He and his wife and son were the three directors of the Ford Motor Company; also they were the sole stockholders. There was a housecleaning, and those who did not see eye to eye with the master got out. The war had done something to Henry; it had taught him a new way to deal with his fellow men. No more crusades, no more peaceships, no more idealists getting hold of him and wasting his time. From now on, he was a businessman, and he held a tight rein on everything. This industry was his. He had made it himself; and what he wanted of the men he hired was that they should do exactly what he told them.

Tough times for the men
. . . Under this new deal, the chassis came to him [the worker] with spindlenuts already screwed on; it was Abner's job to put in a cotter-pin and spread it. The next man wielded a scoop, pasting a gob of brown grease into the cavity; by the time he had smoothed it level, the chassis had moved on to another, who screwed on the hubcap. Abner's job rested his tired legs, but his back began to ache abominably, and his arms were ready to give out from being held up in front of him continually. But he hung on like death and taxes, for he was over forty, the dangerous age for workers in any factory. "We expect the men to do what they are told," wrote Henry.

Mission accomplished
. . . Henry had a seemingly inexhaustible market for his cars. He was employing more than two hundred thousand men, paying wages of a quarter of a billion dollars a year. He had developed fifty-three different industries, beginning alphabetically with aeroplanes and ending with wood-distillation. He bought a broken-down railroad, and made it pay; he bought coal-mines, and trebled their production. He perfected new processes—the very smoke that had once poured from his chimneys was now made into automobile parts.[9]

The following behaviors represent a high level of entrepreneurship:

- You are one of the top producers of results.

- Most jobs you have worked on have resulted in significant contributions.

- You will gamble on good odds anytime.

- You plan work and hold performance to schedule.

- If you want something done, you find a way to get it done.

High performance is stressful, but failure is more so. Entrepreneurship in any field requires good work habits, a belief in oneself, and the willingness to take risks. All three of these qualities depend primarily on the individual. The following action plan will help you maximize entrepreneurship.

Exercise good work habits. The achievement of results requires a positive attitude and the ability to stick with a job until it is done, even when others may give up. A

Polish proverb says, "If there is not enough wind, row." The following poem shows the kind of attitude that is necessary to accomplish difficult tasks:

> Some said it couldn't be done.
> But he, with a chuckle, replied
> That maybe it couldn't, but he would be one
> Who wouldn't say so until he tried.
> So he buckled right in with a bit of a grin,
> If he worried, he hid it.
> He started to sing, as he tackled the thing
> That couldn't be done—and he did it.[10]
> —Edgar Guest

The high performer goes the extra mile. If you have good work habits, your employer will want to keep you, and you will be rewarded both financially and personally as word gets out that you are a valuable asset.

Believe in yourself. Eleanor Roosevelt once said, "No one can make you feel inferior without your consent."[11] The chronology of Abraham Lincoln's career shows the importance of believing in yourself and determined effort:

- in 1831, he failed in business;

- in 1832, he was defeated for the legislature;

- in 1833, he again failed in business;

- in 1836, he had a nervous breakdown;

- in 1843, he was defeated for Congress;

- in 1855, he was defeated for the Senate;

- in 1856, he lost the race for the vice presidency;

- in 1858, he was defeated for the Senate;

- in 1860, he was elected president of the United States.

Be willing to take risks. Entrepreneurship requires courage, which is not the absence of fear, but the ability to overcome fear. Fear can have terrible consequences, as the following story shows:

> In an ancient fable, an oriental monarch met Pestilence going to Baghdad. "What are you going to do there?" asked the King. "I'm going to kill 5,000 people," said Pestilence. On the way back, the monarch met Pestilence again. "You liar," thundered the monarch. "You killed 25,000." "Oh, no," said Pestilence. "I only killed 5,000 people. It was Fear that killed the rest."[12]

Fear of failure can have negative consequences in the work setting. It can paralyze a person to the extent that opportunities are missed and achievement is reduced. As the following poem illustrates, courage is necessary to overcome self-doubt and achieve success:

The Doubter

He had his doubts when he began;
The task had stopped another man;
And he had heard it whispered low,
How rough the road was he must go;
But now on him the charge was laid,
And of himself he was afraid.

He wished he knew how it would end;
He longed to see around the bend;
He had his doubts that he had strength,
Enough to go so far a length;
And all the time the notion grew,
That this was more than he could do.

Of course, he failed. Whoever lives with doubt,
Soon finds his courage giving out;
They only win who face a task,
And say the chance is all I ask;
They only rise who dare the grade,
And of themselves are not afraid.

There are no ogres up the slope;
It is only with human beings that man must cope;
Whoever fears the blow before it's struck,
Loses the fight for lack of pluck;
And only he the goal achieves,
Who truly in himself believes.

—Edgar Guest

Innovation

Innovation is the ability to generate new and usable ideas. The innovator is not satisfied with the status quo, and therefore explores, questions, and studies new ways of doing things. Innovation accounts for advances in all fields of work, from agriculture to architecture. Important products we take for granted today are the result of yesterday's inventions—Thomas Edison's electric light, the

Wright brothers' airplane, and Alexander Graham Bell's telephone are but a few examples. In the field of agriculture, George Washington Carver created more than three hundred synthetic products for the peanut, more than one hundred for the sweet potato, and more than seventy-five for the pecan.

The creative process is not unique to human beings; it can be seen in other animals as well:

> Primatologists put out various foods, such as wheat and potatoes, that were not part of the macaque's natural diet, to attract the animals to feeding grounds near the open seashore where they could more easily be observed. . . . Because a mound of wheat had simply been piled on the beach, the monkeys found it difficult to separate grains of wheat from grains of sand. Year after year, the monkeys painstakingly picked out the grains of wheat with their fingertips— until a young female arrived at the novel solution of scooping a handful of the mixture and running on her hind legs to the sea. When she opened her hands in the water, the heavier sands sank immediately while the wheat grains floated on the surface, where they could easily be scooped up. This method of sifting wheat eventually became a tradition within the group, much as it must have in human groups that early developed the cultural innovation of winnowing wheat to separate the chaff from the grain. Wheat-sifting by macaques represents true protoculture: a modification in behavior different from that of other groups belonging to the same species and faced with the same potentials and limitations in the environment—one that is transmitted throughout the group and from generation to generation.[13]

The following behaviors represent a high level of creativity:

- You continually search for better ways to do things.

- You have changed the whole approach to your work.

- You are well known for your creativity.

- Your ideas are almost always used.

- You are innovative in your ideas and approach to work.

How do you develop creativity and increase innovation? Keep an open mind, have a questioning attitude, and use a new-ideas system.

Keep an open mind. An essential quality of the innovator is openness to change and to new experience. The innovator does not consider creation to be a place, but rather a direction, and does not consider him- or herself to be a completed book, but rather a book in the process of being written.

Charles F. Kettering, the famous inventor, emphasized the importance of keeping an open mind when he wrote:

I don't want men of experience working for me. The experienced man is always telling me why something can't be done. The fellow who has not had any experience doesn't know a thing can't be done—and goes ahead and does it. . . . There exist limitless opportunities in any industry. Where there is an open mind, there will always be a frontier.[14]

The innovative person remembers the bumblebee—nothing that flies is less qualified to do so. The bumblebee's wings are small compared to its large body; yet, despite the laws of aerodynamics, the bumblebee flies. We often hear about an idea that doesn't sound as if it would work. However, *non tentare, non pugnare*—if you haven't tried it, don't knock it. Innovation requires an open mind.

Do any of the following innovation blocks prevent you from being as creative as you could be?

- **Excessive need for order.** Institutions—church, school, industry, and government—provide a sense of order. But it is possible to be too orderly. When everything happens according to plan, innovation is ordered out of existence. As the Hungarians say, "To make an omelet you have to break a few eggs." For creativity, order should be viewed as a tool, not a goal.

- **Reluctance to play.** Creativity requires playfulness, daydreaming, and questioning "What if?" and "Why?" Innovative people play with things, people, and ideas. Those who are afraid to play because they think they will look silly or because they feel guilty about having fun rarely come up with creative ideas.

- **Myopic vision.** Some people pride themselves on seeing things "as they are." But if you see things only as they are, you miss seeing what they could be; this is the essence of innovation. A shoe can be a hammer, a pillow, or something from which to drink water. The playwright George Bernard Shaw once said, "You see things, and you say, 'Why?' But I dream things that never were; and I say, 'Why not?'"

- **Fear of risk.** Society punishes failure, so we become afraid to "stick our necks out." Yet the wisdom of the ages says, "Nothing ventured, nothing gained."

- **Reluctance to exert influence.** If children are taught to be "seen and not heard," they may not want to attract attention or appear to be "different" when they become adults. Most people have the feeling that the majority has to be right. But often, the majority keeps on doing things one way when there is a new and better way available.

- **Closed-mindedness.** What if Christopher Columbus had been as certain as many people in his day that the world was flat? Research has shown that the more people feel they really know something, the less open they are to new information and ideas in that area. This is called the "specialist disease."[15]

Have a questioning attitude. People are creatures of habit. Some habits are good because they help us survive. Good driving habits and hygiene habits are examples. Other habits, such as wasting time or procrastinating, are harmful and prevent success. People may have poor habits and not know it, unless they ask themselves two questions: "Am I doing the right thing?" and "Is there a better way to do it?" Many people sleepwalk through their days, never stopping to ask themselves these two questions. For these individuals, creativity is never realized because it is never considered. The following poem shows the importance of having a questioning attitude:

The Calf Path—The Beaten Path of Beaten Men
One day though an old-time wood,
A calf walked home, as good calves should;
But made a trail,
A crooked trail, as all calves do.
Since then three hundred years have fled,
And I infer the calf is dead.
But still, he left behind his trail,
And thereby hangs my mortal tale.

The trail was taken up the next day,
By a lone dog that passed that way.
And then a wise sheep,
Pursued the trail, over the steep,
And drew the flocks behind him too,
As all good sheep do.
And from that day, over hill and glade,
Through those old woods, a path was made.

This forest path became a lane,
That bent, and turned, and turned again.
This crooked lane became a road,
Where many a poor horse with his load,
Toiled on beneath the burning sun.
And thus a century and a half,
They followed the footsteps of that calf.

> The years passed on in swiftness fleet,
> And the road became a village street.
> And this became a city's thoroughfare.
> And soon the central street was a metropolis.
> And men, two centuries and a half,
> Followed the footsteps of that calf.
>
> A moral lesson this tale might teach,
> Were I ordained, and called to preach.
> For men are prone to go it blind,
> Along the calf paths of the mind;
> And work away from sun to sun,
> To do just what other men have done.
> They follow in the beaten track,
> And out, and in, and forth, and back;
> And still their devious course pursue,
> To keep the paths that others do.
>
> They keep these paths as sacred grooves,
> Along which all their lives they move.
> But how the wise old wood gods laugh,
> Who saw the first old-time calf.
> Ah, many things this tale might teach,
> But I am not ordained to preach.[16]
> — Samuel Foss

Use a new-ideas system. Being open to change, avoiding innovation blocks, and having a questioning attitude are three ingredients of creativity; but a fourth element is necessary—a system is needed to generate new and usable ideas. One good system comes from the English writer Rudyard Kipling. Kipling, who was known for his creativity, was asked how he could come up with so many good ideas—what was the secret of his success? His famous answer was:

> I keep six honest serving-men;
> They taught me all I knew;
> Their names are What and Where and When,
> And How and Why and Who.
> I send them over land and sea;
> I send them east and west;
> But after they have worked for me,
> I give them all a rest.

I let them rest from nine till five,
For I am busy then,
As well as breakfast, lunch, and tea,
For they are hungry men:
But different folk have different views:
I know a person small—
She keeps ten million serving-men,
Who get no rest at all.
She sends 'em abroad on her own affairs,
From the second she opens her eyes—
One million Hows, two million Wheres,
And seven million Whys.[17]

By asking six simple questions—who, what, why, when, where, and how—and by constructively answering these, you can usually find new and workable solutions to any problem.

You can improve if you want to

It is possible to improve performance, and the rewards can be great. Consider the following story:

When Gene Malusko first went to work for his company, he was hired as a laborer. Before long, it was apparent that he would become either a union steward or a work group supervisor. Gene had the ability to work with and through other people. Gene could talk people into things; he was a statesman. Gene chose supervision because he had a family to raise and needed the money. For the next year, he was a successful foreman—he had good relations with his subordinates, and he had a good production record.

Then Gene became interested in advancement. As he considered those who had been promoted in the past, he realized that they had each excelled at obtaining results. The quality and efficiency of their production had stood out over that of the other supervisors. This convinced him to set forth on a self-improvement program to improve entrepreneurship, the delivery of results.

Thereafter, when Gene arrived at work, he began working immediately, and he worked diligently until the job was done. He developed a reputation for making his production quota each day, and he could be counted on to help out in emergencies. Gene was also willing to stick his neck out and take risks when the situation warranted it. He overcame self-doubt with the attitude. "Nothing ventured, nothing gained." With confidence in himself and good work habits, Gene developed a superb record of achievement. Gene exhibited entrepreneurship, and within two years, he was promoted to general foreman.

Gene performed well as a general foreman on the strength of his ability to work with people (statesmanship) and his ability to obtain results (entrepreneurship). After a mere three years in this capacity, he was selected as the youngest superintendent in the history of the company.

Two years later, Gene was talking with a friend about future plans when he stated that his goal was to be a general manager. He wondered aloud, "What do those people have that I don't?" The answer was creativity. A good general manager must work with and through others, which Gene did; must achieve results regardless of obstacles, which Gene did; and must come up with new and usable ideas, which Gene almost never did.

Gene's friend told him about the ideas of Charles Kettering and the importance of keeping an open mind; he pointed out the six common blocks to innovation; he gave him "The Calf Path—The Beaten Path of Beaten Men," emphasizing the need to question things; and finally, he told him about Rudyard Kipling's six honest serving-men, a system of constructive questioning.

Until this time, Gene had not thought much about why things were as they were; he had rarely questioned whether there was a better way to do something; and he had never been given a system for generating new ideas. For Gene, a new dimension of work performance was unveiled, and he set about to improve his creativity.

Each day, Gene would go into his work area and ask six important questions— who, what, why, when, where, and how—to analyze the production bottlenecks and employee problems he encountered. He would ask: Who should do this work, the machine operator or the material handler? What work should be done, milling or planing? Why should this work be done, production or politics? Where should the work be done, in the office or the field? When should the work be done, on the first shift or the second? And how should the work be done, by person or by machine? And, like Kipling, Gene always found a better way.

Gene worked at constructive questioning until it became a habit, and he gained a reputation as a creative person. He added innovation to the qualities of statesmanship and entrepreneurship that he had already developed, and two years later, Gene Malusko was promoted to general manager.[18]

Gene's story is one of professionalism. He learned what was required to perform his job well; he performed good work; yet he constantly tried to improve. He was not complacent. As a result of professional development, Gene Malusko improved the performance of his company and achieved personal rewards as well.

Performance success story—a case in point

Sam Walton, founder of Wal-Mart, was America's richest person, a multibillionaire, when he died, and he was beloved by all who knew him. His prescription for success, as detailed in *Sam Walton: Made in America, My Story,* has three key elements: statesmanship, entrepreneurship and innovation. Walton wrote that success came only through *building a team,* only after *hard work,* and only by *breaking old rules.*

> **Statesmanship**—share the rewards. "If you treat people as your partners, they will perform beyond your wildest dreams." (In the effort to treat others as partners, Sam's reading of people wasn't always 100 percent. Once he attempted to thank big city investors by taking them camping on the banks of Sugar Creek. A coyote started howling and a hoot owl hooted, and half the back-east investors stayed up all night around the campfire because they couldn't sleep.)

> **Entrepreneurship**—commit to your business. "I think I overcame every single one of my personal shortcomings by the sheer passion I brought to my work." (Hard work and risk have a price, as revealed by Sam's youngest child Alice when she once confided to a friend, "I don't know what we are going to do. My daddy owes so much money, and he won't quit opening stores.")

> **Innovation**—Be creative. "If everybody else is doing it one way, there's a good chance you can find your niche by going in a new direction. I guess in all my years, what I heard more than anything else was: a town of less than 50,000 can't support a decent store." (Of course, some say this strategy stemmed from Sam's wife, Helen, who insisted on raising the Walton family in a town with fewer than 10,000 people.)[19]

Would you hire you?

The following exercise looks at fifteen qualities employers like to see in their personnel. They are important in all fields of work and all levels of responsibility.

⊘ Application: Putting Your Best Foot Forward

Evaluate your current job performance by circling the appropriate number (1 is low; 10 is high).

Job knowledge
Success at work begins with job knowledge. Make it your business to know what to do, when to do it, and why you are doing it.

Low   1   2   3   4   5   6   7   8   9   10   High

Dependability
If your work requires being on time, be on time. You should be ten minutes early for the work day if at all possible. Tardiness lowers your image (this includes lunch and work breaks). Also, if you say you will do something, do it. Be known as a person who can be counted on.

Low   1   2   3   4   5   6   7   8   9   10   High

Cooperation
Take interest in other people, and strive to be helpful. Everyone appreciates someone who is willing to lend a hand. Show others you are interested in doing a good job for them. Learn to understand and get along with all types of people.

Low   1   2   3   4   5   6   7   8   9   10   High

Concentration
There are three kinds of people: those who make things happen, those who watch things happen, and those who have no idea what happened. You don't want to be the third kind. Always pay attention to what is going on; that is how you learn. You should try to learn something new every day. People are more interested in those who show initiative and concentration. Don't sleepwalk through your day; this is how accidents occur and opportunities are missed.

Low   1   2   3   4   5   6   7   8   9   10   High

Initiative

If you are not eager to do your job, either you are in the wrong line of work or you have allowed yourself to become lazy. If it is the first, find another job; if it is the second, overcome your laziness. It will pay off. Be a self-starter; don't wait for others to generate a spark in you. It is your life, and you are in control. What you do now will determine your future. Follow the motto: Seize the moment.

Low   1   2   3   4   5   6   7   8   9   10   High

Communication

No one likes excuses after the fact, even if they are legitimate. If you can't accomplish a task as assigned, inform those who should know as soon as possible. The more you communicate, the better your relationships will be.

Low   1   2   3   4   5   6   7   8   9   10   High

Flexibility

Don't be overly rigid. Most jobs require flexibility to get the best results. Be open to changing your approach, your schedule, and even your goals if it will help increase job performance.

Low   1   2   3   4   5   6   7   8   9   10   High

Dedication

You have to be dedicated to your job if you are to succeed. Don't automatically take the attitude that you are being exploited by others. A job is usually a two-way street. You are helping your employer, but you are also acquiring knowledge and experience that will benefit you; also, you are being paid. Most business owners and managers work nearly ten hours a day trying to keep their operations going, and this creates jobs. Employee dedication is needed as well, and it is usually greatly appreciated.

Low   1   2   3   4   5   6   7   8   9   10   High

Resolving conflict

Avoid arguments on the job. If you do become part of a conflict, try to solve the problem in private, as soon as possible, and without hurting anyone. Remember, seeing things from the other person's point of view helps to solve unnecessary conflict.

Low   1   2   3   4   5   6   7   8   9   10   High

Patience

At times, you may feel dissatisfied with your job. If so, wait a reasonable period before deciding whether to change jobs. In the meantime, talking to the people with whom you work may help you feel like part of the group and may help you enjoy what you are doing.

Low   1   2   3   4   5   6   7   8   9   10   High

Personal appearance

Impressions are important, so dress appropriately for work. Maintain excellent personal hygiene, and keep your clothes presentable.

Low   1   2   3   4   5   6   7   8   9   10   High

Conscientious use of time

Avoid taking more break time than you truly need (including paid personal time). Would you like paying someone who is not working? Put yourself in the employer's position, and evaluate yourself. Are you giving a full day's work for a full day's pay?

Low   1   2   3   4   5   6   7   8   9   10   High

Gumption

Always look for something to do. It costs money and time for one person to keep another person busy. If you cannot find something, ask. Never just sit or stand around. Remember, the difference between ordinary and extraordinary is the word *extra*.

Low   1   2   3   4   5   6   7   8   9   10   High

Excellence

Study or practice your work so that you are truly good at it. This will boost your ego and make you more valuable to your employer, which will usually be reflected in your wages. Do not become complacent with current success. Remember, a professional in any field knows what it takes to perform well, but always strives to improve.

Low   1   2   3   4   5   6   7   8   9   10   High

Trustworthiness

Be honest in all of your dealings. Word travels quickly, and a poor reputation can be acquired faster than a good one. Always tell the truth as you believe it to be.

Low   1   2   3   4   5   6   7   8   9   10   High

Source: Steve Martin, Northern Kentucky University, 1984, revised 1997. Based on training materials from the National Association of Homebuilders, Manpower Department, 1025 Connecticut Ave., N.W., Washington, D.C. 10036.

Scoring and interpretation

Add your total score and read the evaluation and discussion that follow.

Score	Evaluation	Discussion
135–150	Outstanding	Extremely high performers receive these scores. These individuals produce top results.
105-134	Very good	Good performers receive these scores. They are solid producers in their organizations.
75–104	Ordinary	People who receive these scores are "doing their jobs"—no more and no less.
15–74	Below standard	These scores reflect problems with ability, experience, motivation, or attitude. Counseling and training should be sought.

Developmental need

Competencies count in the success equation. They can help you if you have them and hurt you if you don't. In my own case, I have never learned *computers*. This has been a handicap all of my professional life, especially in word processing. To avoid grief in the future, I will have to bite the bullet and develop this skill.—Author's file notes (G. M.)

Chapter Nineteen References

1   Source unknown.

2   Michael Korda, *Success!* (New York: Ballantine Books, 1978).

3   Phillip Marvin, *Management Goals: Guidelines and Accountability* (Homewood, Ill.: Dow Jones-Irwin, Inc., 1980), 166-67.

4   Will Forpe and John C. McCollister, *The Sunshine Book: Expressions of Love, Hope and Inspiration* (Middle Village, N.Y.: Jonathan David Publishers, Inc., 1979).

5   Gordon W. Allport, "The Ego in Contemporary Psychology," *Psychological Review* 50 (1943): 466.

6   Forpe and McCollister, *The Sunshine Book*, 112.

7   Benjamin Franklin, *The Complete Poor Richard Almanacks Published by Benjamin Franklin*, vol. 2: 1748–1758 (Barre, Mass.: Imprint Society, 1970), 375, 377.

8   William James, as quoted in J. M. Cohen and J. M. Cohen, *The Penguin Dictionary of Quotations* (New York: Viking Press, 1977), 204.

9   Upton Sinclair, *The Flivver King* (New York: Phaedra, Inc., 1969), 6, 7, 19, 654, 69, 70, 78.

10 Edgar Guest, as quoted in Forpe and McCollister, *The Sunshine Book*, 5.

11 Eleanor Roosevelt, *This is My Story* (New York: Harper and Brothers, 1936).

12 Forpe and McCollister, *The Sunshine Book*, 99.

13 Peter Farb, *Humankind* (New York: Bantam Books, Inc., 1980), 31.

14 *The Reader's Digest Great Encyclopedic Dictionary* (Pleasantville, N.Y.: Reader's Digest Association, 1966), 2039.

15 Robert P. Levoy, "Getting Your Money's Worth from Courses," Professional Practice Consultants.

16 Samuel Foss, "The Calf Path," as found in Peter J. Frost, Vance F. Mitchell, and Walter R. Nord, *Organizational Reality: Reports from the Firing Line,* 3rd ed. (Glenview, Ill.: Scott, Foresman & Company, 1986), 486-87.

17 John Beecroft, *Kipling: A Selection of His Stories and Poems* (Garden City, N.Y.: Doubleday & Company, Inc., 1956), 383-84.

18 Case from the authors' files.

19 Sam Walton, *Sam Walton, Made in America: My Story.* (New York: Doubleday, 1992).

Chapter Twenty

Time Management

What is time?

Voltaire, the French writer-philosopher, asked an interesting question in his book *Zadig or the Book of Fate*: "What, of all things in the world, is the longest and the shortest, the swiftest and the slowest, the most divisible and the most extended, the most neglected and the most regretted, without which nothing can be done, which devours all that is little and enlivens all that is great?"

To this, Zadig answered, "Time." Then he said, "Nothing is larger, since it is the length of eternity; nothing is shorter, since there is never enough of it to satisfy our wants. Nothing is faster for the person who is happy; nothing is slower for one who is sad. In smallness, time is infinitely divisible; in greatness, time has no limit. People neglect time, but they regret the loss of it. There is no action that can be done without time. Time stores in darkness whatever is unworthy, and makes immortal all that is truly great."[1]

Benjamin Franklin once said, "Dost thou love life? Then do not squander time, for it is the stuff that life is made of." If you waste your time, you waste your life. If you master time, you master your life. For what purpose should time be used?

Take Time

Take time to *think*,
it is the source of power.

Take time to *play*,
it is the secret of youth.

Take time to *read*,
it is the basis of knowledge.

Take time to *love*,
it is the essence of life.

Take time for *friends*,
it is the road to happiness.

Take time to *laugh,*
it is the music of the soul.

Take time to *give,*
it is too short to be selfish.

Take time to *work,*
it is the price of success.

Franklin was well known for his wise use of time. To keep himself on track, he would start each morning with the question, "What good shall I do today?" and he would end each day with the question, "What good have I done today?"[2]

Everyone's biggest problem

One of the most important tools in managing stress is effective time management. Check the items that are true of you.

❏ You are always late for meetings and appointments.

❏ You are typically behind in your work, school, or personal responsibilities.

❏ You often feel hurried, harried, and hassled.

❏ You don't have enough time for basics—sleeping, eating, family affairs.

❏ You often feel fatigued—worn out physically and mentally.

❏ You often forget appointments, meetings, and other responsibilities.

❏ You are constantly working.

❏ You can't meet deadlines—even if you are constantly working.

❏ Your activities are fragmented, disjointed, and incomplete.

The more checks you have, the more serious your time management problem is.

Time is both personal and finite. It is *personal* in that the best statement of who you are is the way you spend your time. Your use of time reflects your needs, goals, and personality as does no other single thing. Time is *finite* in that each person has only twenty-four hours a day. Figure 20.1 shows how most people spend their time each day.

Figure 20.1 How You Spend Your Time

Based on surveys and observations of thousands of people, the average person's day looks something like this.

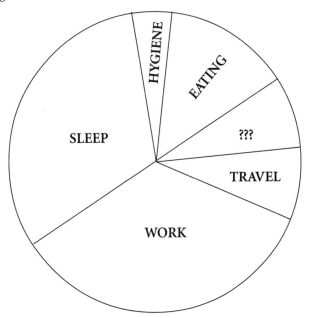

Activity	Hours spent
Sleeping	8
Personal hygiene	1
Preparing and eating meals	3
Traveling	2
Working	8
Total	22

On average, this leaves about two hours each day to do all of the other things that make life worth living. However, most people, by their own accounts, waste at least two hours a day. We have to ask, for what did we exchange our two hours? Did we just put time in, or did we make steps toward our goals in life?

Source: "How We Spend Our Time," *Time Management Center, P.O. Box 5, Grandville, Mich. 49418. Reprinted with permission.*

Getting full benefit from the twenty-four hours you have each day depends on your attitude toward time and on your time management skills.

The importance of attitude

The following shows an attitude toward time and life that will help you get the most out of both:

Just for today . . .
Just for today, I will try to live through this day only and not tackle all of my life's problems at once. I hope I can do something for someone and keep the memory of it for a lifetime.

Just for today, I will try to be happy. This assumes to be true what Abraham Lincoln once said: "Most folks are as happy as they make their minds up to be."

Just for today, I will adjust myself to what is and try not to adjust everything to my own desires. I will take my "chances" as they come and fit myself to them.

Just for today, I will exercise myself in two ways: I will do somebody a good turn and not get found out. I will do at least two things I don't want to do just because they are good for me.

Just for today, I will be agreeable. I will look as fit as I can, talk softly, listen intently, act courteously, criticize not one bit, try not to find fault, and try to regulate no one except myself.

Just for today, I will have a program. I may not follow it exactly, but I will have it. I will try hard to save myself from two pests—hurry and indecision.

Just for today, I will have a quiet moment or two all by myself and relax. During this brief period, somehow, I will try to better myself and try to get a better perspective of my life.

Just for today, I will be unafraid to enjoy what is beautiful and what is common and to believe that as I give to the world and the people in it, so will the world benefit.

—William J. Stewart

Time management skills

The following story shows the importance of time management skills. Does the situation sound familiar?

Bill slid behind the wheel of his car. It was late, and he was very tired. As he thought back over his day, he said to himself, "Man, this job is killing me!" He remembered arriving at work early and seeing the stacks of paperwork and the voice-mail and e-mail messages demanding his attention. At least three of these were "hot items," requiring immediate action. In his briefcase were four letters he had written the night before to give to his secretary and bits of a major report due by week's end. In addition, there was the note in his pocket from his wife: "Call the florist to send flowers for your mother's birthday." Bill remembered the desperation he had felt as he gathered his strength to dive into the problems of the day. He felt like a rat, trapped in a familiar maze and running a habitual treadmill. Finally, where was that coffee? He sure wished he had a cup of coffee. Problems and people were to pour forth in a relentless stream for ten consecutive hours.

Now, as he sat in his car, Bill thought: "The day has not gone well . . . nor has the week. Come to think of it, the whole year has been one crisis after another for the entire operation." Several of his key people seemed to feel "under siege" as well. Others didn't seem to feel anything at all. It was as if they were physically at work, but mentally absent—undedicated and not very productive. Lately, it was as if everyone fell into one of two camps—the unhelpful and the shell-shocked. Neither camp had many smiles or many relaxed moments to savor accomplishments. In fact, big-picture-wise, he himself had trouble identifying the accomplishments of his operation. Bill thought: "Why is this? Why do we lurch from personnel problems to financial crises to production emergencies, one after another? Why do we always seem to be fighting fires?"[3]

Bill's problem is called the "firehouse syndrome." The symptoms are high frustration, overworked employees, burned-out managers, and decreased productivity. The results are high stress levels, low morale, and organizational breakdown. The solution to the firehouse syndrome is better use of one's time. Bill could help his employees, his organization, and himself by improving his time management skills.

Time and the workplace

What are people's time problems at work? These are the fifteen most common:[4]

1. Telephone interruptions

2. Drop-in visitors

3. Meetings

4. Crisis management

5. Lack of objectives, priorities, daily plan

6. Cluttered desk

7. Ineffective delegation

8. Too much attempted at once

9. Lack of communication

10. Inadequate, inaccurate, or delayed information

11. Indecision and procrastination

12. Confused responsibility and authority

13. Inability to say "no"

14. Tasks left unfinished

15. Lack of self-discipline

Complete the following questionnaire to evaluate the time management practices of a work group or organization. Change a few words, and the same time management evaluation can apply to a family.

⊙ Application: Time Management Audit—Are You Wasting Time?

Circle *Usually yes* or *Often no* for each of the following questions.

1. Do all members have a clear understanding of the goals of the group?

   Usually yes   Often no

2. Does everyone have a clear understanding of personal responsibilities and duties in order of priority?

   Usually yes   Often no

3. Is a calendar or bulletin board used to show important schedules and events?

   Usually yes   Often no

4. Are the telephone, e-mail, and other information systems generally effective and timely?

   Usually yes   Often no

5. Is the letter and package mail system generally effective and timely?

   Usually yes   Often no

6. Is the physical layout of work space and equipment generally effective?

   Usually yes   Often no

7. Are regularly scheduled meetings conducted that facilitate communication and teamwork?

   Usually yes   Often no

8. Is the leader sensitive to what she or he does that wastes the group's time or reduces effectiveness?

   Usually yes   Often no

9. Do members maintain appointment books or to-do lists and check off tasks as they are completed?

   Usually yes   Often no

10. Does the group prioritize its activities, focusing on the most important items first?

    Usually yes   Often no

11. Are accurate and easy-to-read clocks convenient to work stations?

    Usually yes   Often no

12. Can people quickly and easily obtain the information they need to conduct day-to-day business?

    Usually yes   Often no

13. Is the flow of work such that things rarely get overlooked and tasks rarely get done twice (such as mail being misplaced or two people writing the same report)?

    Usually yes   Often no

14. Is there a *one-team attitude* among members of the group?

    Usually yes   Often no

15. Are decisions made in a timely manner?

    Usually yes   Often no

16. Is the most effective communication medium used when relating to others—telephone, e-mail, video, letter, report, conference, group discussion, or one-on-one meeting?

    Usually yes   Often no

17. Do meetings start and end on time, with meeting periods lasting no more than 1 1/4 hours between breaks?

    Usually yes   Often no

18. Does the formal/informal structure of the group facilitate quick and accurate information flow?

    Usually yes   Often no

19. Does the group focus on achieving worthwhile goals, rather than simply staying busy?

    Usually yes   Often no

20. Does the group's equipment—cars, computers, tools, etc.—function properly?

    Usually yes   Often no

21. Are money, materials, methods, and people deployed to accomplish important tasks with minimal waste of time?

    Usually yes   Often no

22. Do members write clearly and legibly so that others know what they mean and waste little time deciphering scribbles?

    Usually yes   Often no

23. Is sufficient time allocated to plan, implement, and evaluate the work of the group?

    Usually yes   Often no

24. For group meetings, are a schedule and a list of topics prepared and then addressed?

    Usually yes   Often no

25. Is the group effective at saying no when necessary?

    Usually yes   Often no

26. Are travel and waiting times used productively?

    Usually yes   Often no

27. Are work areas well organized and free of clutter?

    Usually yes   Often no

28. Are interruptions effectively managed?

    Usually yes   Often no

29. Does the group utilize available support services as effectively as possible?

    Usually yes   Often no

30. Does the group periodically ask "What is the best use of our time right now?"—and then act on the answer?

    Usually yes   Often no

Scoring and interpretation

Add the number of "Usually yes" answers you circled to determine the group's score on the Time Management Audit. Then enter the total on the appropriate line on the hourglass in Figure 20.2. Fill in the space below this line to obtain a graphic illustration of the group's time management effectiveness.

If a perfect score (30) was not achieved, go back to the items marked "Often no" and take steps to correct this time management deficiency. This may require the help of others who may be part of the problem or who may be affected by the group's poor time management practices.

Figure 20.2 How Effective Are You?

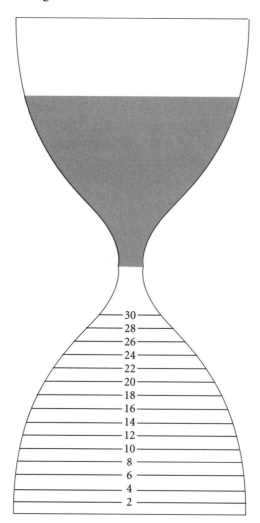

Time management benefits and costs

You will know you have mastered time management when you can sit quietly for at least two or three hours during your week to think about your life, your work, and your personal effectiveness. Every person needs quality time for creative thinking and planning. You won't have this time if you have wasted it.

If you waste an hour a day

If you waste an hour a day on the job, what does that loss mean in dollars and cents? Assuming an eight-hour workday, three weeks of annual vacation, and ten holidays, here are the costs of a *wasted hour per day* over the course of a year at various salary levels:

Salary	Cost
$14,000	$1,750
$16,000	$2,000
$18,000	$2,250
$20,000	$2,500
$25,000	$3,125
$30,000	$3,750
$35,000	$4,375
$40,000	$5,000
$50,000	$6,250
$75,000	$9,375
$100,000	$12,500

Time management principles

We should manage time as if our lives were at stake—because they are. Time is life, and if you waste this precious resource, your life will be less than it could be. The following are principles for preventing or solving time management problems.[5]

- **Agree upon goals.** Good time management begins with goals—knowing what you are supposed to accomplish and in what priority. This should result in an understanding of what you will be accountable for and what others can do to help you succeed.

  A manager in a computer software firm was criticized by the owner for being ineffective. Asked why, the owner replied, "You have failed to keep the systems analyst off my back." The manager was surprised, and responded, "This must have been a hidden purpose of my job. You never told me that before." From that point on, the manager increased his effectiveness by dealing with the complaints and concerns of the systems analyst.[6]

■ **Set priorities.** When opportunities exceed resources, choices must be made. Nowhere is this more apparent than in the use of time. Since time cannot be manufactured, you must decide what to do and what not to do. Concentrate your time, energy, and talents on the most important goals and tasks. Use the ABC method to determine priorities:

Priority A—"Must-do": These are vital goals and tasks. Some may fall in this category because of customer requirements, significant deadlines, management directives, or opportunities for success.

Priority B—"Should-do": These are of medium importance. Goals and tasks in this category may contribute to improved performance but are not essential or do not have critical deadlines.

Priority C—"Could-do": This is the lowest category. While interesting, these goals and tasks could be postponed or scheduled for slack periods.

Your A's, B's, and C's may change over time. Today's B may become tomorrow's A as an important deadline approaches. Likewise, today's A may become tomorrow's C if circumstances change. This shows the importance of using the ABC method regularly—daily or at least weekly. Use Figure 20.3 to practice setting priorities.

Figure 20.3 Setting Priorities

Priority A—"Must-do" goals and tasks

_____

_____

_____

_____

_____

_____

_____

Priority B—"Should-do" goals and tasks

_____

_____

_____

_____

_____

_____

_____

Priority C—"Could-do" goals and tasks

_____

_____

_____

_____

_____

_____

The following story shows how important it is to set priorities:

> A well-known story about setting priorities concerns Charles Schwab when he was president of Bethlehem Steel. He called Ivy Lee, a consultant, and said, "Show me a way to get more things done with my time, and I'll pay you any fee within reason."
>
> "Fine," Lee replied. "I'll give you something in twenty minutes that will step up your output at least fifty percent."
>
> With that, Lee handed Schwab a blank piece of paper, and said: "Write down the six most important tasks that you have to do tomorrow, and number them in order of their importance. Then put this paper in your pocket, and the first thing tomorrow morning look at item one and start working on it until you finish it. Then do item two, and so on. Do this until quitting time, and don't be concerned if you have finished only one or two items. You'll be working on the most important ones first anyway. If you can't finish them all by this method, you couldn't have by any other method, either; and without some system, you'd probably not even have decided which was the most important."
>
> Then Lee said: "Try this system every working day. After you've convinced yourself of the value of the system, have your employees try it. Try it as long as you wish, and then send me a check for what you think it is worth."
>
> Several weeks later, Schwab sent Lee a check for $25,000 with a note proclaiming the advice to be the most profitable he had ever followed. This concept helped Charles Schwab earn $100 million and turn Bethlehem Steel into the biggest independent steel producer in the world.
>
> You may think Charles Schwab was foolish to pay $25,000 for such a simple idea. However, Schwab thought of that consulting fee as one of his best investments. "Sure, it was a simple idea," Schwab said. "But what ideas are not basically simple? For the first time, my entire team and I are getting first things done first."[7]

- **Use a daily to-do list to accomplish your goals.** Write down the tasks you want to accomplish each day, and rank these in order of importance. The small amount of time you invest in doing this will repay you many times over. A point to remember: Make sure your to-do list is on a paper or notebook small enough to carry with you; it should go where you go. If you are ever tempted to keep your to-do list in your head, remember what Ziggy said: "I made a mental note to remember something very important I had to do today . . . but I lost the note."

- **Know your values.** Be sure your goals and to-do list reflect your values. Nothing is more stressful than being hard-working and efficient on tasks that have nothing to do with your value system. For every task, ask yourself, does this support what is really important to me? The sequence is to identify core values, set immediate and long-term goals, and use a prioritized to-do list as a productivity tool. See Figure 20.4.

Figure 20.4 Effective Time Management

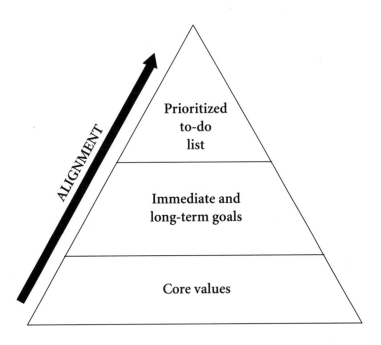

When daily behavior is aligned with goals, and goals support values, you experience optimum control and a sense of integrity.

- **Eliminate time wasters.** Good time management requires combining similar tasks and eliminating unnecessary ones. You should eliminate meetings that serve no useful purpose, eliminate unnecessary paperwork, and strive for efficiency in travel. Why take several trips to town when all errands could be combined? Why take a trip by plane if a fax or a call will accomplish the same purpose? Simplify, always simplify.

- **Make good use of waiting time.** In our complex and interdependent society, we often run into delays—at the repair shop, in the bank, or at the airport. Be prepared to use this time productively. Reading, writing, thinking, talking, resting, and exercising are all preferable to wasting time.

- **Log your day.** Do a time study by tracking what you do each day for a period of one month. It is good to know how you are spending your time, and the analysis may reveal surprises.

  > One bank asked its branch managers to record the time they spent under three headings—time with customers, time with administrative duties, and time with staff. Analysis showed that too much time was spent on internal administration and too little time was spent on marketing and staff development.[8]

- **Learn how, when, and why to say no.** One of the best time management techniques is the effective use of the words "yes" and "no." If saying yes helps accomplish important goals, by all means do so. But if saying yes prevents you from accomplishing more important tasks, learn how to say no in a tactful way. If your supervisor interrupts your work with an additional assignment, discuss how the new task will affect existing ones. Obtain a clear understanding of the priorities of all your assignments.

- **Stock up and clean house.** Having the correct tools and materials, and knowing where they are, saves time and energy. You won't have the stress of losing things if you put them where they belong. Proper supplies and an orderly work area are basic to good time management. A few hours of housecleaning and stocking up several times a year will usually improve efficiency.

- **Provide enough time.** The saying "haste makes waste" is true. If you do not give yourself sufficient time to accomplish a task, mistakes and decreased performance are inevitable. As a rule of thumb, complex meetings involving employee counseling, project planning, and staff development require at least one hour from the moment they begin. A one-hour minimum is usually necessary to establish a productive atmosphere, share basic information, deal with important issues, draw conclusions, make decisions, agree on future steps, and end the work session on a positive note. The corollary to providing enough time is to set "ending times." When tasks are completed and a meeting is over, adjourn.

- **Work when you are fresh.** If you have an especially demanding day ahead, rest up the night before. Otherwise, fatigue may affect judgment and results.

- **Focus your efforts.** A fundamental rule of effective time management is to concentrate on the task at hand. Mistakes can result from trying to do too many things at once. Often it is not the quantity of time spent on a project that counts, but the quality of time. By slowing down—driving slower, eating slower, and honoring the process—effectiveness as well as satisfaction can be increased.

- **Perform undesirable tasks when your energy level is high.** People have the tendency to do what they enjoy, postponing uninteresting or unpleasant jobs until their enthusiasm and energy are so low that these jobs become even less enjoyable, and therefore harder to accomplish. By working on low-interest tasks when your energy is high—whatever time of day that is—you will get more done in the long run. When you complete the uninteresting tasks and turn to interesting assignments, you will feel stimulated and energized.

> **Secret of success**
> One can learn a lot by asking successful people, "What has been the secret of your success?" I once did this with a Medal of Honor recipient and a leader in medical research. He thought for a moment and with a smile and a twinkle in his eye, he said, "I always do what I hate to do first. Then, when I turn to what I love, I have a tremendous burst of energy. When I am doing what I love, the work itself keeps me going."—Author's file notes (G. M.)

- **Prevent interruptions.** Sometimes you have to hole up and work on something without interruptions and without hurting anyone's feelings either. The note on the door can be just the answer:

  > I'm working on an important deadline. I'll be free at 3:00. Thanks.
  > Sorry—Deadline due! Thanks for understanding.
  > If your question can wait—my project won't be late. Free at 3:00.

  Another helpful technique is to leave your door partially open. This communicates the message that you need privacy to do something, but someone may enter if it is important.

- **Don't build a castle when a log cabin will do.** The extra refinement may not be worth the expense when a log cabin will accomplish the same purpose. This principle applies in time management as well; in some instances, the best possible performance may be far better and far more expensive than is necessary. For example, a manager usually should not spend time performing tasks subordinates could do. Even if the manager can do a better job, the loss in efficiency, employee growth, and overall productivity of the work unit may not be worth the extra refinement. Knowing when to be perfect and when to be okay is an important stress management skill.

- **Practice good telephone techniques.** Use a dependable message service or machine. Return all calls. Keep conversations brief. Shorten long-winded calls with a phrase such as, "Before we hang up . . . ," or "Before you get away . . ."

  Avoid taking calls while you are in important meetings and problem-solving sessions. If you are working with others, these interruptions will reduce both efficiency and goodwill.

  Consolidate call-backs. Begin with priority calls and work down the list. Returning calls one half hour before or after lunch, one half hour before the end of the workday, and the first half hour of the following workday is effective for many people. Leave detailed messages on voice mail, including the best time to reach you.

  Initiating telephone calls when others are most available and receptive is another good practice. For example, you should avoid calling a company president on the morning of the monthly board meeting. In general, it is best to initiate telephone calls early in the morning, late in the morning, early in the afternoon, and late in the afternoon of the business day.

  Remember, the telephone can be both a helper and time waster. One study found that 25 percent of the time spent on the telephone was used in waiting.

- **Use efficient mail and paperwork practices.** Set aside a specific time of the day or week to read mail and do paperwork. If you try to read incoming mail and paperwork as it arrives, the quality of your work probably will deteriorate because your efforts will lack a clear focus. A good technique is to reserve the last hour or so of the workday for correspondence and paperwork.

  Effective time management requires handling each piece of paper as few times as possible. Each item should be dispatched in one of the following ways: (1) read the item for information and discard it; (2) make a personal response, such as making a telephone call or dictating a memo, and then file the item; (3) route the item to others for follow-through; (4) store the item for future personal attention.

- **Keep a delegation file.** Time and energy are wasted when managers fail to follow up on tasks they delegate. Relying on memory is not good enough. A good technique is to use a file or calendar to record assignments and review progress.

- **Plan for emergencies.** Keep your car in good repair and keep extra keys in your wallet. Get up fifteen minutes early.

- **Keep a schedule.** Establish a work schedule that is efficient and satisfying, and try to follow it as much as possible. The idea of having a plan for the day is an old one, as shown in Figure 20.5. The following are suggestions for effective time planning:

  Schedule fixed blocks of time first. Start with class time or work time, for instance. These time periods are usually determined in advance. Other activities must be scheduled around them. Then schedule essential daily activities like sleeping and eating. No matter what else you do, you will sleep and eat. Be realistic about the time you need for these functions.

  Include time for errands. The time we spend going to the store, paying bills, and doing laundry is easy to overlook. These little errands can destroy a tight schedule and make us feel rushed and harried all week. Plan for them.

  Schedule time for leisure. Brains that are constantly assaulted with new ideas and new challenges need time off to digest them. Einstein went sailing and played the violin. Take time for activities you enjoy. Recreation deserves a place in your priorities.

  Set realistic goals. Don't set yourself up for failure by telling yourself you can do a four-hour job in two hours. There are only 168 hours in a week. If you schedule 169 hours, you lose before you begin.

  Allow flexibility in your schedule. Recognize that emergencies will happen, so plan for the unexpected. Don't schedule every moment. Give yourself enough time to get between places safely and comfortably.

Figure 20.5 Ben Franklin's Daily Regimen

Morning Question: What good shall I do this day?	5 6 7	Rise, wash and address Powerful Goodness! Contrive day's business and take the resolution of the day; prosecute* the present study, and breakfast.
	8 9 10 11	Work.
Noon	12 1	Read, or overlook accounts, and dine.
	2 3 4	Work.
Evening	5 6	Put things in their places. Supper.
Question: What good have I done today?	7 8 9 10	Music, diversion, or conversation. Examination of the day.
Night	11 12 1 2 3 4 5	Sleep.

*Prosecute: carry on

- **Use meetings effectively.** A meeting is a two-edged sword. It can be useful and productive, or it can be a waste of valuable time. Keep in mind that all who attend meetings are individuals who may have something important to contribute and who are contributing their own valuable time. The following points should be considered when planning and conducting a meeting:

  a. Assure yourself that a meeting is necessary. Know the purpose of the meeting and what you expect to accomplish.

  b. Schedule the meeting far enough in advance to allow participants time to prepare.

c. Inform each participant of the nature of the meeting and the specific role you wish the person to play—providing information, recording minutes, generating ideas, making decisions.

d. Control the size of the meeting by inviting only those individuals who can benefit or contribute.

e. Prepare an agenda, limiting the topics of discussion to a number that can be reasonably handled in one session. Usually, meetings should convene and end within a period of 1-1/4 hours; then people need a break.

f. Advise people in advance if you expect them to make a presentation.

g. Begin and end on time.

h. During the meeting, be specific and clear and use data to support your statements.

i. Try to understand why people act in different ways, and use this knowledge to avoid personal rivalries. When necessary, reject ideas— never people.

j. Know when to delegate. You can remove some of the burden from your shoulders and keep everyone involved as well.

k. Before adjourning, review the purpose of the meeting, the accomplishments, and what participants are to do next.

l. After the meeting, see that minutes are prepared and that everyone gets a copy.[9]

- **Embrace time management.** Some people resist time management practices, but no other single tool has as much potential for improving performance and managing stress.

Time management teacher
In 1969, my boss taught me time management principles. He taught me to clarify values, set goals, and prioritize activities. He taught me the importance of writing things down and checking off tasks completed. He taught me the importance of keeping records and saving papers. None of this organization came naturally to me, but I could see the need. Thirty years later with a precious wife, three grown children, two farms, nine books, two IRS audits, and no missed appointments, I would say time management has been my single best production multiplier and stress reducer. I have been twice as productive and felt twice as much in control because someone cared to share this all-important skill.—Author's file notes (G. M.)

- **Just do it.** Procrastination is a thief. Ultimately, action is required. The good time manager asks, what is the best use of my time right now, and then seizes the moment. As Ben Franklin once wrote, "Well done is better than well said."

Thoughts on beating the clock

Time management expert Nina Tassi knows a lot about stress and time management. Her description of the time-pressured, resource-stretched, and generally exhausted person, pushed and pulled in more ways than is healthy, is the increasing case for more and more people. Her prescription is to adopt time management principles to gain control of your life. The picture she paints of one who does is instructive and motivating.[10]

Seven key traits of people who are at ease with time

1. They never seem to be in a hurry. Even their body language is graceful and purposeful, not jerky and rushed.

2. They experience the present to the fullest, having the capacity to focus on the moment at hand, both in work and in play.

3. They take time to preserve their physical health, emotional well-being, and—importantly—their creative resources.

4. They set priorities and then work the list, which allows them to accomplish more than most other people.

5. They learn from experience and never harbor guilt, regret, or blame.

6. They spend time on relationships. They love to teach and learn from others, as well as care and be cared for.

7. They live value-based lives, making sure their actions support what is truly important to them.

Tassi's research makes it keenly obvious how desirable it is to be a time-integrated person. These individuals are responsible, but also free. By following simple principles of effective time management, they live happy and productive lives with ease and grace.

What is success?

The subject of peak performance isn't complete without considering the meaning of success. In other words: peak performance, yes; but to what end?

The answer, like beauty, is in the eye of each person. Still, one American thinker—Ralph Waldo Emerson—seems to have captured the essence of success for most people:

What is Success?

To laugh often and love much;

To win the respect of intelligent
persons and the affection of children;

To earn the esteem of honest critics
and endure the betrayal of false friends;

To appreciate beauty;

To find the best in others;

To give of one's self without the
slightest thought of return;

To leave the world a better place,
whether by a healthy child, a rescued
soul, a garden patch or a redeemed
social condition;

To have played and laughed with
enthusiasm and sung with exaltation;

To know that even one life has
breathed easier because you have lived;

This is to have succeeded.[11]

Personal Thoughts on Peak Performance

Answer the following questions to personalize the content of Part Seven. Space is provided for writing your thoughts.

- Tennyson wrote in *Ulysses*, "I am part of all that I have met." Describe a time in your life when you performed at the peak of your ability. Discuss the impact it had on others.

- Do you use positive self-talk to keep performance high, or do you allow negative thoughts to reduce your performance?

- Based on the Peak Performance Profile, what characteristics do you share with top performers? What areas need work?

- What are your strengths and weaknesses on the Performance Pyramid? What key steps can you take to maintain or improve your job performance?

- Overall, how would you rate your time management effectiveness? What can you do to improve in this important area?

- What does success mean to you? Describe in your own words.

Chapter Twenty References

1   Voltaire, *Zadig or the Book of Fate* (New York: Garland Publishers, Inc., 1974).

2   William J. Stewart, *Supervision*, University of Cincinnati, 1970.

3   Stan Kossen, *The Human Side of Organizations*, 2nd ed. (New York: Harper and Row, Publishers, Inc., 1978), 203-205.

4   R. Alec Mackenzie, *Teamwork through Time Management: New Time Management Techniques for Everyone in Your Organization* (Chicago: Dartnell, 1990).

5   Lawrence Steinmetz, *The Art and Skill of Delegation* (Reading, Mass.: Addison-Wesley Publishing Co., Inc., 1976); Alan Lakein, "Time Management Ideas," from the film *The Time of Your Life* (Cally Curtis Films, 3384 Peachtree Rd. N.E., Atlanta, GA 30326); Alan Lakein, *How to Get Control of Your Time and Your Life* (New York: Peter H. Wyden, Inc., 1989); and Andrew J. DuBrin, *Contemporary Applied Management* (Plano, Tex.: Business Publications, Inc., 1982), 66-72.

6   DuBrin, *Contemporary Applied Management*, 67.

7   Michael Le Beouf, *Working Smart: How to Accomplish More in Half the Time* (New York: McGraw-Hill, Inc., 1979), 52-54.

8   DuBrin, *Contemporary Applied Management*, 68.

9   Keith Davis, *Human Behavior at Work: Organizational Behavior*, 6th ed. (New York: McGraw-Hill, Inc., 1981), 184-90.

10 Nina Tassi, *Urgency Addiction: How to Slow Down without Sacrificing Success* (New York: Penguin, 1993); and Nina Tassi, "Stop Racing the Clock," *Working Mother*, April 1992, pp. 65-68.

11 Ralph Waldo Emerson, "What Is Success?"; also "What is Success?" by Bessie Anderson Stanley, as found in *Distilled Wisdom: An Encyclopedia of Wisdom in Condensed Form*, ed. Alfred Armand Montapert (Englewood Cliffs, N.J.: Prentice-Hall, 1964).

Part Eight

Stress Prevention

21. Avoid Self-Medication

22. The 1 x 3 x 7 = 21 Plan

The things we think have a tremendous effect upon our bodies. If we can change our thinking, the body frequently heals itself.—C. Everett Koop

What you will learn in Part Eight*

In Part Eight you will learn:

- the danger of tobacco, alcohol, and other drugs;

- the role of the mind in managing stress;

- the need for exercise, rest, and proper nutrition.

* Part Eight is intended to be used as a health reference, not as a medical manual. The information presented is included to help you make informed decisions about your health. It is not intended to be a substitute for any treatment that may be prescribed by your physician. If you suspect that you have a medical problem, you are urged to seek competent medical assistance.

Chapter Twenty-One
✷
Avoid Self-Medication

The danger of substance abuse

The use of tobacco, alcohol, and other drugs is an area of stress management that deserves special attention. These substances can become addictions that increase stress. In excess, they can harm physical health, destroy personal relationships, reduce job success, and generally diminish people's lives.

A small percentage of the population is expert in medicine and pharmacology, but you wouldn't know it when you consider the level of self-prescribed substances used today. The social and economic costs in U.S. society are staggering. Tobacco, alcohol, and other drugs account for more than a half million U.S. deaths a year; and as of 1990, the annual economic cost reached 238 billion dollars—99 billion in alcohol-related costs, 72 billion from smoking, and 67 billion for drug abuse. Tobacco and alcohol are the first and second major substances involved in preventable death in our society.[1]

Tobacco

The year 1997 marked the eighty-fourth anniversary of Camel cigarettes. Coincidentally, it was also the eighty-fourth anniversary of the American Cancer Society. In 1989, the U.S. surgeon general issued a report, Reducing the Health Consequences of Smoking: 25 Years of Progress. It was published 25 years after the initial warnings that cigarettes are responsible for major health problems, especially lung cancer.

Most adults today know that cigarette smoking is a dangerous habit. In fact, cigarettes are the only legal product that causes death when used as intended. Scientific evidence shows the direct biological impact of smoking as a cause of cancer. Indeed, it is estimated that most cases of lung cancer could be prevented if people did not smoke. Cigarettes are also a major contributor to heart disease. A cigarette smoker is ten times more likely to develop lung cancer than a nonsmoker and is twenty times more likely to have a heart attack.

Specific health consequences of cigarette smoking include:

- reduced lung capacity

- faster than normal aging

- increased blood pressure

- stickier blood, increasing the risk of hardening of the arteries, heart attack, and stroke

- constricted blood vessels, making them more rigid

- low birth weight babies and exposure to heart, lung, and brain impairment

- change of blood composition as cells that normally carry oxygen to vital organs instead transport toxic carbon monoxide

- reduced male potency by impairing blood circulation

- harm to skin and bone structure including increased facial wrinkles and raised risk of osteoporosis

- significantly increased risk of cancer[2]

It helps to understand why nicotine is so addictive. Cigarette smoking causes the release of endorphins, natural body substances chemically similar to opiates such as morphine and other painkillers. When endorphin levels increase, you feel more pain free, at ease, and euphoric. The key is to substitute some other, healthful habit that achieves the same effect. Vigorous aerobic exercise seems to do this best. Thus, an exercise program provides an excellent complement to a smoke-ending program.

Another important key is to curtail smoking by young people, since smoking as a habit usually begins during childhood, adolescence, and young adulthood. The Centers for Disease Control and Prevention estimate that every day 3,000 American young people become smokers. Seventy-five percent of adult smokers started before age 18. It is estimated that at present 2.1 million adolescents age 12 through 17 are smokers.[3]

Percentages vary across cultures, but currently 25.6 percent of adult Americans smoke: 28.5 percent of males smoke, while 22.8 percent of females smoke, helping to explain decreased longevity rates for males versus females. Figure 21.1 shows the negative effects of cigarette smoking. The graph compares the death rates for male and female smokers and nonsmokers. *It is an interesting statistic that five and one-half minutes of life expectancy are lost for each cigarette you smoke.* It should also be noted that nonsmokers who are constantly exposed to cigarette smoke have increased risk of developing lung cancer, heart disease, and other ailments. Figure 21.2 shows the benefits of a smoke-free life.

Figure 21.1 Death Rates per 100,000 Population of Smokers vs. Nonsmokers

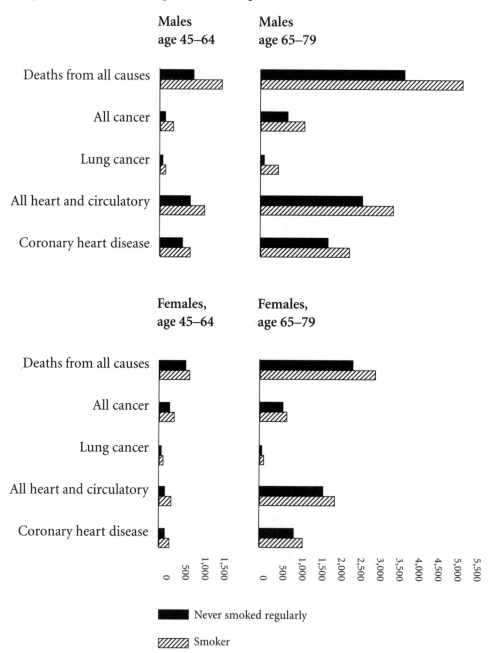

Source: Data from National Cancer Institute Monograph No. 19.

Figure 21.2 Why Quit Smoking?

Within minutes the body starts to heal

- **Within 20 minutes:** Your blood pressure and pulse rate drop to normal. Body temperature of hands and feet increases to normal.

- **Within 8 hours:** The carbon monoxide level in the blood drops to normal and the oxygen level in the blood rises to normal. Smoker's breath disappears.

- **Within 24 hours:** The chance of heart attack decreases.

- **Within 48 hours:** Nerve endings start regrowing. The ability to taste and smell increases.

- **Within 3 days:** You breathe easier.

- **Within 2 weeks to 3 months:** Circulation improves. Walking becomes easier. Lung function increases up to 30 percent.

- **Within 1 to 9 months:** You cough less. Sinus congestion and shortness of breath decrease. The cilia that sweep debris from your lungs grow back. You feel more energetic.

- **Within 1 year:** Excess risk of coronary heart disease is half that of a smoker.

- **Within 3 years:** Your heart attack risk drops to near normal. The risk of death from heart attack and stroke is almost the same as for people who never smoked.

- **Within 5 years:** The lung cancer death rate for former smokers (one pack a day) decreases by almost half. Risk of cancer of the mouth, throat, and esophagus is half that of smokers.

- **Within 10 years:** Lung cancer death rate is similar to a nonsmoker's. Precancerous cells are replaced. Risk of cancer of the mouth, throat, esophagus, bladder, kidney, and pancreas decreases.

Source: American Cancer Society, Centers for Disease Control and Prevention, 1995.

Alcohol

It is a rare person whose life goes untouched by alcohol. It is the most widely used psychoactive drug in the United States.[4] It is associated with thousands of unnecessary deaths every year, often among the young. The overuse of alcohol can seriously damage every organ of the body, from the liver to the brain, and is a significant factor for maladies ranging from heart disease to cancer. Alcohol is the third leading cause of preventable mortality in the United States, after tobacco and diet/activity patterns.[5] As Figure 21.3 shows, the health risks of drinking increase as quantity goes up.

Figure 21.3 Health Risks with Daily Drinking

Up to 1 drink a day for women, 2 drinks a day for men:	No known increased risk
3 per day:	Blood pressure increases; Heart disease increases; Cirrhosis increases for women; Live shorter lives.
4 per day:	Cirrhosis increases for men.
5 per day:	Pancreatitis increases; Much shorter life span.
6 per day:	Cancer of mouth, throat, and digestive system increases; Significantly reduced life expectancy.

Risks add up.
The risks with 6 drinks per day include the
risks for 3, 4, and 5 drinks per day.

Note: This does not include risk of
accidents from intoxication.

Source: Prevention Research Institute, 841 Corporate Drive, Suite 300, Lexington, Kentucky 40503, 1996.

Chemically, alcohol is C_2H_5OH, or ethyl alcohol—a colorless liquid with a sharp, burning taste. Medically, it is a depressant—a drug that slows the activity of the brain and spinal cord. Alcohol is the intoxicating ingredient in alcoholic beverages. Beer and ale are made by fermentation of grains and malt. Hops may be added. Most contain 4–7 percent alcohol. Wine (champagne, Chablis, etc.) is made by fermentation of grapes or other fruit. Regular table or dinner wine contains 9–14 percent alcohol. Dessert or fortified wines, such as port and sherry, contain 18–21 percent alcohol. Liquor such as whiskey, gin, vodka, and rum is made by distillation of a fermented brew of grain, fruit, or molasses. Most distilled liquor contains 40–50 percent alcohol (80–100 proof).

The ancient Romans recognized the difference between people who drank alcohol by choice and those who couldn't control their drinking. Centuries later, the Middle English language distinguished between drunkenness and addiction to drink. In the United States as early as 1784, Dr. Benjamin Rush, the father of American psychiatry and a signer of the Declaration of Independence, described habitual drinking as an involuntary condition, a disease brought on by "spirituous liquors."[6]

Today, the American Medical Association and the U.S Department of Health and Human Services, along with many other professional organizations, promote policies and programs based on the disease concept of alcoholism. In 1990, the National Council on Alcoholism and Drug Dependence and the American Society of Addiction Medicine defined alcoholism as follows:

> Alcoholism is a primary, chronic disease with genetic, psychosocial, and environmental factors influencing its development and manifestations. The disease is often characterized by impaired control over drinking, preoccupation with the drug alcohol, use of alcohol despite adverse consequences, and distortions in thinking, most notably denial. Each of these symptoms may be continuous or periodic.[7]

Consistently heavy drinkers are likely to become psychologically and physically dependent on alcohol. Psychological dependence exists when alcohol becomes so central to a person's thoughts, feeling, and actions that the need to continue its use amounts to a craving or compulsion. Physical dependence is a state in which the body has adapted to the presence of alcohol and withdrawal symptoms erupt if its use is stopped suddenly. Symptoms can include agitation, sleeplessness, profuse sweating, poor appetite, tremors, convulsions, hallucinations, and even death.[8]

Heavy and chronic drinking can harm virtually every organ and system in the body.[9] Excess alcohol:

- is the single most important cause of illness and death from liver disease (alcoholic hepatitis and cirrhosis);

- is associated with cardiovascular diseases, including hypertension, arrhythmia, and stroke;

- contributes to approximately 65 percent of all cases of pancreatitis;

- depresses the immune system and predisposes one to infectious diseases, including respiratory infections, pneumonia, and tuberculosis;

- increases risk for cancer of the upper digestive tract, including the mouth, pharynx, larynx, and esophagus;

- can lead to inadequate functioning of the testes and ovaries, resulting in hormonal deficiencies, sexual dysfunction, and infertility;

- is related to a higher rate of early menopause and a higher frequency of menstrual irregularities (duration, flow, or both) in women.

The use of alcohol is an important factor in many social problems—domestic violence, child abuse, and other human miseries. Alcohol is involved in 50 percent of family disputes in which the police are involved, 70 percent of serious assaults, and 80 percent of murders. William Menninger, founder of the Menninger Clinic, states, "If alcoholism were a communicable disease, a national emergency would be declared."

Figure 21.4 shows the effects of alcoholism on job performance over a period of time. Despite the known problems of alcohol, an estimated 12 million Americans are problem drinkers, and nearly one in three Americans has a person with a drinking problem in the family. The two types of alcohol abusers are steady or constant users, who drink over a long period of time, and binge drinkers, who consume a large amount of alcohol in a short period of time.[10]

Figure 21.4 How an Alcoholic Employee Behaves

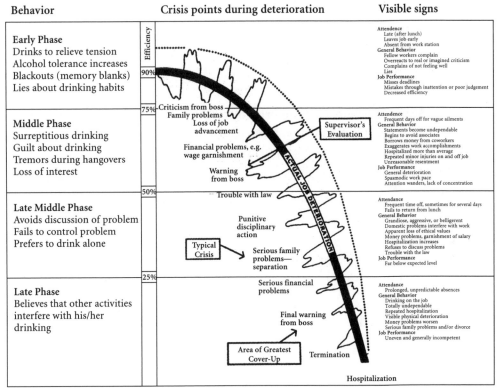

Source: Anthony D. K. Carding, "Booze and Business: Can Your Employees Mix Them?" Administrative Management 30, no. 12 (1969): 21; "How an Alcoholic Employee Behaves," (Milwaukee: CompCare Publications, 1977).

The questions in Figure 21.5 were prepared by the National Council on Alcoholism for evaluating drinking habits. The main factor distinguishing the person who chooses to drink from the one who needs to drink is this: If a person continues to drink even when it destroys something critical to well-being—home, health, career, legal status—the person has crossed over the line and into alcoholism. Proven measures that can help overcome alcoholism include admitting you have a problem, seeking help from qualified others, talking with family and friends, staying away from temptation, keeping a good sense of humor, maintaining constant vigilance, and personal commitment.[11]

Figure 21.5 What Are the Signs of Alcoholism?

The following test can help you review the role alcohol is playing in your life. These questions incorporate many of the common symptoms of alcoholism. This test is intended to help you determine if you or someone you know needs to find out more about alcoholism.

1. Do you drink heavily after a disappointment, a quarrel, or when someone gives you a hard time?   Y   N

2. When you have trouble or feel under pressure, do you drink more heavily than usual?   Y   N

3. Have you noticed that you are able to handle more liquor than you did when you first started drinking?   Y   N

4. Did you ever wake up the "morning after" and discover that you could not remember part of the evening before, even though your friends tell you that you did not "pass out"?   Y   N

5. When drinking with other people, do you try to have a few extra drinks when others will not know it?   Y   N

6. Are there times when you feel uncomfortable if alcohol is not available?   Y   N

7. When you begin drinking, are you in more of a hurry to get the first drink than you used to be?   Y   N

8. Do you sometimes feel guilty about your drinking?   Y   N

9. Are you irritated when your family or friends discuss your drinking?   Y   N

10. Have you noticed an increase in the frequency of memory "blackouts"?   Y   N

11. Do you want to continue drinking after your friends say they have had enough?   Y   N

12. When you are sober, do you regret things you have done or said while drinking?   Y   N

13. Have you tried switching brands or following different plans for controlling your drinking?   Y   N

14. Have you failed to keep promises you have made about controlling or cutting down on your drinking? Y N

15. Have you ever tried to control your drinking by making a change in jobs, or moving to a new location? Y N

16. Do you try to avoid family or close friends while you are drinking? Y N

17. Are you having an increasing number of financial and work problems related to your drinking? Y N

18. Do people seem to be treating you unfairly without good reason? Y N

19. Do you eat very little or irregularly when you are drinking? Y N

20. Do you sometimes have the "shakes" in the morning and find that it helps to take a drink? Y N

21. Have you recently noticed that you cannot drink as much as you once did? Y N

22. Do you sometimes stay drunk for several days at a time? Y N

23. Do you sometimes feel very depressed and wonder whether life is worth living? Y N

24. Sometimes after periods of drinking, do you see or hear things that aren't there? Y N

25. Do you get terribly frightened after you have been drinking heavily? Y N

Interpretation

"Yes" answers indicate the following stages of alcoholism:

Questions 1–8	Early stage
Questions 9–21	Middle stage
Questions 22–25	The beginning of final stage

Source: National Council on Alcoholism Inc., 1987.

To find out more about alcoholism, contact the National Council on Alcoholism (NCA) in your geographic area. In addition, the self-help fellowship of Alcoholics Anonymous (AA) has chapters in nearly every community to help those who want to stop drinking. Al-Anon Family Groups, for people affected by someone else's drinking, also meet in most cities and towns. Local telephone directories list NCA affiliates, AA, and Al-Anon and other resources under "alcohol."

Other drugs

Besides tobacco and alcohol, you should strive for freedom from tranquilizers, sleeping pills, headache medicine, and other central nervous system depressants. Overuse of such drugs can lead to deterioration of healthier coping strategies. You should also avoid dependency on medicines such as antacids, laxatives, and cold remedies and use natural relaxation techniques to normalize body functions.

Too many chemicals of the wrong type in the body usually make a poor situation worse. Indeed, many drugs that are relatively safe taken alone can have adverse reactions when taken in combination with other drugs, including alcohol, and can even cause death. If conditions are serious enough to require medication, by all means seek professional help and obtain the correct medication. Otherwise, avoid the abuse of tobacco, alcohol, and drugs. Remember the adage "two wrongs do not make a right." Go natural.[12]

See Figure 21.6 for a summary of commonly used drugs in the United States today. Included are usual short- and long-term effects and potential for dependency. Figure 21.7 shows addiction tendencies for selected drugs.

Figure 21.6 Use and Abuse of Common Drugs

Type of Drug	Examples and Comments	Slang Names	Usual Forms*	Medical Use	Potential for Excessive Use to Lead to Physical (Ph) Psychological (Ps) Dependence	Common Effects at Peak of Drug Response	Long-term Symptoms	Possible in Overdoses
Depressants "Downers"	Barbiturates (Seconal, Amytal, Luminal), Methaqualone (Quaalude), glutethimide (Doriden), and others. Any drug used to calm or sedate could be in this category.	Barbs, dolls, blue devils, candy, red devils, phennies, ludes, 714s, sopors	Legitimate-looking tablets and capsules.	Treatment of insomnia and tension.	High for both Ph and Ps; varies somewhat between drugs. Ph withdrawal effects can be life threatening.	Anxiety reduction, mild euphoria, impaired judgment.	Addiction, toxic psychosis, possible convulsions.	Death from depression of breathing and from dangerous behavior under influence.
Alcohol	Sedative-hypnotic (whiskey, gin, beer, wine, and others).	Booze, juice	Alcoholic beverages.	Rare; antiseptic	High for both Ph and Ps; varies somewhat between drugs. Ph withdrawal effects can be life threatening.	Loss of inhibitions; impaired speech and judgment; lethargy.	Neurological damage, cirrhosis toxic psychosis, addiction.	Death from depression of breathing and from dangerous behavior under influence.
Opiates**	Narcotic sedatives—heroin, morphine, Dilaudid, codeine, methadone, opium, and others; derived from the seed pods of the poppy plant. Exerts effects by depressing central nervous system.	Horse, H, smack	Injection; legitimate-looking tablets and capsules; powders (white, brown, or gray); smoking.	Treatment of severe pain, diarrhea, and cough; analgesic effects.	High for both Ph and Ps; varies somewhat between drugs. Ph withdrawal effects uncomfortable, but rarely life threatening.	Initially may vomit, then become calm and euphoric; impaired intellectual functioning and coordination; respiratory depression.	Addiction, constipation, loss of appetite, temporary impotency.	Death from depression of breathing; cardiovascular collapse.
Tranquilizers	Drugs, used for calming effect—Valium, Librium, Serax, and others.		Pills, capsules.	Anxiety/tension psychological disorders.	Low for Ph; some Ps.	Relaxation, relief of anxiety and tension, improved functioning.	Drowsiness, blurred vision, skin rash, tremors.	Death possible with abuse or overdose.
Stimulants** "Uppers"	Amphetamines—Benzedrine, Methedrine, Dexedrine; "speed" (methamphetamine); "ripoff speed" (drugs made to look like prescription diet drugs but containing caffeine and other legal stimulants); cocaine (rock, flake, powder forms)—derived from coca leaves.	Pep pills bennies, speed, coke, flake, snow, crack	Legitimate-looking tablets and capsules; crystals of powders (usually white); injection; inhalation.	Amphetamines—control of appetite, mild depression, narcolepsy. Cocaine—local anesthetic.	Ph unlikely but Ps high; severe depression can occur on withdrawal and lead to suicide.	Alertness, "high" feeling, talkativeness; may become irritable, paranoid, and aggressive.	Loss of appetite, anxiety, delusion, panic reaction, aggression, depression.	Amphetamine—chest pain, unconsciousness death from heart rhythm defects and/or convulsions; cocaine; paralysis; cocaine, convulsions.
Caffeine	Stimulant found in coffee, tea, cola beverages, chocolate, cocoa, and some over-the-counter drugs such as aspirin and No-Doz.	Java	Liquid, capsules.	Treatment of migraine headaches, some forms of coma.	Ph no; Ps yes.	Increased alertness; reduction of fatigue.	Insomnia, gastric irritation, habituation.	Severe toxic effects unlikely.

Figure 21.6 Use and Abuse of Common Drugs (continued)

Drug	Description	Slang names	Method / form	Medical uses	Dependence potential	Short-term effects	Long-term effects	Dangers
Tobacco "Nicotine"	Cigarettes, cigars—stimulant	Fag, coffin, nail	Smoking.	None.	Ph high; Ps high.	Alertness, calmness, sociability.	Cardiovascular damage, emphysema, lung cancer, mouth and throat cancer, habituation.	At least 1200 toxic chemicals identified as products of tobacco smoke. Death from cancer or cardiovascular disease common.
Hallucinogens	LSD, mescaline (peyote) psilocybin, DMT, STP, and others. These drugs alter perception of reality.	Acid, window pane, blotter, blue stars, sugar	Tablets, capsules, liquid, or impregnated on blotters, stamps, or pieces of clear gelatin.	None.	No Ph; extent of Ps unknown, probably low.	Loss of coordination, hallucinations, changes in space and time perception may make irrational verbal statements and movements.	Can produce panic reaction, intensify already existing psychosis.	Severe toxic effects unlikely; death can occur from dangerous behavior while under influence.
Deliriants "dissociative anesthetic"	Phencyclidine hydrochloride (PCP) and any drug with actions like belladonna (such as jimsonweed). Produce hallucinations and delirium at doses causing significant toxic effects.	PCP, angel dust	Smoking, tablets, capsules, powder, seeds; may be mixed with other drugs.	None: Animal—human; —immobilizing agent.	Low for Ph; moderate to high Ps.	"Blank stare," confusion, disturbed speech, agitation, hostile behavior, gross incoordination, "floating" sensation.	Violent psychotic behavior, impaired judgment, emotional dependence, coma, or stupor.	Death from heart and breathing system effects or dangerous behavior.
Inhalants: A. Gasoline and solvents B. Nitrous oxide C. Amyl or butyl nitrite	Almost any vaporous liquid or aerosol may be usually found in inhaled for a temporary "high." "Laughing gas," "whippets"—intended for use in charging whipped cream canisters. Rush, "poppers," "amyl," etc.		Nitrous oxide is nitrous oxide as small (2-inch) metal "bullets"; nitrites are strong-smelling solutions generally in small brown bottles.	None, except greatly with agent anesthetic.	Ph and Ps varies with agent judgment and coordination and patterns of use.	Inebriation, impairment of delirium. Laughing episodes and euphoria. Sudden lowering then rising of blood pressure and heart rate, suffocating sensation, flushed "prickly heat" feeling.	Varied—some substances can damage body organs such as liver and kidneys.	Death possible with overdose or long-term use; cause varies with agent.
Marijuana	Derived from the flowers and top leaves of the female Cannabis sativa plant, a weed of the hemp family; concentrated preps of resin are known as hashish and hash oil. Tetrahydrocannabinol (THC) is the active ingredient in marijuana and hashish causing psychogenic reactions.	Grass, joint, reefer, pot, Texas tea, rope, weed	Generally as dark green or brown plant particles; often in plastic bags or as cigarettes.	Treatment of glaucoma, asthma, and those who suffer from nausea and vomiting from cancer therapy.	Ph unlikely; Ps low for most users, moderate to high for a few.	Mild stimulation, followed by relaxed euphoric feeling; red eyes; interference with thinking, judgment, and recent memory.	Possible lung cancer and chronic respiratory disorders, acute panic reactions, habituation.	Death from dangerous behavior while under influence.

* Fake look-alikes exist for many street drugs. No one can be absolutely certain of the quality of any street drug without analysis.
** People who inject drugs under nonsterile conditions run a high risk of contracting AIDS, hepatitis, abscesses, or circulatory disorders.

Source: Adapted from Dennis Coon, Essentials of Psychology, 5th ed. (St. Paul: West Publishing Co., 1991), and James McConnell, Understanding Human Behavior, 7th ed. (New York: Harcourt Brace Jovanovich, 1992).

Figure 21.7 Hooked on Drugs

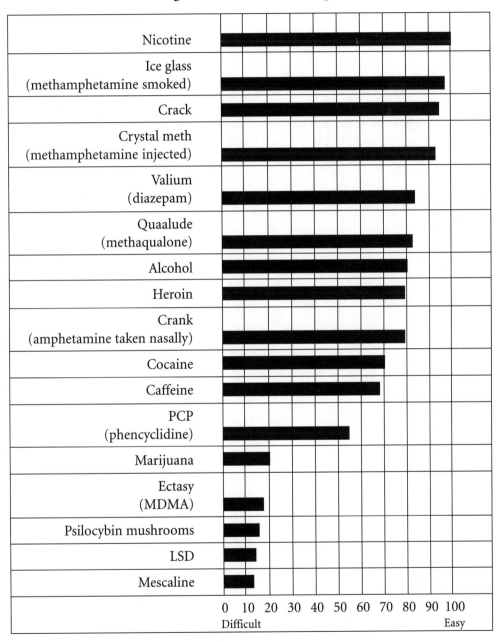

Relative rankings of how easy it is to get hooked on selected drugs.

Source: Lisa Davis, "Why Do People Take Drugs?" Health, *November/December 1990.*

Chapter Twenty-One References

1   Robert Wood Johnson Foundation. Brandeis University, 1992.

2   *Heart and Stroke Facts* (Dallas, Tex.: American Heart Association, 1994).

3   *Heart Attack and Stroke Facts: 1996 Statistical Supplement* (Dallas, Tex.: American Heart Association, 1996).

4   Substance Abuse and Mental Health Services Administration, *National Household Survey on Drug Abuse: Main Findings 1992* (Washington, D.C.: Department of Health and Human Services, 1995), 2.

5   J. McGinnis and W. Foege, "Actual Causes of Death in the United States," *Journal of the American Medical Association* (JAMA), 270, no. 18 (Nov. 10, 1993): 2208.

6   "The Disease of Alcoholism" (National Council on Alcoholism and Drug Dependence, Washington, D.C., 1996).

7   R. Morse and D. Flavin, "The Definition of Alcoholism," *Journal of the American Medical Association* (JAMA), 268, no. 8 (Aug. 26, 1992): 1013.

8   "Facts about Alcohol" (Addiction Research Foundation, Toronto, Canada, 1989).

9   National Institute on Alcohol Abuse and Alcoholism, *Eighth Special Report to U.S. Congress on Alcohol and Death* (Washington, D.C.: Department of Health and Human Services, 1993), xxvii.

10 "Alcohol in Perspective," *Health Letter* (University of California at Berkeley, 1993).

11 Neil Wertheimer, *Total Health for Men* (Emmaus, Pa.: Rodale Press, 1995), 28-34.

12 *Manage Your Stress: Participant's Workbook* (New York: McGraw-Hill, 1980). Table no. 219, "Substance Abuse Treatment Services: 1995"; Table no. 220, "Drug Use by Type of Drug and Age Group: 1979 to 1995," U.S. Bureau of the Census, *Statistical Abstract of the United States: 1997*, 117th ed. (Washington, D. C.: 1997).

Chapter Twenty-Two
☀
The 1 x 3 x 7 = 21 Plan

Seeing your doctor

Too many people spend the first half of life building their wealth and losing their health, only to spend the second half of life losing their wealth to regain their health. You see it all the time: people who ought to know better eat too much, sleep too little, neglect their bodies, and let themselves fall into negative thinking and self-defeating behaviors.

What is the answer? The 1 x 3 x 7 = 21 plan for dealing with stress. By following this weekly plan, you will be better prepared to deal with life's pressures, conflicts, and frustrations. This will reduce physical and emotional wear and tear and will help prevent disease and aging. Note that you should consult your physician before changing health habits, particularly in the areas of exercise and nutrition. Diagnostic tests will enable your doctor to suggest a safe program that will meet your fitness goals.

The importance of blood pressure

When you talk with your doctor, blood pressure will be discussed. Blood pressure is simply the measurement of pressure your circulating blood exerts on the walls of your blood vessels. In order to travel through the miles of blood vessels throughout your body, blood must be under pressure. A problem arises if you have high blood pressure (hypertension). Hypertension means that your heart is having to work too hard to pump blood through the body to nourish tissues and sustain life. Hypertension affects health in the following ways:

- It causes the heart and blood vessels to weaken over time.

- It increases the probability of heart attack, stroke, congestive heart failure, and kidney failure.

- It magnifies the risk of heart attack several times when combined with smoking, high cholesterol, obesity, and diabetes.

Your blood pressure may be high because your heart is sending out an increased amount of blood with each contraction. This can happen if salt (sodium) overload causes you to retain extra fluids, resulting in more volume for your heart to pump. Also, emotions such as fear, anger, and anxiety activate the sympathetic nervous system, which transmits signals that constrict the arteries. When arteries are constricted, blood pressure goes up and can remain high for as long as the stressful situation persists. In addition, recurring states of alarm can cause driving surges of blood that damage the inner linings of the arteries. When the lining is roughened, fats are deposited, narrowing the inside diameter of the blood vessels, thus raising the pressure.

"Arteriosclerosis" is a general term for the thickening and hardening of the arteries. Some hardening of the arteries normally occurs when people grow older. Atherosclerosis, a type of arteriosclerosis, comes from the Greek word *athero* (meaning gruel or paste) and *sclerosis* (hardness). Atherosclerosis is characterized by blockage of the arteries by fatty debris (plaque) containing cholesterol, triglycerides, and other fatty elements. Plaque clings to the arterial walls and narrows the openings that the blood must pass through. Atherosclerosis also involves fibrosis, which is a buildup of scar tissue in the arterial walls themselves. This buildup occurs most frequently in the arteries of the heart, brain, and kidneys, leading to complications that account for the majority of all deaths in the United States.

Blood pressure is measured and reported as millimeters of mercury (mmHg). It is recorded as two numbers, such as 120/80. The first number represents systolic pressure, the pressure in your arteries when your heart is in its pumping phase. The second number represents the diastolic, or resting pressure. Although a reading of 120/80 is considered normal for adults, the first number (systolic pressure) may range 20 points in either direction (from 100 to 140). The second number (diastolic pressure) may range 10 points (from 70 to 90). The World Health Organization's criterion for high blood pressure is 140/90, indicating mild hypertension. Diastolic blood pressure deserves special attention as research indicates a high correlation between elevated diastolic pressure and stroke, congestive heart failure, and coronary heart disease.

One of the problems with high blood pressure is that there are generally no outward symptoms. You can't see it or feel it. This is why it is called "the silent killer." It is a widespread ailment affecting approximately one in five Americans, and it is a contributing factor in about one million deaths each year. More Americans die from cardiovascular disease in a single year than have died collectively in all the wars this country has fought. To avoid being one of the stricken, check your blood pressure at least once a year. Many lives could be saved by this single health habit.

Although hypertension can be caused by genetic factors, most cases can be controlled by changes in living habits. If detected, high blood pressure can usually be corrected through weight control, low fat/low cholesterol diet, reduction of caffeine and alcohol, cessation of smoking, reduced salt consumption, physical exercise, and stress counseling. In some cases, medication is prescribed. If unnoticed and untreated, hypertension is highly damaging and can take years off your life.[1]

Heart disease

Heart disease deserves a special note, as it is the leading cause of death in the United States today, with more than half of the deaths occurring suddenly. What is more, heart disease can develop at an early age. Forty-five percent of U.S. heart attacks occur in people under the age of 65. A study in the *American Journal of Cardiology* reports heart disease, heart attack, and death occurring for people even in their thirties.

Myocardial infarction, or heart attack, occurs when the heart muscle tissue begins to die because its supply of oxygen and other nutrients has been cut off by a blocked artery. If the blood supply is cut off drastically or for a long time, muscle cells suffer irreversible injury and die. Disability or death can result, depending on how much heart muscle has been damaged. The damage caused by a heart attack can be reduced with early treatment, including administering clot-dissolving drugs. As the heart heals, new blood vessels develop to carry additional blood.

The difference between full recovery and permanent damage from a heart attack is often a matter of minutes. The number of minutes before getting medical attention can make the difference between life and death. At least 250,000 people a year die of heart attack within one hour of the onset of symptoms and before they reach the hospital. The following are some of the signs and symptoms to watch for:

- Uncomfortable chest tightness, pressure, or heaviness—not necessarily pain—behind the breastbone in the center of the chest

- Symptoms can last more than a few minutes, or go away and come back

- Spreading discomfort to neck, teeth, jaw, shoulders, arms, or back

- Cold sweat and shortness of breath

- Dizziness, lightheadedness, or feeling faint

- Nausea, often mistaken for indigestion

- Pale, ashen look

With medication and treatment, damage can be reduced significantly if you get help quickly. It is better to risk a false alarm and possible embarrassment than to sit back and wait, hoping the discomfort will disappear. Know in advance which hospital or medical facility is nearest your home or workplace, including 24-hour emergency care. Also keep emergency rescue service numbers next to the telephone and in your pocket, wallet, or purse.

Much of what is known about heart disease comes from the Framingham Heart Study. Since 1949, public health officials have followed the living habits and medical histories of approximately five thousand residents of this Boston suburb. Over the years they have found three major risk factors associated with heart disease: cigarette smoking, high blood pressure, and high cholesterol levels.

Other controllable risk factors identified by Framingham and similar studies include stress, obesity, diabetes, and lack of exercise. There are also several conditions beyond our control that increase the likelihood of a heart attack: age (four out of five deaths from heart attack occur after 65), sex (under age 60, twice as many men as women have heart attacks, although after 60 the numbers begin to level out), and heredity. Jan Breslow, a geneticist at Rockefeller University, estimates that five to ten percent of the population are genetically highly susceptible to heart disease, and that an equal proportion are highly resistant.[2]

Stroke

One of the most terrifying medical experiences a person can have is suffering a stroke. Suddenly, your arm goes numb. You can't speak. Half your body becomes useless. On average, someone suffers a stroke in the United States every minute, and every 3.5 minutes someone dies of one.

Stroke is sudden neurologic damage caused by disturbance of blood circulation to the brain. It is the third leading cause of death in America, behind heart disease and cancer. It strikes a half million people a year and is the major cause of disability in the United States. Key risk factors are high blood pressure, smoking, heart disease, high red blood cell count (that thickens the blood, making clots more likely), and transient ischemic attacks ("little strokes" that occur when a blood clot temporarily clogs an artery and part of the brain doesn't get the blood it needs). All of these conditions are preventable in many cases by a healthful lifestyle. High blood pressure is the most important risk factor for stroke. In fact, stroke risk varies directly with blood pressure.

There are two major types of stroke: (1) Ischemic strokes occur when blood flow to an area of the brain is blocked. This type accounts for 84 percent of all strokes. Of these, 63 percent are caused by a blood clot that forms in a cerebral artery; 37 percent by an embolus, which is a piece of clot broken loose from an artery elsewhere in the body, usually the heart. (2) Hemorrhagic strokes account for 16 percent of all strokes and are caused by a ruptured cerebral blood vessel. Of these, 62.5 percent occur within the brain and 37.5 percent occur on the surface.

The warning signs of a stroke are:

- Sudden weakness or numbness of the face, arm, or leg on one side of the body.

- Sudden dimness or loss of vision, particularly in only one eye.

- Loss of speech, or trouble talking or understanding speech.

- Sudden, severe headaches with no known cause.

- Unexplained dizziness, unsteadiness, or sudden falls, especially accompanied by the previous symptoms.

If you notice one or more signs of stroke, don't wait. See a doctor immediately to prevent severe loss of body functions—if not death. Seeking emergency treatment for stroke at a center conducting stroke research offers the best chance for potentially successful therapy. Most academic medical centers are involved in stroke research and a growing number of community hospitals are becoming involved.[3]

Schedule for checkups

As a minimum, use the following guide for adult physical checkups:

Female over 18 and/or sexually active
- Yearly exam by gynecologist

Female/male, starting at age 20
- Blood pressure checked at least every two years

- A comprehensive eye exam every two to four years

- Medical exams for cancers of the lymph nodes, mouth, skin, testicles, and thyroid as suggested by your physician

- A tetanus-diphtheria booster every 10 years

Female/male, during the 40s
All of the above, plus:

- A complete physical exam with follow-ups as determined by your physician

Female/male, starting at age 50
All of the above, plus:

- A yearly prostate-specific antigen (PSA) test (males)

- A yearly stool test (for colon and rectal cancer)

- A sigmoidoscopy (for colon cancer) every 3 to 5 years

A note about AIDS

As a result of the epidemic of AIDS, in 1995 human immunodeficiency virus (HIV) infection became the eighth leading cause of death in the United States, the fourth leading cause among people aged 25 to 64 years, and the leading killer of men aged 25 to 44, surpassing accidents, heart disease, cancer, suicide, and murder. Risk factors include risky sex practices that lead to exchange of body fluids, intravenous drug use with infected needles, and exposure to tainted blood or blood products. Although men account for eight of every ten cases of AIDS in the United States and intravenous drug use, homosexual sexual practices, and a combination of these two risk factors account for 80 percent of U.S. cases, worldwide the vast majority of HIV infections have been contracted through heterosexual intercourse.

People concerned about AIDS can obtain anonymous screening tests for HIV antibodies at many health departments, hospitals, and clinics. For more information about AIDS, contact the Centers for Disease Control National AIDS Hotline at 1-800-342-AIDS (Spanish language hotline: 1-800-344-SIDA; hotline for the deaf: 1-800-AIDS-TTY).[4]

Preparing for stress

Satchel Paige once asked, "How old would you really be if you didn't know how old you really were?" He believed *true* age had little to do with the date on the calendar and everything to do with the state of your mind and the condition of your body. No matter what your present chronological age is, by following good health habits you can help decrease the speed of biological aging. Your goal should not be to become immortal, but to remain healthy and vigorous for as long as possible and to compress the inevitable period of decline preceding death from several years into a few weeks or months.

The human body is an amazing machine. Like most machines, if you take care of it, it can serve you well. Abuse it, and it will malfunction, age prematurely, and even break down. Harvard medical professor Herbert Benson describes a view of health and well-being akin to a three-legged stool—one is medication, the second is surgery, and the third is self-care. Although most medicine as practiced in America today involves the first two legs, the vast majority of visits to the doctor are in the mind/body and stress-related realm that is often poorly served by drugs and surgery. In the third leg, self-care are nutrition, relaxation, exercise, and the power of belief systems. This is where the 1 x 3 x 7 = 21 plan comes in, as it can add years to your life and life to your years. The following is a discussion of this weekly plan for dealing with stress.

1: Mind over matter

At least one time a day, use positive imagery. Shakespeare wrote, "There is nothing either good or bad, but thinking makes it so." The physical basis for Shakespeare's observation is the fact that the autonomic nervous system cannot differentiate between real and imagined experiences. It acts the same in either case, and this is the reason why voodoo, hypnosis, and other forms of "mind over body" work.

The following is an account of what can happen when a man believes he has been cursed by an enemy and that he will die. It is an example of negative imagery, showing how imagined problems can cause real pain:

> He stands aghast, with his eyes staring at the treacherous pointers, and with his hands lifted as though to ward off the lethal medium, which he imagines is pouring into his body. His cheeks blanch and his eyes become glassy, and the expression of his face becomes horribly distorted. . . . He sways backwards and falls to the ground, and after a short time, appears to be in a swoon. . . . From this time onwards, he sickens and frets, refusing to eat and keeping aloof from the daily affairs of the tribe. Unless help is forthcoming in the shape of a countercharm, death is only a matter of a comparatively short time.[5]

Walter Cannon studied a large number of voodoo deaths and concluded that these deaths result from changes in the body that accompany strong and prolonged emotion. The victim who has been cursed believes he will die and therefore becomes terrified. The fear may be so intense that it results in a heart attack or other bodily disorder, including even death.[6]

The following is a more modern example of the power and consequences of negative imagery:

> A Russian railway employee accidentally locked himself in a refrigerator car. He was unable to escape, and couldn't attract the attention of those outside; so he resigned himself to his fate. As he felt his body becoming numb, he recorded the story of his approaching death in sentences scribbled on the wall of the car.
>
> "I am becoming colder," he wrote. "Still colder, now. Nothing to do but wait. I am slowly freezing to death . . . half asleep now, I can hardly write. . . ." And finally, "These may be my last words." And they were; for when at length the car was opened, they found him dead.
>
> And yet the temperature of the car was only 56°F. The freezing apparatus was, and had been, out of order. There was no physical reason for the employee's death. There was plenty of air; he hadn't suffocated. He was the victim of his own illusion. His conclusions were all wrong. He was so sure he knew.[7]

In contrast to negative imagery, think about the positive aspects of your life and once a day, count your blessings. Examples are the love of your family, your good health, and a satisfying work-life.

Mind-body connection

The interrelatedness of mind and body has been well documented, beginning with the Bible:

> A cheerful heart is a good medicine, but a downcast spirit dries up the bones.
>
> Proverbs 17:22

In the field of medicine, the idea that the mind can affect the body began with Hippocrates himself, when he observed that even the most ill patients sometimes get well, "simply through their contentment with the goodness of the physician."[8]

A holistic approach to mind and body was noted by Plato in the *Republic*. He wrote, "The great error in the treatment of the body is to be ignorant of the whole. For one part can never be well unless the whole is well."[9] This is what the Roman philosopher Seneca meant when he wrote, "A man is never so happy as when his mind, his body, and his heart are in harmony together." What would Plato and Seneca say about today's practice of healing—physicians for the body, therapists for the mind, and clergy for the soul? They would say that no approach alone can cure the whole person.

The fact that the state of the mind affects the condition of the body was well known by William Osler, the nineteenth-century physician who is considered to be the father of modern medicine. "The care of tuberculosis, "said Osler, "depends more on what the patient has in his head than what he has in his chest."[10]

Near the turn of the twentieth century, the American philosopher William James wrote:

> The greatest discovery in our generation is that human beings, by changing the inner attitudes of their minds, can change the outer aspects of their lives![11]

In the 1970s, Jerome Frank, emeritus professor of Johns Hopkins University School of Medicine, observed:

> Nonmedical healing of bodily illness highlights the profound influence of emotions on health and suggests that anxiety and despair can be lethal; confidence and hope, life-giving.[12]

Most recently and eloquently, Norman Cousins summarized the relationship between thought and health and the power of the mind to heal the body:

> The greatest force in the human body is the natural drive of the body to heal itself—but that force is not independent of the belief system, which can translate expectations into physiological change. Nothing is more wondrous about the fifteen billion neurons in the human brain than their ability to convert thoughts, hopes, ideas, and attitudes into chemical substances. Everything begins therefore with belief. What we believe is the most powerful option of all.[13]

Figure 22.1 shows a picture of the health consequences of negative emotions.

Figure 22.1 Emotions, Stress, and Health[14]

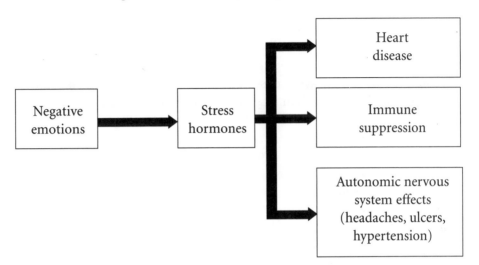

Psychoneuroimmunology

Today's scientists have begun to understand how the mind—activated by hypnosis, placebo, imagery, cognition restructuring, or faith—can change the body's physiology. The new branch of science that studies this interaction is called *psychoneuroimmunology*. In the tradition of Hippocrates, Osler, James, and Cousins, this is not a new idea. What is new is the technical expertise to measure and study changes in the specialized cells of the immune system such as macrophages, B-cells, helper T-cells, suppresser T-cells, and killer T-cells as a function of different mental-emotional states.[15]

The current research in mind/body medicine was kindled by a discovery made in 1974. In that year, Robert Ader of Rochester School of Medicine and Dentistry found evidence that the nervous system and the immune system are intimately connected.[16]

Until Ader's experiments, most anatomists, physicians, and biologists believed that the brain and the immune system were separate entities, neither able to influence the other. Those experiments have been repeated successfully, however, and scientists are finding that there are, indeed, many connections between these systems. Nerve endings have been found in the tissues that produce, develop, and store immune-system cells—the thymus, lymph nodes, spleen, and bone marrow—and immune-system cells have been shown to respond to chemical signals produced by the nervous system. These findings have fueled the new field of psychoneuroimmunology.[17]

Figure 22.2 shows a picture of the basic model of psychoneuroimmunology. The diagram shows how the mind can alter functions of the nervous, endocrine, and immune systems, thus helping to determine whether a person is well or ill.

Figure 22.2 Basic Model of Psychoneuroimmunology[18]

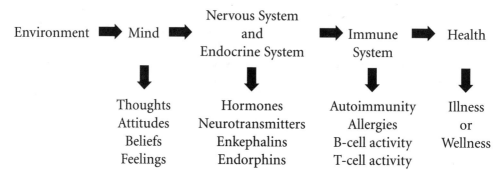

An interesting discovery of modern research is that negative emotions such as grief, despair, hopelessness, depression, and anxiety can impair normal functioning of the immune system. For example, one study found lower-than-normal levels of immune system cells in men whose wives had recently died.[19] This finding may explain the observation that among older people a surviving spouse has a higher-than-expected risk of death during the period of bereavement.

In an exploration of identification phenomena in the bereaved, Zisook, et al., found that 14 percent of their sample admitted to feeling physically ill since their loss, 15 percent felt "just like the person who died," 8 percent had acquired habits of the deceased, 12 percent felt they had the same illness, and 9 percent had pains in the same areas of their bodies as the person who died. In addition to bereaved spouses, unhappily married and recently divorced people also have reduced immune system functions, as do individuals experiencing job loss.[20]

Good health depends on the normal functioning of the immune system. Stress can reduce the immune system's ability to respond to harmful organisms. There are basically three ways that the immune system may become dysfunctional and contribute to stress-related illnesses: (1) underactivity, (2) hyperactivity, and (3) misguided activity. Characteristic diseases caused by these three types of dysfunction are, respectively, cancer, asthma, and rheumatoid arthritis.[21]

What does all this mean as far as health is concerned? It means that the more positive your mental and emotional state, the more responsive and functional your immune system is likely to be. A healthy immune system means that you are likely to experience fewer infections, you may be less likely to fall victim to autoimmune diseases, and you will probably be less susceptible to cancer.

Positive imagery

Because thoughts and emotional states can have a powerful influence on physical health, at least once every day you should use positive imagery. Pause for a few minutes to think about and appreciate the good things in your life—your family, health, job, and friends. You may have had so many problems and bad experiences that you have fallen into the habit of negative thinking. Counteract this by accentuating the positive. Simple statements include: I have a loving family, I am happy and healthy, I am here for a purpose, I am honest and kind, I make a difference.

Some people are prone to negative thinking. You may know a person who always seems to look on the dark side of things. If a cup is half full, it is seen as half empty; if the weather is partly sunny, there are complaints about the clouds. Such a person creates a negative mood that is detrimental to everyone's health and well-being.

You should use pleasant thoughts to counteract negative feelings. The following shows the benefits of positive imagery:

> A youthful looking woman was asked what she used to preserve her attractive appearance. Her reply was, "I use for the lips, truth; for the voice, sweet words; for the eyes, appreciation; for the hand, charity; for the figure, uprightness; and for the heart, I use love."[22]

As you evaluate yourself, are you in the habit of negative thinking? If so, beginning today, and at least once every day, use positive imagery to increase the quality of your life.

X 3 : Perform a death-defying act

Have at least three physical workouts a week. Healthy people incorporate physical exercise into their lifestyles. The importance of exercise has been known for centuries, and modern studies confirm that physical activity has a positive effect on disease prevention and longevity.

As a guideline, you should exercise three to five times a week for thirty to sixty minutes, including warm-up and cool-down activities. This is true for both men and women, regardless of age. Although muscle strength, endurance, flexibility, and body composition (a healthful balance between fat and muscle) are important fitness goals, cardiovascular fitness is the primary goal of these workouts. Thus, brisk walking, jogging, cycling, and swimming are good exercises, as they raise the heart rate high enough to help your cardiovascular system. These types of exercises are called *aerobic* exercises—exercises that are characterized by an increase in the depth and rate of breathing.

Aerobic fitness describes how well you are able to take oxygen from the atmosphere into your lungs and blood, then pump it to your working muscles, and utilize it to oxidize carbohydrates and fats to produce energy.

A general guide is to exercise regularly, starting slowly and building up to three to five sessions per week that double the heart rate for at least twenty minutes of your thirty to sixty minute workout. Fewer than three exercise sessions are insufficient, and more than five are unnecessary for optimum benefit for the average person.[23] The following presents a more specific guide for determining the correct heart rate for cardiovascular fitness:[24]

Target heart rate for cardiovascular fitness
What is an appropriate level of exercise? There is an intensity of activity that is sufficient to develop cardiovascular fitness, but not so strenuous to exceed safe limits. This is called the "target heart rate," measured in beats per minute by the heart (BPM). Your target heart rate is between 60 and 85 percent of your maximum aerobic power. Below 60 percent of this capacity, you achieve little cardiovascular benefit, and above 85 percent, there is little value from the extra intensity.

Maximum aerobic power is the technical name for the point at which, despite your best efforts, your heart and circulatory system cannot deliver any more oxygen to your tissues. Exhaustion soon follows. Almost simultaneously, the heart becomes unable to beat any faster. This constitutes your maximum attainable heart rate.

The best way to determine maximum attainable heart rate is to take an exercise stress test. If this is impractical, an approximation can be determined by subtracting your age from 220. This figure is used to calculate your target heart rate.

To obtain the target heart rate, you should first determine your resting heart rate, the number of beats of the heart per minute while at rest. The accurate measurement of heart rate is important. Locating the pulse requires some practice. Any location where a pulse can be felt is satisfactory. Acceptable sites include: the radial artery, felt at the wrist on the thumb side; the brachial artery, inside the bend of the elbow toward the body side; the femoral artery in the groin; the arteries at the temple; and the carotid artery in the neck (although there is some evidence that pressure here may cause a reflexive slowing of the heart rate).

It is important to measure pulse with the fingers and not the thumb, because using the thumb may lead to an error in counting. Normally, the resting heart rate should be measured after you have been sitting comfortably for thirty minutes. This time period may be impractical in some situations and may be modified, but decreasing it to as little as ten to fifteen minutes may give invalid readings.

After obtaining your resting heart rate, subtract this from your maximum attainable heart rate (220 – age). Then multiply the result by the desired percentage of activity intensity—between 60 and 85 percent. (In general, a sedentary individual should use 60 percent and gradually increase with fitness). Finally, by adding the resting heart rate to this figure, you can calculate your "target heart rate."

Example: Mary is thirty-five years old, has a resting heart rate of 70 beats per minute (BPM), and is relatively sedentary. Her "target heart rate" is found as follows:

220 – 35 = 185 (maximum attainable heart rate)
185 – 70 (resting HR) = 115
115 x .60 (percentage of activity intensity) = 69
69 + 70 = 139 BPM (Heartbeats per minute)
Mary's "target heart rate" for cardiovascular fitness is 139 BPM.

Figure 22.3 presents a line and rule method for determining target heart rate for cardiovascular fitness.

Figure 22.3 Your Target Heart Rate for Cardiovascular Fitness

Sit quietly and count your pulse for one minute. This is your resting heart rate. Then draw a straight line on the chart (below) between your resting heart rate and your age. The point where your line crosses the target heart rate line is your target heart rate. Notice that there are two sets of numbers along the age axis. if you exercise regularly and consider yourself fit, use the high fitness scale. If you are just starting out, use the low fitness scale.

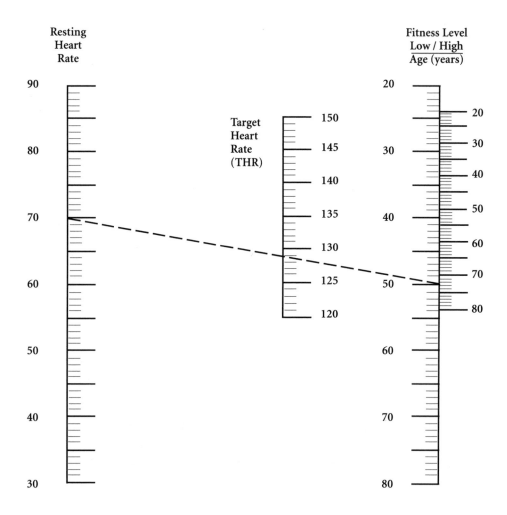

Source: American Health, *April 1987.*

The value of exercise

Modern lifestyles have become increasingly sedentary, both in the workplace and at home. This is out of harmony with our physiology, which evolved to prepare us for an active physical existence. Until recently, daily survival depended on physical fitness.

There are few excuses for not being in good physical shape, and there are important reasons why a person should be in good condition:

- It is not overly difficult.

- It doesn't take too much time.

- It costs very little.

- It has positive value for physical and emotional health.

Scientific evidence supports the value of an active lifestyle involving physical activity: (1) The College Alumni Study, following more than 16,000 Harvard and University of Pennsylvania graduates for more than thirty years, shows that physically active individuals significantly reduce their risk of chronic disease and live longer. (2) Analysis conducted by the Centers for Disease Control shows that active people cut their risk of heart disease in half compared to inactive people. (3) The Aerobics Research Institute reports that moderate activity performed regularly significantly reduces the risk of heart disease and certain types of cancer. (4) Research from the National Heart, Lung, and Blood Institute shows that three out of four hypertensive people experience a reduction in blood pressure through regular exercise.[25]

Physical exercise renews the body and makes it strong in many ways:[26]

- Moderate exercise, especially when combined with weight control, helps reduce hypertension.

- New red corpuscles emerge from the bone marrow and enter the bloodstream, reviving tired blood and increasing energy so that you can enjoy more activities.

- Fatty substances in the blood—cholesterol and triglycerides—are reduced, lessening the risk of arterial blockage that could lead to stroke and heart failure. Total cholesterol level and LDL (bad—Lousy—cholesterol) are lowered, while HDL (good—Helpful—cholesterol) is raised.

- New capillaries open up, increasing the effectiveness of your vascular network. If all the blood vessels in an adult of average height and weight were connected in a line, the length would circle the globe almost two times. The major arteries and veins would be the first twenty feet, and the remaining 49,600 miles would be the arterioles, capillaries, and venules.

- Exercise is an ideal line of defense to prevent and alleviate chronic low-back pain.

- Exercise produces a general sense of well-being, reducing anxiety, depression, tension, and other effects of stress.

- The heart becomes more efficient, increasing the volume of blood pumped with each contraction. This is important when you realize that, weighing approximately a pound and being as small as your fist, this single organ must pump 10 1/2 pints of blood through almost 50,000 miles of blood vessels each day. Each day the average heart beats (expands and contracts) 100,000 times and pumps about 2,000 gallons of blood. During the course of 70 years, an average human heart will beat nearly 2.5 billion times.

- The brain's oxygen-carrying blood supply increases, so you can think more clearly and quickly, thus improving creativity and problem-solving ability.

- Exercise helps combat osteoporosis, the demineralization of the bones so prevalent in older people, especially in women. Weight-bearing exercises such as walking and running help preserve bone density.

- Exercise helps preserve muscle mass, thereby maintaining physical strength.

- Exercise can postpone and reduce the occurrence of non-insulin-dependent diabetes. As many as 16 million Americans are afflicted with adult-onset diabetes, which is most prevalent in sedentary, obese people.

- Exercise improves the ability to obtain needed sleep.

- Exercise is one of the best known ways to improve attitude. It can boost levels of mood-elevating, pain-killing brain chemicals called endorphins and can reduce free-floating anxiety or hostility.

- Exercise adds to life expectancy. According to the Centers for Disease Control, sedentary living is a leading culprit in death from heart attack. Being sedentary raises the risk of fatal heart attack by 50 percent.

Exercise plan

Kenneth Cooper, leading expert on aerobic exercise, identifies a five-step plan for achieving physical fitness:[27]

- Have a thorough medical examination, including a physical stress test.

- Determine your target heart rate for cardiovascular fitness.

- Choose an aerobic exercise you enjoy. Five good ones, in descending order for exercise value, are cross-country skiing, swimming, running (faster than nine miles per hour) or jogging (slower than nine miles per hour), cycling, and brisk walking. Other aerobic options include skating, dancing, stair climbing, and racquet sports.

■ Begin a regular program. Exercise a minimum of three times a week for approximately 30 to 60 minutes.

1. Warm up to elevate body temperature and prepare for more vigorous exercise: 5 minutes jogging in place is ideal.

2. Stretch to loosen muscles and prevent injuries: 5 minutes.

3. Exercise at your target heart rate for at least 20 minutes. (60 to 85 percent of your maximum attainable heart rate). Do not overexert. Signs of overexertion include pains in the chest, dizziness, nausea, severe breathlessness, and loss of muscle control. Follow the principles of moderation and avoid the concept of "no pain, no gain."

4. Cool down by moving slowly: 5 minutes walking is ideal.

5. Stretch to prevent soreness or engage in 10 minutes of calisthenics or weight-training activities to increase muscle strength, endurance, and flexibility; and then finish with stretching.

Figure 22.4 shows the activity, time frame, and typical heart rate associated with each step of a 45-minute period.

Figure 22.4 Activity and Time Frame for Aerobic Exercise (45 minute period)

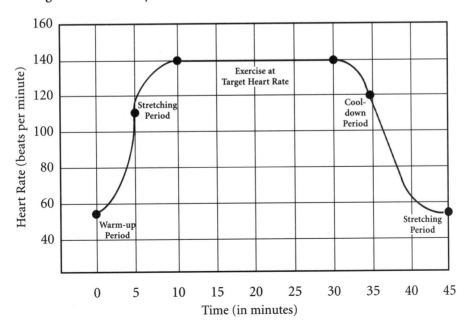

■ Exercising after work and before dinner can help relieve tension that has developed during the day and, as a bonus, typically reduces appetite.

Benefits and options

Mental fitness, in addition to physical fitness, can be improved through exercise. Many people who exercise by cycling, running, or swimming will cram all of the problems of their day into their heads before beginning to exercise. Thirty to 60 minutes later, their minds are clear, and they don't know where their problems are. Their worries are along the roadway, on the jogging path, or at the bottom of the swimming pool.

Exercise for life

What exercises should adults do and how often should they do them?

Activities that emphasize large muscle groups and involve cardiorespiratory endurance are recommended. Aerobic exercises are particularly important for cardiovascular development and maintenance. Other activities (bowling, golf, volleyball, etc.) may be included for enjoyment.

Healthy adults should participate in continuous aerobic activity for approximately twenty minutes. Beginning exercisers should perform at low to moderate levels.

Participation three days a week is recommended. Going beyond three days a week depends on the exercise. Jogging and running may produce orthopedic injuries when done more than three times per week. Three times per week should be enough for calisthenics, stretching, and rhythmic-endurance exercises.

Physical impact activities such as football and basketball carry high injury risks as biological age advances. An alternative is lifetime or carryover sports that can be continued for many years. In this category is one of the best exercise regimens available, simple walking. Hippocrates himself said, "Walking is man's best medicine."[28]

Statistics show that Americans have responded positively to exercise. Participation in regular physical activity gradually increased during the 1960s, 1970s, and 1980s. The top three sport activities in 1995 were exercise walking, swimming, and bicycle riding. A recent Gallup poll shows approximately 60 percent are now involved in some type of regular exercise program, compared with only 24 percent in 1961. To be included in the number who are performing a death-defying act, you should follow three basic principles:

1. **Set aside time.** Make physical exercise a priority and a habit for life.

2. **Do what you enjoy.** Try a number of activities and choose your favorites.

3. **Commit to fitness.** Realize that physical exercise is a foundation for health, happiness, and personal effectiveness in all aspects of life.

Stress prevention

When it comes to exercise, personality plays a part. One professor enjoyed the racquetball league. One day his opponent would be a historian, and the next time he may be playing a biologist. What was interesting was to see how the different disciplines approached the game. The most aggressive competitors were the political science and law school faculty. The mathematicians knew all the angles. And the education department wanted to teach you things—how to serve, etc. Of course, the psychology professor was concerned about people's feelings. Regardless of style, the effect was the same—*good exercise for all.*— Author's file notes (G. M.)

Are you as fit as you should be to cope with the inevitable stresses of life? Are you able to deal effectively with daily physical demands without feeling fatigued? Can you handle an emergency? If not, begin today to improve. You should select an exercise program that you enjoy; do it at least three times a week, and make physical fitness a lifelong habit.

X 7: Give it a rest

Have the equivalent of seven restful nights of sleep per week. Each person needs a different amount and interval of sleep. Some people need fewer than eight hours' sleep each night (Thomas Edison needed five), while others need more (Albert Einstein needed ten). Some people rest best at night, while others spread their rest periods throughout the day. In any case, your body requires adequate rest to revitalize itself and be prepared to cope with stress. For many Americans, the demands of work, family, and an on-the-go lifestyle have combined to make sleep deprivation a major stress problem. Many fall asleep on the job, in school, and even while driving.

As you get older, the time spent in bed typically decreases until approximately age 45 (17 out of 24 hours are spent in bed near birth; 8-1/2 hours at about age 12; an average of 7-1/2 hours between the ages of 25 and 45). After age 45, people usually increase the amount of time they spend in bed to 8-1/2 hours but actually decrease the time spent sleeping. In later years, the average sleeping time is approximately 6-1/2 hours.[29]

Are you a lark or an owl? Most of us can classify ourselves according to whether we are more alert and energetic in the mornings—"larks"—or in the evenings— "owls." Larks tend to wake up early and do their best work in the morning. Owls find it hard to start the day but once up don't hit their peak of productivity until the evening hours. Such differences vary according to many factors, including temperament and personality. For instance, larks tend to be more introverted; owls are more extroverted.[30]

Regardless of the amount or schedule, everyone needs two kinds of sleep—REM (rapid eye movement) and NREM (non-REM). Both are important for physical and mental health. NREM sleep serves a body-restoration function; tissue growth and repair occur during this type of sleep. Without NREM sleep, you would eventually collapse. After you have been deprived of sleep, NREM is usually made up first. Until the deficiency in NREM sleep is satisfied, you will find it difficult to carry out physical tasks.

On the other hand, REM sleep serves a brain-restoration function, helping to restore mental fitness. REM sleep helps in coping with day-to-day psychological stress. Experiments show that subjects exposed to stressful situations have a sharply increased need for REM sleep, during which time they seem to make peace with their traumatic experiences.[31]

There are two major keys to getting the rest you need:

- have a relaxing environment, including a good bed;

- understand the "chicken-and-egg" relationship between muscle tension and the reticular formation, a physiological network of nerves at the base of the brain.

The reticular formation serves as a "switching station" for the higher centers of the brain by letting in stimuli for conscious thought. Unless you relax your muscles, including the muscles of your tongue (which are usually busy forming words), the reticular formation will not switch off, and you will not obtain your needed rest. The "chicken-and-egg" relationship is that muscle relaxation leads to a turned-off reticular formation, which leads to muscle relaxation, which leads to rest and renewal.[32]

Stages of sleep

We spend about one-third of our lives in the state of consciousness called sleep. Actually, sleep occurs in cycles consisting of four stages. See Figure 22.5.[33]

Figure 22.5 Brain Wave Patterns During Stages of Sleep

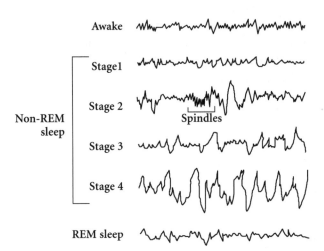

Stage 1 is falling asleep. Brain waves are irregular and they lack the pattern of alpha waves that characterizes the relaxed waking state. The heart rate slows down and muscles relax. The person in stage 1 sleep is easy to waken and may not realize that he has fallen asleep.

Stage 2 sleep shows bursts of brain wave activity called "spindles," so named because their tracings on an EEG chart resemble thread wrapped around an old-fashioned spindle. Stage 2 sleep is deeper than stage 1 sleep.

Stage 3 sleep is even deeper as spindles disappear and long, slow (about one wave per second) delta waves appear. The sleeper is unresponsive to external stimuli and difficult to waken. Heart rate, blood pressure, and temperature continue to go down.

Stage 4 sleep is the deepest level. It is called "delta sleep" because of the prevalence of the slow delta waves. In young adults, delta sleep occurs in fifteen- to thirty-minute periods, interspersed with lighter stages. As one grows older, the amount of delta sleep is reduced.

In the course of a sleep cycle, the sleeper proceeds from stage 1 to 2 to 3 to 4 and back through the stages: 4 to 3 to 2 to 1. When the sleeper gets back to stage 1, the eyes dart and roll around under the closed eyelids. This is the sign that the sleeper is in REM (rapid eye movement) sleep. It is during REM sleep that dreaming occurs.

During a night's sleep, we usually go up and down through the stages, but with each cycle the REM period becomes longer and the deep slow-wave stages become shorter. In later cycles, it is common for the sleeper to go only to stage 2 and then back to REM. These cycles are about 90 minutes in length. See Figure 22.6.

Figure 22.6 A Typical Night's Sleep

Through the course of the night, we cycle through the stages of sleep. The deepest sleep occurs primarily in the first few hours. The REM periods, during which we dream, become longer as morning approaches.

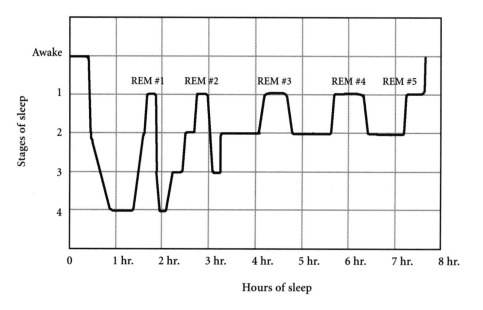

Hours of sleep

Rules for rest

One in three Americans suffers from insomnia, meaning we either have trouble falling asleep or can't stay asleep through the night. About a third of these people call the problem severe. Women are about twice as likely to experience sleep problems as men. The following are ten rules for improving the quality of your sleep and, therefore, being better prepared to deal with stress:[34]

- Sleep only as much as you need to feel refreshed and healthy the next day. Oversleeping can result in fragmented and shallow rest.

- Wake up each morning at a consistent time. A standard wake-up time seems to lead to ease in falling asleep.

- Practice regular physical exercise. Regular physical activity improves sleep over a period of time; however, periodic, one-time exercise sessions do not directly influence sleep the following night.

- A quiet environment is advisable. Loud noise reduces the quality of sleep, even when you cannot remember it the next morning or do not wake up during the night.

- A moderate temperature is recommended for ideal sleep. Both excessive heat and excessive cold disturb sleep.

- Don't go to bed with a full or an empty stomach. A light snack such as warm milk can be helpful, since hunger generally reduces the quality of sleep.

- Avoid sleep medication. Although a sleeping pill may be helpful in some cases, the chronic use of such sleep aids is ineffective and may even be harmful.

- Reduce caffeine intake. Caffeine before sleep disturbs rest, even in people who do not seem to be affected.

- Avoid alcohol consumption. Although alcohol may help a tense person to fall asleep quickly, it results in fragmented, poor-quality sleep.

- If you are having difficulty falling asleep and are feeling angry, frustrated, and tense, it often helps to do something else, such as read or talk until you are relaxed.

An effective technique for falling asleep comes from *The Lives of a Bengal Lancer*. It is simply to draw twenty slow, even breaths, then on the twenty-first hold the breath for a few moments. By the time you have done this three times you will be drowsy.[35]

Meditation

One widely used method to cope with stress is meditation. Practiced during a 10-to-20-minute period once each day, or in shorter, 3-to-5-minute breaks, meditation is an excellent way to decrease muscle tension, reduce emotional strain, and provide physical rest.

Meditation made easy

You don't need mantras or pretzel positions. There are three simple steps to meditation.

1. Sit in a comfortable position in a quiet place.

2. Close your eyes and be still.

3. Breathe deeply, regularly, and comfortably. If you find your mind wandering to the worries of the day, focus on slow, regular breathing.

Essentially, there are two types of meditation: "opening up" and "shutting down." Neither type is inherently better than the other as a stress management technique.[36] "Opening up" concentrates on the five senses of the body: sight, sound, touch, taste, and smell. Through various opening-up exercises, one becomes more conscious of the world, resulting in physical and mental renewal. This type of meditation can be practiced while walking on the beach or lying on the sand.[37]

"Shutting down" is a different type of meditation. Instead of increasing broad sensory awareness, stimulation is reduced by concentrating on one object or activity. Common shutting-down exercises include:

- using deep, regular breathing;

- focusing on one point, such as a flame, the navel, or a star;

- making sounds, such as religious chants;

- mentally repeating special words or "mantras," such as the Eastern "Ommm";

- visually concentrating on one scene or person;

- moving, such as Sufi dancing (whirling dervishes) and fingering of worry beads or the rosary;

- engaging in devotions, such as parables and prayers.[38]

According to the teachings of Buddha, the source of human problems is extreme attachment to the senses and thoughts. Peace can be attained only when one is freed from these attachments, transcending the incessant bombardment of the consciousness so as to experience a quiet body and a unified spirit. Buddha's teachings generally state the simple goals of meditation, which have motivated millions of people for hundreds of years. Although the goals are simple, the fundamentals are often misunderstood, as meditation itself is difficult to define. Meditation can best be understood as a state of mind or consciousness, but it is most often defined in terms of an art or technique.

The art of meditation is the ability to maintain a passive concentration in which alertness and control are maintained, but in a way that is not tension producing. The meditator is not trapped in an altered state of consciousness as is often the case with drugs. Because one has command over emotions, feelings, and memory, physiological processes can be quieted and control can be maintained over the body. Research on meditation has shown that it is accompanied by a marked reduction in the activity of most systems governed by the autonomic nervous system.[39]

There are many popular techniques that aim at inducing a self-transcendent state of consciousness through meditation. The most popular techniques in Western society are based on specific concentration and contemplation practices of ancient yoga and Zen Buddhism.

Yoga, a Sanskrit word meaning "reunion," began thousands of years ago in India as part of Hinduism. It has been transmitted from generation to generation by enlightened masters. Several yoga paths have developed into spiritual schools, and in many instances these paths have become separate disciplines in themselves. Bhakti Yoga, the path of devotion to God, uses devotional chanting and worship. Jaina Yoga, the path of knowledge, teaches wisdom and understanding. Some others are Karma Yoga, the path of action and selfless services; Hatha Yoga, the path of health using exercise as a means to physical and mental harmony; and Raja Yoga, or Royal Yoga, the path of self-realization and enlightenment. According to Palanjali's Sutras, the most authoritative source of yoga philosophy, all other forms of yoga are preparation for meditation and realization of the Raja Pathway, through which the full potential of the soul can be attained. Although yoga practices are used by various religious groups, yoga is not a religion; thus it is free of dogmatism and orthodoxism.[40]

Zen, as originally conceived, was not a philosophy; it had no doctrine. Having no doctrine, it was not a religion and did not deny or affirm the existence of God, a soul, or a spirit. Specific rituals and intellectual inquiries associated with it were merely attempts by various sects to discipline and guide the seeker. Zen seeks to open the mind itself, to make it its own master and free it of unnatural encumbrances. In this sense, Zen is chaotic and unteachable. So, to accomplish the goals of Zen, various disciplines have grown with each teacher who thought of a better method to teach the undisciplined mind to reach this freedom. Meditation is at the core of all the techniques.[41]

Transcendental meditation (TM) is a classic Hindu mantra technique based on the teaching of the Hindu teacher Sankaracharya and made popular by Maharishi Mahesh Yogi through the worldwide organization called Students International Meditation Society. TM is not a religion or a philosophy and does not demand any particular lifestyle of its practitioners. It is described as a technique for expanding conscious awareness and producing a state of restful alertness indicative of self-transcendence. The technique of TM is a simple mantra that is matched to each meditator. The mantras themselves are not unique to TM but come from Sanskrit texts still in use today.[42]

Gil's story

At age nineteen I entered a tubercular sanitarium and during a twelve-year period from age nineteen to age thirty-one I spent five years of complete bed rest. With pneumothorax treatment I had my left lung collapsed for four years, and later my right lung was collapsed for two years. I was very short-winded and had very limited breathing capacity for any activity. I could hold my breath for no more than ten seconds. During my earlier years I did not like physical activities and exercises. In high school I would skip the gym classes, and now I realize I was creating the weak body I had.

At age forty-eight, my former wife and I read a book titled *Yoga, Youth and Reincarnation* by Jess Stearn. We were interested in the reincarnation part. However, we both started working with the yoga postures and disciplines. After three months of working two hours a day, seven days a week, Phyllis lost twenty-five pounds and took two inches off her hips. At that time I wrote to the lady in the book. She invited Phyllis to come to Boston to study with her, which she did. When she returned, Phyllis started teaching yoga classes in Cincinnati that were very successful.

I was exercising daily with a reluctant body and in a short time was improving physically. I continued practicing the postures and disciplines and especially the breathing exercises and started assisting Phyllis in her classes. About a year later, the Deer Park evening school wanted to have a yoga class, and I started teaching there. Soon after that, other places wanted to have yoga; I now have classes three nights a week. All these classes have been in operation from 15 to 20 years.

I was seventy-eight years old last June and, thanks to yoga, I am stronger than I was for the first forty-eight years of my life. I know that yoga can push back limitations and sometimes completely erase them. Yoga can add years to your life, and life to your years. I am happy to be alive—and grateful to all the great, dedicated people I've met over the years.[43]

Biofeedback

Biofeedback is a method of obtaining information about physiological activity occurring in the body. An electronic monitoring device attached to the body detects changes in internal function and communicates these to the person through a tone, light, or meter. Most people, by paying attention to this feedback, can gain some control over functions previously thought to be beyond conscious control, such as body temperature, heart rate, muscle tension, and brain waves. Biofeedback training consists of three stages:

1. Developing increased awareness of a body state or function

2. Gaining control over it

3. Transferring this control to everyday living without use of the biofeedback monitoring instrument

Three basic modalities of biofeedback training are used for stress management and to treat psychosomatic illnesses: muscle tension feedback, skin temperature feedback, and sweat gland activity feedback (also referred to as electrodermal feedback).

The goal of biofeedback for stress reduction is to achieve a state of tranquillity, usually associated with the brain's production of alpha waves (which are slower and more regular than normal waking waves). Most people can produce alpha waves more or less at will after several training sessions.[44] For information on biofeedback in your area, contact college and university psychology departments and, if available, local medical centers.

Relaxation techniques

Relaxation techniques include "scientific relaxation" and the "relaxation response." See page 479 for Herbert Benson's excellent article "The Relaxation Response." Relaxation can be an effective way to prevent and cure headaches, a common symptom of stress.

Headaches are divided into four basic types. Two types are caused by contractions of blood vessels in the scalp. One is called a vascular, or migraine, headache, characterized by throbbing pain that can last for hours or even days. The second is called a cluster headache, characterized by throbbing pain for thirty to forty-five minutes but recurring every couple of hours for days and even weeks at a time. The third type is caused by sustained muscle tension in the forehead, neck, or scalp. This is called a tension headache, and it is the most common type of headache. The fourth type of headache is sinus headache, caused by pressure on swollen, tender sinus linings. The pain occurs around the bridge of the nose as well as the jaw and ears. All of these types of headaches can be helped by using relaxation techniques, including sleep.[45]

Massage and breathing

Massage has been used for centuries to alleviate stress. Massage techniques vary, but the whole idea behind massage is to reduce muscle tension. As muscle tension fades, so does stress. Effleurage massage means "to skim over." In this technique, the most pressure is applied on the upward stroke. Petrissage massage means "to knead," and in this type of massage, the muscles are rubbed against underlying bone. Deep friction massage is done by making small circles using firm pressure, but only using the fingertips. Oils are often used to prevent friction on the skin and to allow the sensation to be experienced primarily in the muscles.[46]

Breathing has been mentioned several times throughout this text. Full and regular breathing is an important line of defense in managing stress. It clears the head and calms the body. There is truth in the saying that if you half-breathe you half-live.

To demonstrate the importance of getting enough rest, ask yourself, "Did I get enough sleep last night?" If you did not, you are probably having to work much harder to read and learn than if you had. The solution is to have the equivalent of seven restful nights of sleep every week. Let this be a standard part of your readiness plan to deal with the stresses of life.

= 21: You are what you eat

Have the equivalent of 21 nutritious meals per week. Strive to get your body weight and composition to a point that pleases you and keep it there. The meals you eat should be spread out, balanced, and proportional to your body size and activity level. On average, men need approximately 2,700 calories per day (900 per meal) and women need about 2,100 calories per day (700 per meal).[47]

There are many theories on nutrition. Miss Piggy says, "Never eat more than you can lift." Better advice comes from the Dietary Guidelines for Americans by the U.S. Department of Agriculture and the U.S. Department of Health and Human Services. The seven dietary guidelines are as follows:[48]

1. Eat a variety of foods.

2. Maintain your ideal weight.

3. Avoid too much fat, saturated fat, and cholesterol. (Dietary fat should account for no more than 30 percent of total calories, down from the current 37 percent rate consumed; less is best.)

4. Eat foods with adequate starch and fiber.

5. Avoid too much sugar.

6. Avoid too much sodium.

7. If you drink alcohol, do so in moderation (a maximum of one drink per day for women, two per day for men).

There is truth in the saying "You are what you eat." Have you ever seen an ill-fed horse? Contrast this with a horse fed a proper diet. The second looks like Man o' War, and the first looks like Mr. Ed. People are no different from horses in this regard. Nutrition affects skin, teeth, and bones, as well as performance. You must be sure that your diet includes vitamins, minerals, carbohydrates, fats, protein, and water and that it reflects the guidelines shown in the Food Guide Pyramid. See Figure 22.7.

Figure 22.7 Food Guide Pyramid—A Guide to Daily Food Choices

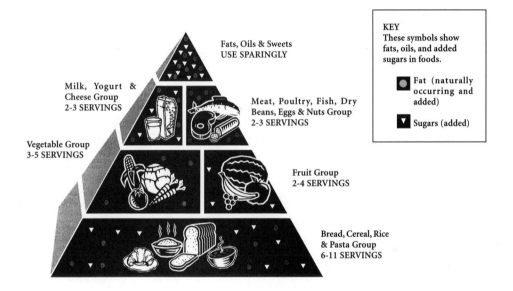

Source: USDA Human Nutrition Information Service, 6505 Belcres Road, Hyattsville, Maryland 20782, 1992.

Although the pyramid encourages us to eat a variety of foods, its strength is that it establishes a hierarchy of importance for foods. The following is an explanation of the pyramid tiers from bottom (most important) to top (least important):

First tier. The base of the pyramid includes the bread, cereal, rice, and pasta group. This group is the largest in the pyramid to encourage people to eat more complex carbohydrates and fiber-rich foods. Enriched cereals and breads, especially whole-grain products, are important sources of carbohydrates, thiamin (B1), iron, niacin, and fiber. These foods provide energy and promote a healthy nervous system.

Second tier. The next level includes the fruit and vegetable groups, where sources of fiber, carbohydrates, and vitamins A and C are found. These help prevent some diseases, heal wounds, improve night vision, and control weight. Collectively, food from the first two tiers should constitute 55 to 60 percent of daily food choices.

Third tier. The dairy and meat groups make up the third tier. Their placement toward the top of the pyramid indicates that these groups should not be emphasized in the diet to the same degree as the previous groups, because they contain saturated fats and a greater amount of total fat. However, dairy foods are excellent sources of calcium, riboflavin (B_2), and protein, providing for strong bones, teeth, and healthy skin, and helping vision. Meats, including lean beef, pork, fish, and poultry, as well as nuts, eggs, and beans, are important sources of protein, niacin, iron, and thiamin. These foods are good for muscles, bones, blood cells, skin, and nerves.

Fourth tier. The last group, fats, oils, and sweets, is graphically represented as the smallest part of the pyramid to encourage us to consume smaller amounts of these foods because they tend to be high in fat, saturated fat, or sugar.[49]

Nutrition and cancer

Is there a relationship between food and cancer? This is a matter of ongoing research and debate. As of now, it appears that certain guidelines can help. See Figure 22.8.[50]

- Do not become obese. This is defined as 20 percent more than one's ideal body weight, considering age, height, and bone structure.

- Reduce the amount of fat in the diet; fat consumption should be less than 30 percent. Twenty percent is even better.

- Eat high-fiber foods such as whole-grain cereals, fruits, and vegetables.

- Eat foods rich in vitamins A and C.

- Eat cruciferous vegetables such as cabbage, cauliflower, broccoli, and brussels sprouts.

- Eat fewer nitrite-preserved foods such as bacon. Also eat less salt and fewer smoke-cured meats and fish.

- Keep alcohol consumption low.

Figure 22.8 Components of Diet and Specific Cancers

Correlations are indicated in the center of the figure: The strongest links are shown in boldface type, weaker ones in regular type, and the weakest ones in italic type.

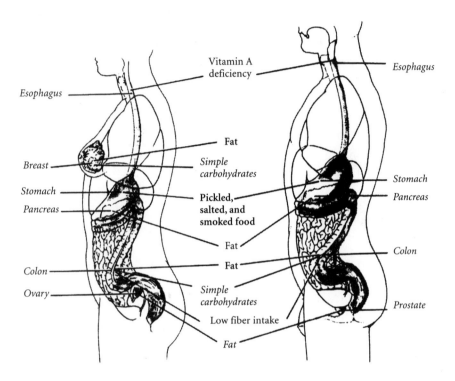

Poor nutrition habits

It is interesting to note that although most people acknowledge that good nutrition is important, their actions do not support their words. The United States pays a health bill of billions per year for illness related to poor nutrition, and it is sad to note that "junk" foods account for more than one-third of the average family's food budget.[51]

Experts agree that many chronic diseases are genetically determined, that is, heredity is important. However, it often takes a trigger for the disease to develop. That trigger in many cases is diet. Four of the ten leading causes of death in the United States—heart disease, certain types of cancer, stroke, and diabetes—are diseases in which diet plays a part.[52] Currently, there are ten poor nutrition habits especially prevalent in America.

Caffeine overload. Many people consume too much caffeine. It is present in much of what we eat and drink. Chocolate, colas, coffee, and tea contain the drug. In addition, caffeine is present in diet, cold, allergy, and headache medicines. By far, coffee and soft drinks are the biggest culprits in U.S. caffeine consumption. See Figure 22.9.

Figure 22.9 Common Sources of Caffeine

	serving size	mg* caffeine
Coffee		
brewed	6 fl. oz.	103
instant	1 rounded tsp.	57
decaffeinated	1 rounded tsp.	2
Tea, brewed 3 minutes	6 fl. oz.	36
Coca-Cola	12 fl. oz.	46
Coca-Cola, Diet	12 fl. oz.	46
Chocolate	1 oz.	12

*mg = milligram

On an individual level, the average U.S. adult consumes 205 gallons of coffee and 51.2 gallons of soft drinks each year. This average is high when you consider that many people do not drink these beverages at all. Thus, some people are doing a lot of extra drinking and may be overstimulated by caffeine.[53]

Drinking too much coffee can be stressful. More than ten cups of coffee (1,000 milligrams of caffeine) in a day can cause toxic symptoms—mild delirium, seeing flashes of light, irregular heartbeat, muscle tension, and rapid trembling. When people "overdose" on caffeine and see lights and hear strange noises, they should know that this is not an out-of-body experience. It may be a sign to cut back on caffeine intake.[54]

What is the solution? Consider cutting back the amount of caffeine consumed, perhaps by drinking decaffeinated beverages. Because caffeine is mildly addictive, you may experience headaches and feel tired or unable to concentrate for a while. These feelings are not uncommon, and they typically disappear. Remember Aristotle's advice: moderation, moderation, all things in moderation.

Too much sugar. One problem with too much sugar is that it promotes tooth decay. Also, while sugar accounts for more than 20 percent of average daily calories, it provides very little nutritional value. When you eat sweets in large quantities, they may take the place of foods that provide more vitamins, minerals, and protein. Also, some people experience the self-inflicted symptoms of hypoglycemia by eating too many sweets. They enjoy the taste of baked goods, ice creams, and candies, but they cannot afford that many calories in their diet. So they resort to going for long periods of time without eating anything at all, then consuming enormous amounts of sugar.[55]

The average American consumes an amount of junk food per year equal to: 300 containers of soda, 200 sticks of chewing gum, 100 pounds of refined sugar, 63 dozen doughnuts, 55 pounds of fats and oils, 50 pounds of cookies and cakes, 20 gallons of ice cream, 10 pounds of candy, and 5 pounds of potato chips.[56]

While our bodies need sugar to live, the best way to get it is from the complex carbohydrates found in vegetables and breads. The solution is to cut back and space out the amount of sweets you consume. Although one piece of pie per day may be fine, a whole pie may be inappropriate, unless you are a marathon runner or a lumberjack and burn off the calories consumed.

Excess salt. Although sodium chloride (salt) is necessary to sustain human life, too much salt can be harmful. Evidence correlates high sodium intake with elevated blood pressure. The average American consumes 3,000 to 6,000 milligrams of sodium a day, far more than the body needs and much higher than the 2,400 milligrams a day recommended by the National Heart, Lung and Blood Institute for a 2,000-calorie diet.[57]

Exactly how a person develops the habit of using too much salt varies, but the case of one retired banker is not unusual: During World War II, he was assigned to the South Pacific as a pilot. The climate was hot, and he wore a heavy flight suit, so he took salt supplements. In addition, he was encouraged to put extra salt on the food he ate. Gradually, he acquired a taste for salt. After the war, his wife, wanting to please him, cooked heavily salted food, as did many spouses. To compound the problem, food companies, wanting to sell their products, began adding salt to canned goods and condiments to satisfy customers. Over time, many American families acquired a preference for a high quantity of salt in their daily diet.

To prevent health problems caused by consuming too much salt, cut back on the quantity you use. Instead, try seasoning with herbs, spices, and fruit juices. Limit intake of salty snacks, condiments, and cured meats. Rinse canned foods like tuna and vegetables to remove salty juices, or use "No salt added" products. Finally, drop back to one or two shakes of the salt shaker instead of six, seven, or eight.

Empty-calorie foods. Many people run the risk of vitamin deficiency from consuming empty-calorie foods and having irregular mealtimes. Nothing can surpass naturally wholesome meals as a solution to this problem. As a safeguard, however, you may want to consider a daily vitamin supplement. Author and fitness expert Kenneth Cooper recommends a balanced diet including vitamins C, E, beta carotene for nonsmokers, vitamins B_{12} and B_6, and folic acid. In his 1997 book *Advanced Nutritional Therapies,* he describes his own regimen—eating five servings of fresh fruits and vegetables each day and several supplements: vitamin C, 500 milligrams twice a day; vitamine E, 400 IUs a day; beta carotene (for nonsmokers) 25,000 IUs a day; vitamin B_{12}, 500 micrograms; vitamin B_6, 50 milligrams; and folic acid, 400 to 800 micrograms. Ask your physician's advice regarding your need for a vitamin supplement. It should be noted that taking too many of some vitamins, such as fat-soluble vitamins A and D, can result in health problems. The principle of moderation applies here as well.[58]

Too much alcohol. Although two-thirds of adults drink alcohol, only 10 percent (those who drink most heavily) drink half of all alcohol consumed.[59] If you drink alcoholic beverages, do so in moderation. Moderation is no more than one drink a day for women, and no more than two drinks a day for men. Alcoholic beverages are high in calories and low in nutrients—12 oz. regular beer (150 calories), 5 oz. table wine (100 calories), 1.5 oz. 80-proof distilled spirits (100 calories). Heavy drinkers frequently develop nutritional deficiencies because of low food intake and poor absorption of nutrients by the body, as well as more serious diseases, including cirrhosis of the liver, inflammation of the pancreas, damage to the brain and heart, and increased risk for many cancers. Women who are pregnant or trying to conceive should refrain from all alcohol use.[60]

Insufficient fiber. Fiber used to be called "roughage" in our grandparents' day. A diet high in fiber fills you up without filling you out, helps lower cholesterol, and may help reduce risk of colon cancer. Nutritionists recommend 20 grams of fiber a day, which includes a diet with plenty of vegetables, fruits, and grain. Eating foods with complex carbohydrates (breads, cereals, pasta, etc.) adds fiber to the diet. Complex carbohydrates contain essential nutrients versus simple carbohydrates (sugar).[61]

Cholesterol. Cholesterol is a fatty substance found in our blood. It doesn't mix with blood and therefore must be transported by proteins. The combination of cholesterol and protein is referred to as a lipoprotein. The two major types of lipoproteins are low-density lipoprotein (LDL) and high-density lipoprotein (HDL). Total cholesterol is the combined amount of LDL and HDL cholesterol in the blood. Cholesterol is measured and reported as milligrams per deciliter of blood (mg/dl).

The American Heart Association identifies a total cholesterol level of less than 200 mg/dl as desirable. This level indicates that cholesterol does not represent a significant risk for developing cardiovascular disease. A cholesterol level of 200–239 mg/dl is considered borderline-high. Cholesterol at this level is considered to be a risk factor. A cholesterol level of 240 mg/dl and above is defined as high and represents a significant risk factor. Estimates are that 96 million American adults (52.1 percent) have blood cholesterol levels of 200 mg/dl and higher, and 37.8 million American adults (20.5 percent) have levels of 240 or above.

LDL is the major carrier of cholesterol in the blood. LDL is labeled as the "bad," or *lousy*, cholesterol because it can clog the arteries and is associated with an increased risk of heart disease. An LDL below 130 mg/dl is desirable; 130–160 mg/dl is borderline-high; and over 160 mg/dl is high-risk. The level of LDL can be reduced with a combination of low-fat diet and prescription drugs.

HDL is the "good," or *helpful*, cholesterol because this type of lipoprotein actually carries cholesterol from the blood to the liver, where it is passed from the body. Desirable levels of HDL are 40–50 mg/dl in men and 50–60 mg/dl in women. The higher the HDL, the lower the risk of heart attack. The level of HDL can be increased by exercise.

An important measure of cholesterol is the ratio of total blood cholesterol to HDL cholesterol (total/HDL). When we divide our total blood cholesterol by the HDL cholesterol, we have increased risk if the number is above 4.5. A value lower than 4.5 indicates that the levels of HDL are high enough to provide a protective effect that lowers the risk of developing heart disease.[62]

Researchers have identified a third type of cholesterol that should be considered in the cholesterol equation. Its scientific name is Lipoprotein (a), or Lp(a). High levels in the blood can significantly increase risk of heart disease. Although Lp(a) levels are believed to be primarily determined by heredity and there is no sure way to reduce high levels of it, new evidence suggests that aspirin, which thins the blood, may mitigate its effects. The combination of high Lp(a) and high LDL produces an especially high risk of premature heart disease, indicating an active program of low-fat diet and drug treatment.[63]

To lower cholesterol through diet, the Harvard Healthletter recommends increasing consumption of a range of foods rich in vitamin B_6, vitamin B_{12}, and folic acid, all of which work to convert the amino acid called homocysteine into a form the body can use. Excess levels of homocysteine damage the lining of arteries and allow the build up of cholesterol which can lead to patch blockages. Also, cut back on bacon, eggs, butter, cheese, and other high-fat dairy and meat products. These standard items of the American diet are our primary sources of saturated fat and cholesterol. They can raise the blood's cholesterol to excessive levels, and this promotes atherosclerosis, the most common form of heart disease.

Atherosclerosis involves the buildup of plaque along the inner walls of the arteries. Plaque is composed of fat, cholesterol, calcium, and cellular debris. Plaque deposits, compounded by a buildup of scar tissue in the arterial walls (fibrosis), eventually cause the vessel walls to become so hard and thick that blood moves with difficulty through the narrowed channels, and this can cause chest pain (angina) and a heart attack.

Although the exact process by which atherosclerosis occurs is not well understood, there is no doubt that without high levels of cholesterol in the blood, it just does not occur. In Japan, where smoking rates are higher than in the United States and where high blood-pressure levels are as frequent, there are only an eighth as many heart attacks. A striking difference between the two populations is their blood cholesterol levels. Studies of Japanese who migrated to Hawaii and California and adopted American eating habits showed that their cholesterol levels increased, as did their rates of heart attack.

In 1984 the National Heart, Lung and Blood Institute released a ten-year study on cholesterol showing that if you have a high blood cholesterol level, for every 1 percent you lower it, you lower your chance of having a heart attack by 2 percent.[64] The average American has a blood cholesterol of 210 to 220 mg/dl. According to the National Institutes of Health, adults over the age of thirty should have serum cholesterol counts under 200.[65]

If your cholesterol is high, it is important to reduce consumption of high-cholesterol foods and turn to grains, fruits, vegetables, and other natural low-fat sources of nutrition. A switch from a meat-based diet to a starch-based diet (rice and many vegetables) provides the same volume of food with one-fourth the calories. A helpful rule is to maintain a diet that contains less than 30 percent fat. Also, lower cholesterol through doing aerobic exercise, stopping smoking, maintaining a healthy weight, and drinking only in moderation.

Weight problems. Obesity is defined as being 20 percent over one's ideal body weight, considering age, height, and bone structure. By this standard, a U.S. government 1988-94 benchmark study of weight revealed 35 percent of adults (33 percent of men and 36 percent of women) in the United States were obese. *Mild obesity* refers to a body weight 20 to 40 percent above ideal weight; *moderate obesity*, 40 to 100 percent above ideal weight; and *severe obesity*, 100 percent or more above ideal weight.[66]

The dangers of obesity have been identified by the U.S. Surgeon General's *Health Report* and the National Research Council's *Diet and Health Report*. A panel of experts convened by the National Institutes of Health has developed a consensus statement regarding the health implications of obesity. The panel cited the strong association between obesity and high blood pressure, Type II diabetes, and high blood cholesterol levels. Obese women are more likely than normal-weight women to die from cancer of the uterus, breast, ovaries, and gallbladder. Obese men are more likely to die from cancer of the colon, prostate, and rectum. As a result of its effect on longevity and its high positive association with severe, chronic disease, obesity is regarded as a serious health problem.[67]

The good news is that obesity can be corrected. According to Shape Up America!, a health organization founded by former Surgeon General C. Everett Koop, even the first several pounds one loses can be important for reversing or delaying the onset of certain diseases. A ten-pound loss tends to lower blood pressure by about four points, and this amount can be significant. For high-tech help in losing weight, contact the Shape Up America! "Cyberkitchen" at www.shapeup.org. By entering your age, height, weight, normal activity level, and gender, you will be told changes to make in your diet and physical activity in order to lose one pound a week.

Figure 22.10 will help you determine your ideal weight. It also shows how many calories you can afford based on your activity level.

Figure 22.10 What Should You Weigh?

Adult women of average build can compute their ideal weight by multiplying their height in inches by 3.5 and then subtracting 105 from the product. Thus, an average build woman who is five feet four inches tall should weigh about 119 pounds (64 x 3.5 – 105 = 119). For men of average build, the formula is height in inches times four, minus 125. An average build five foot ten inch man should weigh about 155. If you have a large frame, add 10 pounds to the total; for a small frame, subtract 10 pounds.

It is reasonable to make allowances for bone structure and muscularity; even if Woody Allen and Rosie Grier were the same height, they should not weigh the same amount. But be careful that in making these allowances, you don't mistake fat for muscle. And remember that if you are 130 pounds overweight, it is unlikely that the difference is all in your bones.

Are you overeating or undereating?
You can use the following system for determining your calorie allowance. Begin by rating yourself on the scale below:

13	very inactive
14	slightly inactive
15	moderately active
16	relatively active
17	frequently, strenuously active

If you are an office worker or homemaker and you rarely exercise, you should rate yourself a 13. If your physical exercise consists of occasional games of golf or an afternoon walk, you are a 14. A score of 15 means that you exercise in moderation—jogging, calisthenics, tennis. A 16 means that you are almost always on the go, seldom sitting down or standing still for long. Do not give yourself a 17 unless you frequently engage in heavy labor and other strenuous exercise. Most adult Americans rate themselves 13 or 14.

To calculate the number of calories you need to maintain your ideal weight, multiply your activity rating by your ideal weight. A 200-pound office worker, for example, needs 2,600 calories a day, while a 200-pound athlete needs 3,400 calories.

To estimate how many calories you are getting now, multiply your current weight times your activity level. For example, if your weight is constant at 140 pounds and you are inactive, you are consuming about 1,820 calories a day (13 times 140).

Subtract the number of calories you need for your ideal weight from the number of calories you are consuming, and you will know the size of your energy imbalance.

Source: Adapted from Michael J. Mahoney and Kathryn Mahoney, "Fight Fat with Behavior Control," Psychology Today 9, no.12 (May 1976): 39–43, 92–94.

The most-used way to determine ideal weight ranges are the tables prepared by the insurance industry. Figure 22.11 is one example of such a table. These tables relate weight and height to how long policyholders lived, not to their health, vitality, or appearance.

Figure 22.11 Metropolitan Life Insurance Company Height and Weight Tables*

Height	Men Weight (lb)			Height	Women Weight (lb)		
	Small Frame	Medium Frame	Large Frame		Small Frame	Medium Frame	Large Frame
5'1"	123-129	126-136	133-145	4'9"	98-108	106-118	115-128
5'2"	125-131	128-138	135-148	4'10"	100-110	108-120	117-131
5'3"	127-133	130-140	137-151	4'11"	101-112	110-123	119-134
5'4"	129-135	132-143	139-155	5'0"	103-115	112-126	122-137
5'5"	131-137	134-146	141-159	5'1"	105-118	115-129	125-140
5'6"	133-140	137-149	144-163	5'2"	108-121	118-132	128-144
5'7"	135-143	140-152	147-167	5'3"	111-124	121-135	131-148
5'8"	137-146	143-155	150-171	5'4"	114-127	124-138	134-152
5'9"	139-149	146-158	153-175	5'5"	117-130	127-141	137-156
5'10"	141-152	149-161	156-179	5'6"	120-133	130-144	140-160
5'11"	144-155	152-165	159-183	5'7"	123-136	133-147	143-164
6'0"	147-159	155-169	163-187	5'8"	126-139	136-150	146-167
6'1"	150-163	159-173	167-192	5'9"	129-142	139-153	149-170
6'2"	153-167	162-177	171-197	5'10"	132-145	142-156	152-173
6'3"	157-171	166-182	176-202	5'11"	135-148	145-159	155-176

*Ranges show weights in pounds at ages 25–59 based on lowest mortality. The tables have been adjusted to represent weights without clothes and heights without shoes.

Source: Adapted from the 1983 Metropolitan Height and Weight Tables. Reprinted courtesy of the Metropolitan Life Insurance Company.

In 1990 the federal Departments of Agriculture and Health and Human Services issued a new edition of dietary guidelines. The healthy weights are somewhat more than the weights listed in the Metropolitan Life Insurance guidelines. In addition, weights for older persons are higher than for younger adults, because studies suggest that people can gain a little weight with age without added health risk.

So how can you tell if your weight is OK? First, find out whether you have a medical condition or a family history of conditions as diabetes and high blood pressure, which are better controlled at a lower weight. Second, determine how much fat is in the risky location around your middle. Stand up straight and measure the most narrow part of your upper body at about the level of your natural waist, not your navel. (Don't pull in your stomach and don't pull the measuring tape so tight that it compresses your skin.) Then measure the widest part of your hips and buttocks. (Don't pull the tape too tightly.) Divide the waist measure by the hip measure. For example, if your waist measurement is 35 and your hip measurement is 42, your waist-to-hip ratio is: 35 divided by 42 equals 0.83. In general, a man's waist measurement should not exceed his hip measurement (more than 1.0) and a woman's waist measurement should not be more than 80 percent of her hip measurement. See the waist-to-hip ratio chart in Figure 22.12 for interpretation.

Figure 22.12 Waist-to-Hip Ratio Chart

Risk Level	Men	Women
Low	Less than 0.85	Less than 0.75
Moderate	0.85 to 1.00	0.75 to 0.80
High	More than 1.00	More than 0.80

Source: The American Heart Association, "What's Your FQ?" in cooperation with the YMCA and YWCA.

The next step is to check your weight against the table in Figure 22.11. If you do not have a medical condition or family history of weight-related health problems, such as high blood pressure or diabetes, and if you are in the moderate- or low-risk level on the waist-to-hip ratio chart, you can be more relaxed about where you are in your weight range.

The location of fat is important. The body has two primary sites: one at the hips and one in the abdomen. Fat at the hips, which is more common in women and is more difficult to lose, is stored primarily for special purposes, like extra energy needs during pregnancy and nursing. You are described as having a pear-shaped figure if your fat is located primarily at the hips. Fat distributed in the abdomen, chest, nape of the neck, and lower back increases the risk for heart disease, stroke, Type II diabetes, and some forms of cancer. You are described as having an apple-shaped figure if your fat is concentrated around the middle.

Poor eating style. In addition to the type and amount of food you eat, your eating style can affect your physical and psychological health. Twenty-five years ago there was no official psychiatric diagnosis for behaviors that are now collectively called eating disorders. The most common are anorexia nervosa and bulimia.

Anorexia nervosa is primarily a disturbance not in appetite, but rather in a person's sense of self-identity and autonomy. The anorexic struggles desperately to control weight in order to combat an underlying sense of helplessness. People with anorexia nervosa have a distorted self-image; they think they are overweight, even when they have become emaciated. This condition can lead to starvation and even death.[68]

Individuals with bulimia go on repeated eating binges, followed by self-induced vomiting or laxative abuse. They rapidly consume large amounts of food, usually sweets, stopping only because of severe abdominal pain, sleep, or social circumstances. They then induce vomiting to relieve guilt and control their weight. In severe cases, bulimics may spend hours every day gorging themselves and vomiting. Like anorexia, bulimia primarily afflicts women in their teens and twenties and may continue intermittently over a period of years.[69]

The following eating habits are recommended for enjoying food and controlling weight:[70]

- Eat in the company of others.

- Eat slowly, never on the run (such as while driving).

- Take smaller portions.

- Wait five minutes before taking seconds.

- Choose foods you enjoy.

- Don't use food as your only reward or pleasure.

- Don't save the best for last; begin with your favorites.

- Do not clean your plate as a matter of duty.

- Eat only when you are hungry.

- Store food out of sight.

- Eat poached, broiled, or baked foods instead of fried foods.

- Eat several times each day, not just once.

Inappropriate dieting. Many people fall into a pattern of excessive weight gain and loss, and some go on diets that are hazardous to their health. The fact is, crash diets won't keep you thin and may even be harmful. Here are four reasons why:

1. The body quickly adapts to a lower food intake by lowering its metabolic rate and thus resists burning off fat.

2. The weight lost in the early part of a strict diet program is not fat, but mostly water.

3. If you consume less than 1,000 to 1,200 calories a day, you lose muscle tissue as well as fat.

4. Very-low-calorie diets don't teach you how to eat on a regular basis. Therefore, you eventually return to your "old" habits, which returns you to your "old" self.

The best way to get rid of fat is to moderately reduce caloric intake (no more than 500 calories below your normal requirements) and moderately increase physical activity, such as aerobic exercise three to five times a week.

A balanced diet that includes a wide variety of low-fat foods will ensure proper nutrition and will help establish new eating patterns. Exercise burns more calories and builds muscle tissue, ensuring that your muscle-to-fat ratio will improve.[71]

Good eating habits are important for effective stress management. You simply cannot exist on coffee, sugar, and irregular, low-nutrition meals without experiencing harmful effects. As you consider your own nutrition habits, do you see a need to improve? If the answer is yes, begin today to eat a variety of foods in proportion to your size and activity level and avoid caffeine overload, high cholesterol intake, too much sugar, excess salt, and empty-calorie foods.

Stress readiness plan

It is unlikely that you, as an individual, can significantly reduce the stress caused by modern society. Also, you may not be able to reduce the stress related to your job, marriage, or family right this minute. However, what you can do is develop as many defenses as possible to combat the negative effects of pressure, conflict, and frustration in your life and work. Thinking positive and healthful thoughts is one way. Getting regular physical exercise is another way. Getting enough sleep is another. Following good nutrition habits is a fourth way to give you the edge against the wear and tear of inevitable stress. Weekly, you should follow the 1 x 3 x 7 = 21 plan.

> **Personal case**
> In 1976 I moved from administration into full-time teaching. From a professional standpoint, I was moving from one assignment I enjoyed to another that I enjoyed. But from a personal standpoint, it proved to be a positive development, because it provided the opportunity to review the past, evaluate the present, and plan for the future, especially in the area of personal health.
>
> I realized that I had lapsed into habits and patterns that were taking their toll and would be destructive if they weren't changed. High blood pressure readings reinforced what I already knew when I looked in the mirror or huffed and puffed up the stairs—I needed to get my physical act together.
>
> Walking the track early in my "comeback," I thought of my schedule of family, work, meetings, etc., and I realized a weekly plan would work best. It would be effective and doable. That's when the 1 x 3 x 7 = 21 plan took form.— Author's file notes (G. M.)

What about you—will you follow through? You will if you want to; in other words, you will if you are motivated. And if you are motivated, you can change the habits of a lifetime. You can do the seemingly impossible, as the following story shows.

Graveyard story

There once was a young man visiting a cemetery. It became late in the day, and it started to rain, so he decided to leave. As he was walking toward the gate, he tripped over a headstone, and fell six feet into an open grave.

The young man clawed desperately at the sides of the grave. But the walls were steep, the rain was heavy, and it was dark, so he could not get out. Realizing he was trapped, he knelt in a corner, pulled his jacket over his head, and waited for the rain to subside.

After a while, the young man heard a noise at the other end of the grave. He looked out from under his jacket and saw that another man had fallen into the same open grave. He saw that he too was frightened and was frantically trying to climb the wall of the grave.

The first young man felt sorry for the second. He could understand his fear, and from his own experience, he knew there was no way out of the grave. So he decided to help.

Slowly, the young man stood up, walked over to the newcomer, reached out, and put his hand on his shoulder. He said, "You can't get out of here."

But he did! He got out of there . . . *because he was motivated.*

Personal Thoughts on Stress Prevention

Answer the following questions to personalize the content of Part Eight. Space is provided for writing your thoughts.

- Everyone has more than one age. Chronologically, how old are you (date on birth certificate)? Biologically, how old do you feel (based on vitality)? What forces and events have influenced your current level of vitality?

- In evaluating yourself, which elements of the 1 x 3 x 7 = 21 plan do you need to improve?

  a. Do you need to think more positive thoughts?

  b. Do you need to improve your physical fitness? (Strength? Endurance? Flexibility? Cardiovascular fitness? Body composition?)

  c. Do you need relaxation and better sleep habits?

  d. Do you need to improve your diet and nutrition?

Chapter Twenty-Two References

[1] *Heart and Stroke Facts* (Dallas, Tex.: American Heart Association, 1994); and Daniel A. Girdano and George S. Everly Jr., *Controlling Stress and Tension*, 2nd ed. (Englewood Cliffs, N.J.: Prentice-Hall, 1986), 37-42.

[2] Patrick Huyghe, "Your Heart: A Survival Guide," *Science Digest*, April 1985, pp. 31-35, 84; Robert S. Eliot, From *Stress to Strength: How to Lighten Your Load and Save Your Life* (New York: Bantam, 1994); and *Heart Attack and Stroke Facts: 1996 Statistical Supplement* (Dallas, Tex.: American Heart Association, 1996).

[3] Gary Hauser, National Stroke Foundation and the National Stroke Foundation, 1995; and *Heart Attack and Stroke Facts: 1996 Statistical Supplement*.

[4] U.S. Bureau of the Census, Table "Death by Age and Leading Cause: 1995," *Statistical Abstract of the United States: 1998, 118th ed.* (Washington, D.C., 1998); and Neil Wertheimer, *Total Health for Men* (Emmaus, Pa.: Rodale Press, 1995), 24-27.

[5] Herbert Basedow, *The Australian Aboriginal* (Adelaide, Australia: Preece and Sons, 1925).

[6] Dennis Coon, *Introduction to Psychology: Exploration and Application*, 2nd ed. (St. Paul, Minn.: West, 1980), 277; also C. Peterson and L. M. Bossio, *Health and Optimism: New Research on the Relationship between Positive Thinking and Physical Well-being* (New York: Free Press, 1991).

[7] Gordon W. Lippitt, *Quest for Dialogue* (Washington, D.C.: Development Publications, 1966), Z1.

[8] Wesley D. Smith, *The Hippocratic Tradition* (Ithaca, N.Y.: Cornell University Press, 1972).

[9] Plato, *Plato's Republic Book I*, commentary by Gilbert P. Rose (Bryn Mawr, Pa.: Bryn Mawr College, 1983); and Julia Annas, *An Introduction to Plato's Republic* (Oxford: Clarendon Press, 1981).

[10] William Osler, *The Principles and Practice of Medicine* (New York: Appleton, 1912).

[11] William James, *The Principles of Psychology* (New York: Henry Holt, 1890).

[12] Jerome D. Frank, *Psychotherapy and the Human Predicament* (New York: Schocken, 1978).

[13] Norman Cousins, *The Healing Heart: Antidotes to Panic and Helplessness* (New York: Norton, 1983).

[14] H. S. Friedman and S. Booth-Knewley, "The 'Disease Prone Personality': A Meta-Analytic View of the Construct," *American Psychologist* 42 (1987), in Ronald E. Smith, Psychology (Minneapolis/St. Paul: West, 1993): 539-55.

[15] Marvin Stein and Andrew H. Miller, "Stress, the Immune System, and Health and Illness," and Edward S. Katkin, Susan Dermit, and Susan F.K. Wine, "Psychophysiological Assessment of Stress," in Leo Goldberger and Shlomo Brenitz, eds., Handbook of Stress: *Theoretical and Clinical Aspects* (New York: Free Press, 1993), 127-41; 142-57.

[16] R. Ader, D. L. Felten, and H. Cohen, eds., *Psychoneuroimmunology*, 2nd ed. (San Diego: Academic Press, 1991); and R. Ader and S. B. Friedman, "Differential Early Experiences and Susceptibility to Transplanted Tumors in the Rat," *Journal of Comparative Physiology* 59 (1965): 361-64.

[17] Stein and Miller, "Stress, the Immune System, and Health and Illness," 127-41; and Katkin, Dermit, and Wine, "Psychophysiological Assessment of Stress," 142-57.

[18] Stein and Miller, "Stress, the Immune System, and Health and Illness," 127-41; and Katkin, Dermit, and Wine, "Psychophysiological Assessment of Stress," 142-57.

[19] M. Stein, S. J. Schleifer, and S. E. Keller, "Brain, Behavior and Immune Processes," in R. Michels and J. O. Cavenar Jr., eds., *Psychiatry*, vol. 2 (Philadelphia: Lippincott, 1985).

20 Stein, Schleifer, and Keller, "Brain, Behavior and Immune Processes"; and S. Zisook, R. A. Devand, and C. Lick, "Measuring Symptoms of Grief and Bereavement," *American Journal of Psychiatry* 139 (1982): 1590-93.

21 Bowers and Kelly, 1979.

22 Will Forpe and John McCollister, *The Sunshine Book: Expressions of Love, Hope and Inspiration* (Middle Village, N.Y.: Jonathan David Publishers, 1979), 95.

23 P. O. Astrand, *Health and Fitness* (Woodbury, N.Y.: Barron's Educational Series, 1977), 58; and Charles T. Kuntzleman, *Your Active Way to Weight Control* (Box 8644, Clinton, Iowa: 1980), 12-19.

24 Michael E. Gray, *What About Your Body's Fitness?* (Burlington, N.C.: Carolina Biological Supply Co., 1982), 10-11.

25 James M. Rippe, "Let's Get Moving/Start Walking," *Newsweek*, Feb. 27, 1995, p. 4.

26 U.S. Surgeon General's report, Physical Ac*tivity and Health*, 1996; *Heart Attack and Stroke Facts* (Dallas, Tex.: American Heart Association, 1996); John H. Postlethwait and Janet L. Hopson, *The Nature of Life*, 2nd ed. (New York: McGraw Hill, 1992), 452-53; Astrand, Health and Fitness, 17-30; *The Better Health Handbook* (Irvine, Calif.: Plus Products, 1979), 5-13; Kuntzleman, *Your Active Way to Weight Control*, 1-8; and Bud Getchell and Wayne Anderson, *Being Fit: A Personal Guide* (New York: John Wiley and Sons, Inc. 1982), 46-48.

27 Kenneth H. Cooper, *The New Aerobics* (New York: Evans and Co., 1970), 9-51; and Kenneth H. Cooper, *Dr. Kenneth H. Cooper's Antioxidant Revolution* (Nashville: Nelson, 1994).

28 Gray, "What About Your Body's Fitness?" Northern Kentucky University, 1992.

29 *Bethesda Hospitals: Stress Management* (St. Louis: Department of Health Promotion, St. Louis University Medical Center), 105.

30 Richard Restak, *The Brain* (New York: Bantam, 1984).

31 Peter Farb, *Humankind* (Boston: Houghton-Mifflin, 1974), 290-99; and Ronald E. Smith, *Psychology* (Minneapolis/St. Paul: West, 1993), 235-40.

32 Farb, *Humankind*, 290-99; Horace Winchell Magoun, *The Waking Brain*, 2nd ed. (Springfield, Ill.: Thomas Publisher, 1963); and Smith, *Psychology*, 235-40.

33 Smith, *Psychology*, 235-36.

34 Wertheimer, *Total Fitness for Men*, 308; and *Bethesda Hospitals: Stress Management*, 106.

35 Francis Yeats-Brown, *The Lives of a Bengal Lancer* (New York: Viking, 1931).

36 I. David Welsch, Donald C. Medirous, and George A. Tate, *Beyond Burnout* (Englewood Cliffs, N.J.: Prentice-Hall, Inc., 1982), 260-67.

37 Welsch, Medirous, and Tate, *Beyond Burnout*, 260-67.

38 Welsch, Medirous, and Tate, *Beyond Burnout*, 260-67.

39 George Mandler, "Thought, Memory, and Learning," in Goldberger and Brenitz, *Handbook of Stress*, 40-55; and Gordon Edlin and Eric Golantz, *Health and Wellness: Holistic Approach*, (Boston: Jones and Bartlett, 1992), 32-33, 35.

40 Godfrey Devereaux, *The Elements of Yoga* (Rockport, Mass.: Element, 1994).

41 Kenneth Kraft, *Zen, Tradition and Transition* (New York: Grove Press, 1988).

42 Maharishi Mahesh Yogi, *Science of Being and the Art of Living: Transcendental Meditation* (New York: Meridian, 1995).

43 Gil Steinberger, Cincinnati, Ohio, 1997. Reprinted with permission.

44 John M. Stoyva and John G. Carlson, "A Coping/Rest Model of Relaxation and Stress Management," in Goldberger and Brenitz, *Handbook of Stress*, 724-56.

45 Green and Shellenberger, *The Dynamics of Health and Wellness*, chs. 4 and 15; and Stoyva and Carlson, "A Coping/Rest Model of Relaxation and Stress Management," 734-38.

46 Edlin and Golantz, *Health and Wellness*, 568-69.

47 Kuntzelman, *Your Active Way to Weight Control*, 4-5; and *Building a Better Diet* (U.S. Department of Agriculture, Food and Nutrition Service, Program Aid no. 1241, September 1979).

48 *Dietary Guidelines for Americans* (Washington, D.C.: U.S Department of Agriculture and the U.S. Department of Health and Human Services, 1992).

49 *Building a Better Diet.*

50 Edlin and Golantz, *Health and Wellness*, 350-61.

51 *The Better Health Handbook*, 5-13.

52 T. M. Collins, *Comprehensive Health Care for Everyone: A Guide for Mind, Body, and Spirit* (Nevada City, Calif.: Blue Dolphin Publishing, 1995).

53 *Food Consumption Prices, and Expenditures—1997 Annual Data, 1970-1995*, Table no. 232, "Per Capita Consumption of Selected Beverages by Type: 1980-1995," U.S. Department of Agriculture, Economic Research Service, (Washington, D.C.)

54 Lowell Ponte, "All About Caffeine," *Reader's Digest* 123 (January 1983): 72-76.

55 *Fast Food and the Four Basic Food Groups* (Rosemont, Ill.: National Dairy Council, 1984); and Edward A. Charlesworth and Ronald G. Nathan, *Stress Management: A Comprehensive Guide to Wellness* (Houston: Biobehavioral Publishers and Distributors, Inc., 1982), 443-57.

56 Wertheimer, *Total Health for Men*, 15.

57 *The Good Health Fact Book* (Pleasantville, N.Y.: Reader's Digest, 1992); and Robert H. Garrison Jr. and Elizabeth Somer, *The Nutrition Desk Reference* (New Canaan, Conn.: Keats Publishing, 1995); and National Heart, Lung, and Blood Institute Information Center, P.O. Box 30105, Bethesda, MD 20824-0105, 1996.

58 *Fast Food and the Four Basic Food Groups*; Charlesworth and Nathan, *Stress Management*, 443-57; and *The Good Health Fact Book.*

59 National Institute on Alcohol Abuse and Alcoholism, *Sixth Special Report to U.S. Congress on Alcohol and Health* (Washington, D.C.: Department of Health and Human Services, 1987), 3.

60 *Dietary Guidelines for Americans: Alcohol and Your Health* (U.S. Department of Agriculture and U.S. Department of Health and Human Services, 1996); C. Baum-Baicker, "The Psychological Benefits of Moderate Alcohol Consumption: A Review of the Literature," *Drug and Alcohol Dependence* 15 (1985) 305-22; and R. D. Moore and T. A. Pearson, "Moderate Alcohol Consumption and Coronary Heart Disease: A Review," *Medicine* 65, no. 4 (1986): 242-67.

61 *The Good Health Fact Book.*

62 *Heart and Strokes Facts;* and *Heart Attack and Stroke Facts: 1996 Statistical Supplement*, (Dallas: American Heart Association, 1996).

63 Christine Gorman, "Bad News on Cholesterol," *Time*, September 2, 1996, p. 58.

64 National Heart, Lung and Blood Institute (1984).

65   *The Good Health Fact Book.*

66   Wertheimer, *Total Health for Men*, 393; and Collins, *Comprehensive Health Care for Everyone.*

67   U.S. Surgeon General, *Nutrition and Health* (Washington, D.C.: Department of Health and Human Services, 1988); and National Research Council, *Diet and Health.*

68   D. Blake Woodside, *A Review of Anorexia Nervosa and Bulimia Nervosa* (St. Louis: Mosby, 1995).

69   Woodside, *A Review of Anorexia Nervosa and Bulimia Nervosa.*

70   *The Good Health Fact Book.*

71   Wiley Piazza, "Wellness Notes," Northern Kentucky University, 1994.

Part Eight Reading

The Relaxation Response

The case for the use of the Relaxation Response by healthy but harassed individuals is straightforward. It can act as a built-in method of counteracting the stresses of everyday living which bring forth the fight-or-flight response. We have also shown how the Relaxation Response may be used as a new approach to aid in the treatment and perhaps prevention of diseases such as hypertension. In this chapter, we will review the components necessary to evoke the Relaxation Response and present a specific technique that we have developed at Harvard's Thorndike Memorial Laboratory and Boston's Beth Israel Hospital. We again emphasize that, for those who may suffer from any disease state, the potential therapeutic use of the Relaxation Response should be practiced only under the care and supervision of a physician.

How to bring forth the relaxation response

. . . we reviewed the Eastern and Western religious, cultic, and lay practices that led to the Relaxation Response. From those age-old techniques we have extracted four basis components necessary to bring forth that response:

(1) *A Quiet Environment*
Ideally, you should choose a quiet, calm environment with as few distractions as possible. A quiet room is suitable, as is a place of worship. The quiet environment contributes to the effectiveness of the repeated word or phrase by making it easier to eliminate distracting thoughts.

(2) *A Mental Device*
To shift the mind from logical, externally oriented thought, there should be a constant stimulus: a sound, word, or phrase repeated silently or aloud; or fixed gazing at an object. Since one of the major difficulties in the elicitation of the Relaxation Response is "mind wandering," the repetition of the word or phrase is a way to help break the train of distracting thoughts. Your eyes are usually closed if you are using a repeated sound or word; of course, your eyes are open if you are gazing. Attention to the normal rhythm of breathing is also useful and enhances the repetition of the sound or word.

(3) *A Passive Attitude*
When distracting thoughts occur, they are to be disregarded and attention redirected to the repetition or gazing; *you should not worry about*

Source: Herbert Benson, M.D., with Miriam Z. Klipper, The Relaxation Response, *ch. 7. Copyright © by William Morrow and Company, Inc. By permission of the publisher.*

how well you are performing the technique, because this may well prevent the Relaxation Response from occurring. Adopt a 'let it happen" attitude. *The passive attitude is perhaps the most important element in eliciting the Relaxation Response. Distracting thoughts will occur. Do not worry about them. When these thoughts do present themselves and you become aware of them, simply return to the repetition of the mental device. These other thoughts do not mean you are performing the technique incorrectly. They are to be expected.*

(4) A Comfortable Position
A comfortable posture is important so that there is no undue muscular tension. Some methods call for a sitting position. A few practices use the cross-legged "lotus" position of the Yogi. If you are lying down, there is a tendency to fall asleep. As we have noted previously, the various postures of kneeling, swaying, or sitting in a cross-legged position are believed to have evolved to prevent falling asleep. You should be comfortable and relaxed.

It is important to remember that there is not a single method that is unique in eliciting the Relaxation Response. For example, Transcendental Meditation is one of the many techniques that incorporate these components. However, we believe it is not necessary to use the specific method and specific *secret,* personal sound taught by Transcendental Meditation. *Tests at the Thorndike Memorial Laboratory by Harvard have shown that a similar technique used with any sound or phrase or mantra brings forth the same physiological changes noted during Transcendental Meditation:* decreased oxygen consumption; decreased carbon-dioxide elimination; decreased rate of breathing. In other words, using the basis necessary components, any one of the age-old or the newly derived techniques produces the same physiologic results regardless of the mental device used. The following set of instructions, used to elicit the Relaxation Response, was developed by our group at Harvard's Thorndike Memorial Laboratory and was found to produce the same physiologic changes we had observed during the practice of Transcendental Meditation. This technique is now being used to lower blood pressure in certain patients. A noncultic technique, it is drawn with little embellishment from the four basic components found in the myriad of historical methods. We claim no innovation but simply a scientific validation of age-old wisdom. The technique us our current method of eliciting the Relaxation Response in our continuing studies at the Beth Israel Hospital of Boston.

1) *Sit quietly in a comfortable position.*

2) *Close your eyes.*

3) *Deeply relax all your muscles, beginning at your feet and progressing up to your face. Keep them relaxed.*

4) *Breathe through your nose. Become aware of your breathing. As you breath out, say the word, "ONE," silently to yourself. For example, breathe IN . . . OUT, "ONE"; IN . . . OUT, "ONE"; etc. Breathe easily and naturally.*

5) Continue for 10 to 20 minutes. You may open your eyes to check the time, but do not use an alarm. When you finish, sit quietly for several minutes, at first with your eyes closed and later with your eyes opened. Do not stand up for a few minutes.

6) *Do not worry about whether you are successful in achieving a deep level of relaxation. Maintain a passive attitude and permit relaxation to occur at its own pace. When distracting thoughts occur, try to ignore them by not dwelling upon them and return to repeating "ONE." With practice, the response should come with little effort. Practice the technique once or twice daily, but not within two hours after any meal, since the digestive processes seem to interfere with the elicitation of the Relaxation Response.*

The subjective feelings that accompany the elicitation of the Relaxation Response vary among individuals. The majority of people feel a sense of calm and feel very relaxed. A small percentage of people immediately experience ecstatic feelings. Other descriptions that have been related to us involve feelings of pleasure, refreshment, and well-being. Still others have noted relatively little change on a subjective level. Regardless of the subjective feelings described by our subjects, we have found that the physiologic changes such as decreased oxygen consumption are taking place.

There is no education requirement or aptitude necessary to experience the Relaxation Response. Just as each of us experiences anger, contentment, and excitement, each has the capacity to experience the Relaxation Response. It is an innate response within us. Again, there are many ways in which people bring forth the Relaxation Response, and your own individual considerations may be applied to the four components involved. You may wish to use the technique we have presented but with a different mental device. You may use a syllable or phrase that may be easily repeated and sounds natural to you.

Another technique you may wish to use is a prayer from your religious tradition. Choose a prayer that incorporates the four elements necessary to bring forth the Relaxation Response. We believe every religion has such prayers. We would re-emphasize that we do not view religion in a mechanistic fashion simply because a religious prayer brings forth this desired physiologic response. Rather, we believe, as did William James, that these age-old prayers are one way to remedy an inner incompleteness and to reduce inner discord. Obviously, there are many other aspects to religious beliefs and practices which have little to do with the Relaxation Response. However, there is little reason not to make use of an appropriate prayer within the framework of your own beliefs if you are most comfortable with it.

Your individual considerations of a particular technique may place different emphasis upon the components necessary to elicit the Relaxation Response and also may incorporate various practices into the use of the technique. For example, for some a quiet environment with little distractions is crucial. However, others prefer to practice the Relaxation Response in subways or trains. Some people choose always to practice the Relaxation Response in the same place and at a regular time.

Since the daily use of the Relaxation Response necessitates a slight change in life-style, some find it difficult at first to keep track of the regularity with which they evoke the Response. In our investigations of the Relaxation Response, patients should use a calendar. Each time they practice the Relaxation Response, they make a check on the appropriate date.

It may be said, as an aside, that many people have told us that they use our technique for evoking the Relaxation Response while lying in bed to help them fall asleep. Some have even given up sleeping pills as a result. It should be noted, however, that when you fall asleep using the technique, you are not experiencing the Relaxation Response, you are asleep. As we have shown, the Relaxation Response is different from sleep.

Personal experiences with the relaxation response

Several illustrations of how people include the practice of the Relaxation Response in their daily lives should answer the question that you may now be posing: "How do I find the time?" One businessman evokes the Relaxation Response late in the morning for ten or fifteen minutes in his office. He tells his secretary that he's "in conference" and not to let in any calls. Traveling quite a bit, he often uses the Relaxation Response while on the airplane. A housewife practices the Relaxation Response after her husband and children have left for the day. In the late afternoon, before her husband comes homes, she again evokes the Response, telling her children not to disturb her for twenty minutes. Another woman, a researcher, usually awakes ten or twenty minutes earlier in the morning in order to elicit the Relaxation Response before breakfast. If she wakes up too late, she tries to take a "relaxation break" rather than a coffee break at work. She finds a quiet spot and a comfortable chair while her coworkers are out getting coffee. On the subway, a factory worker practices the Relaxation Response while commuting to and from work. He claims he has not yet missed his stop. A student uses the Relaxation Response between classes. Arriving fifteen minutes early, he uses the empty classroom and says he is not bothered by the other students entering the room. If the classroom is in use, he simply practices the response sitting in the corridor.

The regular use of the Relaxation Response has helped these people to be more effective in their day-to-day living. The business man feels he is "clearing the cobwebs" that have accumulated during the morning. He also states he often hears new perspectives on perplexing business problems. The housewife, before regularly eliciting the Relaxation Response, found it very difficult to face the prospects of preparing dinner and getting the family organized for another day. She now feels more energetic and enjoys her family more. The researcher no longer requires two cups of coffee in the morning to get started at work, and the factory worker notes he "unwinds" going home. The student says he is more attentive and hardly ever falls asleep during lectures. He even attributes better grades to his regular elicitation of the Relaxation Response.

The examples of when people practice the Relaxation Response are numerous. You must consider not only what times are practical but also when you feel the use of the Relaxation Response is most effective. We believe the regular use of the Relaxation response will help you better deal with the distressing aspects of modern life by lessening the effects of too much sympathetic nervous system activation. By this increase control of your bodily reactions, you should become more able to cope with your uncertainties and frustrations.

The following two descriptions of people who have regularly used the Relaxation Response for specific problems show how they feel the Relaxation Response has been of help to them. A young man, who suffered from severe anxiety attacks, reports that he often felt fearful, nervous and shaky, tense and worried. After practicing the Relaxation Response for two months, he rarely suffered from attacks of anxiety. He felt considerably more calm and relaxed. Usually, he practiced the technique regularly twice a day, but he would also practice it when he began to feel anxious. By applying the technique in such a manner he found he could alleviate these oncoming feelings. In short, he felt that the practice of the Relaxation Response had significantly improved his life.

Our second illustration is from a woman with moderate hypertension. She has a strong family history of high blood pressure, and the regular practice of the Relaxation Response has lowered her blood pressure. She has been practicing the technique using the word "ONE" for over fourteen months. Her own words best convey what the response has meant to her.

> The Relaxation Response has contributed to many changes in my life. Not only has it made me more relaxed physically and mentally, but also it has contributed to changes in my personality and way of life. I seem to have become calmer,

more open and receptive especially to ideas which either have been unknown to me or very different from my past way of life. I like the way I am becoming more patient, overcoming some fears especially around my physical health and stamina. I feel stronger physically and mentally. I take better care of myself. I am more committed to my daily exercise and see it as an integral part of my life. I really enjoy it, too! I drink less alcohol, take less medicine. The positive feedback which I experience as a result of the Relaxation Response and the lowered blood pressure reading make me feel I am attempting to transcend a family history replete with hypertensive heart disease.

I feel happier, content, and generally well when I use the Relaxation Response. There is a noticeable difference in attitude and energy during those occasional days in which I have had to miss the Relaxation Response.

Intellectually and spiritually, good things happen to me during the Relaxation Response. Sometimes I get insights into situations or problems which have been with me for a long time and about which I am not consciously thinking. Creative ideas come to me either during or as a direct result of Relaxation Response. I look forward to the Relaxation Response twice and sometimes three times a day. I am hooked on it and love my addiction.

We should also comment about the side effects of the Relaxation Response. Any technique used to evoke the Relaxation Response trains you to let go of meaningful thoughts when they present themselves and to return to the repetition of the sound, the prayer, the word "ONE," or the mantra. Traditional psychoanalytic practice, on the other hand, trains you to hold on to free-association thoughts as working tools to open up your subconscious. Thus, there is a conflict between the methods of the Relaxation Response and those used in psychoanalysis. Persons undergoing psychoanalysis may have a difficulty in disregarding distracting thoughts and assuming a passive attitude, and it may therefore be more difficult for them to elicit the Relaxation Response.

A basis teaching of many meditational organizations is that if a little meditation is good, a lot would be even better. This argument encourages followers to meditate for prolonged periods of time. From our personal observations, many people who meditate for several hours every day for weeks at a time tend to hallucinate. It is difficult, however, to draw a direct association between the Relaxation Response and this undesirable side effect because we do not know whether the people experiencing these side effects were predisposed to such problems to start with. For example, proponents of some meditative techniques evangelistically promise relief from all mental and physical suffering and tend to attract people who have emotional problems. There may be a preselection of people who come to learn these techniques because they already have emotional disturbances.

Furthermore, the excessive daily elicitation of the Relaxation Response for many weeks may lead to hallucinations as a result of sensory deprivation. *We have not noted any of the above side effects in people who bring forth the Relaxation Response once or twice daily for ten or twenty minutes a day.*

One should not use the Relaxation Response in an effort to shield oneself or withdraw from the pressures of the outside world which are necessary for everyday functioning. *The fight-or-flight response is often appropriate and should not be thought of as always harmful. It is a necessary part of out physiologic and psychological makeup, a useful reaction to many situations in our current world.* Modern society has forced us to evoke the fight-or-flight response repeatedly. We are not using it as we believe our ancestors used it. That is, we do not always run, nor do we fight when it is elicited. However, our body is being prepared for running or for fighting, and since this preparation is not always utilized, we believe anxieties, hypertension, and its related disease ensue. The Relaxation Response offers a natural balance to counteract the undesirable manifestations of the fight-or-flight response. We do not believe that you will become a passive and withdrawn person and less able to function and compete in our world because you regularly elicit the Relaxation Response. Rather, it has been out experience that people who regularly evoke the Relaxation Response claim they are more effective in dealing with situations that probably bring forth the fight-or-flight response. We believe you will be able to cope better with difficult situations by regularly allowing your body to achieve a more balanced state through the physiologic effects of the Relaxation Response. You can expect this balanced state to last a long as you regularly bring forth the response. Within several days after stopping its regular use, we believe, you will cease to benefit from its effects, *regardless* of the technique employed, be it prayer, Transcendental Meditation or the method proposed in this book.

Questions

1. Have there been times and circumstances in your life when you could use the relaxation response? Discuss.

2. Have your experiences physical, psychological, or behavioral signs of stress that could be relieved by the relaxation response? Discuss.

Conclusion

In searching for a metaphor for *Stress: Living and Working in a Changing World*, we decided upon the hourglass. We chose this symbol because each person has a certain amount of life to spend. How much we have, what we do with it, and how fast we spend it are underlying themes of this book. Henry David Thoreau once wrote, "The cost of a thing is the amount of what I call 'life' which is required to be exchanged for it, immediately or in the long run."

Review

When a book is finished, there has usually been so much material covered and time lapsed that a review can be helpful. John Dewey once wrote, "After the facts have been forgotten, what remains is education." The following is the *education*, or central Do's, Don'ts, and Points to Remember for each part of this book.

Part 1: Understanding Stress

Do	➡	know what stress is, its causes and effects
Don't	➡	deny the signs of stress, ignoring symptoms until the consequences are great
Remember	➡	one of life's developmental tasks is to manage stress effectively, constructively, and healthfully

Part 2: Personality and Stress

Do	➡	use wisdom of the ages as coping techniques for dealing with stress
Don't	➡	be a hot reactor, living life in a state of constant alarm and vigilance, leading to exhaustion and ultimate breakdown
Remember	➡	know what is important, prioritize your activities, accentuate the positive, keep things in perspective, and practice TLC in all of your relationships

Part 3: Stress Across the Life Span

Do	➡	know that life is a series of challenges that must be met for personal growth
Don't	➡	rest on past successes, or give up hope for the future, thinking things will never change
Remember	➡	every life is like a novel, each chapter being written in the ink of the moment

Part 4: Personal Stress

Do	➡	know yourself and be true to your values
Don't	➡	live an unexamined life, failing to fulfill your potential as a human being
Remember	➡	everyone needs a purpose in life, something important yet to be done

Part 5: Interpersonal Stress

Do	➡	show trust and respect in your relations with others
Don't	➡	take people for granted
Remember	➡	one has to give love to get love, and as you sow, so you reap

Part 6: Job Stress

Do	➡	make your work so satisfying that it is inseparable from your play
Don't	➡	ignore attitude problems in yourself or others
Remember	➡	do what you love and success will follow

Part 7: Peak Performance

Do	➡	become what you can be, or you will be doomed to be unhappy
Don't	➡	waste time; your time is your life
Remember	➡	attitude counts—as you think, so you feel; as you feel, so you do. Peak performance begins with a positive mental attitude

Part 8: Stress Prevention

Do	➡	think positive thoughts, stay physically fit, get enough rest, and eat healthfully
Don't	➡	use self-medication as a coping technique
Remember	➡	you may not be able to change the world right this minute or all by yourself, but you can be mentally and physically prepared to deal with stress—follow the 1 x 3 x 7 = 21 readiness plan

Challenge to change

People have to want to change or they never will; and they have to commit to change or they never do. The following Stress Management Contract can help you bridge the gap between theory and practice, between thought and action. Completed alone or with another person, it serves as both a motivation and tracking tool for applying the lessons of this book.

◎ Application: Stress Management Contract

The following is a contract to be self-written or developed with another person. It can be a useful tool to manage stress and cope with change. In the spaces provided, include the things you intend to do. Then, review this contract every week for at least one month to see how much progress you have made. You should make a new Stress Management Contract at least once every year.

Wisdom of the ages

Coping behaviors of the stress-resistant person include:

Follow the principle "moderation, all things in moderation." I will:

_____

_____

Set priorities, using the 80/20 rule. I will: _____

_____

_____

Don't try to be superhuman. I will: _____

_____

_____

Escape for a while. I will: _____

_____

_____

Use a decompression chamber technique. I will: _____

_____

_____

Talk with others. I will: _____

_____

_____

Go easy with criticism. I will: _____

_____

_____

Manage emotions. I will: _____

_____

_____

Enjoy the little things in life. I will: _____

_____

_____

Help another person. I will: _____

_____

_____

Handle hassles healthfully. I will: _____

_____

_____

Have a hobby. I will: _____

_____

_____

Accentuate the positive. I will: _____

_____

_____

Improve job proficiency. I will: _____

_____

_____

Keep a sense of humor. I will: _____

_____

_____

Trust in time. I will: _____

_____

_____

1 x 3 x 7 = 21 plan

A readiness plan to prepare for inevitable stress and cope with change includes:

1: Positive imagery. I will: _____

_____

_____

x 3 : Exercise. I will: _____

_____

_____

x 7: Relaxation. I will: _____

_____

_____

= 21: Nutrition. I will: _____

_____

_____

Healthy relationships

To increase positive relationships, I will: _____

_____

_____

Signature: _____

Partner: _____

Date: _____

Discussion

By practicing wisdom of the ages, following the 1 x 3 x 7 = 21 plan, and increasing the TLC you give and receive in your relations with others, you can prevent the burnout phenomenon—physical, psychological, and spiritual fatigue—both on the job and in the home. You can understand and deal successfully with stress and experience a dramatic increase in the length and quality of your life. In a word, the principles and techniques of stress management will help you succeed in your life and live to enjoy it.

Note from the authors

Our professional involvement with the subject of stress was triggered by three events: a lecture on "Executive Health and Stress" by Hans Selye in 1980; a demonstration grant on "Stress in Mass Transit" for the U.S. Department of Transportation in 1981; and a train-the-trainer project with AT&T in 1982, "Stress Coping Skills for Turbulent Times—Surviving the Break-up." These three activities showed us the importance of the subject and the good that can come from stress education.

In the years since, we have remained active in the field. Stress and change continue to interest us. We study and teach it on a regular basis. But as an old saying goes, sometimes there is a slip between the cup and the lip, and sometimes we fail our own course. Still, we try—we live, we learn, and we try our best to manage stress in our own changing lives.

We have found that the lessons in this book apply in our own lives as well. There is hardly a mistake we have not made or a bad habit we haven't been friends with sometime or another. So this book is for all of us. Perhaps you, as we, will revisit the pages and share it with others. A book, if it is read at the right time, can change the course of all that follows.

Selye's lessons

It is fitting to conclude a book on stress with the ideas of Hans Selye, who devoted his life to understanding and teaching this important subject. Selye recommends eight points that can change your life:

1. Regardless of how much you want to be loved, it is useless to try to befriend someone who continuously rejects you.

2. Face the fact that there is no such thing as perfection. Your highest goal is to be the best you can be.

3. Returning to a more simple lifestyle can add more pleasure to life than all the wealth and extravagance you've been struggling to obtain.

4. Before you waste a lot of energy trying to fight your way out of a situation, ask yourself, is it really worth fighting for?

5. Focus only on what is good in your life, forgetting anything painful or ugly.

6. When you face your most difficult hour, try to recall and dwell on a past success. A sense of frustration can totally immobilize you. You can avoid this by concentrating on even the slightest bright spot in your past.

7. Never try to detour from unpleasant tasks. Face them as soon as possible so that you can move on to more enjoyable things.

8. There are no pat answers or special formulas for success that will fit everyone. Choose from a wide variety of advice only those things that fit your own unique personality.[1]

The road ahead

If there is a central message in *Stress: Living and Working in a Changing World*, it is the prescription to *live life fully at good stress speed*. This motto to live by yields the greatest good for the greatest number over the longest period with the least regrets.

Living life fully implies a purpose or meaning in life, adherence to high values, and a dedication to people and ideals beyond oneself. *Good stress speed* implies spending one's resources at an optimal rate, neither too fast nor too slow.

We close this book with a wish and a charge: We wish you good speed, with the emphasis on *good*, and we charge you to remember—*Life is a marathon, not a sprint.*

Conclusion Reference

1 Charles T. Kuntzleman, *Maximizing Your Energy and Personal Productivity* (Chaska, Minn.: Nordic Press, 1992).

Appendix A—Estimated Average Length of Life in Years, by Race and Sex

Area and year	All races Both sexes	Male	Female	White Both sexes	Male	Female	All other Both sexes	Total Male	Female	Black Both sexes	Black Male	Female
U.S. Projections:												
2010	77.4	74.1	80.6	78.6	75.5	81.6	(NA)	(NA)	(NA)	70.4	65.1	75.5
2005	76.9	73.5	80.2	77.9	74.7	81.0	(NA)	(NA)	(NA)	69.9	64.5	75.0
2000	76.4	73.0	79.7	77.4	74.2	80.5	(NA)	(NA)	(NA)	69.7	64.6	74.7
U.S.[1]												
1996	76.1	73.0	79.0	79.8	73.8	79.6	(NA)	(NA)	(NA)	70.3	66.1	74.2
1995	75.8	78.9	76.5	76.5	73.4	79.6	71.9	67.9	75.7	69.6	65.2	73.9
1994	75.7	72.3	79.0	76.4	73.2	79.6	71.7	67.5	75.8	69.6	64.9	74.1
1993	75.5	72.2	78.8	76.3	73.1	79.5	71.5	67.3	75.5	69.2	64.6	73.7
1992	75.8	72.3	79.1	76.5	73.2	79.8	71.8	67.7	75.7	69.6	65.0	73.9
1991	75.5	72.0	78.9	76.3	72.9	79.6	71.5	67.3	75.5	69.3	64.6	73.8
1990	75.4	71.8	78.8	76.1	72.7	79.4	71.2	67.0	75.2	69.1	64.5	73.6
1989[2]	75.1	71.7	78.5	75.9	72.5	79.2	70.9	66.7	74.9	68.8	64.3	73.3
1988[2]	74.9	71.4	78.3	75.6	72.2	78.9	70.8	66.7	74.8	68.9	64.4	73.2
1987[2]	74.9	71.4	78.3	75.6	72.1	78.9	71.0	66.9	75.0	69.1	64.7	73.4
1986[2]	74.7	71.2	78.2	75.4	71.9	78.8	70.9	66.8	74.9	69.1	64.8	73.4
1985[2]	74.7	71.1	78.2	75.3	71.8	78.7	71.0	67.0	74.8	69.3	65.0	73.4
1984[2]	74.7	71.1	78.2	75.3	71.8	78.7	71.1	67.2	74.9	69.5	65.3	73.6
1983[2]	74.6	71.0	78.1	75.2	71.6	78.7	70.9	67.0	74.7	69.4	65.2	73.5
1982[2]	74.5	70.8	78.1	75.1	71.5	78.7	70.9	66.8	74.9	69.4	65.1	73.6
1981[2]	74.1	70.4	77.8	74.8	71.1	78.4	70.3	66.2	74.4	68.9	64.5	73.2
1980	73.7	70.0	77.4	74.4	70.7	78.1	69.5	65.3	73.6	68.1	63.8	72.5
1979	73.9	70.0	77.8	74.6	70.8	78.4	69.8	65.4	74.1	68.5	64.0	72.9
1978	73.5	69.6	77.3	74.1	70.4	78.0	69.3	65.0	73.5	68.1	63.7	72.4
1977	73.3	69.5	77.2	74.0	70.2	77.9	68.9	64.7	73.2	67.7	63.4	72.0
1976	72.9	69.1	76.8	73.6	69.9	77.5	68.4	64.2	72.7	67.2	62.9	71.6
1975	72.6	68.8	76.6	73.4	69.5	77.3	68.0	63.7	72.4	66.8	62.4	71.3
1974	72.0	68.2	75.9	72.8	69.0	76.7	67.1	62.9	71.3	66.0	61.7	70.3
1973	71.4	67.6	75.3	72.2	68.5	76.1	66.1	62.0	70.3	65.0	60.9	69.3
1972[3]	71.2	67.4	75.1	72.0	68.3	75.9	65.7	61.5	70.1	64.7	60.4	69.1
1971	71.1	67.4	75.0	72.0	68.3	75.8	65.6	61.6	69.8	64.6	60.5	68.9
1970	70.8	67.1	74.7	71.7	68.0	75.6	65.3	61.3	69.4	64.1	60.0	68.3
1969	70.5	66.8	74.4	71.4	67.7	75.3	64.5	60.6	68.6	—	—	—
1968	70.2	66.6	74.1	71.1	67.5	75.0	64.1	60.4	67.9	—	—	—
1967	70.5	67.0	74.3	71.4	67.8	75.2	64.9	61.4	68.5	—	—	—
1966	70.2	66.7	73.9	71.1	67.5	74.8	64.2	60.9	67.6	—	—	—
1965	70.2	66.8	73.8	71.1	67.6	74.8	64.3	61.2	67.6	—	—	—
1964	70.2	66.8	73.7	71.0	67.7	74.7	64.2	61.3	67.3	—	—	—
1963[4]	69.9	66.6	73.4	70.8	67.4	74.4	63.7	61.0	66.6	—	—	—
1962[4]	70.1	66.9	73.5	70.9	67.7	74.5	64.2	61.6	66.9	—	—	—
1961	70.2	67.1	73.6	71.0	67.8	74.6	64.5	62.0	67.1	—	—	—
1960	69.7	66.6	73.1	70.6	67.4	74.1	63.6	61.1	66.3	—	—	—
1959	69.9	66.8	73.2	70.7	67.5	74.2	63.9	61.3	66.5	—	—	—
1958	69.6	66.6	72.9	70.5	67.4	73.9	63.4	61.0	65.8	—	—	—
1957	69.5	66.4	72.7	70.3	67.2	73.7	63.0	60.7	65.5	—	—	—
1956	69.7	66.7	72.9	70.5	67.5	73.9	63.6	61.3	66.1	—	—	—
1955	69.6	66.7	72.8	70.5	67.4	73.7	63.7	61.4	66.1	—	—	—
1954	69.6	66.7	72.8	70.5	67.5	73.7	63.4	61.1	65.9	—	—	—
1953	68.8	66.0	72.0	69.7	66.8	73.0	62.0	59.7	64.5	—	—	—
1952	68.6	65.8	71.6	69.5	66.6	72.6	61.4	59.1	63.8	—	—	—
1951	68.4	65.6	71.4	69.3	66.5	72.4	61.2	59.2	63.4	—	—	—
1950	68.2	65.6	71.1	69.1	66.5	72.2	60.8	59.1	62.9	—	—	—
1949	68.0	65.2	70.7	68.8	66.2	71.9	60.6	58.9	62.7	—	—	—
1948	67.2	64.6	69.9	68.0	65.5	71.0	60.0	58.1	62.5	—	—	—
1947	66.8	64.4	69.7	67.6	65.2	70.5	59.7	57.9	61.9	—	—	—
1946	66.7	64.4	69.4	67.5	65.1	70.3	59.1	57.5	61.0	—	—	—
1945	65.9	63.6	67.9	66.8	64.4	69.5	57.7	56.1	59.6	—	—	—
1944	65.2	63.6	66.8	66.2	64.5	68.4	56.6	55.8	57.7	—	—	—
1943	63.3	62.4	64.4	64.2	63.2	65.7	55.6	55.4	56.1	—	—	—
1942	66.2	64.7	67.9	67.3	65.9	69.4	56.6	55.4	58.2	—	—	—

Appendix A—Estimated Average Length of Life in Years, by Race and Sex (continued)

Area and year	All races			White			All other					
								Total			Black	
	Both sexes	Male	Femlae	Both sexes	Male	Female	Both sexes	Male	Female	Both sexes	Male	Female
1941	64.8	63.1	66.8	66.2	64.4	68.5	53.8	52.5	55.3	—	—	—
1940	62.9	60.8	65.2	64.2	62.1	66.6	53.1	51.5	54.9	—	—	—
1939	63.7	62.1	65.4	64.9	63.3	66.6	54.5	53.2	56.0	—	—	—
1938	63.5	61.9	65.3	65.0	63.2	66.8	52.9	51.7	54.3	—	—	—
1937	60.0	58.0	62.4	61.4	59.3	63.8	50.3	48.3	52.5	—	—	—
1936	58.5	56.6	60.6	59.8	58.0	61.9	49.0	47.0	51.4	—	—	—
1935	61.7	59.9	63.9	62.9	61.0	65.0	53.1	51.3	55.2	—	—	—
1934	61.1	59.3	63.3	62.4	60.5	64.6	51.8	50.2	53.7	—	—	—
1933	63.3	61.7	65.1	64.3	62.7	66.3	54.7	53.5	56.0	—	—	—
1932	62.1	61.0	63.5	63.2	62.0	64.5	53.7	52.8	54.6	—	—	—
1931	61.1	59.4	63.1	62.6	60.8	64.7	50.4	49.5	51.5	—	—	—
1930	59.7	58.1	61.6	61.4	59.7	63.5	48.1	47.3	49.2	—	—	—
1929	57.1	55.8	58.7	58.6	57.2	60.3	46.7	45.7	47.8	—	—	—
Death-registration states												
1928	56.8	55.6	58.3	58.4	57.0	60.0	46.3	45.6	47.0	—	—	—
1927	60.4	59.0	62.1	62.0	60.5	63.9	48.2	47.6	48.9	—	—	—
1926	56.7	55.5	58.0	58.2	57.0	59.6	44.6	43.7	45.6	—	—	—
1925	59.0	57.6	60.6	60.7	59.3	62.4	45.7	44.9	46.7	—	—	—
1924	59.7	58.1	61.5	61.4	59.8	63.4	46.6	45.5	47.8	—	—	—
1923	57.2	56.1	58.5	58.3	57.1	59.6	48.3	47.7	48.9	—	—	—
1922	59.6	58.4	61.0	60.4	59.1	61.9	52.4	51.8	53.0	—	—	—
1921	60.8	60.0	61.8	61.8	60.8	62.9	51.5	51.6	51.3	—	—	—
1920	54.1	53.6	54.6	54.9	54.4	55.6	45.3	45.5	45.2	—	—	—
1919	54.7	53.5	56.0	55.8	54.5	57.4	44.5	44.5	44.4	—	—	—
1918	39.1	36.6	42.2	39.8	37.1	43.2	31.1	29.9	32.5	—	—	—
1917	50.9	48.4	54.0	52.0	49.3	55.3	38.8	37.0	40.8	—	—	—
1916	51.7	49.6	54.3	52.5	50.2	55.2	41.3	39.6	43.1	—	—	—
1915	54.5	52.5	56.8	55.1	53.1	57.5	38.9	37.5	40.5	—	—	—
1914	54.2	52.0	56.8	54.9	52.7	57.5	38.9	37.1	40.8	—	—	—
1913	52.5	50.3	55.0	53.0	50.8	55.7	38.4	36.7	40.3	—	—	—
1912	53.5	51.5	55.9	53.9	51.9	56.2	37.9	35.9	40.0	—	—	—
1911	52.6	50.9	54.4	53.0	51.3	54.9	36.4	34.6	38.2	—	—	—
1910	50.0	48.4	51.8	50.3	48.6	52.0	35.6	33.8	37.5	—	—	—
1909	52.1	50.5	53.8	52.5	50.9	54.2	35.7	34.2	37.3	—	—	—
1908	51.1	49.5	52.8	51.5	49.9	53.3	34.9	33.8	36.0	—	—	—
1907	47.6	45.6	49.9	48.1	46.0	50.4	32.5	31.1	34.0	—	—	—
1906	48.7	46.9	50.8	49.3	47.3	51.4	32.9	31.8	33.9	—	—	—
1905	48.7	47.3	50.2	49.1	47.6	50.6	31.3	29.6	33.1	—	—	—
1904	47.6	46.2	49.1	48.0	46.6	49.5	30.8	29.1	32.7	—	—	—
1903	50.5	49.1	52.0	50.9	49.5	52.5	33.1	31.7	34.6	—	—	—
1902	51.5	49.8	53.4	51.9	50.2	53.8	34.6	32.9	36.4	—	—	—
1901	49.1	47.6	50.6	49.4	48.0	51.0	33.7	32.2	35.3	—	—	—
1900	47.3	46.3	48.3	47.6	46.6	48.7	33.0	32.5	33.5	—	—	—

[1] Alaska included in 1959 and Hawaii in 1960.
[2] Life table values are revised and, therefore,may differ from those published in "Vital Statistics of the United States", Vol. II, Mortality, Part A for 1989 and earlier years; see Technical Appendix.
[3] Deaths based on a 50-percent sample
[4] Figures by race exclude data for residents of New Jersey; see Technical Appendix

Center for Health Statistics, U.S. Life Tables and Actuarial Tables, 1959–61, 1979–71, and 1979–81; Vital Statistics of the United States, annual, 1998 , 118th ed., and unpublished data. (Washington, D.C.: 1998).

Appendix B—Life Expectancy Tables

Table B.1: Life Expectancy at Birth, at 65 Years of Age, and at 75 Years of Age, according to Race and Sex: United States, Selected Years 1900–95

Specified age and year	All races Both sexes	Male	Female	White Both sexes	Male	Female	Black Both sexes	Male	Female
At birth									
1900 [1,2]	47.3	46.3	48.3	47.6	46.6	48.7	[3]33.0	[3]32.5	[3]33.5
1950 [2]	68.2	65.6	71.1	69.1	66.5	72.2	60.7	58.9	62.7
1960 [2]	69.7	66.6	73.1	70.6	67.4	74.1	63.2	60.7	65.9
1970	70.8	67.1	74.7	71.7	68.0	75.6	64.1	60.0	68.3
1980	73.7	70.0	77.4	74.4	70.7	78.1	68.1	63.8	72.5
1984	74.7	71.1	78.2	75.3	71.8	78.7	69.5	65.3	73.6
1985	74.7	71.1	78.2	75.3	71.8	78.7	69.3	65.0	73.4
1986	74.7	71.2	78.2	75.4	71.9	78.8	69.1	64.8	73.4
1987	74.9	71.4	78.3	75.6	72.1	78.9	69.1	64.7	73.4
1988	74.9	71.4	78.3	75.6	72.2	78.9	68.9	64.4	73.2
1989	75.1	71.7	78.5	75.9	72.5	79.2	68.8	64.3	73.3
1990	75.4	71.8	78.8	76.1	72.7	79.4	69.1	64.5	73.6
1991	75.5	72.0	78.9	76.3	72.9	79.6	69.3	64.6	73.8
1992	75.8	72.3	79.1	76.5	73.2	79.8	69.6	65.0	73.9
1993	75.5	72.2	78.8	76.3	73.1	79.5	69.2	64.6	73.7
1994	75.7	72.3	79.0	76.4	73.3	79.6	69.6	64.9	73.9
1995	75.8	72.5	78.9	76.5	73.4	79.6	69.6	65.2	73.9
1996	76.1	73.0	79.0	76.8	73.8	79.6	70.3	66.1	74.2
Projection: 2000	76.4	73.0	79.7	77.4	74.2	80.5	69.7	64.6	74.7
At 65 years									
1900-1902 [1,2]	11.9	11.5	12.2	—	11.5	12.2	—	10.4	11.4
1950 [2]	13.9	12.8	15.0	—	12.8	15.1	13.9	12.9	14.9
1960 [2]	14.3	12.8	15.8	14.4	12.9	15.9	13.9	12.7	15.1
1970	15.2	13.1	17.0	15.2	13.1	17.1	14.2	12.5	15.7
1980	16.4	14.1	18.3	16.5	14.2	18.4	15.1	13.0	16.8
1984	16.8	14.5	18.6	16.8	14.6	18.7	15.4	13.2	17.2
1985	16.7	14.5	18.5	16.8	14.5	18.7	15.2	13.0	16.9
1986	16.8	14.6	18.6	16.9	14.7	18.7	15.2	13.0	17.0
1987	16.9	14.7	18.7	17.0	14.8	18.8	15.2	13.0	17.0
1988	16.9	14.7	18.6	17.0	14.8	18.7	15.1	12.9	16.9
1989	17.1	15.0	18.8	17.2	15.1	18.9	15.2	13.0	16.9
1990	17.2	15.1	18.9	17.3	15.2	19.1	15.4	13.2	17.2
1991	17.4	15.3	19.1	17.5	15.4	19.2	15.5	13.4	17.2
1992	17.5	15.4	19.2	17.6	15.5	19.3	15.7	13.5	17.4
1993	17.3	15.3	18.9	17.4	15.4	19.0	15.5	13.4	17.1
1994	17.4	15.5	18.9	—	—	—	—	—	—
At 75 years									
1980	10.4	8.8	11.5	10.4	8.8	11.5	9.7	8.3	10.7
1984	10.7	9.0	11.8	10.7	9.0	11.8	10.3	8.9	11.4
1985	10.6	9.0	11.7	10.6	9.0	11.7	10.1	8.7	11.1
1986	10.7	9.1	11.7	10.7	9.1	11.8	10.1	8.6	11.1
1987	10.7	9.1	11.8	10.7	9.1	11.8	10.1	8.6	11.1
1988	10.6	9.1	11.7	10.7	9.1	11.7	10.0	8.5	11.0
1989	10.9	9.3	11.9	10.9	9.3	11.9	10.1	8.6	11.0
1990	10.9	9.4	12.0	11.0	9.4	12.0	10.2	8.6	11.2
1991	11.1	9.5	12.1	11.1	9.5	12.1	10.2	8.7	11.2
1992	11.2	9.6	12.2	11.2	9.6	12.2	10.4	8.9	11.4
1993	10.9	9.5	11.9	11.0	9.5	12.0	10.2	8.7	11.1
1994	11.0	9.6	11.9	—	—	—	—	—	—

[1] Death registration area only. The death registration area increased from 10 States and the District of Columbia in 1900 to the coterminous United States in 1933.

[2] Includes deaths of persons who were not residents of the 50 States and the District of Columbia.

[3] Figure is for the all other population.

NOTES: Final data for the 1980's are based on intercensal population estimates. Provisional data for 1993-94 were calculated using 1990's-based postcensal population estimates. See Appendix I, National Center for Health Statistics and Department of Commerce.

SOURCES: U.S. Bureau of the Census: U.S. Life Tables 1890, 1901, 1910, and 1901-1910, by Glover JW. Washington. U.S. Goverment Printing Office, 1921; Centers for Disease Control and Prevention, National Center for Health Statistics: Vital Statistics Rates in the United States, 1940-1960, by Grove RD and Hetzel AM. DHEW Pub. No. (PHS) 1677, Public Health Service. Washington. U.S. Government Printing Office, 1968. Gardner P and Hudson BL. Advance report of final mortality statistics, 1993. Monthly vital statistics report; vol 44 no 7, suppl. Hyattsville, Maryland. 1996; Annual summary of births, marriages, divorces, and deaths: United States, 1993 and 1994. Monthly vital statistics report; vols 42 and 43 no 13. Hyattsville, Maryland: Public Health Service. 1994 and 1995; Unpublished data from the Division of Vital Statistics; Data for 1960 and earlier years for the black population were computed by the Office of Research and Methodology from data compiled by the Division of Vital Statistics.

Appendix B (continued)

Table B.2: Expectation of Life at Selected Ages by Race and Sex:
Death-registration States, 1900–02, and United States, 1959–61, 1979–81, 1990, 1991, and 1994

		White		All other Total		Black	
Specified age and year	Total	Male	Female	Male	Female	Male	Female
At birth:							
Projection: 2000	76.4	73.0	79.7	77.6	74.2	80.5	69.7 74.7
1994	75.7	73.3	79.6	(NA)	(NA)	64.9	73.9
1991	75.5	72.9	79.6	67.3	75.5	64.6	73.8
1990	75.4	72.7	79.4	67.0	75.2	64.5	73.6
1979-81	73.88	70.82	78.22	65.63	74.00	64.10	73.88
1969-71	70.75	67.94	75.49	60.98	69.05	69.00	68.32
1959-61	69.89	67.55	74.19	61.48	66.47	—	—
1900-1902	49.24	48.23	51.08	—	—	32.54	35.04
At age 1 year:							
1994	75.3	72.8	79.1	(NA)	(NA)	65.1	73.9
1991	75.2	72.5	79.1	67.4	75.5	64.9	73.9
1990	75.1	72.3	78.9	67.2	75.3	65.8	73.8
1979-81	73.82	70.70	77.98	66.01	74.31	64.60	73.31
1969-71	71.19	68.33	75.66	62.13	70.01	61.24	69.37
1959-61	70.75	68.34	74.68	63.50	68.10	—	—
1900-1902	55.20	54.61	56.39	—	—	42.46	43.54
At age 20 years:							
1994	56.8	54.4	60.4	(NA)	(NA)	47.1	55.5
1991	56.8	54.1	60.4	49.3	57.0	46.9	55.4
1990	56.6	54.0	60.3	49.0	56.8	46.7	55.3
1979-81	55.46	52.45	59.44	47.87	55.88	46.48	54.90
1969-71	53.00	50.22	57.24	44.37	51.85	43.49	51.22
1959-61	52.58	50.25	56.29	45.78	50.07	—	—
1900-1902	42.79	42.19	43.77	—	—	35.11	36.89
At age 65 years:							
1994	17.4	15.6	19.1	(NA)	(NA)	13.6	17.2
1991	17.4	15.4	19.2	14.3	17.9	13.4	17.2
1990	17.2	15.2	19.1	14.0	17.8	13.2	17.2
1979-81	16.51	14.26	18.55	13.83	17.60	13.29	17.13
1969-71	15.00	13.02	16.93	12.87	15.99	12.53	15.67
1959-61	14.39	12.97	15.88	12.84	15.12	—	—
1900-1902	11.86	11.51	12.23	—	—	10.38	11.38

Center for Health Statistics, U.S. Life Tables and Actuarial Tables, 1959–61, 1979–71, and 1979–81; Vital Statistics of the United States, annual, 1998 , 118th ed., *and unpublished data. (Washington, D.C.: 1998).*

Appendix C
Expectation of Life and Expected Deaths, by Race, Sex, and Age: 1994

Age/1990	Expectation of life in years					Expected deaths per 1,000 alive at specified age[1]				
		White		Black			White		Black	
(years)	Total	Male	Female	Male	Female	Total	Male	Female	Male	Female
At birth	75.8	73.4	79.6	65.2	73.9	7.57	6.98	5.55	16.22	13.74
1	75.4	72.9	79.0	65.3	73.9	0.58	0.57	0.44	1.10	0.82
2	74.4	72.0	78.1	64.3	73.0	0.43	0.41	0.33	0.79	0.66
3	73.4	71.0	77.1	63.4	72.0	0.33	0.31	0.26	0.60	0.53
4	72.5	70.0	76.1	62.4	71.0	0.27	0.26	0.21	0.49	0.42
5	71.5	69.1	75.1	61.5	70.1	0.23	0.23	0.18	0.43	0.34
6	70.5	68.1	74.1	60.5	69.1	0.21	0.22	0.16	0.40	0.28
7	69.5	67.1	73.1	59.5	68.1	0.20	0.21	0.15	0.36	0.24
8	68.5	66.1	72.2	58.5	67.1	0.18	0.19	0.14	0.31	0.21
9	67.5	65.1	71.2	57.5	66.1	0.16	0.17	0.13	0.25	0.21
10	66.6	64.1	70.2	56.6	65.2	0.15	0.15	0.12	0.20	0.21
11	65.6	63.1	69.2	55.6	64.2	0.16	0.16	0.13	0.20	0.23
12	64.6	62.1	68.2	54.6	63.2	0.21	0.22	0.16	0.32	0.26
13	63.6	61.2	67.2	53.6	62.2	0.31	0.35	0.21	0.59	0.31
14	62.6	60.2	66.2	52.6	61.2	0.45	0.54	0.28	0.95	0.38
15	61.6	59.2	65.2	51.7	60.2	0.61	0.74	0.35	1.37	0.43
16	60.7	58.3	64.4	50.8	59.3	0.75	0.94	0.42	1.77	0.50
17	59.7	57.3	63.3	49.5	58.3	0.87	1.09	0.47	2.11	0.57
18	58.8	56.4	62.3	48.9	57.3	0.94	1.20	0.48	2.36	0.62
19	57.8	55.4	61.3	48.0	56.4	0.96	1.26	0.47	2.54	0.67
20	56.9	54.5	60.4	47.2	55.4	1.01	1.32	0.45	2.72	0.72
21	55.9	53.6	59.4	46.3	54.4	1.05	1.38	0.44	2.91	0.77
22	55.0	52.7	58.4	45.4	53.5	1.06	1.42	0.43	3.07	0.84
23	54.1	51.7	57.4	44.6	52.8	1.10	1.43	0.44	3.17	0.92
24	53.1	50.8	58.5	43.7	51.6	1.11	1.43	0.46	3.25	1.02
25	52.2	49.9	55.5	42.9	50.6	1.12	1.42	0.48	3.30	1.12
26	51.2	48.9	54.5	42.0	49.7	1.13	1.41	0.50	3.37	1.23
27	50.3	48.0	53.6	41.1	48.7	1.17	1.44	0.53	3.49	1.34
28	49.3	47.1	52.6	40.3	47.8	1.23	1.53	0.56	3.69	1.45
29	48.4	46.2	51.6	39.4	46.9	1.32	1.65	0.60	3.94	1.57
30	47.5	45.0	50.6	38.0	46.0	1.42	1.79	0.64	4.21	1.70
31	46.5	44.3	49.7	37.7	45.0	1.51	1.92	0.68	4.49	1.70
32	45.6	43.4	48.7	36.9	44.1	1.61	2.04	0.73	4.76	1.97
33	44.7	42.5	47.7	36.1	43.2	1.70	2.14	0.79	5.02	2.12
34	43.8	41.8	46.8	35.3	42.8	1.79	2.23	0.85	5.28	2.27
35	42.8	40.7	45.8	34.5	41.4	1.89	2.32	0.92	5.55	2.43
36	41.9	39.8	44.9	33.6	40.5	1.99	2.42	0.99	5.84	2.60
37	41.0	38.8	43.9	32.8	39.6	2.10	2.53	1.06	6.19	2.78
38	40.1	37.9	42.9	32.0	38.7	2.22	2.66	1.13	6.56	2.97
39	39.2	37.0	42.0	31.2	37.8	2.34	2.79	1.20	6.99	3.18
40	38.3	36.1	41.0	30.5	36.9	2.47	2.94	1.28	7.45	3.40
41	37.3	35.3	40.1	29.7	36.1	2.62	3.10	1.37	7.92	3.63
42	36.4	34.4	39.2	28.9	35.2	2.76	3.27	1.47	8.40	3.86
43	35.5	33.5	38.2	28.2	34.3	2.92	3.45	1.59	8.88	4.10
44	34.6	32.6	37.3	27.4	33.5	3.07	3.60	1.72	9.37	4.34
45	33.8	31.7	36.2	26.7	32.8	3.25	3.80	1.87	9.88	4.60
46	32.9	30.8	35.4	25.9	31.7	3.46	4.02	2.04	10.43	4.89
47	32.0	29.9	34.5	25.2	30.9	3.70	4.30	2.24	11.02	5.21
48	31.1	29.1	33.5	24.5	30.1	4.00	4.64	2.47	11.67	5.56
49	30.2	28.2	32.6	23.7	29.2	4.33	5.04	2.75	12.38	5.95
50	29.3	27.3	31.7	23.0	28.4	4.74	5.49	3.05	13.15	6.37
51	28.5	26.5	30.8	22.3	27.6	5.16	5.99	3.39	13.97	6.84
52	27.6	25.8	29.8	21.6	26.8	5.82	6.52	3.75	14.82	7.35
53	26.8	24.8	29.0	21.0	26.0	6.11	7.10	4.12	15.68	7.93
54	25.9	24.0	28.1	20.3	25.2	6.64	7.73	4.52	16.58	8.58
55	25.1	23.2	27.3	19.6	24.4	7.21	8.41	4.96	17.48	9.26

Appendix C (continued)
Expectation of Life and Expected Deaths, by Race, Sex, and Age: 1994

Age/1990 (years)	Expectation of life in years					Expected deaths per 1,000 alive at specified age[1]				
	Total	White Male	White Female	Black Male	Black Female	Total	White Male	White Female	Black Male	Black Female
56	24.3	22.2	26.4	19.0	23.6	7.84	9.17	5.44	18.48	9.99
57	23.5	21.6	25.5	18.3	22.8	8.58	10.07	5.99	19.93	10.82
58	22.7	20.8	24.7	17.7	22.1	9.45	11.14	6.62	21.32	11.78
59	21.9	20.0	23.9	17.0	21.3	10.42	12.36	7.33	23.17	12.83
60	21.1	19.3	23.0	16.4	20.6	11.50	13.70	8.11	25.29	14.01
61	20.4	18.5	22.2	15.9	19.9	12.62	15.11	8.93	27.45	15.24
62	19.6	17.8	21.4	15.3	19.2	13.77	16.59	9.79	29.36	16.40
63	18.9	17.1	20.6	14.7	18.5	14.92	18.12	10.67	30.84	17.44
64	18.2	16.4	19.8	14.2	17.8	16.11	19.73	11.59	32.02	18.42
65	17.4	15.7	19.1	13.6	17.1	17.35	21.43	12.57	32.99	19.34
70	14.1	12.5	15.4	11.0	13.9	26.18	32.69	19.52	48.22	29.73
75	11.0	9.7	12.0	8.8	11.1	39.26	49.26	30.73	65.70	41.08
80	8.3	7.2	8.9	6.8	8.4	60.15	75.57	49.53	89.94	59.43
85 & over	6.0	5.2	6.3	5.1	6.2	1,000.00	1,000.00	1.000.00	1,000.00	1,000.00

[1]Based on the proportion of the cohort who are alive at the beginning of an indicated age interval who will die before reaching the end of that interval. For example, out of every 1,000 people alive and exactly 50 years old at the beginning of the period, between 4 and 5 (4.76) will die before reaching their 51st birthdays.

Source: U.S. Center for Health Statistics, Vital Statistics of the United States, annual, 1998 , 118th ed., *and unpublished data. (Washington, D.C.: 1998).*

Appendix D—Other Sources for Managing Stress

There are many resources for people who are experiencing stress in their lives. The following are suggestions about where to go if you or a family member ever needs help.

Where to go	Cost	Comments
Family doctor	Variable	Some family doctors feel comfortable helping their patients with stress-related problems. Ask if your doctor counsels patients on stress. If not, ask for a referral.
Church	No cost	Your church may have counselors on staff. If not, they can put you in touch with people who can help.
Company personnel, wellness, or health departments	No cost or nominal cost	More and more companies are offering stress management workshops at the work site. Check with your personnel, wellness, or health department to see if your company offers such programs.
Community stress workshops	No cost or nominal cost	Community centers, colleges, and associatons such as the YMCA/YWCA often hold stress education workshops.
Community mental health center	Variable	Look up "Mental Health Centers" in the Yellow Pages of your telephone directory.
Counselor	Variable	Counselors can have different backgrounds. Psychiatrists are medical doctors and have an "M.D." after their names. Psychologists have a "Ph.D." or "Psy.D." after their names.
		Other counselors have masters degrees, including social work (M.S.W.), nursing, education, theology, and psychology.
		Other counselors hold bachelor of science (B.S.) and bachelor of arts (B.A.) degrees, and can be highly effective.
		The best ways to find a good counselor are: (1) word of mouth referral from friends, and (2) referral from professionals, such as your doctor or employee health nurse.

Index